THE BIG FAT ALGEBRA 2 WORKBOOK

WORKMAN PUBLISHING
NEW YORK

Workman Kids
Workman Publishing
Hachette Book Group, Inc.
1290 Avenue of the Americas
New York, NY 10104
workman.com

Workman Kids is an imprint of Workman Publishing, a division of Hachette Book Group, Inc.
The Workman name and logo are registered trademarks of Hachette Book Group, Inc.

Designer: Abby Dening
Graphic Illustrator: Abby Dening
Illustrator: Kim Ku
Written by: Robert Vigneri and Dr. Steve Warner
Reviewed by: Julie Dilday

Library of Congress Cataloging-in-Publication Data is available.

ISBN: 978-1-5235-2593-5

First Edition September 2025 IMSF

Distributed in Europe by Hachette Livre,
58 rue Jean Bleuzen, 92 178 Vanves Cedex, France.

Distributed in the United Kingdom by Hachette Book Group, UK,
Carmelite House, 50 Victoria Embankment, London EC4Y 0DZ.

Printed in Shenzhen, China, on responsibly sourced paper.

10 9 8 7 6 5 4 3 2 1

WELCOME TO THE BIG FAT ALGEBRA 2 WORKBOOK.

This workbook is designed to support you as you work your way through *Everything You Need to Ace Algebra 2 in One Big Fat Notebook* or your Algebra 2 class. Consider the *Notebook* your main source and this *Workbook* extra practice.

Each chapter in this *Workbook* supports the content of a corresponding chapter in the *Notebook*. It begins with a brief recap of the key concepts, followed by examples solved step by step. Then there's a series of extra practice problems for you to solve that will help you really understand the concept.

The solution section in the back of this workbook guides you through each step of finding the solution for every question. No more trying to figure out where you went wrong. The path to the correct answer is clearly laid out.

Whether you're reviewing for a test or need to strengthen your problem-solving skills, look no further than this workbook. You'll encounter the same fun, easy-to-understand language that you love in *Everything You Need to Ace Algebra 2 in One Big Fat Notebook*.

Both books provide you with everything you need to ACE that Algebra 2 class!

CONTENTS

$$\frac{y_2 - y_1}{x_2 - x_1}$$

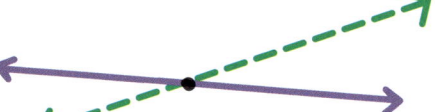

$g(x)$ $f(x)$

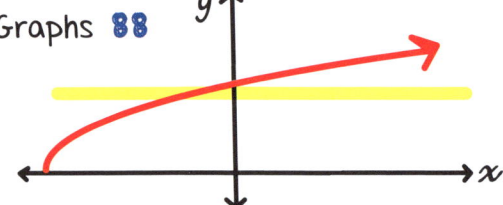

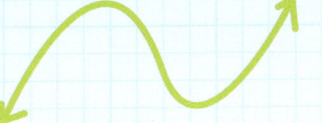

$$\frac{3q-9a}{11q^2a-33qa^2}$$

SIMPLIFYING IS BEST

$|x|$

$$f(x) = e^x$$

UNIT 7: EXPONENTIAL and LOGARITHMIC FUNCTIONS 257

$$\log_4 64 = 3$$

UNIT 8: TRIGONOMETRIC FUNCTIONS 287

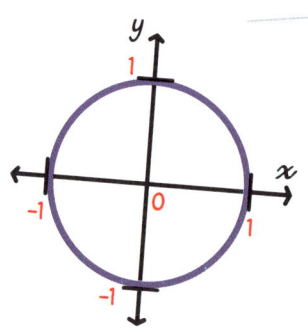

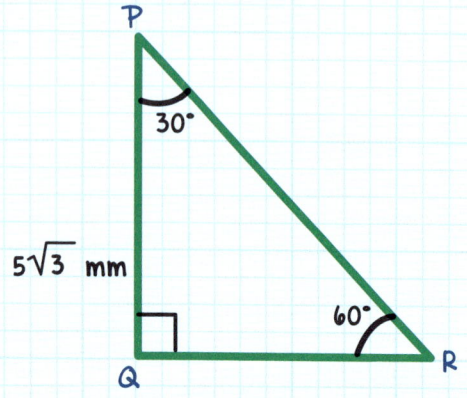

SOLUTIONS:
Answer Key 351

x

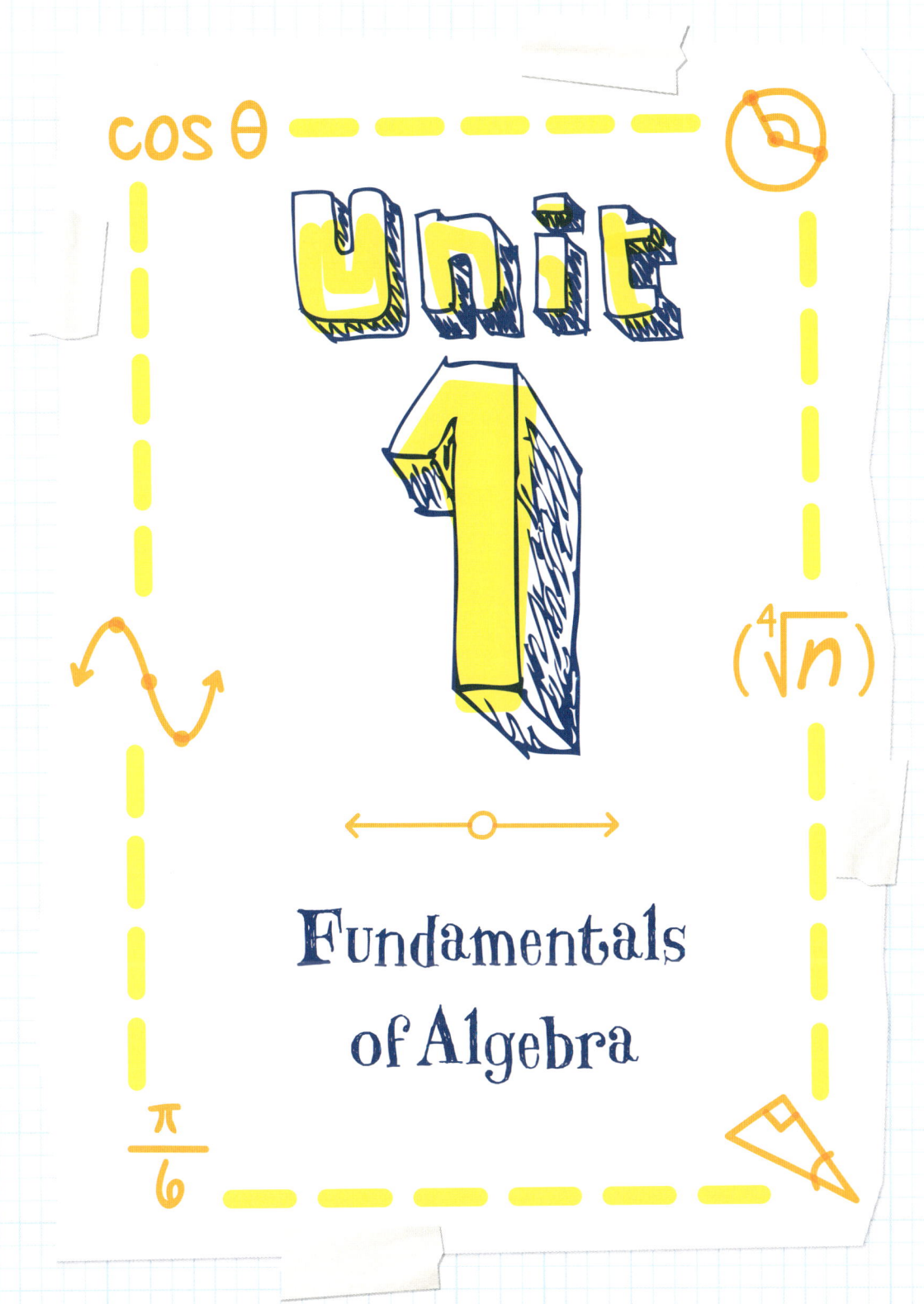

Unit 1

Fundamentals of Algebra

SOLVING LINEAR EQUATIONS AND INEQUALITIES

A **LINEAR EQUATION** can be written in the form $Ax + By = C$, where A, B, and C are real numbers.

To **solve** a linear equation means to find *all* solutions to the equation.

> In this book, solutions will always be real numbers.

We can solve linear equations by isolating the variable on one side of the equation.

EXAMPLE: Solve: $-14d + 54 = -3(2d - 5) + 7$

$-14d + 54 = -3(2d - 5) + 7$ Apply the Distributive Property.

$-14d + 54 = -6d + 15 + 7$ Combine like terms.

$-14d + 54 = -6d + 22$

$-14d + 6d + 54 = -6d + 6d + 22$ Combine like terms.

$-8d + 54 = 22$

$-8d + 54 - 54 = 22 - 54$ Subtract 54 from both sides.

$-8d = -32$

$-8d \div (-8) = -32 \div (-8)$ Divide by 8 on both sides.

$d = 4$

An **INEQUALITY** is a mathematical sentences consisting of two expressions separated by one of the **inequality symbols**.

Solving a linear inequality is exactly the same as solving a linear equation with one extra rule: When we **MULTIPLY** or **DIVIDE** both sides by a *negative* number, we must **REVERSE** the direction of the inequality sign.

INEQUALITY SYMBOL	MEANING
<	less than
>	greater than
≤	less than or equal to
≥	greater than or equal to

There are three ways to represent the solution of an inequality: **INEQUALITY NOTATION**, **INTERVAL NOTATION**, and **GRAPHICAL NOTATION**.

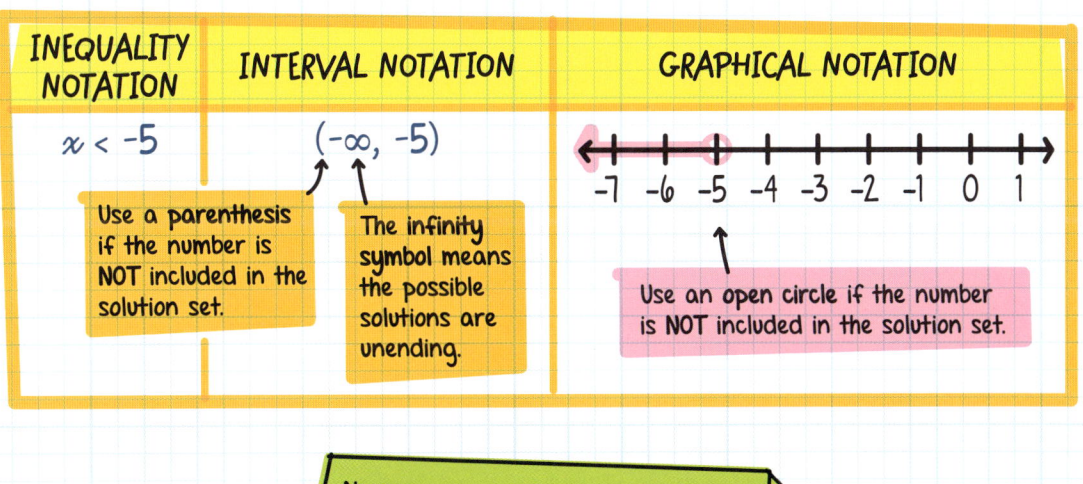

INEQUALITY NOTATION	INTERVAL NOTATION	GRAPHICAL NOTATION
$x < -5$	$(-\infty, -5)$	

Use a parenthesis if the number is NOT included in the solution set.

The infinity symbol means the possible solutions are unending.

Use an open circle if the number is NOT included in the solution set.

Always use a parenthesis with infinity.

INEQUALITY NOTATION	INTERVAL NOTATION	GRAPHICAL NOTATION
$x \geq 0$	$[0, \infty)$ Use a bracket if the number IS included in the solution set.	Use a closed circle if the number IS included in the solution set

EXAMPLE: Solve $-40m - 2(m + 7) \leq -140$. Represent the solution set using inequality notation, interval notation, and graphical notation.

STEP 1: Solve the inequality in exactly the same way you would solve a linear equation.

$-40m - 2(m + 7) \leq -140$ Apply the Distributive Property.

$-40m - 2m - 14 \leq -140$ Combine like terms.

$-42m - 14 \leq -140$

$-42m - 14 + 14 \leq -140 + 14$ Add 14 to both sides.

$-42m \leq -126$

$-42m \div (-42) \leq -126 \div (-42)$ Divide by -42 on both sides.

$m \geq 3$

Remember to reverse the inequality when you divide by a negative number.

STEP 2: Represent the solution set. Use inequality notation, interval notation, and graphical notation.

INEQUALITY NOTATION	INTERVAL NOTATION	GRAPHICAL NOTATION
$m \geq 3$	$[3, \infty)$	 -3 0 3 5

THINK:
M is greater than or equal to 3, which means 3 IS included in the solution. So, the solution will have a bracket, or a closed circle.

EXAMPLE: Gerald's Grocery Store is sponsoring a carnival to raise money for the community food pantry. The carnival sponsorship will cost the store $14,000, and tickets will sell for $12 per person. How many tickets must be sold if the store wants to raise at least $50,000 after the $14,000 sponsorship cost?

STEP 1: Write an inequality to represent the situation.

"At least" tells us that the amount of money the store wants to raise is *greater than or equal to* ($\geq$) $50,000.

Define the variable or unknown: Let t = the number of tickets sold.

The $14,000 sponsorship cost is constant.

Inequality: *(price per ticket) (number of tickets)* − sponsorship cost ≥ least amount of dollars the store wants to raise

$12t − $14,000 ≥ $50,000

STEP 2: Solve the inequality.

12t − 14,000 ≥ 50,000

12t − 14,000 + 14,000 ≥ 50,000 + 14,000

12t ≥ 64,000

12t ÷ 12 ≥ 64,000 ÷ 12

t ≥ 5,333.$\overline{3}$

So, at least 5,334 tickets must be sold for the store to raise at least $50,000.

THINK:
You cannot have "0.$\overline{3}$ ticket."
So, round down to 5,334.

DETERMINE IF THE GIVEN VALUES ARE SOLUTIONS TO THE GIVEN EQUATION.

1. $\dfrac{3x}{4} + 25 = 9 - y$ $\qquad x = -8$ and $y = -10$

2. $7(13r + 2) = 40r - 88$ $\qquad r = -2$

3. $\dfrac{2mn}{mn} + 5 = 8m - 8n$ $\qquad m = 5$ and $n = 4$

SOLVE EACH LINEAR EQUATION.

4. $116 = 71 - 5g$

5. $11x - 3 = 6(x + 12)$

6. $\dfrac{10y - 4}{8} = -32$

SOLVE EACH EQUATION FOR THE INDICATED VARIABLE.

7. $V = \dfrac{1}{3}bh$ for h

8. $a = \dfrac{4}{5}c(b - d)$ for c

WRITE AND SOLVE AN EQUATION TO ANSWER THE QUESTION.

9. In its first month, a new wellness app generated 381,000 buyers. If the app owner receives $45 in revenue from advertisers for every 3,000 buyers, how much revenue did the owner receive in the app's first month?

SOLVE EACH INEQUALITY. REPRESENT EACH SOLUTION USING INEQUALITY NOTATION, GRAPHICAL NOTATION, AND INTERVAL NOTATION.

10. $-15 - 9s \leq 30$

11. $3(2 - w) - 4 > 17$

SOLVE THE INEQUALITY. REPRESENT THE SOLUTION USING INEQUALITY NOTATION AND INTERVAL NOTATION.

12. $\frac{3}{8} \geq 1\frac{1}{4}d - \frac{1}{2}$

WRITE AND SOLVE AN INEQUALITY TO ANSWER THE QUESTION. REPRESENT THE SOLUTION USING INTERVAL NOTATION.

13. Ms. Dana is preparing for the annual spring luncheon. After spending $548 on food and $213 on decorations, she had at least $67 in her wallet. If she paid in cash for the food and decorations, what is the least amount Ms. Dana could have started with? (Assume that Ms. Dana did not have any coins in her wallet.)

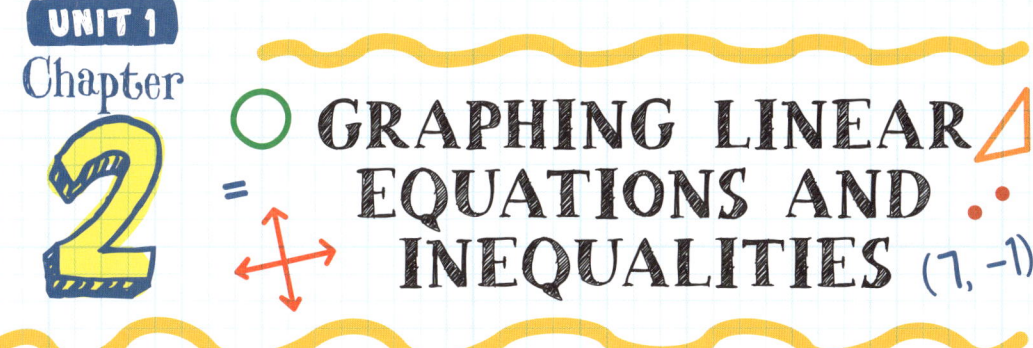

○ GRAPHING LINEAR △ EQUALIONS AND ∴ INEQUALITIES (7, –1)

SLOPE measures the steepness of a line. It is the ratio of the *vertical change* (RISE) to the *horizontal change* (RUN).

$$\text{Slope } (m) = \frac{\text{Rise}}{\text{Run}}$$

Slope can be positive, negative, zero, or undefined.

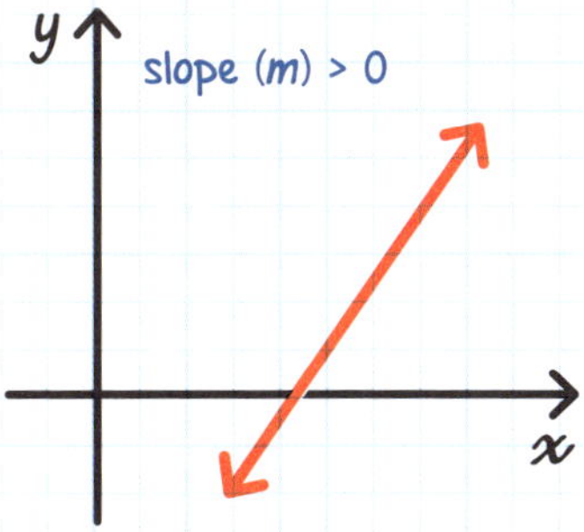

slope (m) > 0

Positive slope

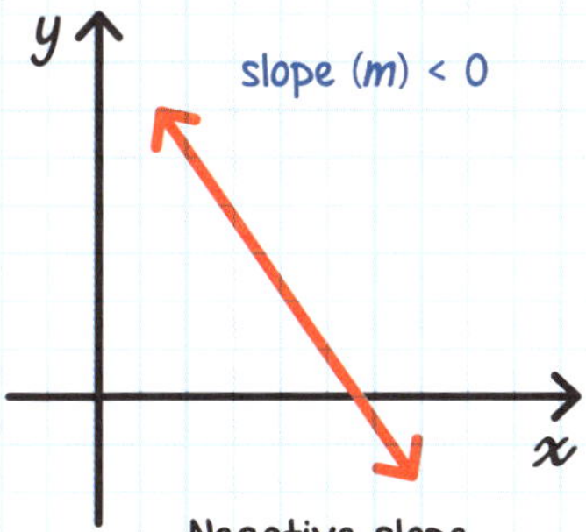

slope (m) < 0

Negative slope

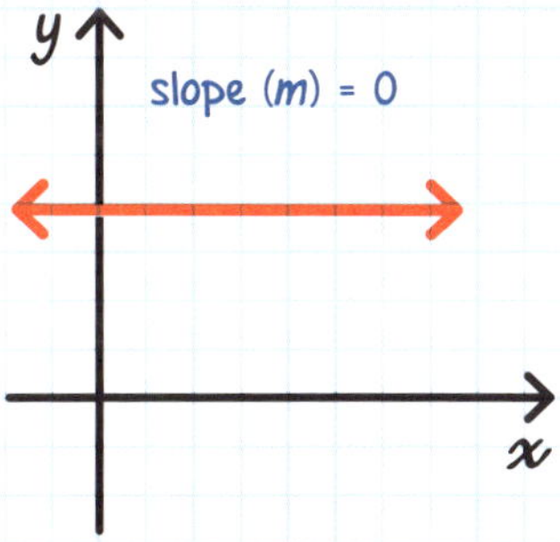

slope (m) = 0

Zero slope

slope (m): undefined

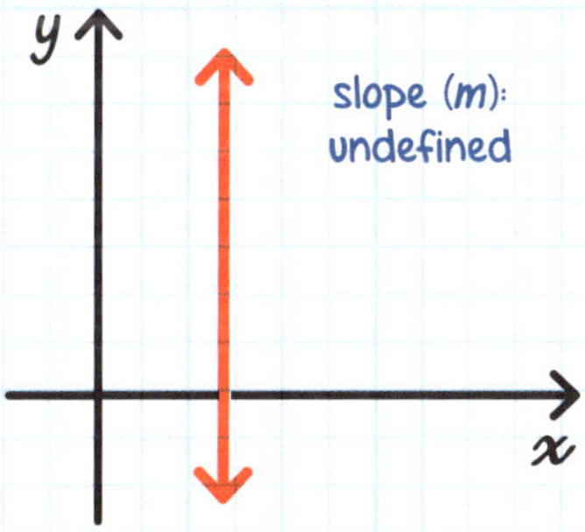

Undefined slope

> Parallel lines have the same slope.
>
> Perpendicular lines have slopes that are negative reciprocals of each other.

Using the Slope Formula

To find the slope of a line, plug the coordinates of two points on the line into the **SLOPE FORMULA**.

$$m = \frac{\text{Rise}}{\text{Run}} = \frac{y_2 - y_1}{x_2 - x_1}$$

EXAMPLE: Use the slope formula to find the slope of the line that passes through the points A $(-1, -3)$ and B $(3, 5)$. Then classify the slope of the line.

STEP 1: Find the values of x_1, y_1, x_2, and y_2.

Use the given coordinates: $(x_1, y_1) = (-1, -3)$ and $(x_2, y_2) = (3, 5)$.

STEP 2: Substitute the values into the slope formula:

$$m = \frac{y_2 - y_1}{x_2 - x_1} = \frac{5 - (-3)}{3 - (-1)} = \frac{8}{4} = \frac{2}{1} = 2$$

STEP 3: Classify the slope of the line.

Since $m > 0$, the line has a positive slope.

Note: The line RISES from left to right.

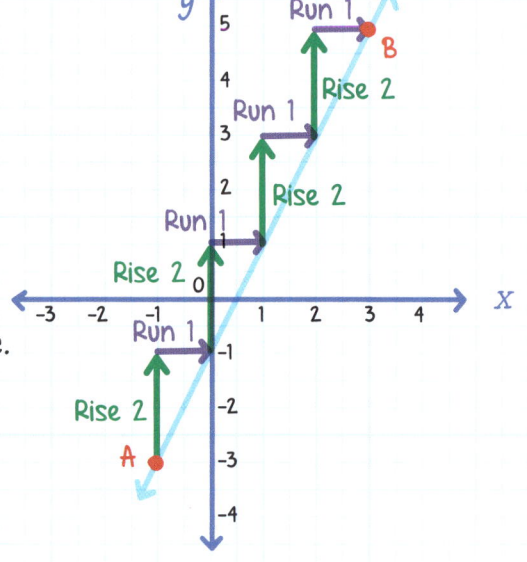

Writing the Equation of a Line

An equation of a line can be written in many different forms. Two of them are slope-intercept form and point-slope form.

SLOPE-INTERCEPT FORM uses the slope and the *y*-intercept.

$$y = mx + b$$

slope

y-intercept

If a line has a **slope of** 4 and a **y-intercept of** (0, 8), the equation in slope-intercept form is $y = 4x + 8$.

EXAMPLE: Find the coordinates of the *x*-intercept and *y*-intercept of the graph of $y = -\frac{1}{4}x + 5$.

STEP 1: Find the *y*-intercept.

The equation is in slope-intercept form, so we have $b = 5$. That means *y*-intercept is (0, 5).

STEP 2: Find the *x*-intercept.

The *x*-intercept is where the line intersects the *x*-axis, so the *y*-coordinate at this point is 0.

$y = -\frac{1}{4}x + 5$

$0 = -\frac{1}{4}x + 5$ Substitute 0 for *y*.

$0 - 5 = -\frac{1}{4}x + 5 - 5$

$-5 = -\frac{1}{4}x$

$-5 \cdot (-4) = -\frac{1}{4}x \cdot (-4)$

$20 = x$

Therefore, the *x*-intercept is (20, 0).

POINT-SLOPE FORM uses the slope and the coordinates of a point on the line.

the coordinates of a specific point

$$y - y_1 = m(x - x_1)$$

slope

EXAMPLE: A line passes through the points (-15, 2) and (3, 11). Find an equation of the line and write it in slope-intercept form and point-slope form.

STEP 1: Use the slope formula to find the slope of the line.

$m = \dfrac{y_2 - y_1}{x_2 - x_1}$ slope formula

$m = \dfrac{11 - 2}{3 - (-15)}$ Substitute the given points.

$m = \dfrac{9}{18} = \dfrac{1}{2}$

STEP 2: Substitute the slope and one point into the point-slope form.

The slope is $m = \dfrac{1}{2}$ and one of the points is (3, 11).

$y - y_1 = m(x - x_1)$ point-slope form

$y - 11 = \dfrac{1}{2}(x - 3)$ Substitute the slope and the coordinates of the point.

$y - 11 = \dfrac{1}{2}(x - 3)$ point-slope form

STEP 3: To write the equation in slope-intercept form, use the point-slope form and isolate y.

$y - 11 = \dfrac{1}{2}(x - 3)$ point-slope form

$$y - 11 = \frac{1}{2}x - \frac{3}{2}$$

$$y - 11 + 11 = \frac{1}{2}x - \frac{3}{2} + 11$$

$$y = \frac{1}{2}x + \frac{19}{2} \quad \text{slope-intercept form}$$

Graphing Linear Inequalities

To graph a linear inequality, we first graph the corresponding linear equation. Then shade the side of the boundary line that represents the solution set.

EXAMPLE: Graph the inequality $6x - 3y < 18$.

STEP 1: Rewrite the inequality as an equation and graph it.

$$6x - 3y < 18 \quad \longrightarrow \quad 6x - 3y = 18$$

To graph the equation, find the x- and y-intercepts of the line. To do that, substitute $x = 0$ and solve for y; and then substitute $y = 0$ and solve for x.

y-intercept	$x = 0$	$6(0) - 3y = 18$ $-3y = 18$ $-3y \div (-3) = 18 \div (-3)$ $y = -6$	$y = -6$	$(0, -6)$
x-intercept	$y = 0$	$6x - 3(0) = 18$ $6x = 18$ $6x \div 6 = 18 \div 6$ $x = 3$	$x = 3$	$(3, 0)$

Plot the *x*- and *y*-intercepts on a coordinate plane.

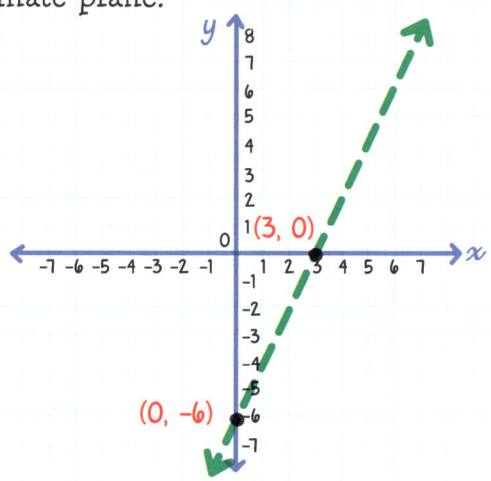

STEP 2: Determine whether the line should be *solid* or *dashed*. Then draw the line connecting the *x*- and *y*-intercepts.

> If the inequality has a ≥ or ≤ the boundary line is solid.
>
> If the inequality has a > or < the boundary line is dashed.

Since the inequality $6x - 3y < 18$ has a < sign, the boundary line should be *dashed*.

THINK:
A dashed line is like an open circle on a number line.

STEP 3: Shade the region that makes the inequality true.

Test the point $(0, 0)$ to see if it is a solution to the given inequality.

$$6x - 3y < 18$$

$$6(0) - 3(0) < 18 \quad \text{Substitute } (0,0)$$

$$0 < 18 \quad \text{True}$$

> We can test ANY point not on the boundary line, but (0, 0) is easiest. If the point (0, 0) lies on the line, we must choose a different point.

Since the inequality is TRUE, we shade the region that *DOES* contain $(0, 0)$.

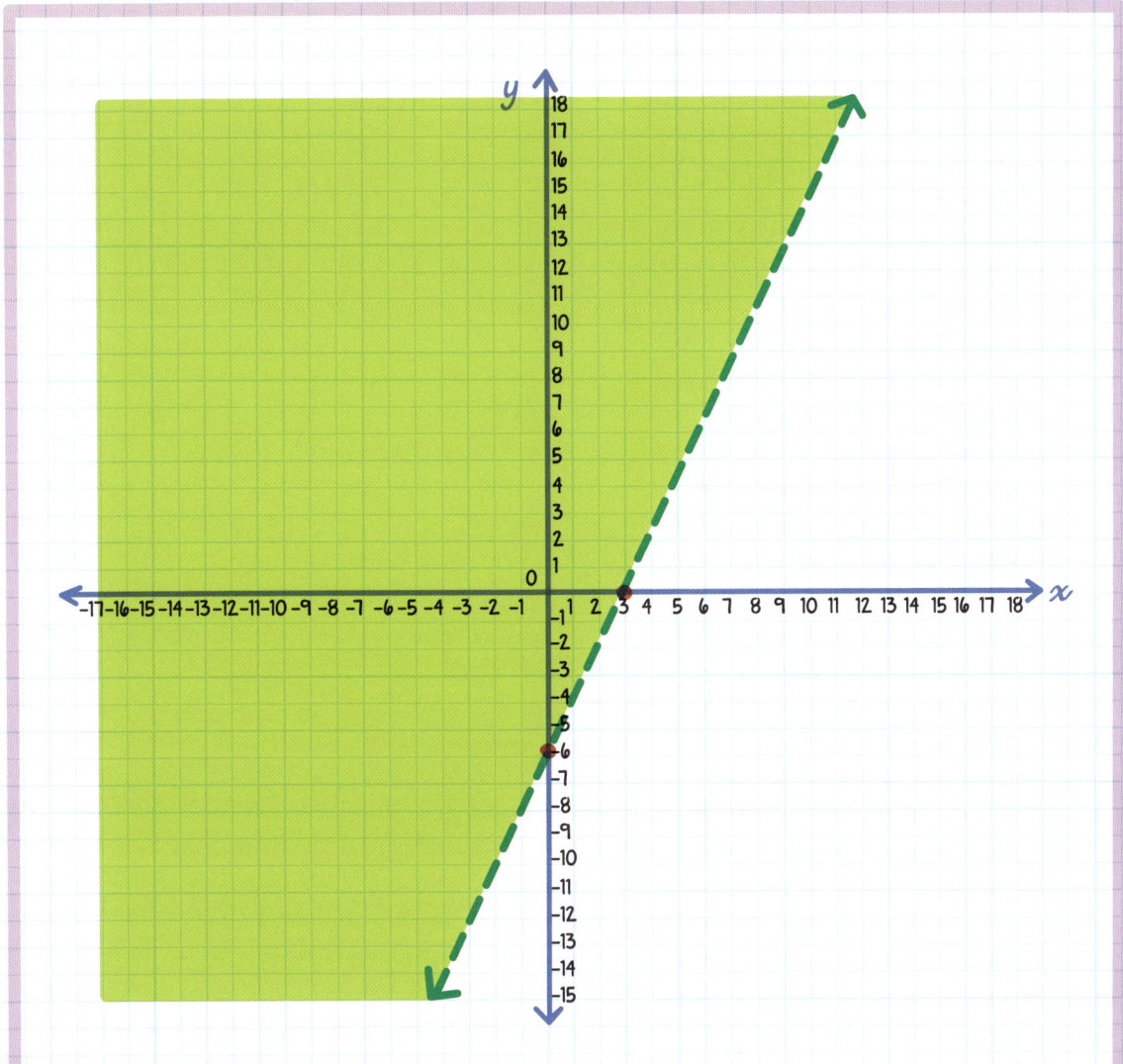

USE WHAT YOU KNOW ABOUT SLOPE AND GRAPHING LINEAR EQUATIONS TO ANSWER QUESTIONS 1 THROUGH 6.

1. Find the slope of the line.

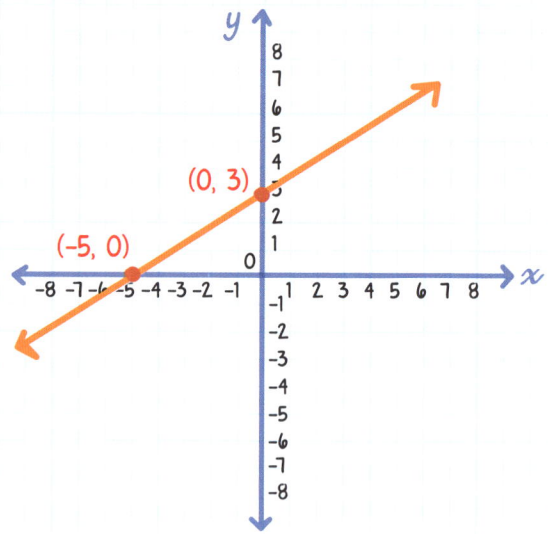

2. Draw a line that has a slope of $\frac{4}{7}$ and a *y*-intercept of (0, –4).

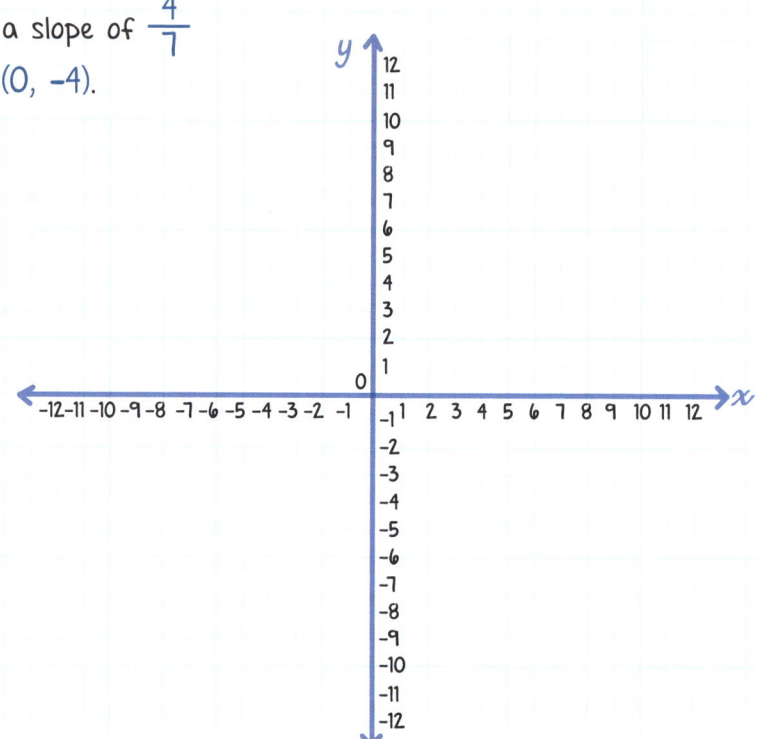

3. Determine the slope of the line that passes through the points $(4, -6)$ and $(2, 4)$.

4. Determine the slope of the line that passes through the points $(7, -5)$ and $(9, -3)$.

5. Find the coordinates of the x-intercept and the y-intercept of $y = 7x - 3$.

6. The equation of a line is $y - 6 = 8(x - 2)$. Find the slope of the line and the coordinates of a point that the line passes through.

7. A line passes through the points $(-5, 9)$ and $(19, 27)$. Find an equation of the line in point-slope form and slope-intercept form.

USE THE GIVEN LINES TO ANSWER QUESTIONS 8 THROUGH 10.

> Line j passes through the points M (-4, -12) and F (5, 15).
>
> Line p passes through the points L (-9, 3) and N (6, -2).

8. Find the slope of line j and the slope of line p.

9. If both lines were plotted on the same coordinate plane, what could you conclude about these lines?

10. Write an equation for each line in slope-intercept form.

11. Graph the inequality $y \geq \dfrac{1}{2}x + 4$.

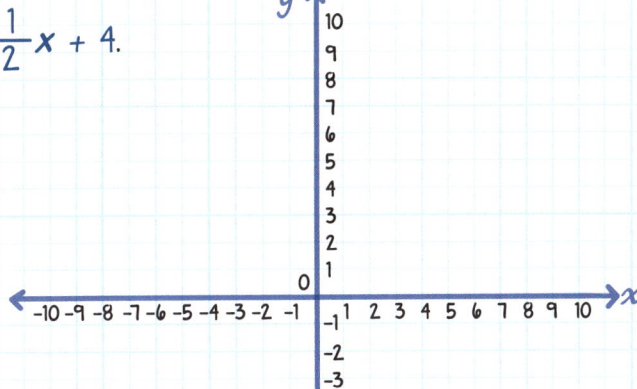

12. Graph the inequality
    $-9x - 3y < 6$.

13. Graph the inequality
    $y + \dfrac{1}{3}x \leq 4$.

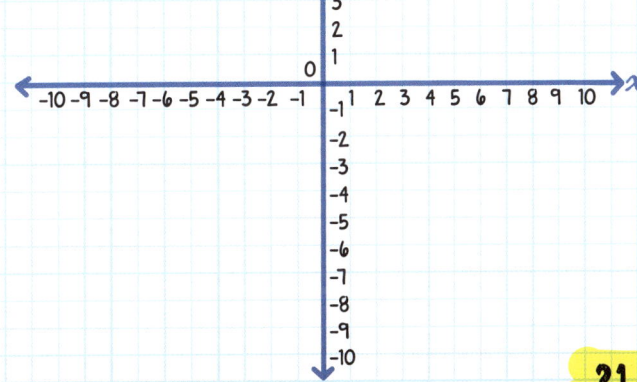

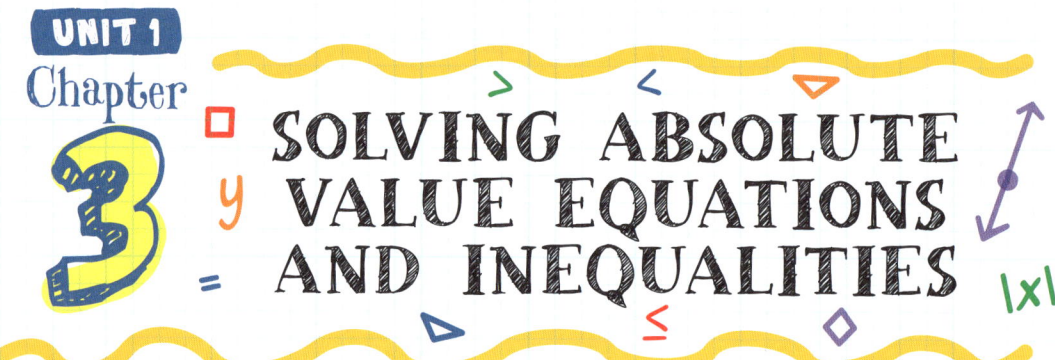

SOLVING ABSOLUTE VALUE EQUATIONS AND INEQUALITIES

The **ABSOLUTE VALUE** of x, written $|x|$, is the distance between 0 and x on the number line.

THINK:
The absolute value of a number is *always* positive because a distance cannot be negative.

To solve an absolute equation algebraically, rewrite it as two linear equations.

$$|x - 18| = 25$$

$x - 18 = 25$	$x - 18 = -25$
$x - 18 + 18 = 25 + 18$	$x - 18 + 18 = -25 + 18$
$x = 43$	$x = -7$

Geometrically, $|x - y|$ is the distance between x and y. This means $|x - y| = |y - x|$.

For $|x - 18| = 25$, the distance between x and 18 is 25.

So, x is 25 less than 18 *or* 25 more than 18.

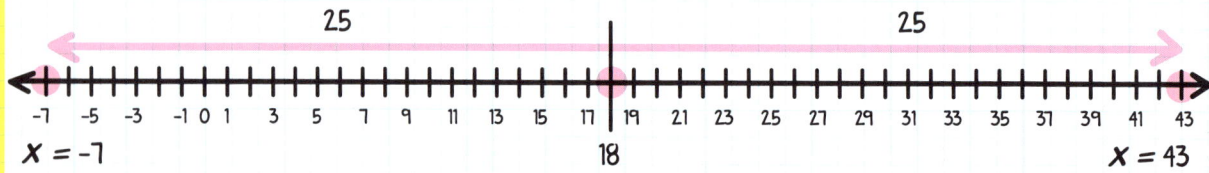

$X = -7$

18

$X = 43$

22

EXAMPLE: Solve for x: $|x - 10| = 2$ algebraically and geometrically.

STEP 1: Solve algebraically. Rewrite the equation as two linear equations and solve for x.

$x - 10 = 2$	$x - 10 = -2$
$x - 10 + 10 = 2 + 10$	$x - 10 + 10 = -2 + 10$
$x = 12$	$x = 8$

STEP 2: Solve geometrically.

The distance between x and 10 is 2.

So, x is 2 less than 10 *or* 2 more than 10.

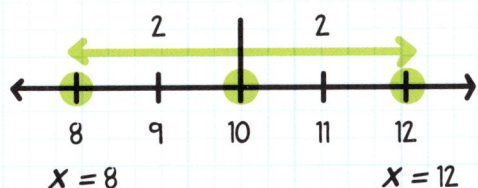

$|x - 10| = 2$

$|12 - 10| = |8 - 10| = 2$

Solutions: $x = 12$ and $x = 8$

So, the solutions to the absolute value equation are $x = 12$ and $x = 8$.

Absolute Value Inequalities

> If c is a positive real number, then $|x| < c$ is equivalent to $-c < x < c$.
>
> Similarly, $|x| \leq c$ is equivalent to $-c \leq x \leq c$.

We can rewrite an absolute value inequality as the *conjunction* of two linear inequalities.

$$|x| < 5$$

$$x > -5 \quad and \quad x < 5$$

This means that the solution set of $|x| < 5$ is the set of all real numbers that are to the right of -5 and to the left of 5 on the number line.

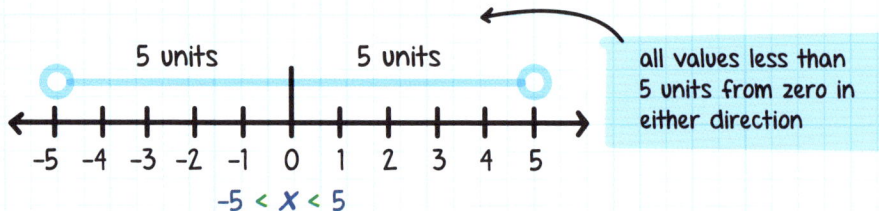

all values less than 5 units from zero in either direction

So, the solution set contains all real numbers *between* -5 and 5 (but *not* including -5 or 5).

In **inequality notation** this is $-5 < x < 5$.

In **interval notation** this is $(-5, 5)$.

EXAMPLE: Solve for x: $|x + 3| < 14.5$. Rewrite the absolute value inequality as linear inequalities without absolute values.

$-14.5 < x + 3 < 14.5$
$-14.5 - 3 < x + 3 - 3 < 14.5 - 3$
$-17.5 < x < 11.5$

So, the solution set contains all real numbers between -17.5 and 11.5.

Inequality notation: $-17.5 < x < 11.5$ **Interval notation:** $(-17.5, 11.5)$

If c is a positive real number, then $|x| > c$ is equivalent to $x < ^-c$ or $x > c$.

Similarly, if c is a positive real number, then $|x| \geq c$ is equivalent to $x \leq ^-c$ or $x \geq c$.

We can rewrite $|x| > 5$ as two linear inequalities.

$$x < ^-5 \quad or \quad x > 5$$

This means that x can be any real number to the left of -5 or to the right of 5 on the number line.

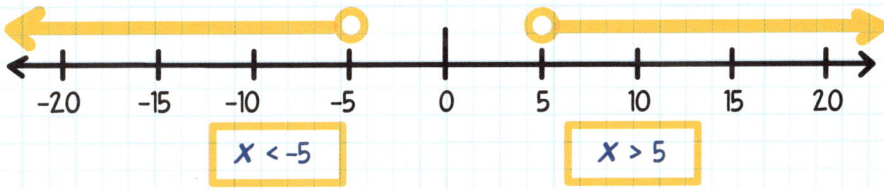

So, the solution set of $|x| > 5$ is the set of all real numbers that are either less than -5 or greater than 5. This solution set can be written using interval notation as $(-\infty, -5) \cup (5, \infty)$.

union symbol

EXAMPLE: Solve for x: $|x + 9| \geq 5$.

STEP 1: Rewrite the absolute value inequality as two linear inequalities.

$$x + 9 \leq -5 \qquad x + 9 \geq 5$$

STEP 2: Solve algebraically.

$$x + 9 \leq -5 \qquad\qquad x + 9 \geq 5$$
$$x + 9 - 9 \leq -5 - 9 \qquad x + 9 - 9 \geq 5 - 9$$
$$x \leq -14 \qquad\qquad x \geq -4$$

So, the solution set contains all real numbers less than or equal to -14 *or* greater than or equal to -4.

Inequality notation: $x \leq -14$ or $x \geq -4$

Interval notation: $(-\infty, -14] \cup [-4, \infty)$

Some absolute value inequalities have no solutions. Write your answer with the empty set symbol: ∅.

Some absolute value inequalities have infinitely many solutions. Write your answer in interval notation or inequality notation.

SOLVE FOR x GEOMETRICALLY.

1. $|x - 6| = 4$

2. $|x - 3| = 12$

3. $|x - 7| = 9$

SOLVE FOR x ALGEBRAICALLY.

4. $9|x + 2| = 27$

5. $2 + 5|x - 6| = 12$

6. $|x - 3| - 9 = 17$

7. $|x - 8| = |-x + 3|$

SOLVE FOR x GEOMETRICALLY. WRITE THE SOLUTION SET USING INTERVAL NOTATION.

8. $|x| > 6$

9. $|x| < 12$

10. $|x| \geq 5$

SOLVE FOR x ALGEBRAICALLY. WRITE THE SOLUTION SET USING INTERVAL NOTATION.

11. $|8x - 1| - 7 \geq 18$

12. $|x + 1| \leq 3$

13. $|12x - 4| < 18$

14. $7|3x - 5| + 14 > 21$

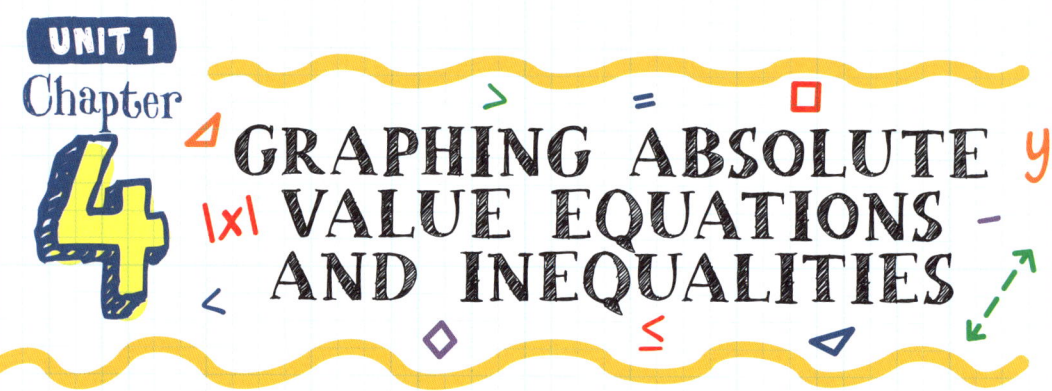

UNIT 1
Chapter 4
GRAPHING ABSOLUTE VALUE EQUATIONS AND INEQUALITIES

Characteristics of the graph of $y = |x|$:

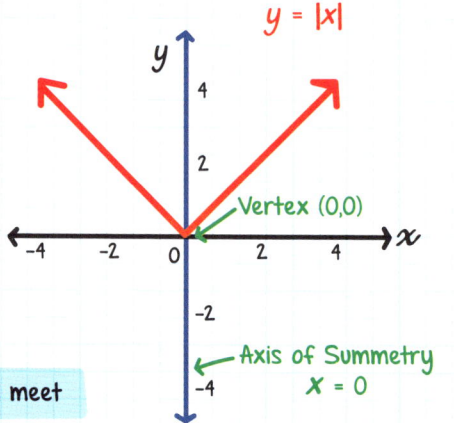

$y = |x|$

Vertex (0,0)

Axis of Summetry $x = 0$

▶ V-shaped

▶ Opens upward

▶ Symmetrical

▶ Vertex at the origin $(0, 0)$

the point of the V, where the two rays meet

Characteristics of the graph of $y = -|x|$:

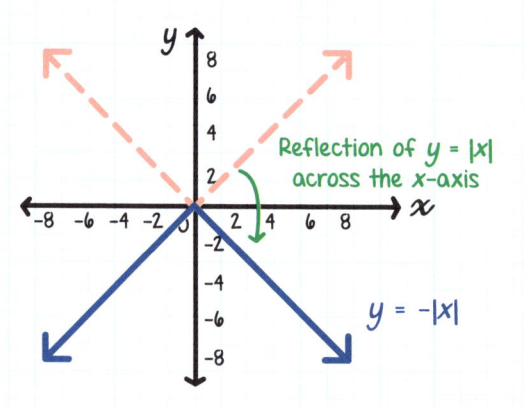

Reflection of $y = |x|$ across the x-axis

$y = -|x|$

▶ V-shaped

▶ Opens downward

▶ Symmetrical

▶ Vertex at the origin $(0, 0)$

▶ Reflection of the graph of $y = |x|$ across the x-axis

The **standard form** of an absolute value equation is:

$$y = a|x - h| + k$$

h and *k* are the *x* and *y* coordinates of the vertex.

The value of *a* determines how wide or narrow the graph is. The sign of *a* tells us whether the graph opens *upward* (a > 0) or *downward* (a < 0).

This equation has a graph that is <u>identical</u> to the graph of $y = |x|$, *except:*

▶ It is translated so that its vertex lies at the point *(h, k)*.

▶ It is expanded or contracted, depending on $|a|$.

▶ If *a* < 0, then it is reflected across the *x*-axis.

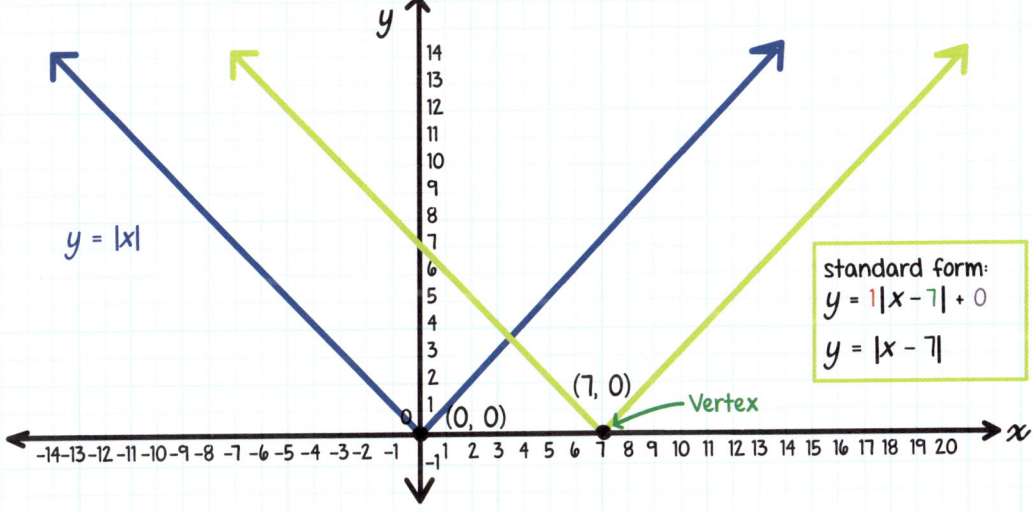

y = |x|

standard form:
$y = 1|x - 7| + 0$
$y = |x - 7|$

(0, 0)
(7, 0)   Vertex

You can use the standard form to graph an absolute value equation.

EXAMPLE: Graph $y = -|x-5| + 10$ using the standard form of an absolute value equation.

standard form: $y = a|x-h| + k$

$\qquad\qquad y = -1|x-5| + 10$

$a = -1$: Since $a < 0$, the graph opens *downward*.

$(h, k) = (5, 10)$: The vertex lies at $(5, 10)$.

To graph, plot the vertex $(5, 10)$, and then use the fact that $a < 0$ to draw the two rays.

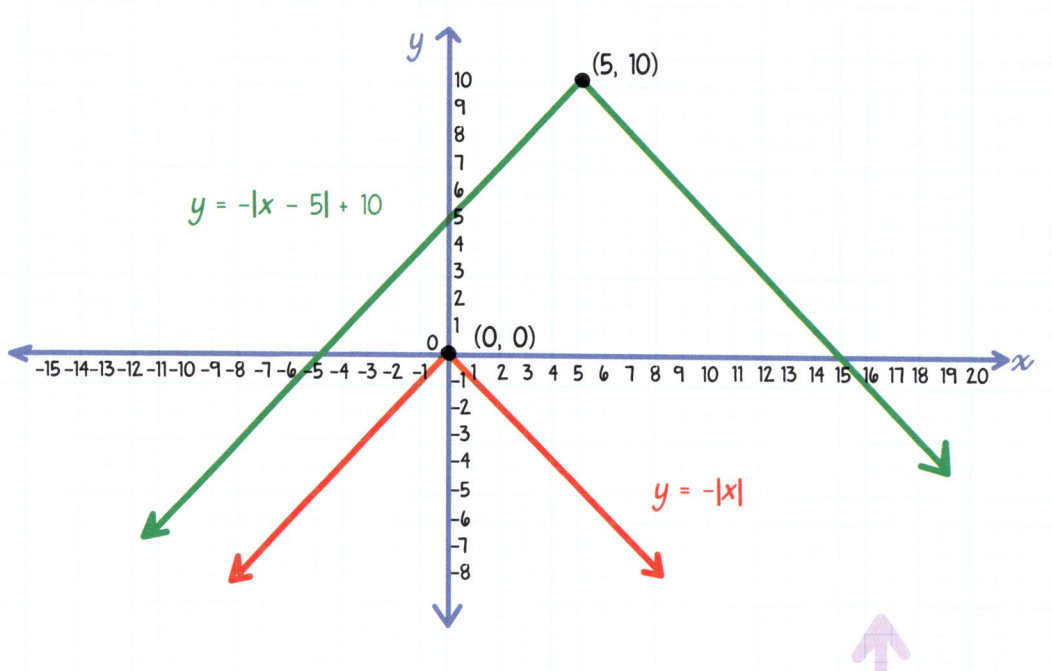

Graphing Absolute Value Inequalities

For the graph of an absolute value inequality, the solution set is either the region above the V or the region below the V.

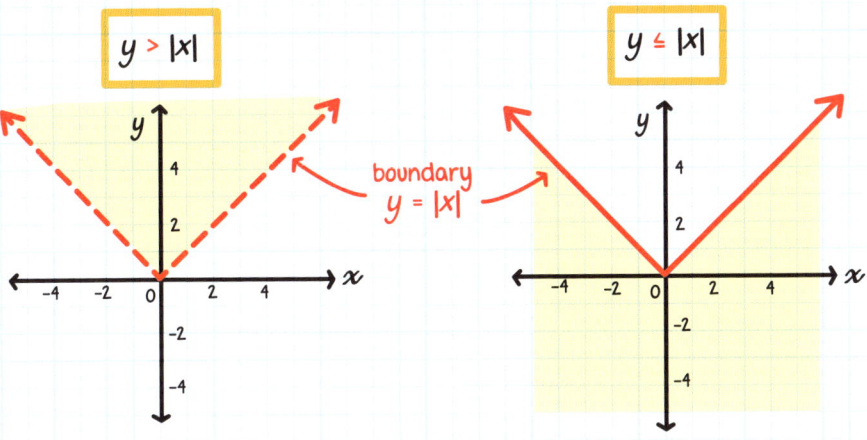

$$y > |x|$$

$$y \leq |x|$$

boundary
$$y = |x|$$

EXAMPLE: Graph $y < |x-8| - 14$.

STEP 1: Rewrite the inequality as an equation in standard form.

$$y < |x-8| - 14 \longrightarrow y = 1|x-8| - 14$$

$a > 0$, so the graph opens *upward*.

The vertex lies at (8, –14).

To graph, plot the vertex (8, –14), and then use the fact that $a > 0$ to draw the two rays.

STEP 2: Determine whether the boundary line should be *solid* or *dashed*.

< or > = dashed
≤ or ≥ = solid

Since the inequality $y < |x-8| - 14$ has a < sign, the boundary line should be *dashed*.

STEP 3: Shade the region that makes the inequality true.

Test $(0, 0)$ to see if it is a solution.

$y < |x - 8| - 14$

$0 \overset{?}{<} |0 - 8| - 14$ Substitute $(0, 0)$.

$0 \overset{?}{<} 8 - 14$

$0 \overset{?}{<} -6$ **False**

Since the inequality is FALSE, shade the region that does NOT contain $(0, 0)$. This is the region *below* the V-shaped graph.

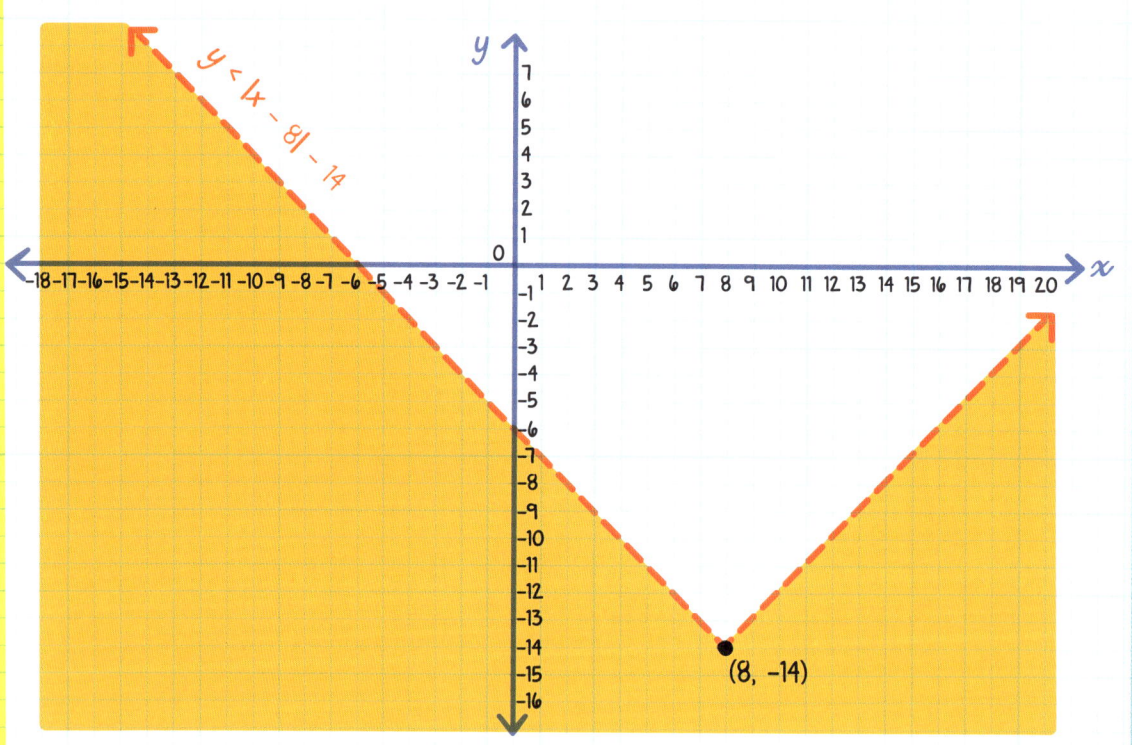

$(8, -14)$

GRAPH THE ABSOLUTE VALUE EQUATION.

1. $y = |x + 4|$

2. $y = -|x| + 7$

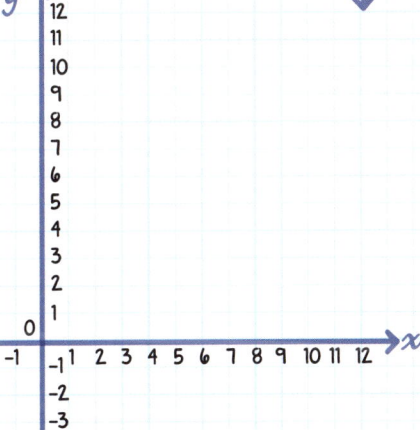

YAY!

3. $y = |x - 2| - 1$

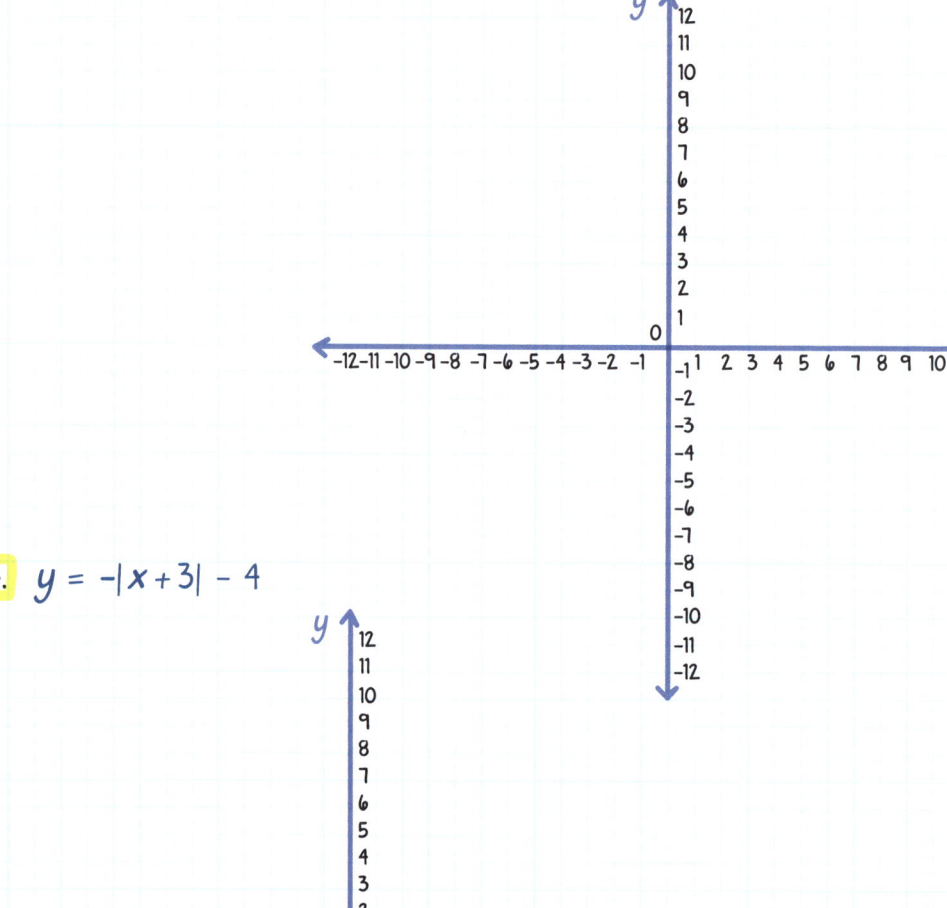

4. $y = -|x + 3| - 4$

GRAPH THE ABSOLUTE VALUE INEQUALITY.

5. $y > |x| + 3$

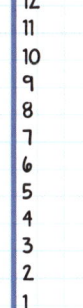

6. $y \leq |x - 6|$

7. $y \geq |x+8| - 1$

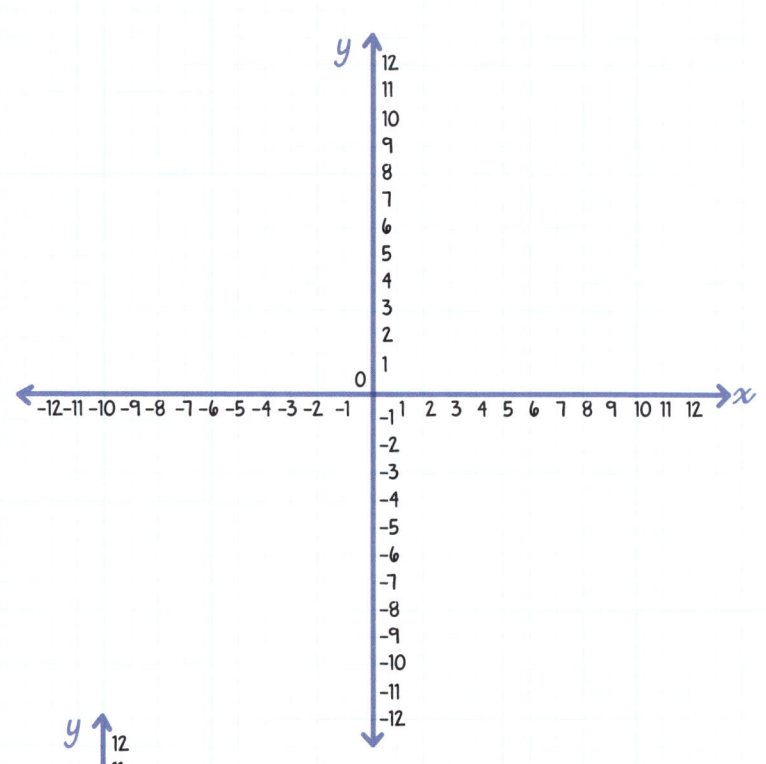

8. $y < |x-7| + 2$

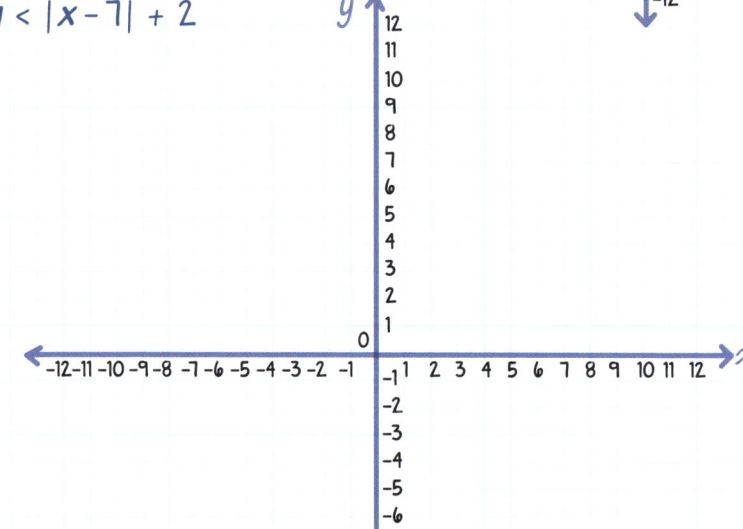

9. Graph the equations $y = |x| - 2$ and $y = -|x - 2|$ on the same coordinate plane. Then compare the graphs. How are they alike? How are they different?

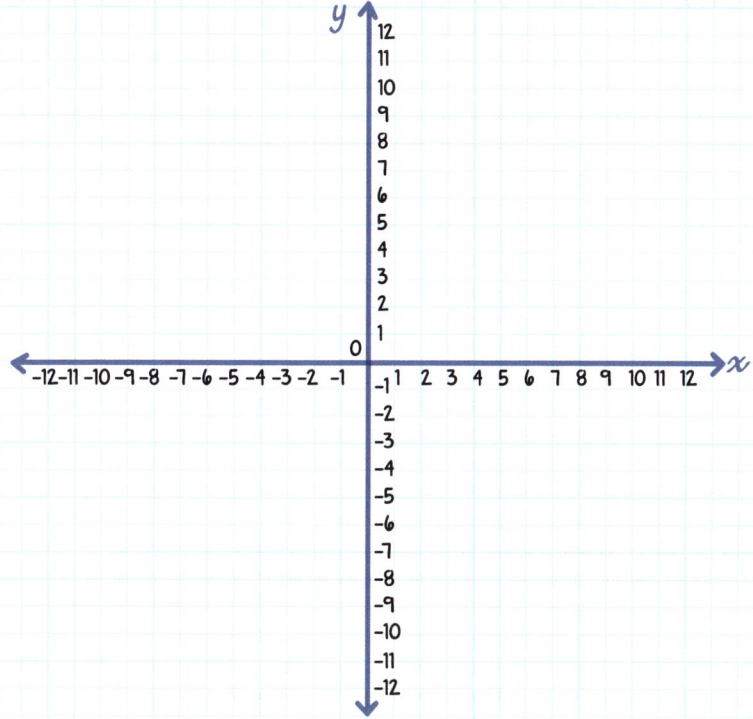

UNIT 1
Chapter 5 — SOLVING LINEAR SYSTEMS

A **LINEAR SYSTEM** is a set of two or more equations that share variables.

A solution to a linear system is a pair of values you can substitute for the variables to satisfy all equations.

To solve a linear system means to find all possible solutions of the system.

You can solve a linear system with the **SUBSTITUTION METHOD** by plugging one equation into another.

EXAMPLE: Use the **substitution method** to solve the following linear system.

$x - 0.5y = 1$ Equation 1
$6x + 4y = 20$ Equation 2

STEP 1: Solve one of the equations for one of the variables.

$x - 0.5y = 1$ Solve Equation 1 for x.
$x - 0.5y + 0.5y = 1 + 0.5y$
$x = 1 + 0.5y$

STEP 2: Substitute the rewritten equation for x in Equation 2.

$6x + 4y = 20$ Equation 2

$6(1 + 0.5y) + 4y = 20$

$6 + 3y + 4y = 20$

$6 + 7y = 20$

STEP 3: Solve for y.

$6 + 7y = 20$

$6 - 6 + 7y = 20 - 6$

$7y = 14$

$7y \div 7 = 14 \div 7$

$y = 2$

STEP 4: Find the value of x by substituting the y-value into Equation 1.

$x = 1 + 0.5y$ This form of Equation 1 is the easiest to work with because x is already isolated.

$x = 1 + 0.5(2)$

$x = 1 + 1$

$x = 2$

There is exactly one solution: $x = 2$ and $y = 2$, or $(x, y) = (2, 2)$.

STEP 5: Check the answer by making sure that *both* equations are satisfied by the x- and y-values.

Equation 1	Equation 2
$2 - 0.5(2) \stackrel{?}{=} 1$	$6(2) + 4(2) \stackrel{?}{=} 20$
$1 = 1$ ✓	$20 = 20$ ✓

You can solve a linear system with the **ELIMINATION METHOD** by eliminating one of the variables.

EXAMPLE: Use the **elimination method** to solve the following linear system.

$$3x - 5y = 27 \quad \text{Equation 1}$$
$$7x + 8y = 4 \quad \text{Equation 2}$$

STEP 1: Choose a variable to eliminate. Let's eliminate x.

Multiply Equation 1 by 7 and Equation 2 by -3, so that when the two equations are added together x will be eliminated.

Equation 1: $7(3x - 5y = 27)$
$$21x - 35y = 189$$

$$21x - 35y = 189 \quad \text{Equation 1}$$
$$-21x - 24y = -12 \quad \text{Equation 2}$$

Equation 2: $-3(7x + 8y = 4)$
$$-21x - 24y = -12$$

STEP 2: Add the two equations to eliminate x. Then solve for y.

$$21x - 35y = 189$$
$$-21x - 24y = -12$$
$$\overline{}$$
$$0 - 59y = 177$$
$$\frac{-59y}{-59} = \frac{177}{-59}$$
$$y = -3$$

YOU'VE BEEN ELIMINATED.

STEP 3: Find the value of x by substituting $y = -3$ into either equation. Let's use Equation 2.

$8y = 4 - 7x$ Equation 2

$8(-3) = 4 - 7x$ Substitute $y = -3$.

$-24 = 4 - 7x$

$-24 - 4 = 4 - 4 - 7x$

$-28 = -7x$

$$\frac{-28}{-7} = \frac{-7x}{-7}$$

$x = 4$

STEP 4: Check the answer by substituting $x = 4$ and $y = -3$ into *both* equations.

Equation 1	Equation 2
$3(4) - 5(-3) \overset{?}{=} 27$	$7(4) + 8(-3) \overset{?}{=} 4$
$4 = 4$ ✓	$-24 = -24$ ✓

Both equations are satisfied, so this system has exactly one solution: $(x, y) = (4, -3)$.

We can use linear systems to solve real-world problems.

EXAMPLE: A caterer pays $112 for 28 pounds of white potatoes and 40 pounds of sweet potatoes. If the total cost of 1 pound of white potatoes and 1 pound of sweet potatoes is $3.25, how much did the caterer pay for white potatoes? How much did the caterer pay for sweet potatoes?

STEP 1: Write a system of linear equations to model the problem.

Let x = the cost per pound of white potatoes.
Let y = the cost per pound of sweet potatoes.

$$28x + 40y = 112 \quad \text{Equation 1} \longleftarrow \text{Equation for total cost.}$$
$$x + y = 3.25 \quad \text{Equation 2} \longleftarrow \text{Equation for total number of potatoes.}$$

Let's use the substitution method to solve this linear system.

STEP 2: Solve Equation 2 for y.

$$x + y = 3.25$$
$$x - x + y = -x + 3.25$$
$$y = -x + 3.25$$

STEP 3: Substitute the right-hand side of the new Equation 2 for y in Equation 1 and solve for x (the cost per pound for white potatoes).

$$28x + 40y = 112$$
$$28x + 40(-x + 3.25) = 112$$
$$28x - 40x + 130 = 112$$
$$-12x + 130 = 112$$
$$-12x = -18 \longrightarrow x = 1.50$$

So, the value of x is 1.50 This means that the cost of 1 pound of white potatoes is $1.50.

STEP 4: Find the value of y (the cost per pound of sweet potatoes) by substituting $x = 1.50$ into one of the original equations. Let's substitute into Equation 2.

$$x + y = 3.25 \longrightarrow 1.50 + y = 3.25 \longrightarrow y = 1.75$$

So, the value of y is 1.75. This means that the cost of 1 pound of sweet potatoes is $1.75.

STEP 5: Check the answer by substituting the x- and y-values we just found into the original equations.

Equation 1	Equation 2
$28(1.50) + 40(1.75) \overset{?}{=} 112$	$1.50 + 1.75 \overset{?}{=} 3.25$
$112 = 112$ ✓	$3.25 = 3.25$ ✓

Therefore, the caterer paid $42 for 28 pounds of white potatoes $(28 \cdot 1.50 = 42)$ and $70 for 40 pounds of sweet potatoes $(40 \cdot 1.75 = 70)$.

We can solve a **SYSTEM OF LINEAR INEQUALITIES** graphically.

EXAMPLE: Graph the system of linear inequalities to find the solution set.

$$\begin{cases} -2x + 4y \geq -12 & \text{Inequality 1} \\ x + 8y < 16 & \text{Inequality 2} \end{cases}$$

STEP 1: Rewrite each inequality as an equation in slope-intercept form.

Inequality 1	Inequality 2
$-2x + 4y \geq -12$	$x + 8y < 16$
$-2x + 4y = -12$	$x + 8y = 16$
$y = \dfrac{1}{2}x - 3$	$y = -\dfrac{1}{8}x + 2$
slope $(m) = \dfrac{1}{2} = \dfrac{\text{rise}}{\text{run}}$	slope $(m) = -\dfrac{1}{8} = \dfrac{\text{rise}}{\text{run}}$
y-intercept = $(0, -3)$	y-intercept = $(0, 2)$

STEP 2: Determine whether each line should be solid or dashed. Then, graph both lines on the same coordinate plane.

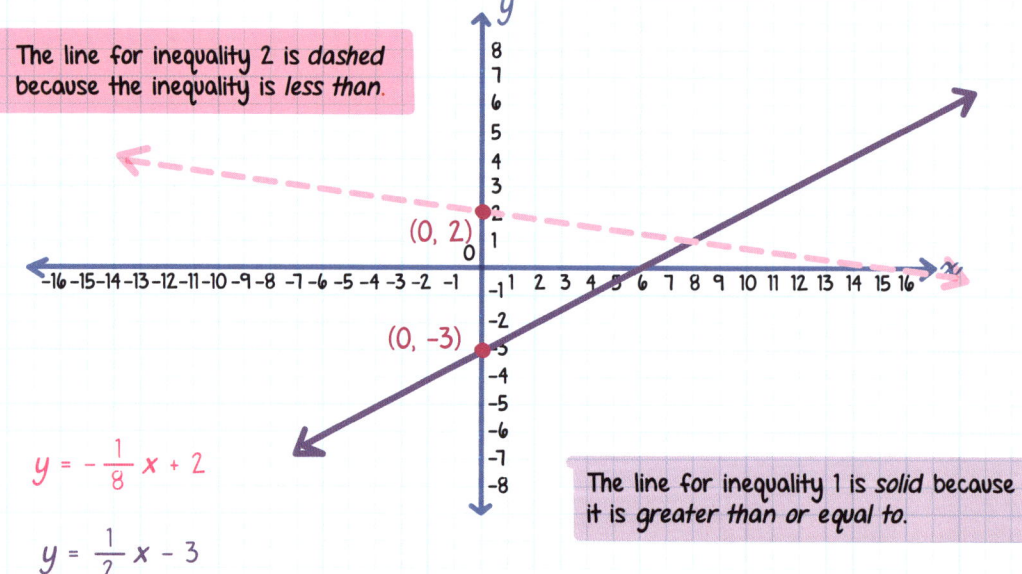

The line for inequality 2 is *dashed* because the inequality is *less than*.

$(0, 2)$

$(0, -3)$

$y = -\dfrac{1}{8}x + 2$

$y = \dfrac{1}{2}x - 3$

The line for inequality 1 is *solid* because it is *greater than or equal to*.

STEP 3: Shade the region that makes each individual inequality true by testing points on each side of the corresponding boundary line.

Inequality 1 Test point: $(0, 0)$	Inequality 1 Test point: $(0, -8)$
$-2x + 4y \geq -12$	$-2x + 4y \geq -12$
$-2(0) + 4(0) \geq -12$	$-2(0) + 4(-8) \geq -12$
$0 \overset{?}{\geq} -12$ ✓ True	$0 - 32 \geq -12$
	$-32 \overset{?}{\geq} -12$ ✗ False
Shade the region that contains $(0, 0)$.	Do *not* shade the region that contains $(0, -8)$.

Inequality 2 Test point: $(0, 0)$	Inequality 2 Test point: $(0, 8)$
$x + 8y < 16$	$x + 8y < 16$
$0 + 8(0) < 16$	$0 + 8(8) < 4$
$0 \overset{?}{<} 16$ ✓ True	$64 \overset{?}{<} 4$ ✗ False
Shade the region that contains $(0, 0)$.	Do *not* shade the region that contains $(0, 8)$.

STEP 4: Identify the solution of the system.

The solution set is the region that is shaded for *both* inequalities. This region contains the points that satisfy both inequalities.

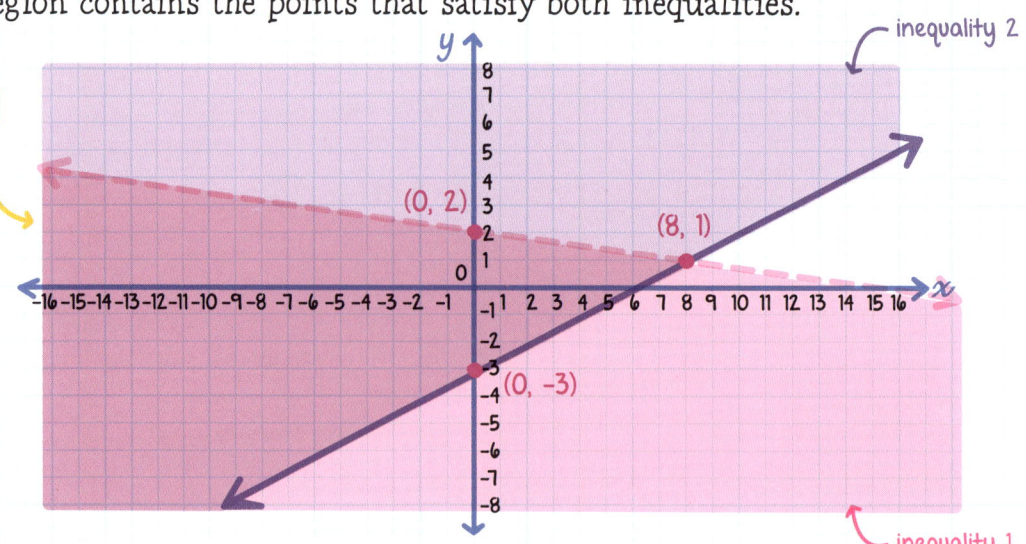

The point $(0, 0)$ is in both regions. That solution is in the region that is shaded by both inequalities.

Since the point of intersection $(8, 1)$ satisfies *only* Inequality 1, place an open circle on that point.

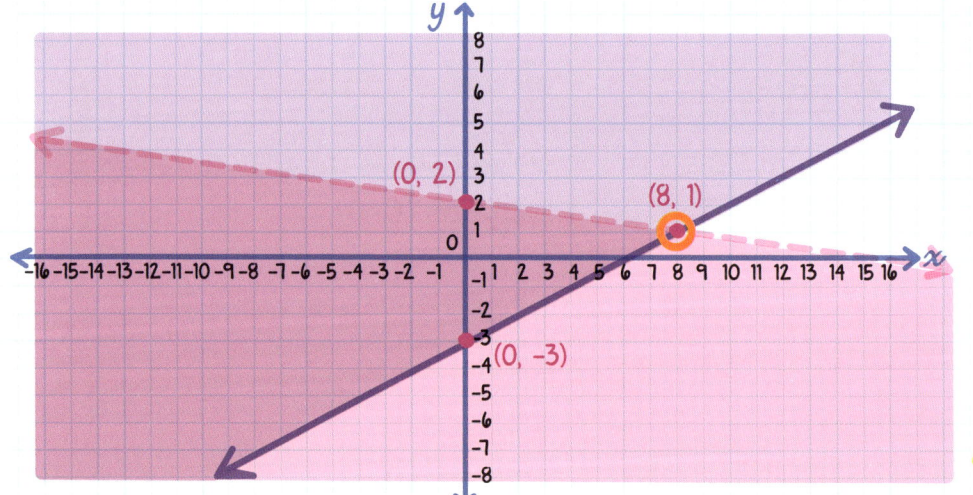

SOLVE EACH LINEAR SYSTEM BY SUBSTITUTION.

1. $\begin{cases} 8x - y = 13 \\ 4y = 12 \end{cases}$

2. $\begin{cases} 3x + 5y = 5 \\ 6x + 2y = 34 \end{cases}$

3. $\begin{cases} x + 7y = 21 \\ 2x - 4y = -12 \end{cases}$

SOLVE EACH LINEAR SYSTEM BY ELIMINATION.

4.
$$\begin{cases} -6x + 2y = 5 \\ -2x + 2y = 5 \end{cases}$$

5.
$$\begin{cases} 4x + y = 3 \\ -4x - y = 14 \end{cases}$$

6. $\begin{cases} -\dfrac{1}{2}x + 2y = 8 \\ \\ 5x + 6y = 24 \end{cases}$

GRAPH EACH SYSTEM OF LINEAR INEQUALITIES TO FIND THE SOLUTION SET.

7. $\begin{cases} 6x + 7y > 9 \\ x - 5y < 14 \end{cases}$

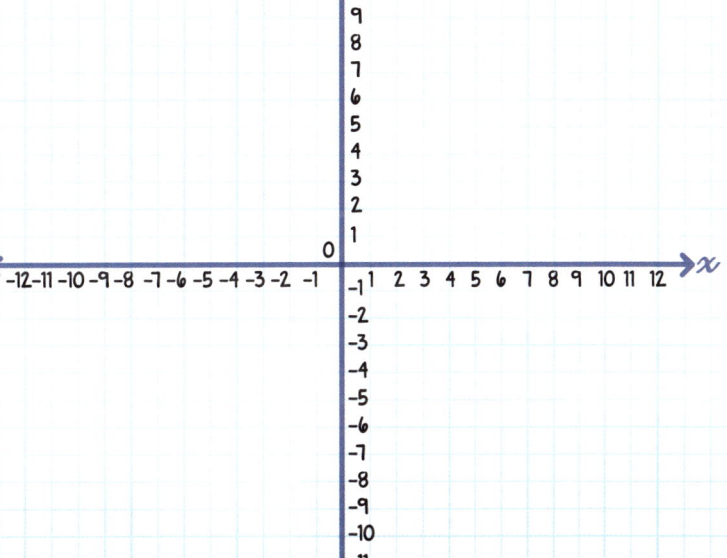

8. $\begin{cases} -x + 6y < 11 \\ y \geq 5 \end{cases}$

9. $\begin{cases} 2y < 8 \\ 11x + 9y > -13 \end{cases}$

10. Principal Johnson is ordering pizza for the senior class pizza party. A cheese pizza is $16 and a pepperoni pizza is $19. He orders 56 pizzas in total and spends $971. How many cheese pizzas did Principal Johnson order? How many pepperoni pizzas did he order?

THINK:
You have two totals, so you can make two equations. Each kind of pizza is a variable.

UNIT 1
Chapter 6

EXPONENTS AND ROOTS

An **EXPONENT** (or **POWER**) is the amount of times a number is multiplied by itself. The number is called the **BASE**.

exponent

$$4^3 = 4 \times 4 \times 4 = 64$$

base

Use these exponent rules to evaluate expressions with exponents.

NEGATIVE EXPONENT RULES

$x^{-a} = \dfrac{1}{x^a}$, where $x \neq 0$

Take reciprocals to write the negative exponents as positive exponents.

$\dfrac{1}{x^{-a}} = \dfrac{x^a}{1} = x^a$, where $x \neq 0$

$\left(\dfrac{x}{y}\right)^{-a} = \left(\dfrac{y}{x}\right)^a = \left(\dfrac{y^a}{x^a}\right)$, where $x \neq 0$ and $y \neq 0$

Use caution when working with negative bases! $-3^6 \neq (-3)^6$

OTHER EXPONENT RULES

Zero Exponent Rule	Power Rule
$x^0 = 1$, where $x \neq 0$	$(x^a)^b = x^{(a \cdot b)}$
Product Rule	Power of Product Rule
$x^a \cdot x^b = x^{(a + b)}$	$(x \cdot y)^a = x^a \cdot y^a$
Quotient Rule	Power of Quotient Rule
$\dfrac{x^a}{x^b} = x^a \div x^b = x^{(a - b)}$, where $x \neq 0$	$\left(\dfrac{x}{y}\right)^a = \dfrac{x^a}{y^a}$, where $y \neq 0$

EXAMPLE: Simplify: $\left(\dfrac{x^2 x^4}{y}\right)^{-3}$. Write the final answer without any negative exponents.

First, simplify the expression inside the parentheses.

$\dfrac{x^2 x^4}{y} = \dfrac{x^{2+4}}{y} = \dfrac{x^6}{y}$ product rule

Next, rewrite the negative exponent as a positive exponent.

$= \left(\dfrac{x^6}{y}\right)^{-3} = \left(\dfrac{y}{x^6}\right)^3$ Take the reciprocal.

Then, use exponent rules to simplify.

$= \dfrac{y^3}{(x^6)^3}$ power of quotient rule

$= \dfrac{y^3}{x^{18}}$ power rule

So, $\left(\dfrac{x^2 x^4}{y}\right)^{-3}$ simplifies to $\dfrac{y^3}{x^{18}}$.

A **RADICAL** is an expression that uses a root, like a square root.

To **SQUARE** a number, raise it to the power of 2: $10^2 = 100$

10 is called a **SQUARE ROOT** of 100. In general, if $x^2 = y$, then x is a square root of y. If x is positive, we can write $x = \sqrt{y}$.

To **CUBE** a number, raise it to the power of 3: $6^3 = 216$.

If $x^3 = y$, then x is a **CUBE ROOT** of y and we can write $x = \sqrt[3]{y}$.

When the square root of an integer is also an integer, the initial integer is called a **PERFECT SQUARE**.

16 is a perfect square because $\sqrt{16}$ = 4. 16 and 4 are both integers.

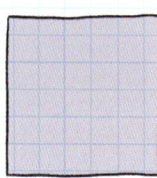

If the cube root of an integer is also an integer it's called a **PERFECT CUBE**.

125 is a perfect cube because $\sqrt[3]{125}$ = 5. 125 and 5 are both integers.

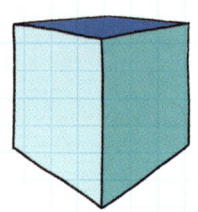

Taking the nth root of a number is the "opposite" of raising a number to the nth power.

For example: $\sqrt[5]{-7{,}776} = -6$

Use these rules to simplify square root expressions:

$$\sqrt{x^2} = |x| \qquad (\sqrt{x})^2 = x$$

Square Root Product Rule	$\sqrt{x \cdot y} = \sqrt{x} \cdot \sqrt{y}$
Square Root Quotient Rule	$\sqrt{\dfrac{x}{y}} = \dfrac{\sqrt{x}}{\sqrt{y}}$

Simplifying Square Root Expressions

THINK:

A square root expression is simplified if:

- No radicand has a factor that is a perfect square.
- There are no radicals in a denominator.
- There are no negative exponents.

EXAMPLE: Simplify $-7\sqrt{12}$.

STEP 1: Rewrite 12 as a product of two factors so that at least one of the factors is a perfect square.

$-7\sqrt{12}$

$= -7\sqrt{4 \cdot 3}$ 4 is a perfect square.

$= -7 \cdot \sqrt{4} \cdot \sqrt{3}$ Use the square root product rule.

THINK:

$-7\sqrt{12}$ means to multiply -7 and $\sqrt{12}$. In other words, $-7\sqrt{12} = -7 \cdot \sqrt{12}$.

STEP 2: Multiply:

$= -7 \cdot \sqrt{4} \cdot \sqrt{3}$ $\sqrt{4} = 2$

$= -7 \cdot 2 \cdot \sqrt{3}$

$= -14\sqrt{3}$

So, $-7\sqrt{12}$ can be simplified to $-14\sqrt{3}$.

SIMPLIFYING IS BEST

USE WHAT YOU KNOW ABOUT EXPONENTS AND ROOTS
TO SIMPLIFY EACH OF THE FOLLOWING EXPRESSIONS.

1. $(-4)^3$

2. $(3x^3y^2)^2$

3. $(-\sqrt{16})^0 + \dfrac{6^{-2}}{3}$

4. $-\left(\dfrac{5}{8}\right)^{-2}$

5. $\sqrt{49}$

6. $\sqrt[4]{-256}$

7. $\sqrt[3]{512}$

8. $\sqrt{84}$

9. $\sqrt{18}$

10. $\dfrac{24b^3h^4}{8bh^2}$

11. $\sqrt{121x^4y^5}$

12. $\sqrt{36x^6y^7}$

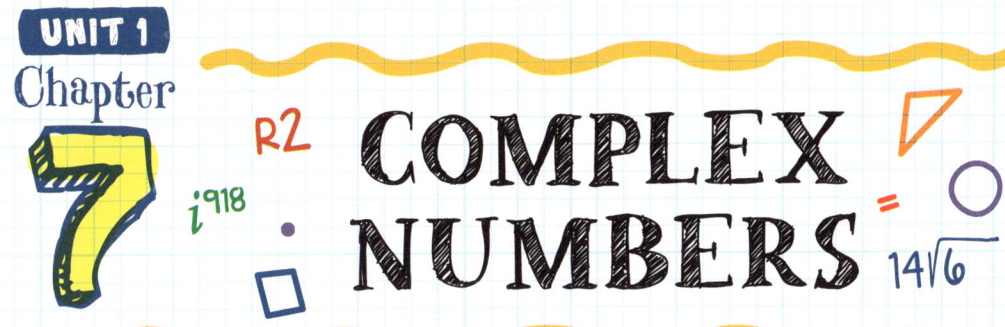

R2

COMPLEX NUMBERS

i^{918}

$= \bigcirc$

$14\sqrt{6}$

The **IMAGINARY UNIT** i is defined as $\sqrt{-1}$.

When we raise i to a positive number, there are only four possible answers: 1, i, -1, or $-i$.

$i^2 = \sqrt{-1} \cdot \sqrt{-1} = -1$

$i^3 = i^2 \cdot i = -1 \cdot i = -i$

$i^4 = i^2 \cdot i^2 = (-1) \cdot (-1) = 1$

$i^5 = i^4 \cdot i = 1 \cdot i = i$

To determine the value of i raised to *any* positive power, divide the exponent by 4 and identify the remainder.

EXAMPLE: Evaluate i^{27}.

STEP 1: Divide 27 (the exponent) by 4. Indicate the remainder.

$27 \div 4 = 6$ R3

STEP 2: Since the remainder is 3, find the value of i^3.

$i^3 = -i$

So, $i^{27} = i^3 = -i$.

Evaluate i^{918}.

STEP 1: Divide 918 (the exponent) by 4. Indicate the remainder.

$918 \div 4 = 229$ R2

STEP 2: Since the remainder is 2, find the value of i^2.

$i^2 = -1$

So, $i^{918} = i^2 = -1$.

EXAMPLE: Evaluate the two expressions.

$$-11i^2 - 3i^2 \qquad\qquad (-11i^2)(-3i^2)$$

STEP 1: Combine like terms.

$-11i^2 - 3i^2$

$= -14i^2$

STEP 2: Substitute $i^2 = -1$.

$= -14 \cdot (-1)$

$= 14$

So, $-11i^2 - 3i^2 = 14$.

STEP 1: Multiply.

$(-11i^2)(-3i^2)$

$= 33i^4$

STEP 2: Substitute $i^4 = 1$.

$= 33 \cdot 1$

$= 33$

So, $(-11i^2)(-3i^2) = 33$.

A **COMPLEX NUMBER** consists of a real number and an imaginary part.

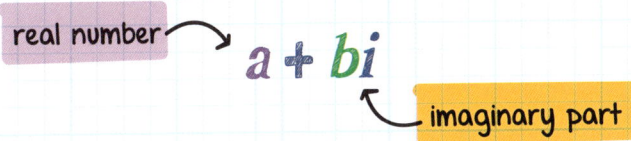

real number → $a + bi$ ← imaginary part

We can **ADD** two complex numbers by adding first their real parts and then their imaginary parts.

EXAMPLE: Evaluate the expression $(8 + 10i) + (32 + 9i)$. Write the complex number in standard form.

$(8 + 10i) + (32 + 9i)$
$= (8 + 32) + (10 + 9)i$
$= 40 + 19i$

So, the sum of the two complex numbers in standard form is $40 + 19i$.

We can **MULTIPLY** two complex numbers with the following formula:
$(a + bi)(c + di) = (ac - bd) + (ad + bc)i$

EXAMPLE: Evaluate the expression $(8 + 10i)(32 + 9i)$. Write the complex number in standard form.

$(8 + 10i)(32 + 9i)$
$= (8 \cdot 32 - 10 \cdot 9) + (8 \cdot 9 + 10 \cdot 32)i$
$= (256 - 90) + (72 + 320)i$
$= 166 + 392i$

THINK:
You could also use the FOIL method to multiply. Just replace i^2 with -1 when you simplify.

We can **DIVIDE** two complex numbers by multiplying both the numerator and the denominator by the **CONJUGATE** of the denominator.

The conjugate of the complex number $a + bi$ is the complex number $a - bi$. When we multiply these two conjugates, we get:

$$(a + bi)(a - bi) = a^2 + b^2$$

EXAMPLE: Write the quotient $\dfrac{5 + 3i\sqrt{6}}{8 + 2i\sqrt{6}}$ in standard form.

STEP 1: Multiply both the numerator and the denominator by the conjugate of the denominator.

$$\frac{(5 + 3i\sqrt{6})}{(8 + 2i\sqrt{6})} \cdot \frac{(8 - 2i\sqrt{6})}{(8 - 2i\sqrt{6})}$$

Since the denominator is the product of conjugates, we can use the formula $(a + bi)(a - bi) = a^2 + b^2$.

$$\frac{(5 + 3i\sqrt{6})}{(8 + 2i\sqrt{6})} \cdot \frac{(8 - 2i\sqrt{6})}{(8 - 2i\sqrt{6})} = \frac{40 - 10i\sqrt{6} + 24i\sqrt{6} + 36}{64 + (2\sqrt{6})^2}$$

STEP 2: Simplify the numerator and denominator and rewrite the answer in standard form.

$$= \frac{40 - 10i\sqrt{6} + 24i\sqrt{6} + 36}{64 + 4 \bullet 6}$$

$$= \frac{76 + 14i\sqrt{6}}{64 + 24}$$

$$= \frac{76 + 14i\sqrt{6}}{88}$$

$= \dfrac{76}{88} \div \dfrac{4}{4} + \dfrac{14\sqrt{6}}{88} i \div \dfrac{2}{2}$ Reduce each fraction.

$= \dfrac{19}{22} + \dfrac{7\sqrt{6}}{44} i$

So, the quotient of the two complex numbers in standard form is $\dfrac{19}{22} + \dfrac{7\sqrt{6}}{44} i$.

EVALUATE THE POWER OF i. THE FINAL ANSWER SHOULD HAVE NO EXPONENT.

1. i^{158}

2. i^{227}

3. i^{469}

SIMPLIFY THE EXPRESSION.

4. $3i\sqrt{-49}$

5. $4\sqrt{-76}$

6. $-5i^9 + 7i^9$

7. $16i^{18} - 5i^{18}$

EVALUATE THE EXPRESSION AND WRITE THE COMPLEX NUMBER IN STANDARD FORM.

8. $(4 + 2i) + (8 + 7i)$

9. $(13 + 3i) - (9 + 11i)$

10. $(2 - 4i)(6 + 7i)$

11. $\dfrac{8 - 6i}{2 + 7i}$

12. $\dfrac{3 + 4i}{10 - 5i}$

Unit 2

Functions

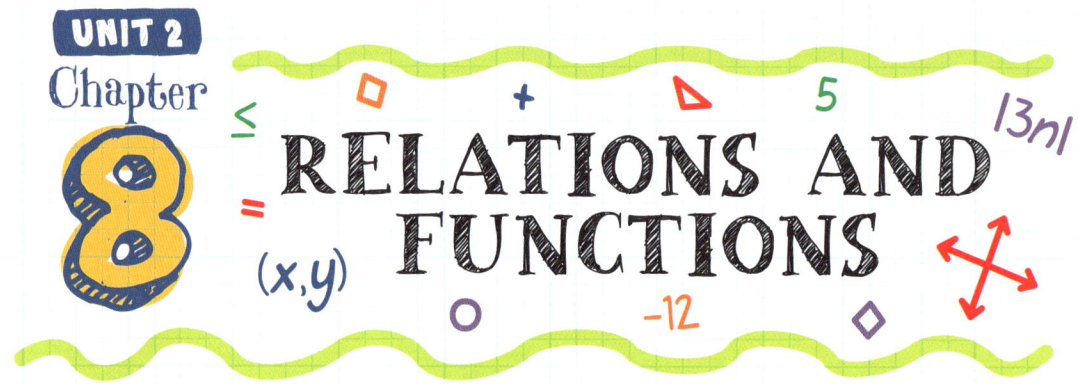

UNIT 2

Chapter 8

RELATIONS AND FUNCTIONS

A **RELATION** is a set of ordered pairs (*x*, *y*).

The **DOMAIN** of a relation is the set of all *x*-values (inputs).

The **RANGE** of a relation is the set of all *y*-values (outputs).

A **FUNCTION** is a relation that has *exactly one* output for each input. If a relation has multiple outputs for one input, it is NOT a function.

EXAMPLE: Is the relation {(-11, 11), (-8, -6), (-5, 8), (-11, -5)} a function?

The domain of this relation is {-11, -8, -5} and the range of this relation is {-6, -5, 8, 11}.

Make an input/output table for this relation.

x-value (input)	y-value (output)
-11	11
-8	-6
-5	8
-11	-5

Ask yourself: Does each input value (in the domain) have only one output value (in the range)? No.

The *x*-value -11 has two outputs: 11 and -5.

This relation is a *not* a function because the input -11 has more than one output (11 and -5).

The **VERTICAL LINE TEST** determines if the graph of a relation is a function. If *any* vertical line touches more than one point on the graph, then it is NOT a function.

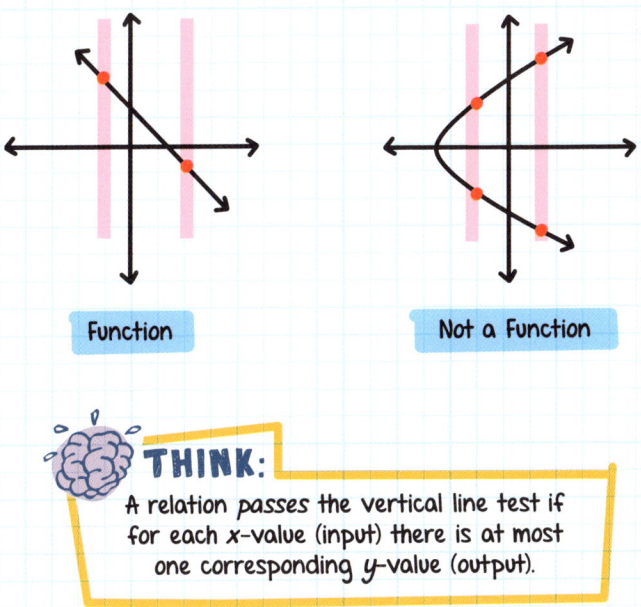

Function

Not a Function

THINK:
A relation *passes* the vertical line test if for each *x*-value (input) there is at most one corresponding *y*-value (output).

In **FUNCTION NOTATION** the **dependent variable** is written as $f(x)$. x is the **independent variable**.

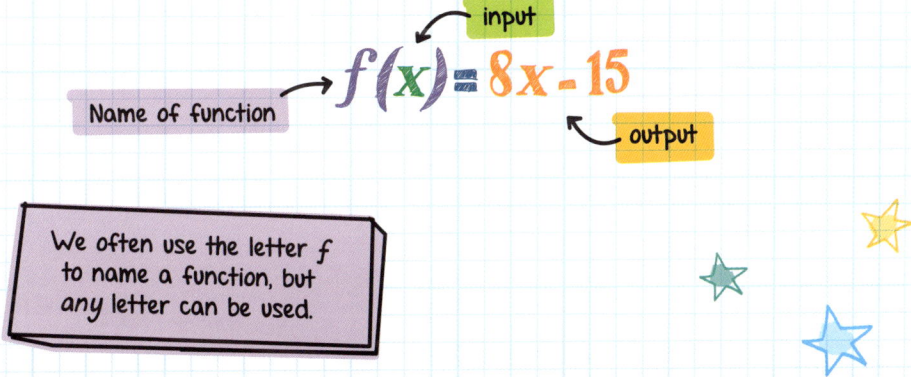

input

$$f(x) = 8x - 15$$

Name of function

output

We often use the letter f to name a function, but any letter can be used.

To evaluate a function, substitute a given value for the independent variable x.

Evaluate $f(x) = x^2 - 7x + 12$ when $x = -4$.

$f(x) = x^2 - 7x + 12$

$f(-4) = (-4)^2 - 7(-4) + 12$ Substitute -4 for x.

$f(-4) = 16 + 28 + 12$

$f(-4) = 56$

Therefore, $f(-4) = 56$.

We can substitute any algebraic expression for x.

EXAMPLE: Evaluate $g(x) = \dfrac{6x + 8}{2}$ when $x = 3c + 2d$.

$g(x) = \dfrac{6x + 8}{2}$

$g(3c + 2d) = \dfrac{6(3c + 2d) + 8}{2}$ Substitute 3c+2d for x.

$g(3c + 2d) = \dfrac{18c + 12d + 8}{2}$ Apply the Distributive Property.

$g(3c + 2d) = \dfrac{18c}{2} + \dfrac{12d}{2} + \dfrac{8}{2}$ Rewrite as three addends.

$g(3c + 2d) = \dfrac{9c}{1} + \dfrac{6d}{1} + \dfrac{4}{1}$ Simplify each addend.

$g(3c + 2d) = 9c + 6d + 4$

Therefore, $g(3c + 2d) = 9c + 6d + 4$.

To graph a function, follow these steps. Let's use the function $f(x) = 2x - 4$ as an example.

STEP 1: Make a table of input/output values.

THINK:
Substitute the x-value into the function and solve to find the y-value.

x-value (input)	$f(x) = 2x - 4$	y-value (output)	$(x, f(x))$
-4	2(-4) – 4	-12	(-4, -12)
-2	2(-2) – 4	-8	(-2, -8)
0	2(0) – 4	-4	(0, -4)
2	2(2) – 4	0	(2, 0)
4	2(4) – 4	4	(4, 4)

STEP 2: Plot the ordered pairs on the coordinate plane and connect them with a line.

THINK:
You could also graph the function by finding the x- and y-intercepts and drawing a line between them.

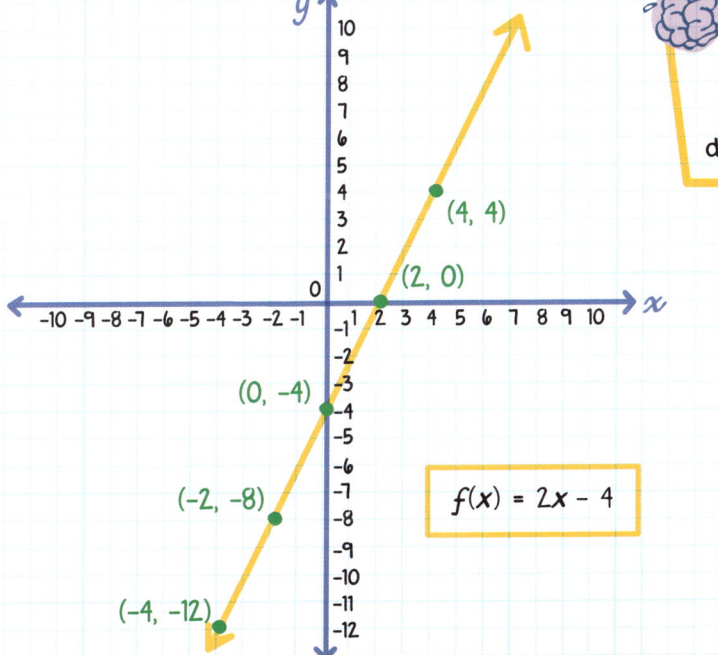

$f(x) = 2x - 4$

Using a Graph to Find the Range

We can identify the range of a function with a restricted domain by drawing its graph.

EXAMPLE: Graph the following function and identify its range.

$f(x) = |3x - 2|, -6 \leq x \leq 6.$

This is the restricted domain.

STEP 1: Make a table of input/output values.

x-values need to be within the domain.

x-value (input)	$f(x) = |3x - 2|$	y-value (output)	$(x, f(x))$
-6	$|3(-6) - 2|$	20	(-6, 20)
-4	$|3(-4) - 2|$	14	(-4, 14)
-2	$|3(-2) - 2|$	8	(-2, 8)
0	$|3(0) - 2|$	2	(0, 2)
2	$|3(2) - 2|$	4	(2, 4)
4	$|3(4) - 2|$	10	(4, 10)
6	$|3(6) - 2|$	16	(6, 16)

STEP 2: Plot the ordered pairs on the coordinate plane and connect them with a line.

The V-shaped graph will have endpoints (-6, 20) and (6, 16).

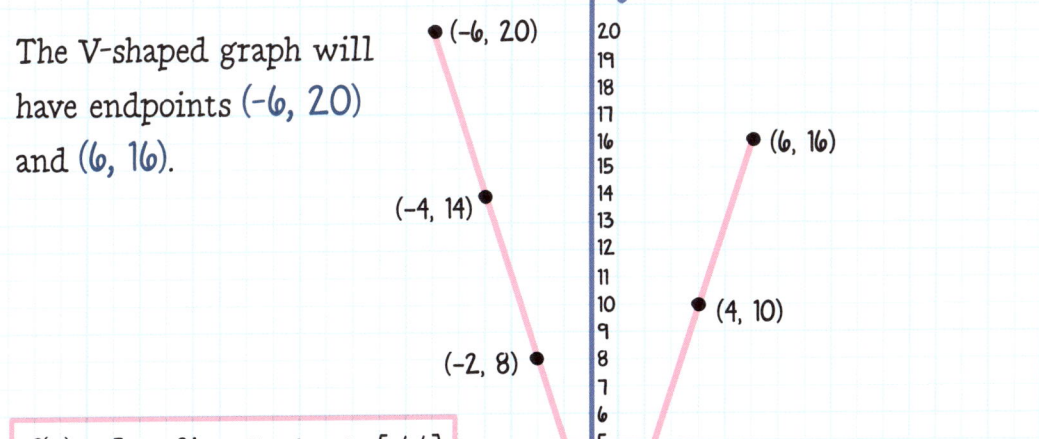

$f(x) = |3x - 2|$ on the domain $[-6, 6]$

The graph shows that the range is [0, 20].

Characteristics of Functions

When a function is graphed on the coordinate plane, we can identify where it is decreasing, constant, and increasing.

A function is DECREASING over an interval if the graph moves *downward* from left to right.

A function is INCREASING over an interval if the graph moves *upward* from left to right.

A function is CONSTANT over an interval if the graph is a *horizontal line*.

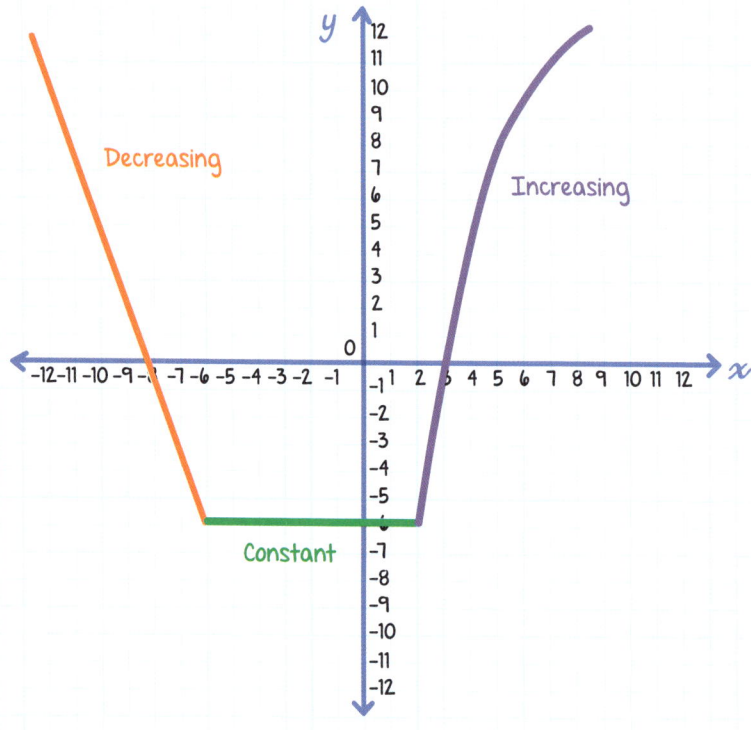

WRITE THE DOMAIN AND THE RANGE OF EACH GIVEN RELATION. THEN STATE WHETHER EACH OF THE GIVEN RELATIONS IS A FUNCTION.

1. (−9, 0), (−9, 1), (−5, 8), (7, 2), (14, 15)

2. (−14, −13), (6, 1), (19,−8), (45, −12), (63, 54)

STATE WHETHER EACH GRAPHED RELATION IS A FUNCTION.

3.

4.

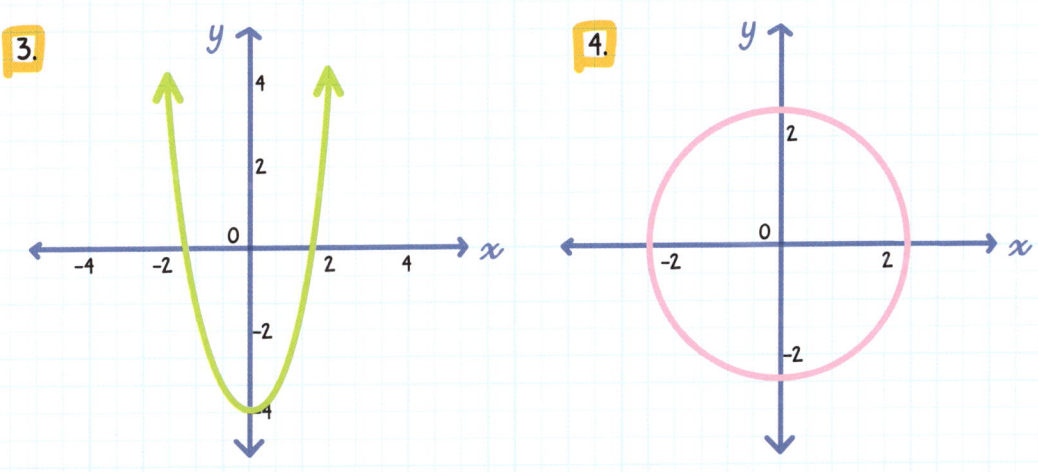

5. Graph the function $f(x) = \frac{2}{7}x + 4$. Identify the x- and y-intercepts of f.

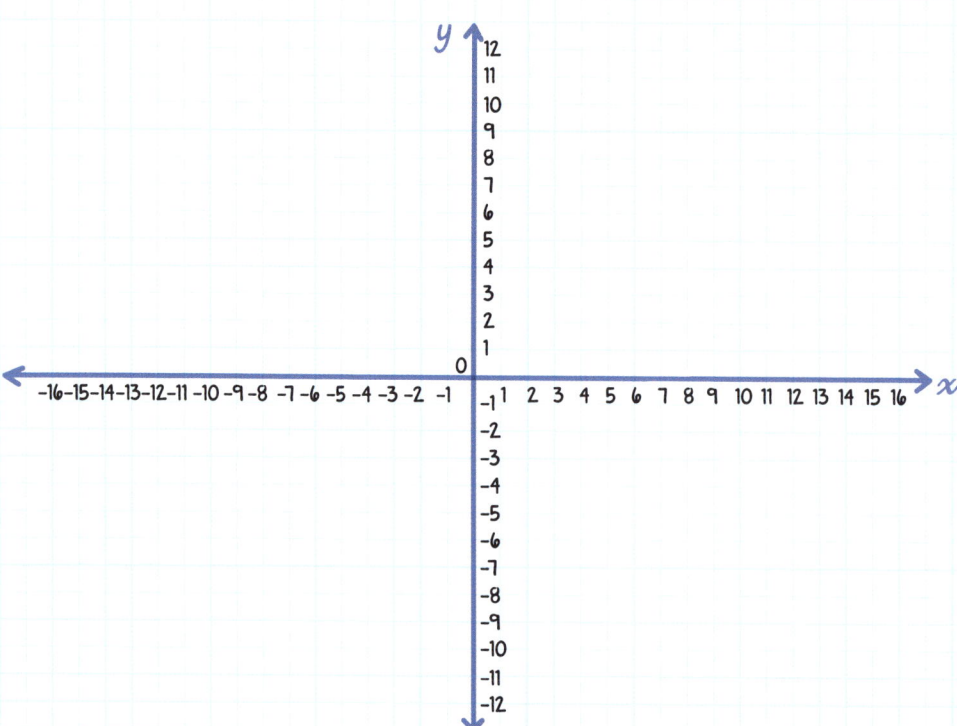

EVALUATE EACH FUNCTION AT THE GIVEN VALUE.

6. $k(g) = \frac{9g+7}{5} - 1; \; g = 2$

7. $p(k) = k - 6m; \; k = m - 3d$

FIND THE VALUE OF THE VARIABLE.

8. If $p(x) = \frac{1}{3}x + 12$, find the value of x given that $p(x) = 9$.

9. If $d(k) = -4 + \frac{1}{4}k$, find the value of k given that $d(k) = 24$.

10. For the given graph, state the domain, range, and intervals over which the function is increasing, decreasing, and constant.

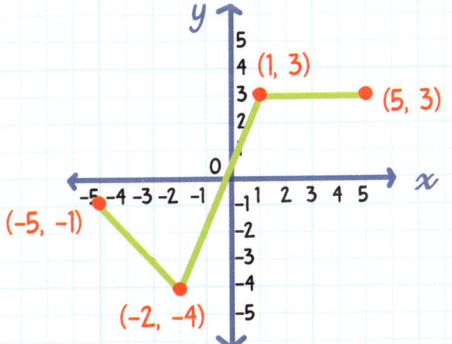

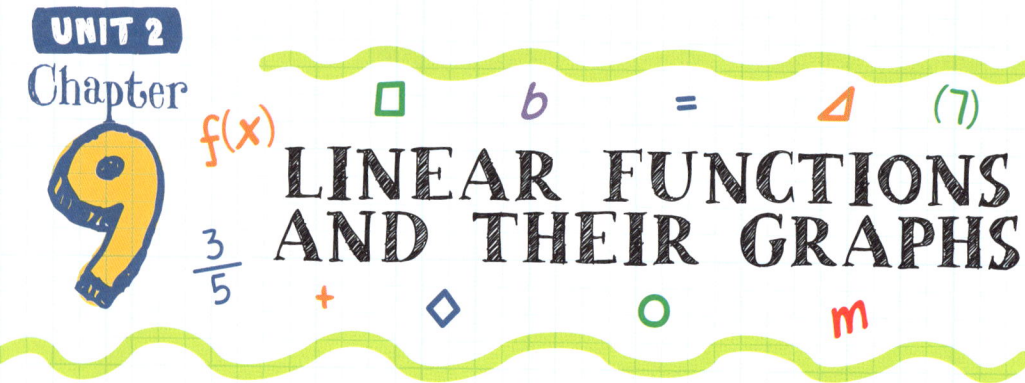

UNIT 2

Chapter 9

LINEAR FUNCTIONS AND THEIR GRAPHS

A **LINEAR FUNCTION** is a function whose graph is a line.
It has the form:

$$f(x) = mx + b$$

slope

y-intercept (0, b)

An **EXPLICIT DEFINITION** of a function is an equation with $f(x)$ isolated on the left-hand side of the equation.

A linear function can be described using an equation, a graph, a table, two points, or a description.

EXAMPLE: Use the graph to write a linear equation.

STEP 1: Find the slope.

Choose two points from the graph and plug them into the slope formula.

$(x_1, y_1) = (-1, 2)$

$(x_2, y_2) = (-2, 6)$

$$m = \frac{y_2 - y_1}{x_2 - x_1} = \frac{6 - 2}{-2 - (-1)} = \frac{4}{-1} = -4$$

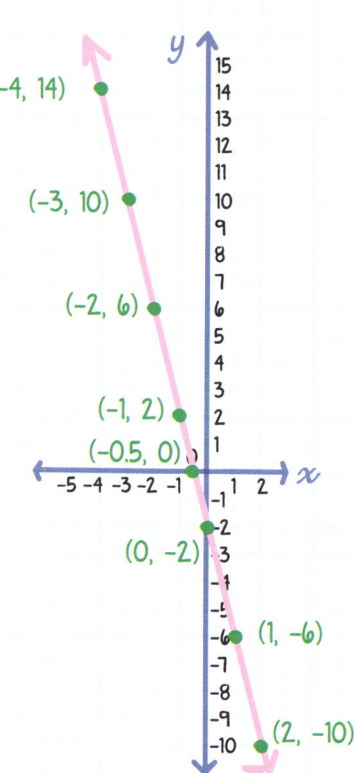

(−4, 14)
(−3, 10)
(−2, 6)
(−1, 2)
(−0.5, 0)
(0, −2)
(1, −6)
(2, −10)

STEP 2: Use the slope and y-intercept to write an equation of the line in slope-intercept form: $y = mx + b$.

slope: $m = -4$
y-intercept: $(0, -2)$

$y = -4x + (-2)$

STEP 3: Write the equation as a function.

$f(x) = -4x - 2$

Replace y with $f(x)$.

Comparing Linear Functions

Given functions f and g, the graphs of these two functions can tell us when $f(x) = g(x)$, $f(x) > g(x)$, and $f(x) < g(x)$.

EXAMPLE: The graphs of functions f and g are given below. Determine all x-values where $f(x) = g(x)$, where $f(x) > g(x)$, and where $f(x) < g(x)$.

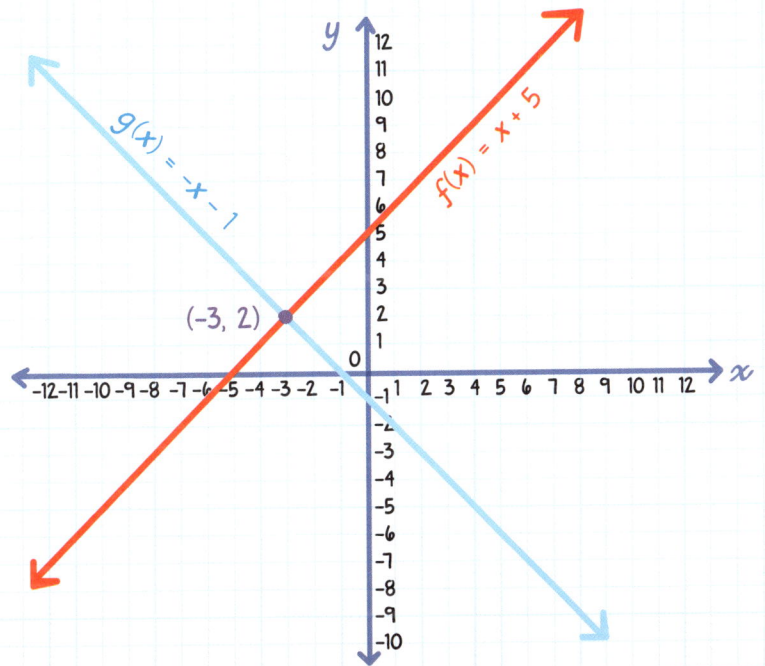

STEP 1: Determine where $f(x) = g(x)$.

$f(x)$ equals $g(x)$ when the two graphs INTERSECT.

On the graph, we see that the point of intersection is $(-3, 2)$.

So, $f(x) = g(x)$ at $x = -3$.

STEP 2: Determine where $f(x) > g(x)$.

$f(x)$ is greater than $g(x)$ when the graph of f is ABOVE the graph of g.

On the graph, we see that this occurs to the right of $x = -3$.

So, $f(x) > g(x)$ on $(-3, \infty)$.

STEP 3: Determine where $f(x) < g(x)$.

$f(x)$ is less than $g(x)$ when the graph of f is BELOW the graph of g.

On the graph. we see that this occurs to the left of $x = -3$.

So, $f(x) < g(x)$ on $(-\infty, -3)$.

DIRECT VARIATON is a relationship between two variables expressing that one is a constant multiple of the other.

Direct Variation Equation:

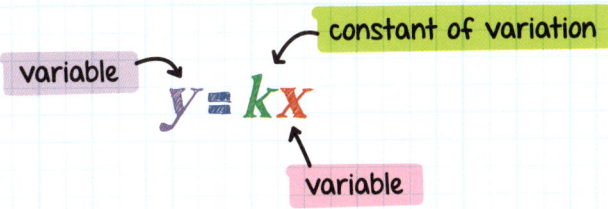

constant of variation

variable

$$y = kx$$

variable

In the equation $y = 10x$, y is a constant multiple of x. The constant of variation is 10.

This is a table of values for $y = 10$. Notice that every time the x-value increases by 1, the y-value increases by 10.

x	1	2	3	4
y	10	20	30	40

On a graph, the constant of variation is the slope (or the rate of change).

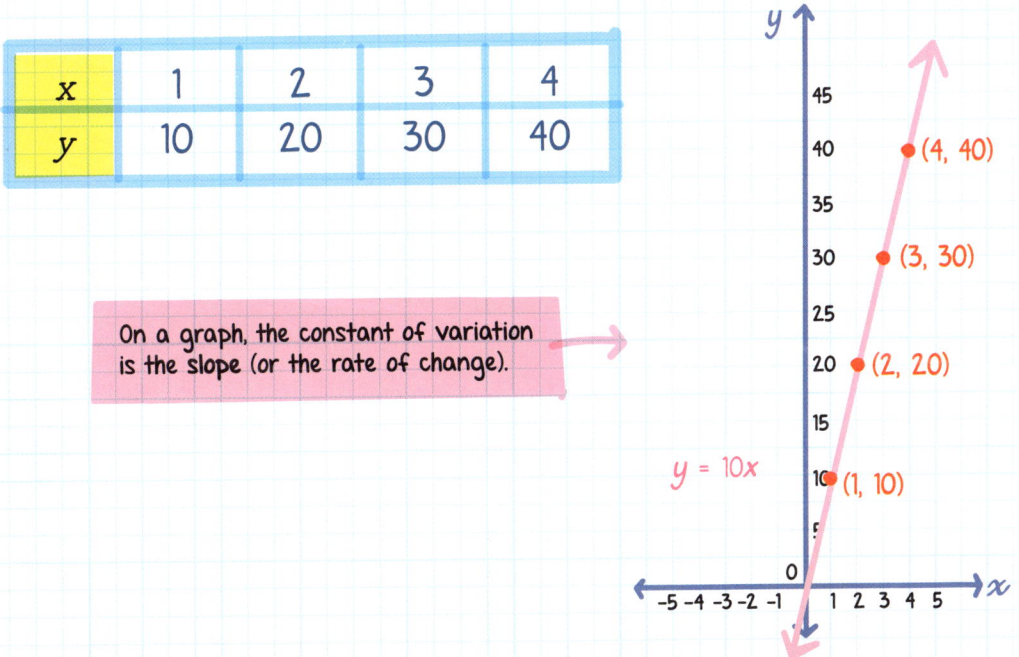

$y = 10x$

(4, 40)

(3, 30)

(2, 20)

(1, 10)

EXAMPLE: If $y = kx$ and $y = 12$ when $x = 15$, then what is y when $x = 25$?

Here are four approaches to solving this problem.

Method 1: We are given that $y = 12$ when $x = 15$, so that $12 = k(15)$, or $k = \frac{12}{15} = \frac{4}{5}$. Therefore $y = \frac{4x}{5}$. When $x = 25$, $y = \frac{4(25)}{5} = 20$.

Method 2: Since y varies directly as x, $\frac{y}{x}$ is a constant. So, we can write the following ratio: $\frac{12}{15} = \frac{y}{25}$. Cross multiplying gives $300 = 15y$, so that $y = \frac{300}{15} = 20$.

Method 3: The graph of $y = f(x)$ is a line passing through the points $(0, 0)$ and $(15, 12)$. The slope of this line is $\frac{12 - 0}{15 - 0} = \frac{12}{15} = \frac{4}{5}$. Writing the equation of the line in slope-intercept form, we have $y = \frac{4}{5}x$.

As in Method 1, when $x = 25$, we have $y = \frac{4(25)}{5} = 20$.

Method 4: To get from $x = 15$ to $x = 25$, multiply x by $\frac{5}{3}$. Because y varies directly as x, it is directly proportional to x. So, we must also multiply y by $\frac{5}{3}$. We get $\frac{5}{3}(12) = 20$.

USE WHAT YOU KNOW ABOUT LINEAR FUNCTIONS AND THEIR GRAPHS TO ANSWER THE FOLLOWING QUESTIONS.

1. Write an explicit definition of the linear function whose graph is shown.

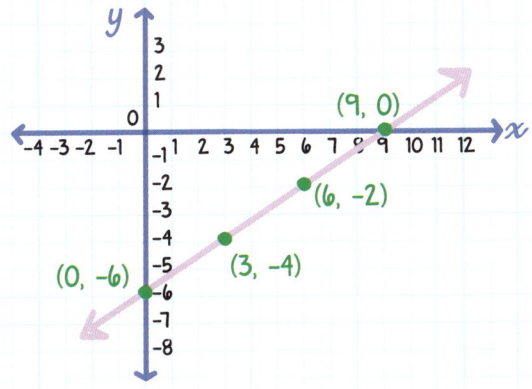

2. Write an explicit definition of the linear function whose graph is shown.

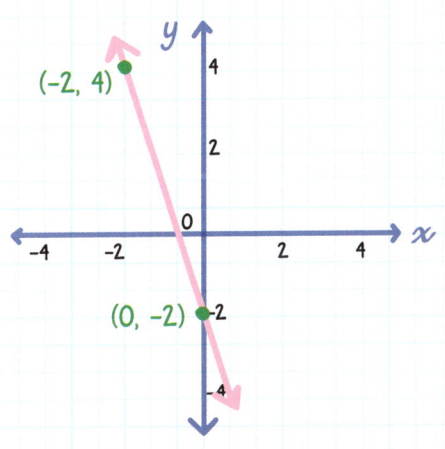

3. For the graphs of the two linear functions f and g, determine all x-values where $f(x) = g(x)$, where $f(x) > g(x)$, and where $f(x) < g(x)$.

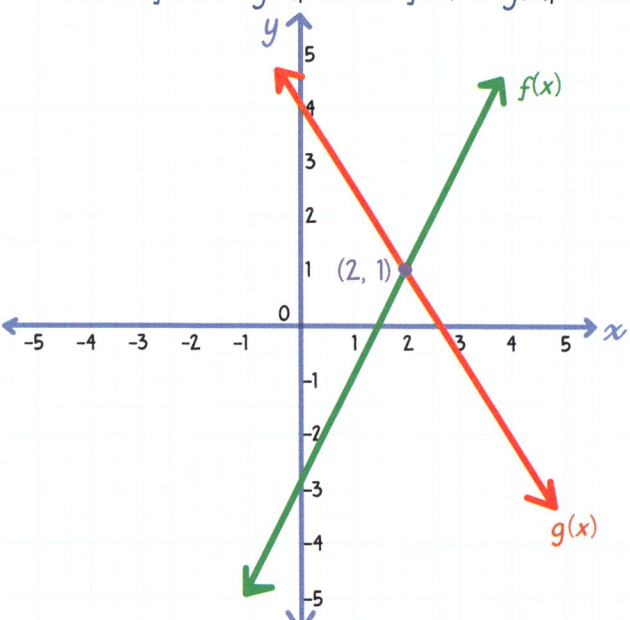

4. For the graphs of the two linear functions f and g, determine all x-values where $f(x) = g(x)$, where $f(x) > g(x)$, and where $f(x) < g(x)$.

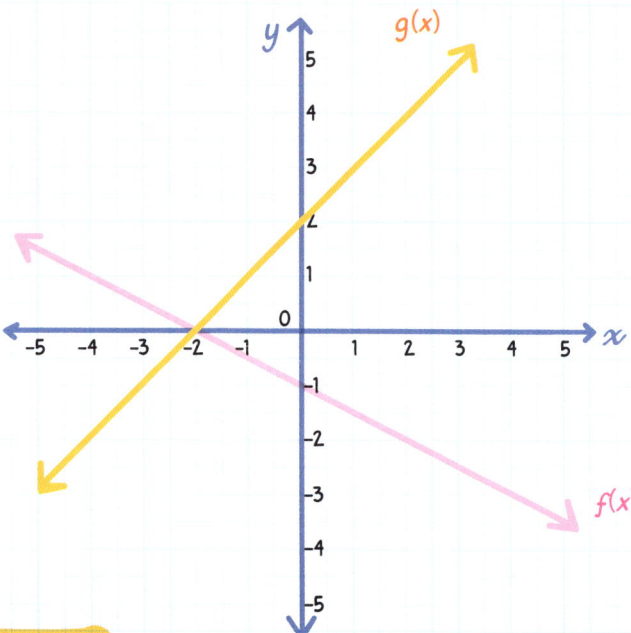

5. If $y = px - 1$ and $y = 7$ when $x = 4$, then what is y when $x = 16$?

6. If $y = dx$ and $y = 15$ when $x = 3$, then what is y when $x = 9$?

7. The amount of a cashier's paycheck varies directly with the number of hours the cashier works. If the cashier worked 21 hours in one week and made $273, how many hours did they work the following week if they made $455?

8. The price of a bus ticket varies directly with how many stops a passenger is on the bus for. If a passenger gets off at the sixth stop, the ticket costs $4.50. How much would a ticket cost if a passenger gets off at the seventeenth stop?

Chapter 10 ABSOLUTE VALUE FUNCTIONS AND THEIR GRAPHS

(0,9)

The **ABSOLUTE VALUE FUNCTION** is defined as:

$$g(x) = |x| = \sqrt{x^2} = \begin{cases} x \text{ if } x \geq 0 \\ -x \text{ if } x < 0 \end{cases}$$

Domain: $(-\infty, \infty)$

Range: $[0, \infty)$

The absolute value function is *decreasing* on $(-\infty, 0)$ and *increasing* on $(0, \infty)$.

The graph of the absolute value function looks like the letter V.

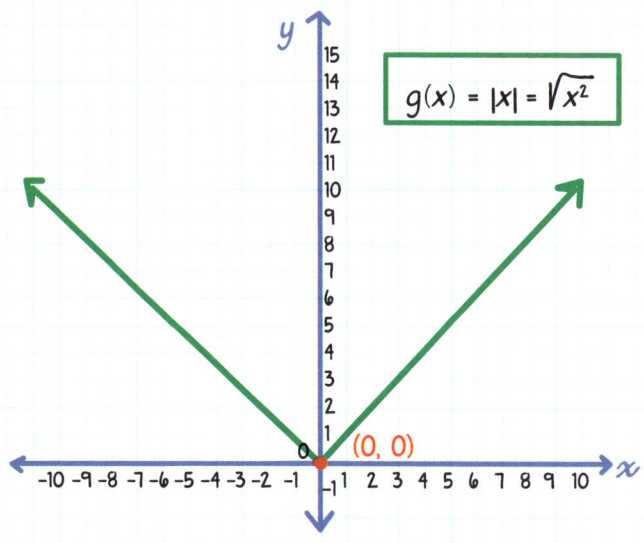

$$g(x) = |x| = \sqrt{x^2}$$

(0, 0)

The **standard form** of an absolute value function with vertex (h, k) is:

$f(x) = a|x - h| + k$.

We can use the standard form to graph an absolute value function.

EXAMPLE: Graph $f(x) = |x + 2|$.

STEP 1: Identify the vertex.

The function in standard form: $f(x) = |x - 2| + 0$.

The vertex is (h, k). Here, $h = -2$, and $k = 0$.

Therefore, the vertex is $(-2, 0)$.

STEP 2: Plot the vertex $(-2, 0)$. Then create a table of values to find at least two more points on either side of the vertex.

For illustration purposes, we will choose 4 more points.

x	$f(x) = |x + 2|$	$y = f(x)$	(x, y)	
4	$f(x) = |4 + 2|$	6	(4, 6)	
0	$f(x) = |0 + 2|$	2	(0, 2)	
-2	$f(x) = |-2 + 2|$	0	(-2, 0)	← vertex
-4	$f(x) = |-4 + 2|$	2	(-4, 2)	
-8	$f(x) = |-8 + 2|$	6	(-8, 6)	

STEP 3: Plot the vertex $(-2, 0)$. Then, plot the other points and connect them to form a V-shaped graph.

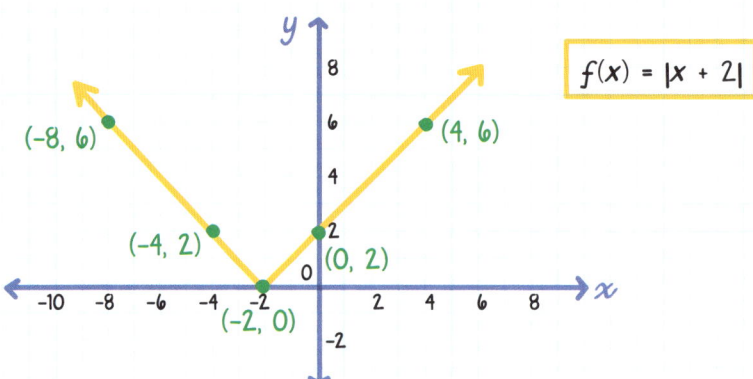

We can also write an equation of an absolute value function in standard form given only its graph.

EXAMPLE: Write the standard form of the absolute value function shown in the graph.

STEP 1: Substitute the coordinates of the vertex into the standard form of the absolute value function.

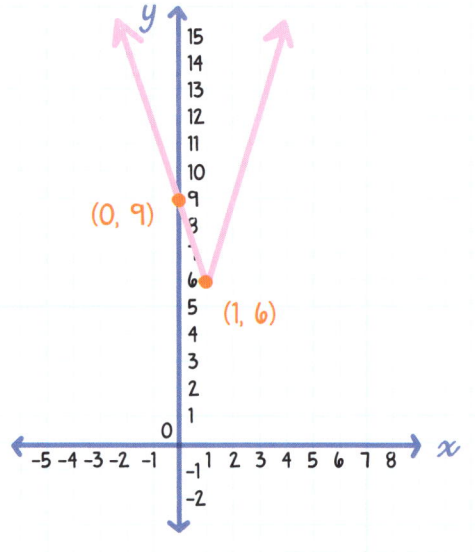

Standard form:

$f(x) = a|x - h| + k$, with vertex (h, k)

Vertex: $(1, 6)$

$f(x) = a|x - 1| + 6$

STEP 2: To find the value of **a**, substitute any other point from the graph and solve for **a**.

Substitute point: $(0, 9)$

$f(x) = a|x-1| + 6$

$9 = a|0-1| + 6$ Substitute $(0, 9)$.

$9 = a|-1| + 6$

$9 = a + 6$

$3 = a$

STEP 3: Substitute the value of **a** into the standard form of the absolute value function.

$f(x) = 3|x-1| + 6$

So, for the given graph, the absolute value function in standard form is $f(x) = 3|x-1| + 6$.

1. Graph $f(x) = -|x-9| + 2$.

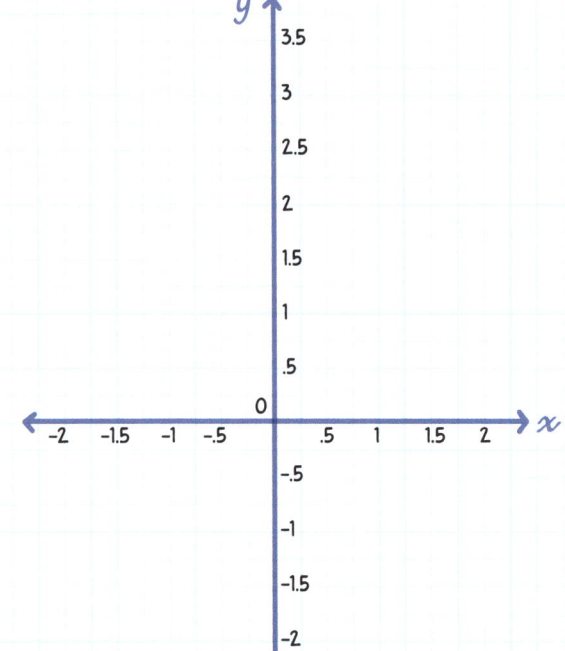

2. Graph $f(x) = |6x+3|$.

3. Graph $f(x) = -\left|\dfrac{3}{4}x\right|$.

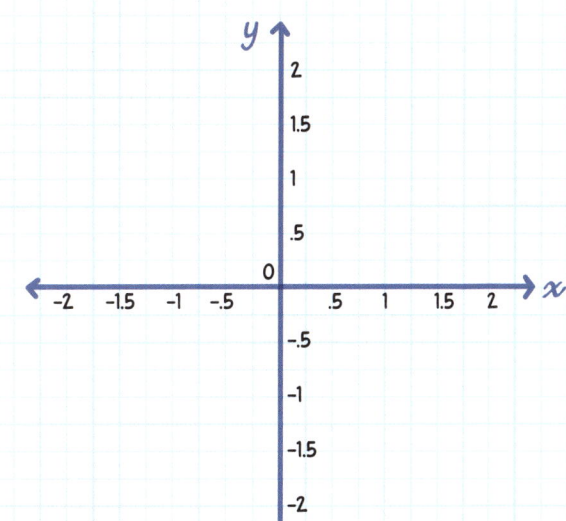

4. Graph $f(x) = \left|\dfrac{1}{3}x\right| + 2$.

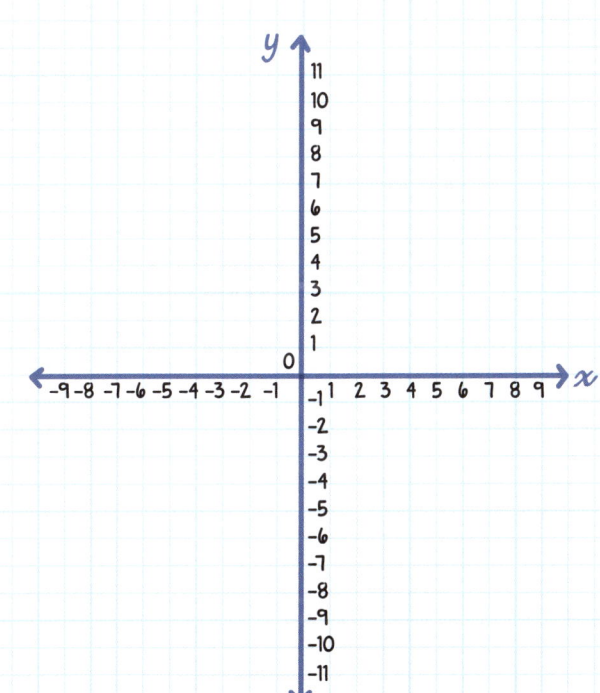

5. Graph $f(x) = 2|x-6|$.

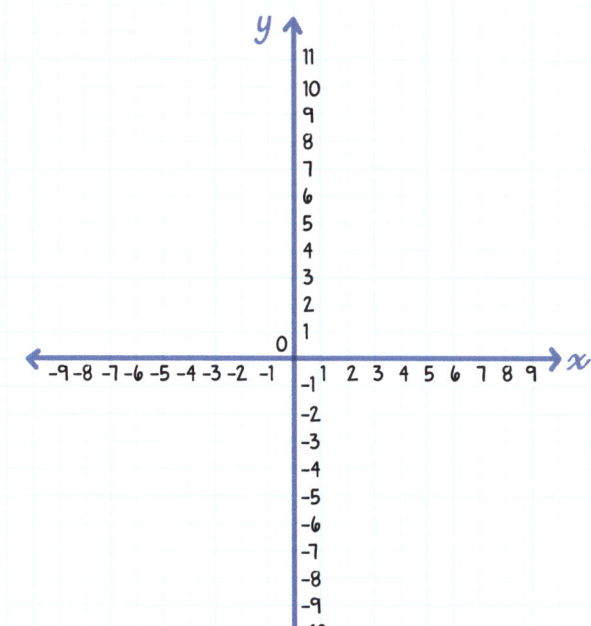

6. Graph $f(x) = \left|-\dfrac{3}{5}x\right|$.

WRITE THE STANDARD FORM OF THE GIVEN ABSOLUTE VALUE FUNCTION.

7.

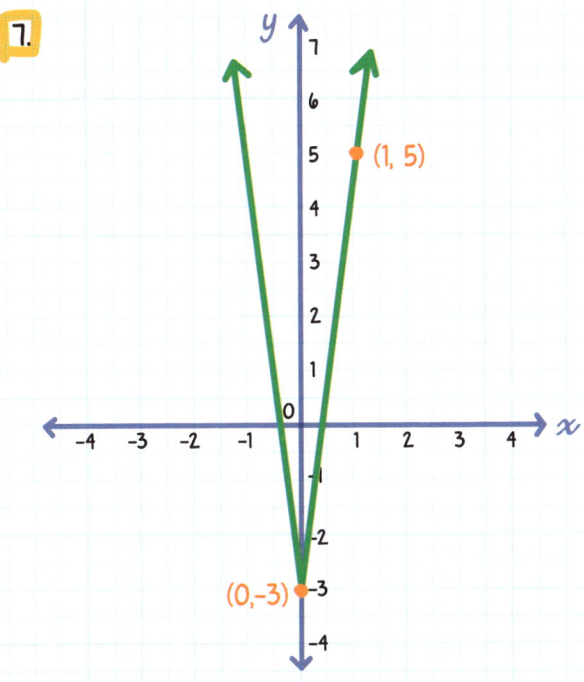

(1, 5)

(0,−3)

8.

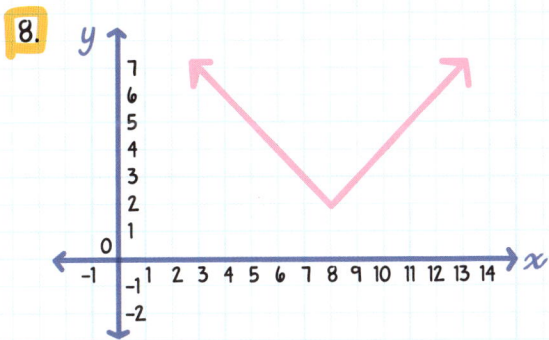

9.

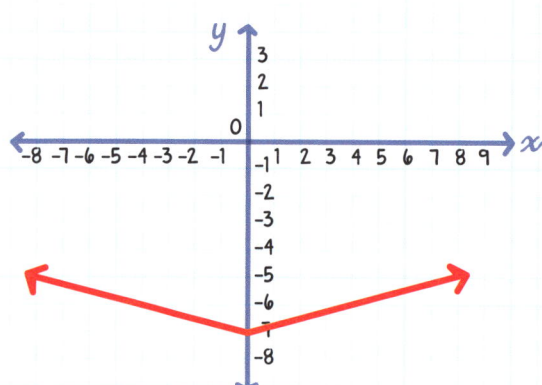

10. The organizers of a bike race are planning the path of a race through a local park. They sketch the path using two rays on a coordinate plane. The starting point of the path is at (0, 8), the path continues straight until (8, 0), and then it turns sharply and continues until its ending point at (18, 10).

A. Write an absolute value function in standard form that represents the race path.

B. The organizers want to place a water station on the path at (10, 2). Is this exact location possible?

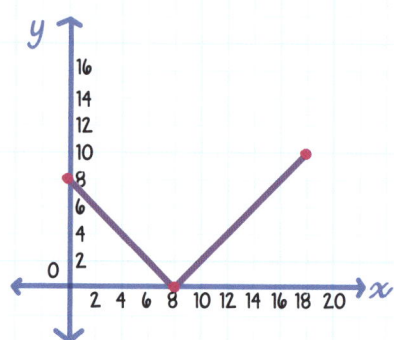

UNIT 2

Chapter 11

TRANSFORMATIONS OF FUNCTIONS

$(-x)^2$ $\dfrac{3}{7}$

A **TRANSFORMATION** of a function is a movement that does *not* change the basic shape of the graph.

Reflections flip a graph across a line.

$y = -f(x)$	$y = f(-x)$
Reflect $f(x)$ across the x-axis.	Reflect $f(x)$ across the y-axis.

Translations shift the graph up, down, right, or left.

$y = f(x) + k$	$y = f(x) - k$
Shift $f(x)$ up k units.	Shift $f(x)$ down k units.
$y = f(x + k)$	$y = f(x - k)$
Shift $f(x)$ left k units.	Shift $f(x)$ right k units.

Dilations stretch or shrink a graph. They can be horizontal or vertical.

$y = kf(x)$

If k is greater than 1, stretch $f(x)$ vertically by a factor of k.

If k is less than 1, shrink $f(x)$ vertically by a factor of k.

$y = f(kx)$

If k is greater than 1, shrink $f(x)$ horizontally by a factor of k.

If k is less than 1, stretch $f(x)$ horizontally by a factor of k.

We can use what we know about basic transformations to predict how the graph of a function will look on the coordinate plane.

For example, to graph $g(x) = x^2 + 6$, we can start with the graph of $f(x) = x^2$, and shift it *up* 6 units.

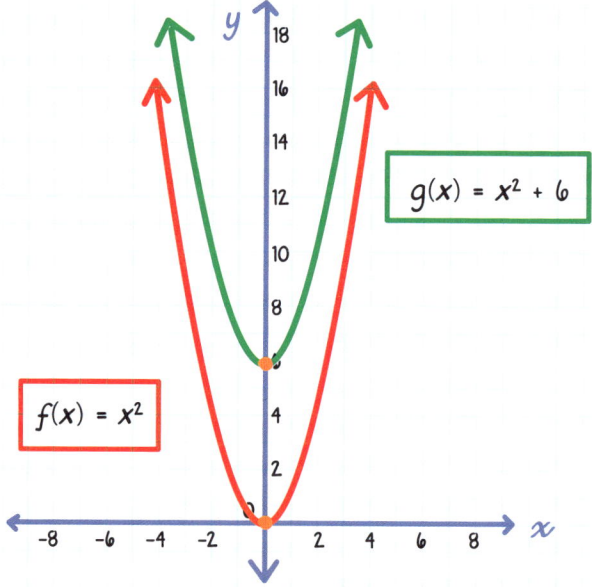

$g(x) = x^2 + 6$

$f(x) = x^2$

A function is **even** if $f(x) = f(-x)$ for all x-values. This means the graph would be symmetrical across the y-axis.

For example, $f(x) = x^2$ is an even function because
$f(-x) = (-x)^2 = x^2 = f(x)$.

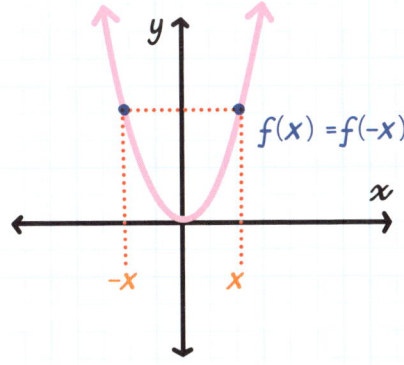

$f(x) = f(-x)$

$-x$ x

How do you know the graph is symmetrical across the y-axis? If you folded it in half, both sides would line up evenly.

We read this as "negative f of negative x."

A function is **odd** if $f(x) = -f(-x)$ for all x-values. This means the graph is symmetrical across the origin.

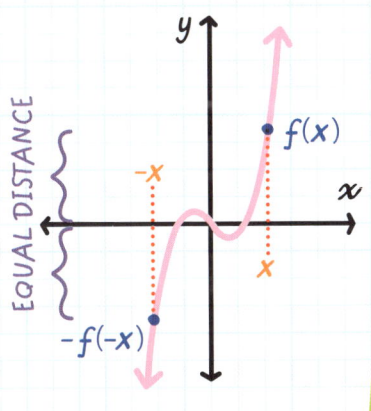

EQUAL DISTANCE

$f(x)$

$-x$

x

$-f(-x)$

How do you know the graph is symmetrical across the origin? You can rotate it 180°, and both halves will match exactly.

Most functions are neither even nor odd. The only function that is both even *and* odd is the **zero function** given by $f(x) = 0$.

USE WHAT YOU KNOW ABOUT TRANSFORMATIONS OF FUNCTIONS TO ANSWER THE FOLLOWING QUESTIONS.

1. Write an explicit definition of the function that shifts the graph of $f(x) = x$ down 3 units.

2. Write an explicit definition of the function that shifts the graph of $g(x) = \sqrt{x}$ to the right 2 units and up 7 units.

3. Write an explicit definition of the function that shifts the graph of $p(x) = x$ up 11 units.

4. Write an explicit definition of the function that reflects the graph of $d(x) = |x + 2|$ across the x-axis.

5. Write an explicit definition of the function that vertically stretches the graph of $f(x) = x^2$ by a factor of 4.

6. Write an explicit definition of the function that vertically shrinks the graph of $f(x) = x^2$ by a factor of $\frac{2}{7}$.

7. Graph $g(x) = |x+4| + 1$ using the graph of the parent function $f(x) = |x|$.

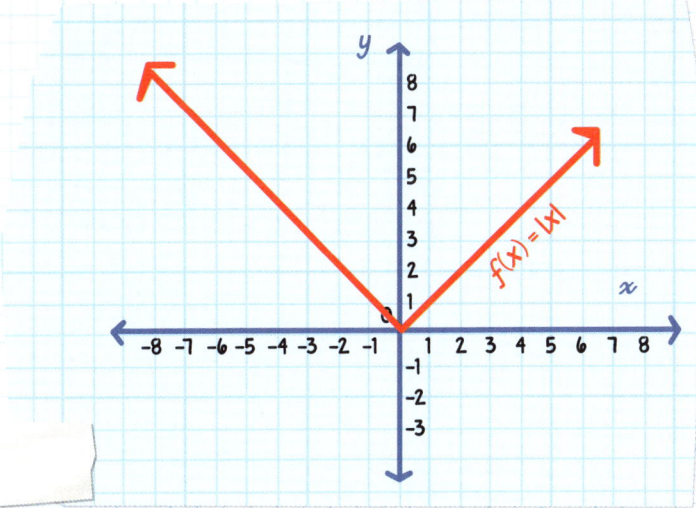

8. Graph $p(x) = -|x-11|$ using the graph of the parent function $d(x) = |x|$.

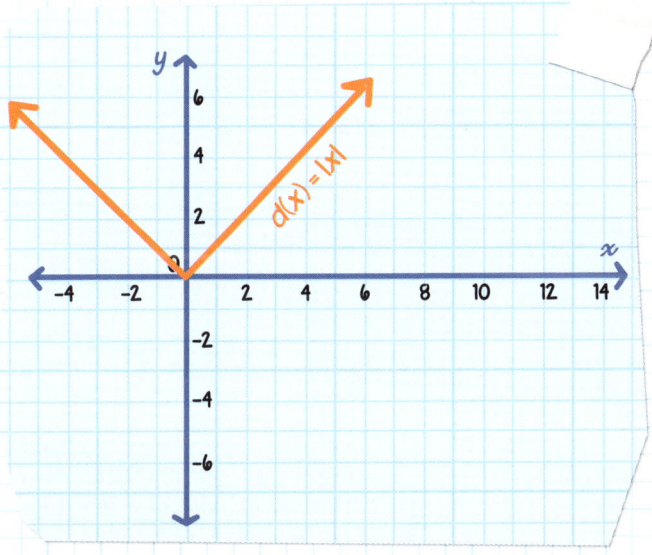

9. Graph $h(x) = (x - 6)^2 + 4$ using the graph of the parent function $j(x) = x^2$.

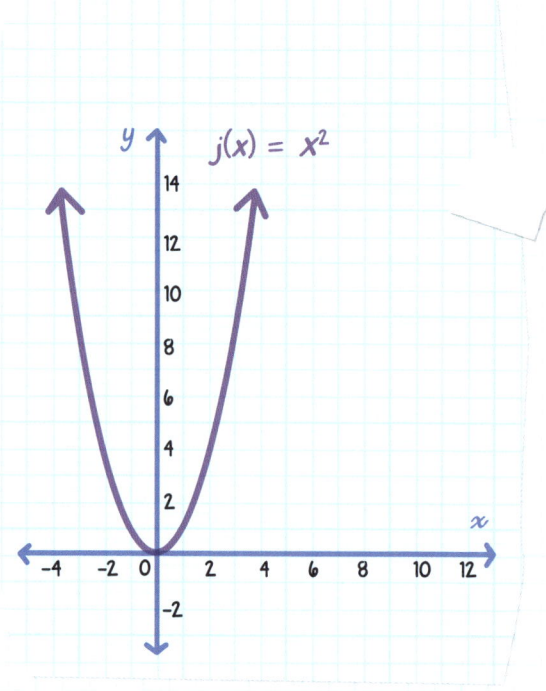

10. Graph $k(x) = \frac{1}{2}\sqrt{x}$ using the graph of the parent function $f(x) = \sqrt{x}$.

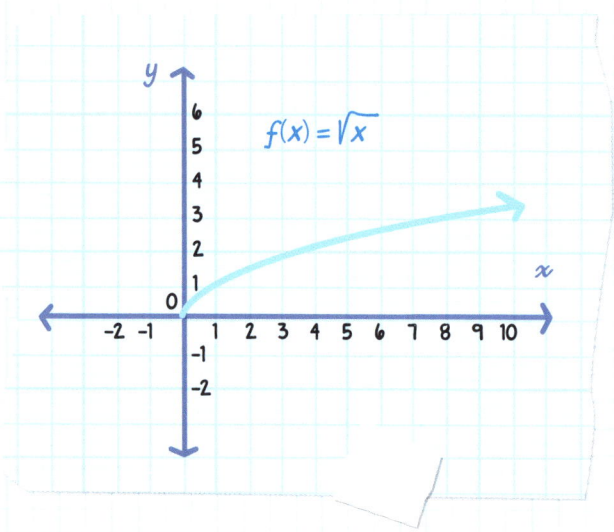

I LOVE TRANSFORMATIONS!

11. Write an explicit definition of the function represented using the parent function $g(x) = \sqrt{x}$.

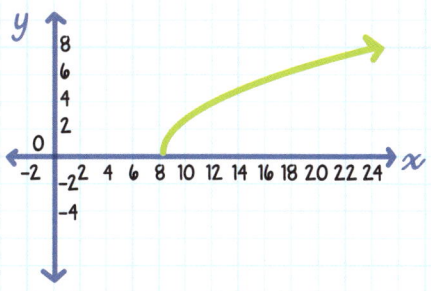

12. Write an explicit definition of the function represented using the parent function $g(x) = x^2$.

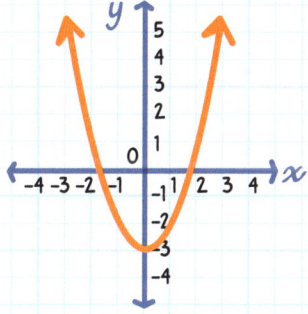

13. Determine whether each function represented by the given graph is even, odd, both, or neither. Justify your answer.

A.

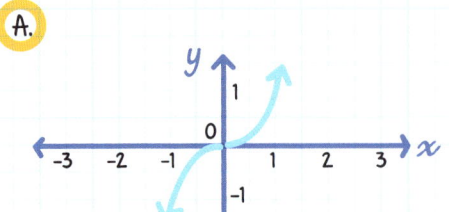

B.

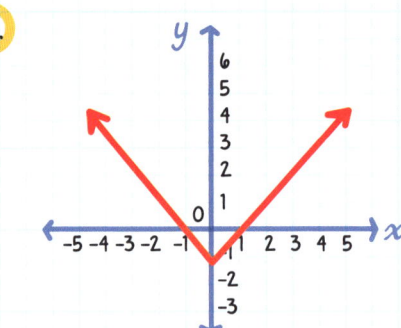

C.

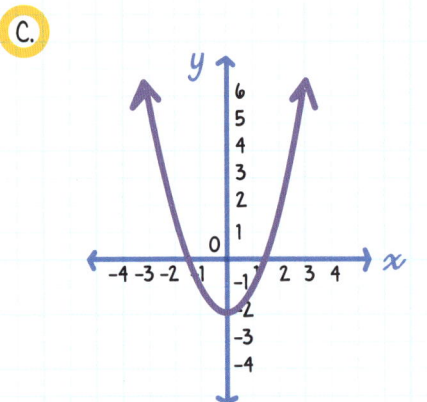

D.

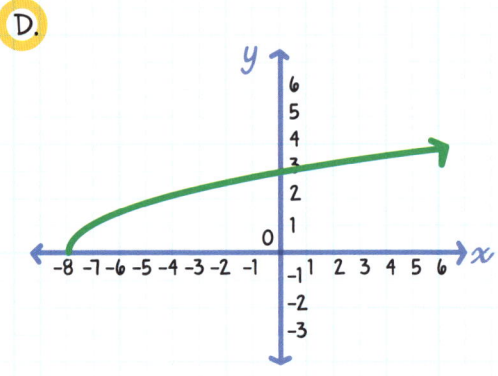

OPERATIONS ON FUNCTIONS

We can add, subtract, multiply, and divide functions using these rules:

Sum $(f + g)(x) = f(x) + g(x)$

Difference $(f - g)(x) = f(x) - g(x)$

Product $(fg)(x) = f(x)g(x)$

Quotient $\left(\dfrac{f}{g}\right)(x) = \dfrac{f(x)}{g(x)}$ where $g(x) \neq 0$

The **natural domain** of the function $f(x) = x$ is all real numbers: $(-\infty, \infty)$.

Unless the domain of a given function is specified, we can assume the natural domain:

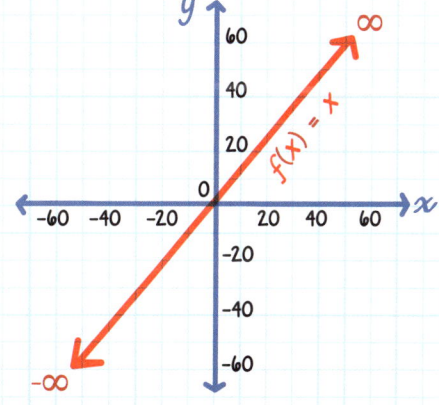

For each operation, substitute the given values of $f(x)$ and $g(x)$ and solve.

EXAMPLE: If $f(x) = 8x - 13$ and $g(x) = -7x$, find $f + g$, $f - g$, fg, and $\frac{f}{g}$. Then state their domains.

Sum: $(f + g)(x) = f(x) + g(x)$

$(8x - 13) + (-7x)$ Substitute $f(x)$ and $g(x)$.

$8x - 13 - 7x$

$x - 13$

So, $(f + g)(x) = x - 13$
Domain: $(-\infty, \infty)$

Product: $(fg)(x) = f(x)g(x)$

$(8x - 13)(-7x)$

$-56x^2 + 91x$

So, $(fg)(x) = -56x^2 + 91x$
Domain: $(-\infty, \infty)$

Difference: $(f - g)(x) = f(x) - g(x)$

$(8x - 13) - (-7x)$

$15x - 13$

So, $(f - g)(x) = 15x - 13$
Domain: $(-\infty, \infty)$

Quotient: $\left(\frac{f}{g}\right)(x) = \frac{f(x)}{g(x)}$

$\frac{8x - 13}{-7x}$

$-\frac{8}{7} + \frac{13}{7x}$

So, $\left(\frac{f}{g}\right)(x) = -\frac{8}{7} + \frac{13}{7x}$

Domain: $(-\infty, 0) \cup (0, \infty)$

Composition of Functions

The **COMPOSITE** or **COMPOSITION** of two functions is generated when one function is "substituted" into the other function.

$$(f \circ g)(x) = f(g(x))$$

The symbol for composition is this small circle.

The outputs of $g(x)$ become the inputs of $f(x)$.

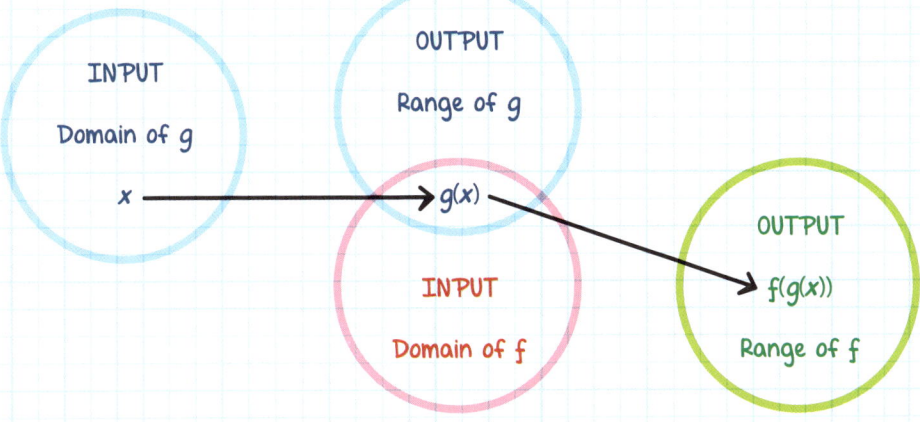

INPUT

Domain of g

OUTPUT

Range of g

x

$g(x)$

INPUT

Domain of f

OUTPUT

$f(g(x))$

Range of f

EXAMPLE: Given $f(x) = \sqrt{x}$ and $g(x) = \sqrt{8-x}$, evaluate $(f \circ g)(x)$. The domain of g is $(-\infty, 8]$.

$$(f \circ g)(x) = f(g(x)) = f(\sqrt{8-x}) = \sqrt{\sqrt{8-x}} = \sqrt[4]{8-x}$$

Domain of $f \circ g$: $(-\infty, 8]$

We can evaluate a composition of functions at a specific value of the independent variable (input) without having to find the composition of the two functions.

EXAMPLE: Given $f(x) = x^2 - 7$ and $g(x) = 5x$, evaluate the following.

1. $(f \circ g)(3)$

$= f(g(3))$
$= f(5 \cdot 3)$ ← Substitute $x = 3$ in $g(x)$: $5x = 5 \cdot 3$
$= f(15)$
$= 15^2 - 7$ ← Substitute $x = 15$ in $f(x)$: $x^2 - 7 = 15^2 - 7$
$= 225 - 7$
$= 218$

$(f \circ g)(3) = f(g(3)) = 218$

2. $(g \circ f)(0.6)$

$= g(f(0.6))$
$= g((0.6)^2 - 7)$ ← Substitute $x = 0.6$ in $f(x)$: $x^2 - 7 = (0.6)^2 - 7$
$= g(-6.64)$
$= 5(-6.64)$ ← Substitute $x = -6.64$ in $g(x)$: $5x = 5 \cdot (-6.64)$
$= -33.2$

$(g \circ f)(0.6) = g(f(0.6)) = -33.2$

Sometimes we need to identify the two functions that make up a composition of functions.

EXAMPLE: Find two functions that can be composed to form the following function: $f(x) = \sqrt{3x^2 + 14}$.

We need to define an "inside" and an "outside" function.

Let the "outside" function be $g(x) = \sqrt{x}$. Then the "inside" function is $h(x) = 3x^2 + 14$.

Check to see that the composition of $g(x)$ and $h(x)$ equals $f(x)$.

$(g \circ h)(x) = g(h(x)) = g(3x^2 + 14) = \sqrt{3x^2 + 14} = f(x)$

So, $f = g \circ h$.

FOR QUESTIONS 1 THROUGH 4, LET $f(x) = 2x + 9$ AND $g(x) = x^2 - 3$. PERFORM THE GIVEN OPERATION AND FIND THE DOMAIN OF THE RESULTING FUNCTION. USE INTERVAL NOTATION FOR THE DOMAIN.

1. $f + g$

2. $f - g$

3. fg

4. $\dfrac{f}{g}$

FOR QUESTIONS 5 THROUGH 8, LET $f(x) = -4\sqrt{x + 2}$ AND $g(x) = 7x$. PERFORM THE GIVEN OPERATION AND FIND THE DOMAIN OF THE RESULTING FUNCTION. USE INTERVAL NOTATION FOR THE DOMAIN.

5. $f + g$

6. $f - g$

7. fg

8. $\dfrac{f}{g}$

FOR QUESTIONS 9 THROUGH 12, LET $f(x) = \sqrt{x + 1}$, $g(x) = 6x^2$ AND $h(x) = -5x^2$. PERFORM THE GIVEN OPERATION AND FIND THE DOMAIN OF THE RESULTING FUNCTION. USE INTERVAL NOTATION FOR THE DOMAIN.

9. $(f \circ g)(x)$

10. $(f \circ h)(x)$

11. $(g \circ f)(x)$

12. $(g \circ h)(x)$

13. Given $f(x) = -x^2 - 4$ and $g(x) = 12x$, evaluate each of the following:

    A. $(f \circ g)(4)$

    B. $(g \circ f)(\frac{1}{2})$

14. Let $f(x) = \dfrac{\sqrt{2x-8}}{3}$. Find two functions g and h such that $f = g \circ h$.

Chapter 13

INVERSE FUNCTIONS

If the ordered pairs in a relation are reversed, then the new set of ordered pairs is called the **INVERSE RELATION**.

Relation R: {(-6, -7), (-3, 5), (0, 4), (5, 9)}

Inverse relation R⁻¹: {(-7, -6), (5, -3), (4, 0), (9, 5)}

Inverse Functions

Remember: In all functions, each input has *only* one output.

In a one-to-one function, each output comes from *only* one input.

On a graph, we can use the **HORIZONTAL LINE TEST** to see if a function is one-to-one. If *every* horizontal line hits the graph at just one point, then the graph represents a one-to-one function.

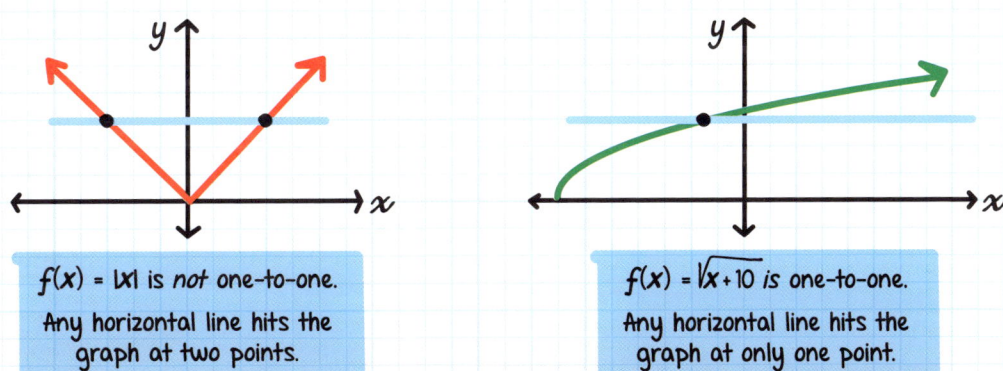

$f(x) = |x|$ is *not* one-to-one.
Any horizontal line hits the graph at two points.

$f(x) = \sqrt{x+10}$ is one-to-one.
Any horizontal line hits the graph at only one point.

Finding the Inverse of a One-to-One Function

To find f^{-1}:

▶ Write the rule for f: $y = f(x)$.

▶ Interchange x and y: $x = f(y)$.

▶ Solve for y: $y = f^{-1}(x)$.

THINK: Only *one-to-one* functions have inverses that are also functions.

EXAMPLE: Find the inverse of the following function and state its domain. $f(x) = -3x + 12$.

STEP 1: Write the original function.

$f(x) = -3x + 12$

STEP 2: Replace $f(x)$ with y.

$y = -3x + 12$

STEP 3: Interchange x and y.

$x = -3y + 12$

STEP 4: Solve for y.

$x = -3y + 12$

$x - 12 = -3y$ ← Divide both sides by -3.

$-\dfrac{1}{3}x + \dfrac{12}{4} = y$

$-\dfrac{1}{3}x + 4 = y$

So, the inverse of $f(x) = -3x + 2$ is $f^{-1}(x) = -\dfrac{1}{3}x + 4$.
Domain: $(-\infty, \infty)$

Finding the Graph of an Inverse Function

Let's look at two functions that are inverses of each other:
$f(x) = 8x - 1$ and $g(x) = \frac{x+1}{8}$, and graph them on the coordinate plane.

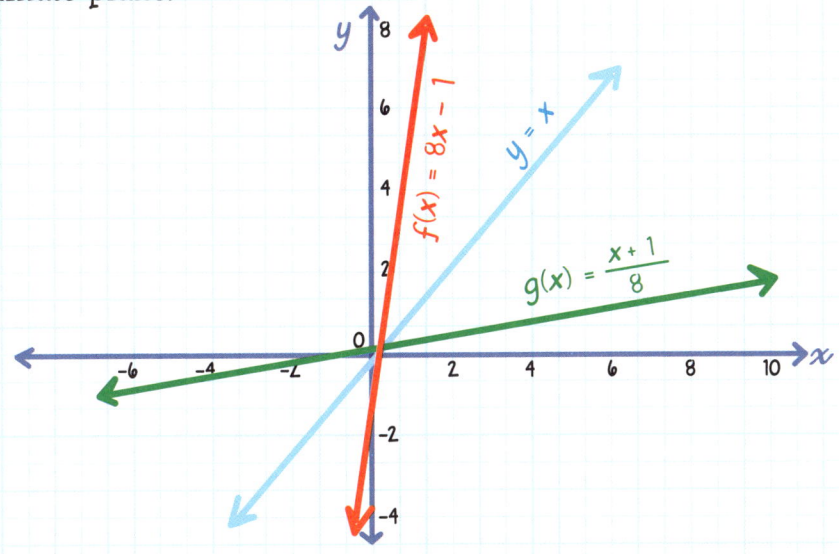

Notice the graph of $g(x) = \frac{x+1}{8}$ is obtained by taking the *symmetrical image* of $f(x) = 8x - 1$ across the diagonal line $y = x$.

EXAMPLE: Given the function $f(x) = -5x + 10$, graph f^{-1}. Then find the rule and the domain of f^{-1}.

STEP 1: Graph the function $f(x) = -5x + 10$.

This is a linear function in slope-intercept form, so we can graph it using the y-intercept $(0, 10)$ and the slope $(m = -5)$.

STEP 2: Reflect points on the graph of f across the line $y = x$.

THINK:
You only need to interchange the coordinates of two points (x, y) to draw the line that is the graph of the inverse function.

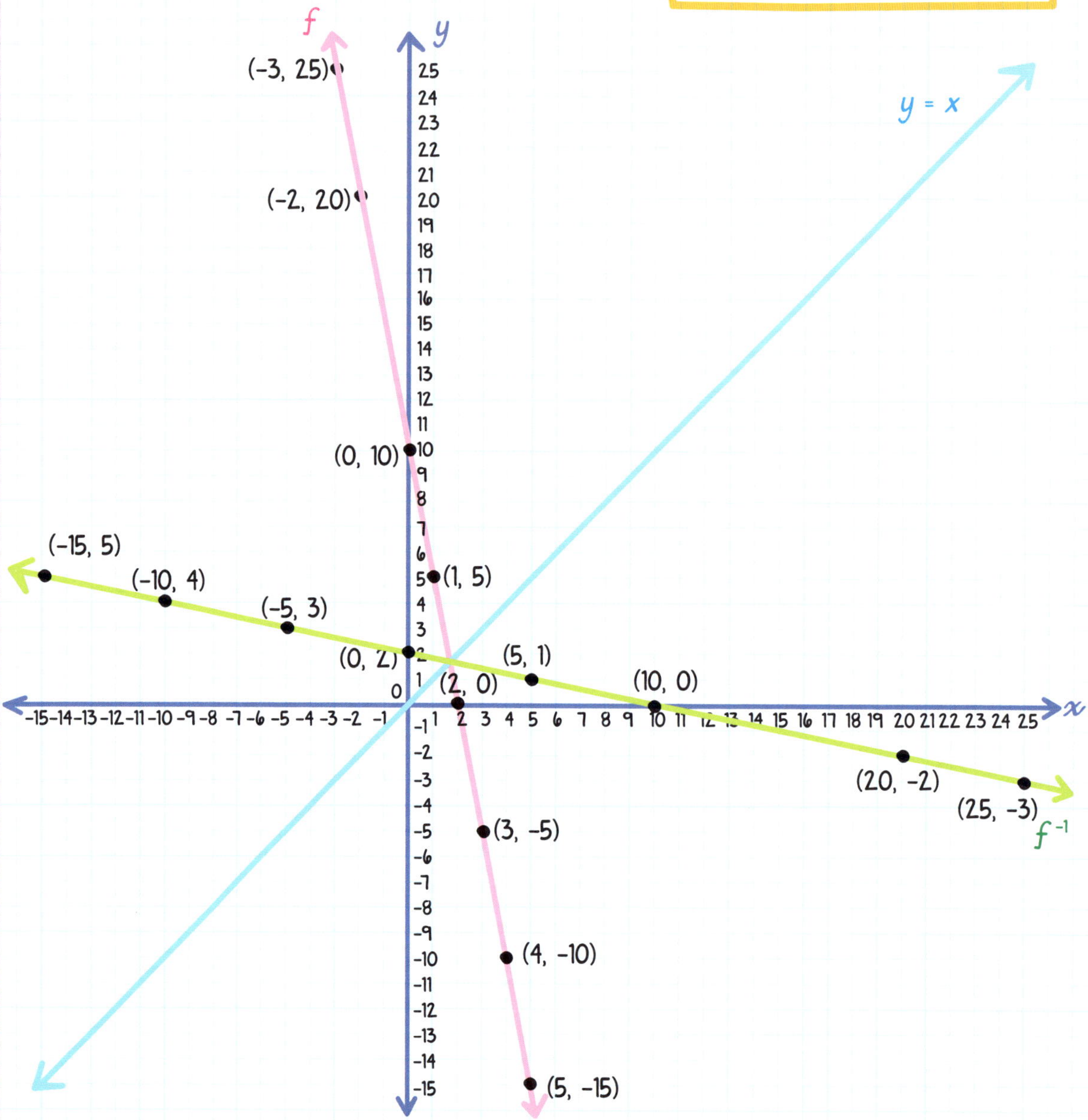

f

$y = x$

$(-3, 25)$
$(-2, 20)$
$(0, 10)$
$(1, 5)$
$(-15, 5)$
$(-10, 4)$
$(-5, 3)$
$(0, 2)$
$(5, 1)$
$(2, 0)$
$(10, 0)$
$(20, -2)$
$(25, -3)$
f^{-1}
$(3, -5)$
$(4, -10)$
$(5, -15)$

x
y

STEP 3: To write the inverse function, we can use the slope-intercept formula: $y = mx + b$.

To find the slope, we'll use two points: $(0, 2)$ and $(10, 0)$.

$$m = \frac{y_2 - y_1}{x_2 - x_1} = \frac{0 - 2}{10 - 0} = \frac{-2}{10} = \frac{-1}{5}$$

The y-intercept is $(0, 2)$, so $b = 2$.

$$y = -\frac{1}{5}x + 2$$

So, the inverse is $f^{-1}(x) = -\frac{1}{5}x + 2$. Domain: $(-\infty, \infty)$

DETERMINE IF THE GIVEN RELATION IS A ONE-TO-ONE FUNCTION.

1.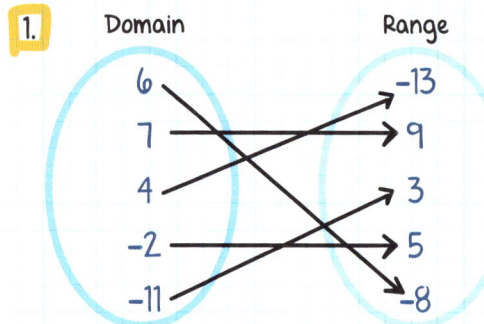

2.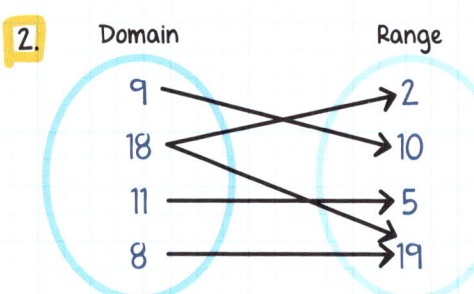

3. Graph A   Graph B

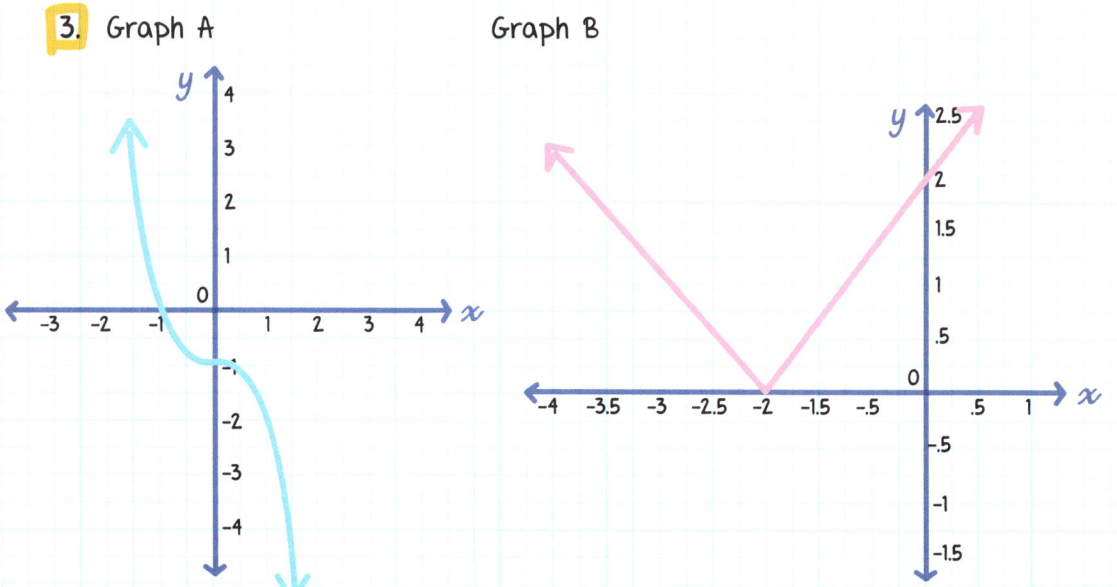

4. The domain and range of function g are shown in the mapping diagram below. What are the domain and range of g^{-1}?

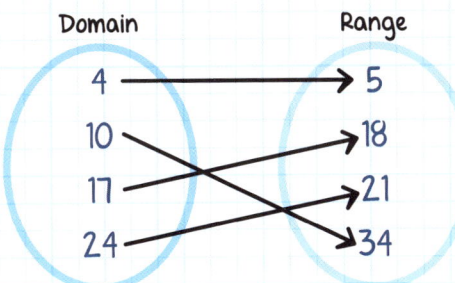

Domain   Range

4 ⟶ 5
10 ⟶ 18
17 ⟶ 21
24 ⟶ 34

5. Given that f is a one-to-one function, if $f^{-1}(3) = 15$, find $f(15)$.

6. Given that f is a one-to-one function, if $f^{-1}(-8.5) = 4$, find $f(4)$.

7. Given $f(x) = 7x + 9$ and $g(x) = \dfrac{x - 9}{7}$, determine whether f and g are inverses of each other.

8. Find the inverse of the following function and state its domain.
   $f(x) = 2x + 15$.

9. Find the rule and the domain for the inverse function of $f(x) = x^3 - 8$.

10. Given the function $f(x) = -2x + 14$, graph the inverse function. Then find the inverse function and state its domain.

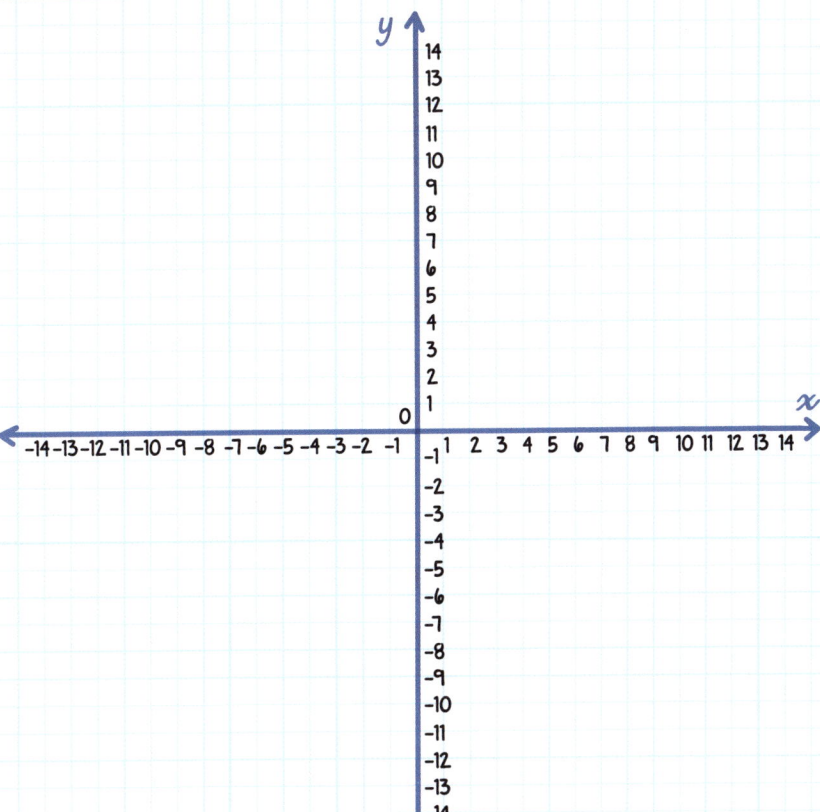

11. Given the function $f(x) = 12x - 6$, graph the inverse function. Then find the inverse function and state its domain.

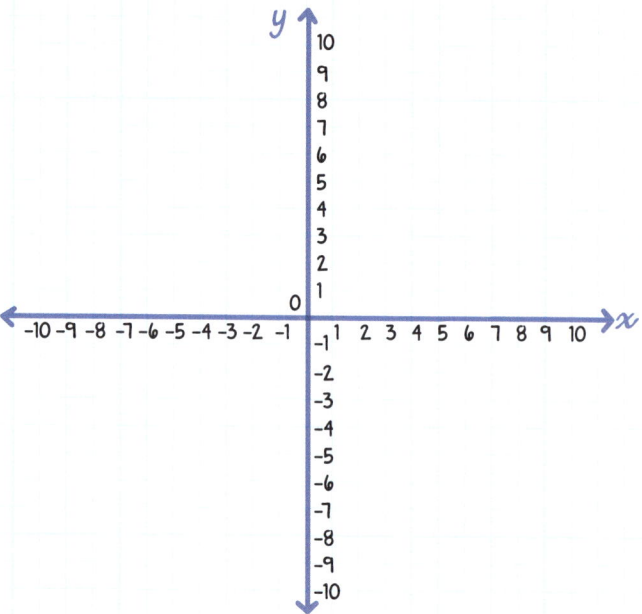

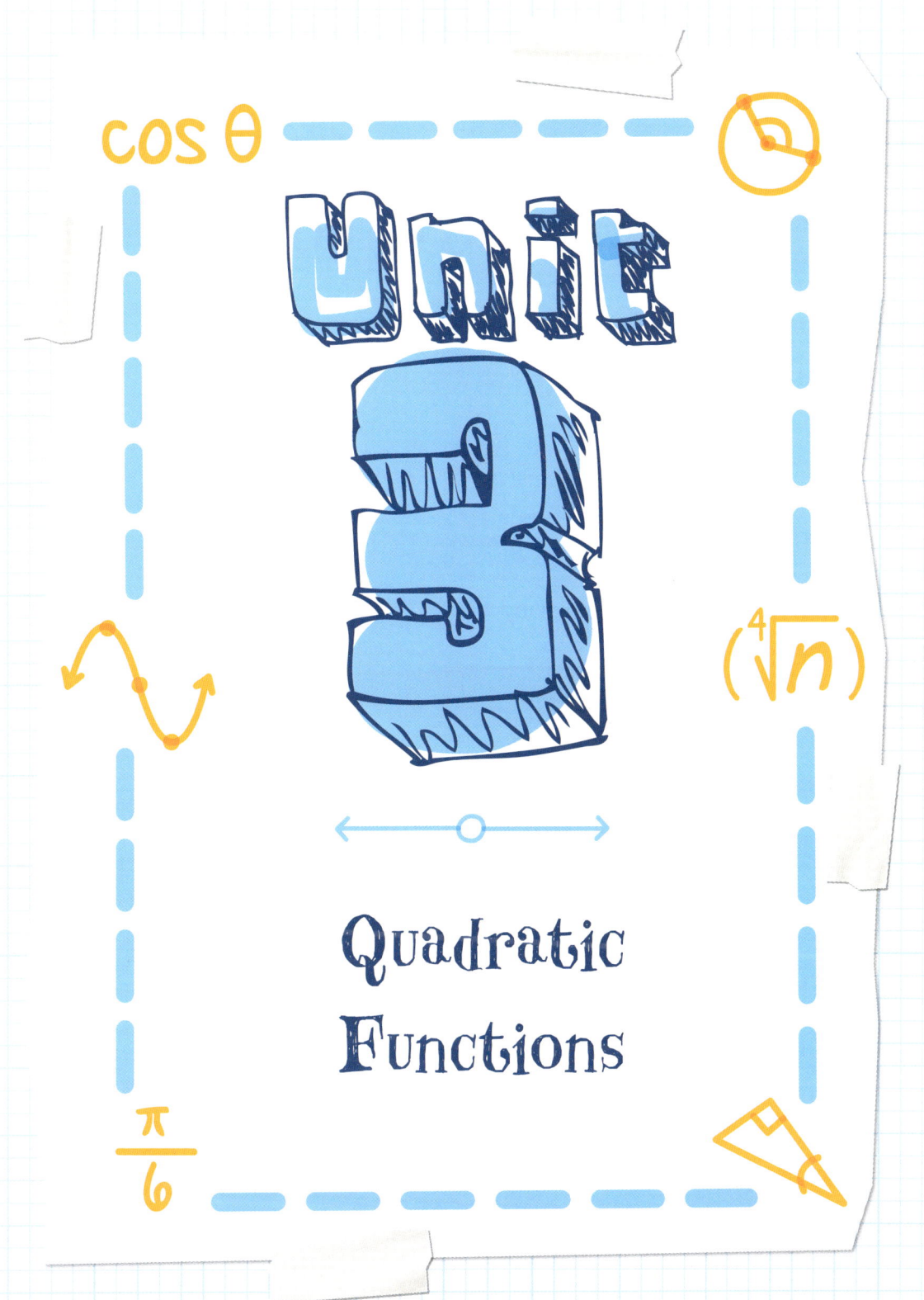

cos θ

$\left(\sqrt[4]{n}\right)$

$\dfrac{\pi}{6}$

Unit 3

Quadratic Functions

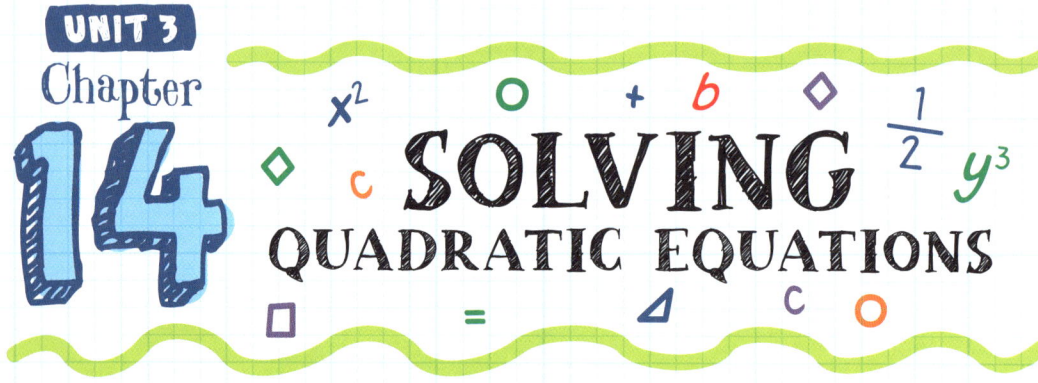

SOLVING QUADRATIC EQUATIONS

A **QUADRATIC EQUATION** can be written in the form:

$$ax^2 + bx + c = 0, \text{ where } a \neq 0.$$

There are several ways to solve a quadratic equation.

We solve a quadratic equation by **FACTORING**.

> The common factoring methods are:
> - Finding the greatest common factor (GCF).
> - Grouping into two or more groups that <u>can</u> be factored.
> - Trinomial factoring.
>
> For a refresher on these methods, see Chapter 18, Factoring Polynomials.

Once the factoring is completed, we use the **ZERO-PRODUCT PRINCIPLE**, which says that if a product is equal to zero, then one of the factors must also be equal to zero.

EXAMPLE: Find the solutions of $4x^2 + 22x = -10$. Use factoring.

STEP 1: Write the quadratic equation in the form $ax^2 + bx + c = 0$.

$4x^2 + 22x = -10$ quadratic equation

$4x^2 + 22x + 10 = -10 + 10$

$4x^2 + 22x + 10 = 0$

STEP 2: Factor the left-hand side of the equation.

For this equation, we can use a combination of trinomial factoring and grouping.

▶ Identify the coefficients.

$4x^2 + 22x + 10 = 0$ Coefficients: $a = 4$, $b = 22$, $c = 10$

▶ Multiply $a \cdot c$.

$4 \cdot 10 = 40$

▶ List the positive integer factors of the product, 40, in pairs:

$1 \cdot 40$, $2 \cdot 20$, $4 \cdot 10$, and $5 \cdot 8$

▶ Determine if one of these factor pairs adds to the coefficient $b = 22$.

$2 + 20 = 22$

▶ Rewrite the middle term, $22x$, as $2x + 20x$.

$4x^2 + 22x + 10$

$= 4x^2 + 2x + 20x + 10$

▶ Factor the expression, first by grouping, then by the greatest common factor (GCF).

$(4x^2 + 2x) + (20x + 10)$ Group the terms.

$= 2x(2x + 1) + 10(2x + 1)$ Find the GCF.

▶ Use GCF factoring one more time.

$2x(2x + 1) + 10(2x + 1)$

$= (2x + 10)(2x + 1)$

STEP 3: Solve the equation by using the Zero-Product Principle: Set each factor equal to zero and solve.

$2x + 10 = 0$ or $2x + 1 = 0$ Apply the Zero-Product Principle.

$x = -5$ or $x = -\dfrac{1}{2}$

STEP 4: Check that each solution satisfies the equation.

$4(-5)^2 + 22(-5) = -10$	$4(-\dfrac{1}{2})^2 + 22(-\dfrac{1}{2}) = -10$
$-10 = -10$ ✅	$-10 = -10$ ✅

The solutions of the given quadratic equation are $x = -5$ and $x = -\dfrac{1}{2}$.

The **SQUARE ROOT PROPERTY** states if $a^2 = b$, then $a = \pm\sqrt{b}$.

EXAMPLE: Find the solutions of $2(x + 3)^2 - 15 = 27$. Use the Square Root Property.

STEP 1: Isolate the squared expression.

$2(x + 3)^2 - 15 = 27$
$2(x + 3)^2 = 42$
$(x + 3)^2 = 21$

YOU CAN ALWAYS COUNT ON ME.

STEP 2: Apply the Square Root Property.

$x + 3 = \pm\sqrt{21}$

STEP 3: Finish solving for x.

$x + 3 - 3 = -3 \pm\sqrt{21}$

$x = -3 + \sqrt{21}$ or $x = -3 - \sqrt{21}$

STEP 4: Check that each solution satisfies the equation.

$2((-3 + \sqrt{21}) + 3)^2 - 15 = 27$	$2((-3 - \sqrt{21}) + 3)^2 - 15 = 27$
$2(\sqrt{21})^2 - 15 = 27$	$2(-\sqrt{21})^2 - 15 = 27$
$2 \cdot 21 - 15 = 27$	$2 \cdot 21 - 15 = 27$
$27 = 27$ ✔	$27 = 27$ ✔

The solutions of the quadratic equation are $x = -3 + \sqrt{21}$ and $x = -3 - \sqrt{21}$.

COMPLETING THE SQUARE: Beginning with the quadratic expression $x^2 + bx$, we can obtain a perfect square by adding $(\frac{b}{2})^2$.

EXAMPLE: Find the solutions of $x^2 + 4x - 96 = 0$ by completing the square.

STEP 1: Bring the constant to the right-hand side of the equal sign.

$x^2 + 4x - 96 = 0$
$x^2 + 4x - 96 + 96 = 0 + 96$

STEP 2: Identify b, the coefficient of x. Take half of b and square the result.

$x^2 + 4x = 96 \quad b = 4$

$(\frac{b}{2})^2 = (\frac{4}{2})^2 = 2^2 = 4$

STEP 3: Add the result from Step 2 to both sides of the equation.

$x^2 + 4x + 4 = 96 + 4$

$x^2 + 4x + 4 = 100$

STEP 4: Rewrite the left side of the equation as a perfect square and apply the Square Root Property.

$x^2 + 4x + 4 = 100$
$(x + 2)^2 = 100$
$x + 2 = \pm 10$ Apply the Square Root Property.

STEP 5: Rewrite as two equations and solve for x.

$x + 2 = 10$ or $x + 2 = -10$

$x = 8$ $x = -12$

STEP 6: Check that each solution satisfies the equation.

$8^2 + 4(8) - 96 = 0$	$(-12)^2 + 4(-12) - 96 = 0$
$0 = 0$ ✔	$0 = 0$ ✔

The solutions of the quadratic equation are $x = 8$ and $x = -12$. ←

QUADRATIC FORMULA: $x = \dfrac{-b \pm \sqrt{b^2 - 4ac}}{2a}$

EXAMPLE: Find the solutions of the quadratic equation $x^2 - 4x + 9 = 0$. Use the quadratic formula.

STEP 1: Identify the coefficient of each term.

$x^2 - 4x + 9 = 0$ Coefficients: $a = 1$, $b = -4$, $c = 9$

STEP 2: Substitute the coefficients a, b, and c into the quadratic formula.

$x = \dfrac{-b \pm \sqrt{b^2 - 4ac}}{2a}$ quadratic formula

$x = \dfrac{-(-4) \pm \sqrt{(-4)^2 - 4(1)(9)}}{2(1)}$

$$= \frac{4 \pm \sqrt{16 - 36}}{2}$$

$$= \frac{4 \pm \sqrt{-20}}{2}$$

$$= \frac{4 \pm \sqrt{-1 \cdot 4 \cdot 5}}{2}$$

$$= \frac{4 \pm 2i\sqrt{5}}{2}$$

$$= 2 \pm i\sqrt{5} \quad \leftarrow \text{ The solutions are complex.}$$

The solutions of the quadratic equation are $x = 2 + i\sqrt{5}$ and $x = 2 - i\sqrt{5}$.

In the quadratic formula, the expression under the radical is called the **DISCRIMINANT** (D).

$$D = b^2 - 4ac$$

▶ If $D > 0$, the quadratic equation has **two distinct real solutions**.

▶ If $D = 0$, the quadratic equation has **one real solution**.

▶ If $D < 0$, the quadratic equation has **zero real solutions** and **two complex solutions** that are conjugates.

EXAMPLE: Given the quadratic equation $10 = x - 2x^2$, find the number of solutions, determine whether the solutions are real or complex, and verify that the answer is correct by finding the solutions.

STEP 1: Write the equation in the form $ax^2 + bx + c$. Identify the coefficients.

$$10 = x - 2x^2$$
$$0 = -2x^2 + x - 10 \quad \text{Coefficients: } a = -2, \ b = 1, \ c = -10$$

STEP 2: Calculate the discriminant.

$$D = b^2 - 4ac$$
$$D = 1^2 - 4(-2)(-10)$$
$$D = 1 - 80 \quad \text{Since } D < 0, \text{ the quadratic equation has zero}$$
$$D = -79 \quad \quad \text{real solutions and two complex solutions.}$$

STEP 3: Use the quadratic formula to verify that there are no real solutions.

$$x = \frac{-b \pm \sqrt{b^2 - 4ac}}{2a} \quad \text{quadratic formula}$$

$$x = \frac{-1 \pm \sqrt{1^2 - 4(-2)(-10)}}{2(-2)} \quad \text{Substitute the coefficients.}$$

$$x = \frac{-1 \pm \sqrt{1 - 80}}{-4}$$

$$= \frac{-1 \pm \sqrt{-79}}{-4}$$

$$= \frac{-1 \pm \sqrt{-1 \cdot 79}}{-4}$$

$$= \frac{-1 \pm i\sqrt{79}}{-4}$$

So, the equation has zero real solutions and two complex solutions:
$$x = \frac{1}{4} - \frac{1}{4} i\sqrt{79} \text{ and } x = \frac{1}{4} + \frac{1}{4} i\sqrt{79}.$$

FACTOR TO FIND THE SOLUTIONS OF THE QUADRATIC EQUATIONS.

1. $x^2 - 2x = 3$

2. $12 = x^2 - 4x$

3. $x^2 - 11x + 28 = 0$

4. $2x^2 + 21x = -40$

USE THE SQUARE ROOT PROPERTY TO FIND THE SOLUTIONS OF THE QUADRATIC EQUATIONS.

5. $2(x + 6)^2 - 10 = 8$

6. $4x^2 = 324$

COMPLETE THE SQUARE TO FIND THE SOLUTIONS OF THE QUADRATIC EQUATIONS.

7. $x^2 + 4x = 12$

8. $x^2 - 20x - 21 = 0$

9. $x^2 - 8x = 20$

USE THE QUADRATIC FORMULA TO FIND THE SOLUTIONS OF THE QUADRATIC EQUATIONS.

10. $\frac{1}{2}x^2 - 5x = 9$

11. $-6x^2 + 4x + 16 = 0$

FIND THE NUMBER OF REAL SOLUTIONS FOR EACH EQUATION.

12. $3x^2 + 6x = -15$

13. $x^2 + 7x + 2 = 0$

14. $-2x^2 - 4x + 10 = 0$

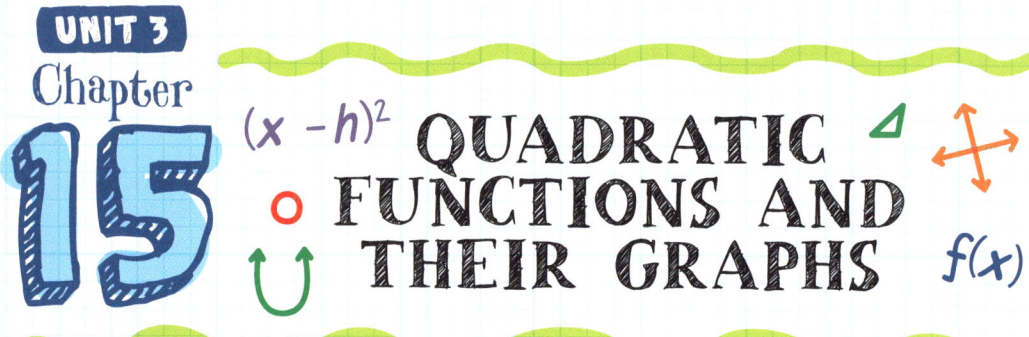

Chapter 15

$(x - h)^2$ QUADRATIC FUNCTIONS AND THEIR GRAPHS $f(x)$

A **QUADRATIC FUNCTION** is written in the general form:

$$f(x) = ax^2 + bx + c, \text{ where } a \neq 0.$$

The graph of a quadratic function is a **PARABOLA**. The sign of the leading coefficient a tells us which direction the parabola opens.

▶ If $a > 0$, it opens *upward*.   ▶ If $a < 0$, it opens *downward*.

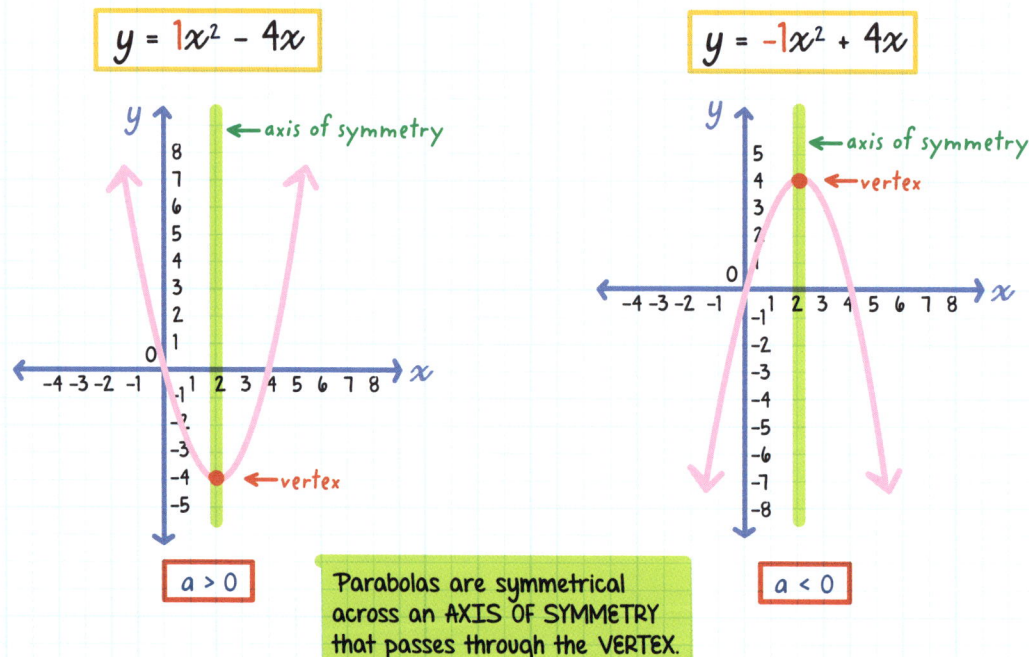

$y = 1x^2 - 4x$ $y = -1x^2 + 4x$

← axis of symmetry   ← axis of symmetry
                                    ← vertex

← vertex

$a > 0$ $a < 0$

Parabolas are symmetrical across an AXIS OF SYMMETRY that passes through the VERTEX.

The **AXIS OF SYMMETRY** equation is:

$$x = -\frac{b}{2a}$$

THINK:

A parabola's axis of symmetry passes through its vertex, so the expression $-\frac{b}{2a}$ equals the value of the x-coordinate of the vertex (h, in the vertex form).

The **VERTEX FORM** of a quadratic function is:

$$f(x) = a(x - h)^2 + k$$

Coordinates of the vertex (h, k)

EXAMPLE: Rewrite the function $f(x) = 2x^2 - 2x - 24$ in vertex form. Find the vertex and axis of symmetry of the function. Then describe the function's graph.

STEP 1: To rewrite the function in vertex form, we will use the method of completing the square.

▶ Factor $2x^2 - 2x$.

$f(x) = 2x^2 - 2x - 24$
$f(x) = 2(x^2 - x) - 24$

▶ Complete the square inside the parentheses.

In the quadratic expression $x^2 - x$, the coefficient $b = -1$. To complete the square, we square half the value of b and add it to the expression.

$f(x) = 2(x^2 - x) - 24$

$f(x) = 2(x^2 - x + (\frac{-1}{2})^2) - 24 - 2((\frac{-1}{2})^2)$ Subtract $2(\frac{-1}{2})^2$ to balance the equation.

▶ Combine the constant terms.

$$f(x) = 2(x^2 - x + (\tfrac{1}{2})^2) - 24 - 2(\tfrac{1}{4})$$

$$f(x) = 2(x^2 - x + (\tfrac{1}{2})^2) - 24 - \tfrac{1}{2}$$

$$f(x) = 2(x^2 - x + (\tfrac{1}{2})^2) - \tfrac{49}{2}$$

▶ Factor the perfect square.

$$f(x) = 2(x - \tfrac{1}{2})^2 - \tfrac{49}{2} \quad \longleftarrow \quad \text{vertex form}$$

STEP 2: Identify the vertex using the vertex form of the equation.

$$f(x) = (x - \tfrac{1}{2})^2 + (-\tfrac{49}{2})$$

vertex: $(\tfrac{1}{2}, -\tfrac{49}{2})$

STEP 3: Find the axis of symmetry using the equation: $(x = -\tfrac{b}{2a})$.

$x = -\dfrac{-2}{2(2)}$ Substitute $b = -2$ and $a = 2$ (from the quadratic equation in standard form).

$x = -\dfrac{-2}{4}$

$x = \dfrac{1}{2}$

THINK:
The x-coordinate of the vertex is the axis of symmetry.

STEP 4: Describe the function's graph.

▶ The parabola opens upward. $(a > 0)$

▶ The vertex is $(\tfrac{1}{2}, -\tfrac{49}{2})$

▶ The axis of symmetry is $x = \tfrac{1}{2}$.

The **discriminant** (D) tells us how many x-intercepts the graph of a quadratic function has.

▶ If $D > 0$, the parabola has **two x-intercepts**.

▶ If $D = 0$, the parabola has **one x-intercept**.

▶ If $D < 0$, the parabola has **no x-intercepts**.

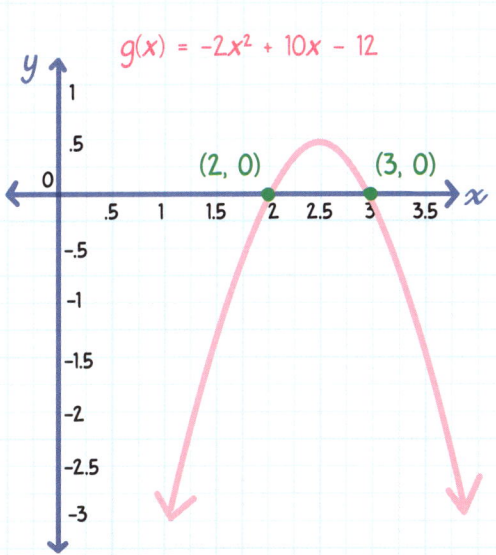

$g(x) = -2x^2 + 10x - 12$

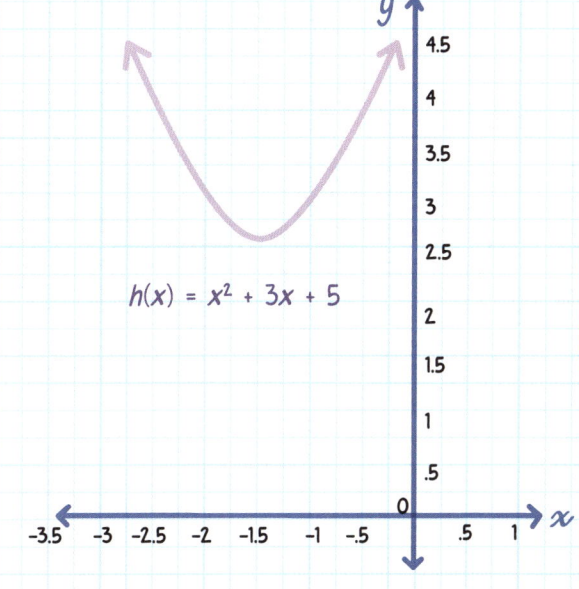

$h(x) = x^2 + 3x + 5$

This graph has two x-intercepts. That means the discriminant is positive.

This graph has no x-intercepts. That means the discriminant is negative.

EXAMPLE: Find the x-intercepts of $f(x) = -x^2 + 11x - 18$.
Use graphing.

STEP 1: Find the axis of symmetry.

$y = -1x^2 + 11x - 18$ ← $a = -1, b = 11, c = -18$

Substitute a and b into the formula.

$x = -\dfrac{b}{2a} = -\dfrac{11}{2(-1)} = \dfrac{11}{2} = 5.5$ ← axis of symmetry

STEP 2: Make a table of x- and y-values.

The axis of symmetry is $x = 5.5$, so start with an x-value of 5.5 in the center of the table, and choose several x-values less than 5.5 and several x-values greater than 5.5.

x	$y = -x^2 + 11x - 18$	y	(x, y)
0	$-0^2 + 11(0) - 18$	-18	(0, -18)
2	$-2^2 + 11(2) - 18$	0	(2, 0)
3	$-3^2 + 11(3) - 18$	6	(3, 6)
4	$-4^2 + 11(4) - 18$	10	(4, 10)
5.5	$-5.5^2 + 11(5.5) - 18$	12.25	(5.5, 12.25)
7	$-7^2 + 11(7) - 18$	10	(7, 10)
8	$-8^2 + 11(8) - 18$	6	(8, 6)
9	$-9^2 + 11(9) - 18$	0	(9, 0)
11	$-11^2 + 11(11) - 18$	-18	(0, -18)

STEP 3: Plot the points and draw a smooth curve through them.

STEP 4: Identify the x-intercepts of the quadratic function.

The x-intercepts of the graph are (2, 0) and (9, 0).

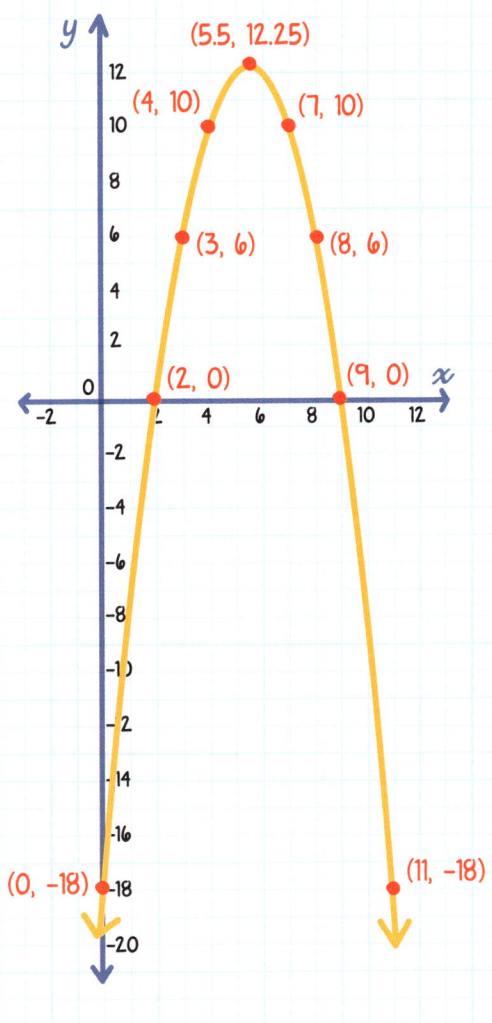

REWRITE THE FUNCTION IN VERTEX FORM. IDENTIFY THE VERTEX, AND THE AXIS OF SYMMETRY. THEN DESCRIBE THE GRAPH.

1. $f(x) = 3x^2 + 12x - 12$

2. $g(x) = -x^2 - 18x + 3$

3. $h(x) = 2x^2 - 4x + 8$

GRAPH THE QUADRATIC FUNCTION TO FIND THE x-INTERCEPTS.

4. $f(x) = 2x^2 + 8x + 10$

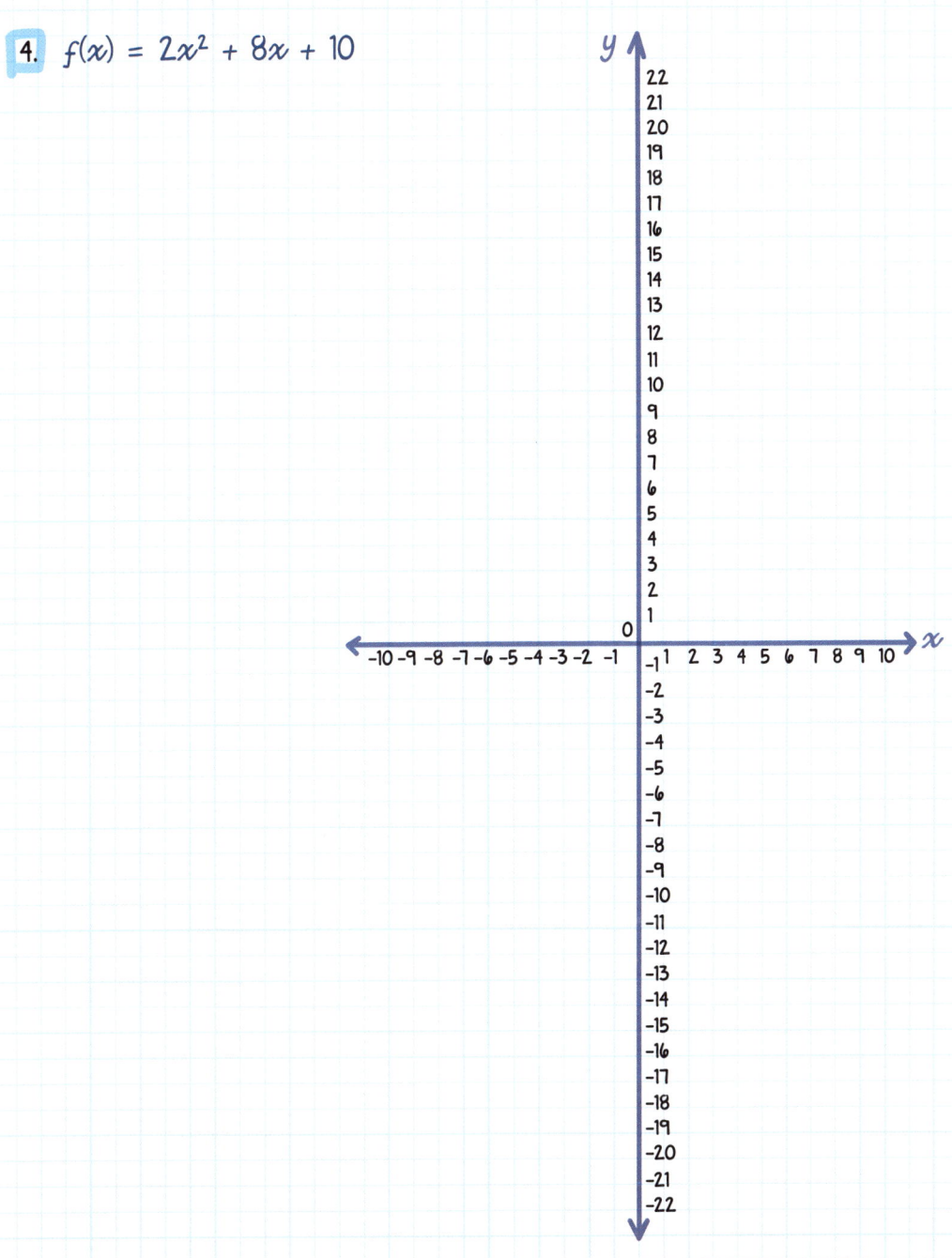

5. $p(x) = x^2 - 7x - 8$

NONLINEAR SYSTEMS OF EQUATIONS

UNIT 3
Chapter 16

(10)

A **NONLINEAR SYSTEM** is two or more equations, at least one of which is nonlinear.

The solution to a system is a point (x, y) that satisfies each equation in the system.

EXAMPLE: Solve the given system of equations. Use substitution.

$$\begin{cases} -16 + y = -x^2 & \text{Equation 1} \\ y = x^2 - 4x - 32 & \text{Equation 2} \end{cases}$$

STEP 1: In Equation 2, y is isolated on the left side of the equation. Therefore, we can substitute $y = x^2 - 4x - 32$ for y in Equation 1.

$-16 + y = -x^2$ Equation 1

$-16 + (x^2 - 4x - 32) = -x^2$

$x^2 - 4x - 48 = -x^2$

$x^2 + x^2 - 4x - 48 = -x^2 + x^2$

$2x^2 - 4x - 48 = 0$

$2(x^2 - 2x - 24) = 0$ Factor.

$2(x - 6)(x + 4) = 0$

$x - 6 = 0$ or $x + 4 = 0$ Zero-Product Principle

$x = 6$ or $x = -4$

STEP 2: Find the corresponding values of y by substituting $x = 6$ and $x = -4$ into one of the equations. Let's use Equation 2.

$y = x^2 - 4x - 32$	$y = x^2 - 4x - 32$
$y = 6^2 - 4(6) - 32$	$y = (-4)^2 - 4(-4) - 32$
$y = 36 - 24 - 32$	$y = 16 + 16 - 32$
$y = -20$	$y = 0$

So, the solutions appear to be $x = 6$, $y = -20$ and $x = -4$, $y = 0$.

STEP 3: Check that the solutions satisfy both original equations.

Equation 1:	Equation 2:
$-16 + y = -x^2$	$y = x^2 - 4x - 32$
solution: $x = 6$, $y = -20$	solution: $x = 6$, $y = -20$
$-16 + (-20) \stackrel{?}{=} -6^2$	$-20 \stackrel{?}{=} 6^2 - 4(6) - 32$
$-16 - 20 \stackrel{?}{=} -36$	$-20 \stackrel{?}{=} 36 - 24 - 32$
$-36 = -36$ ✅	$-20 = -20$ ✅

Equation 1:	Equation 2:
$-16 + y = -x^2$	$y = x^2 - 4x - 32$
solution: $x = -4$, $y = 0$	solution: $x = -4$, $y = 0$
$-16 + 0 \overset{?}{=} -(-4)^2$	$0 \overset{?}{=} (-4)^2 - 4(-4) - 32$
$-16 + 0 \overset{?}{=} -16$	$0 \overset{?}{=} 16 + 16 - 32$
$-16 = -16$ ✔	$0 = 0$ ✔

So, the solutions to the system of equations are $x = 6$, $y = -20$ and $x = -4$, $y = 0$. The solutions can also be written as the points $(6, -20)$ and $(-4, 0)$.

EXAMPLE: Solve the given system of equations. Use elimination.

$$\begin{cases} 4x^2 - 4y^2 = 36 & \text{Equation 1} \\ x^2 + y^2 = 9 & \text{Equation 2} \end{cases}$$

STEP 1: Eliminate one of the variables.

Let's eliminate x by multiplying the second equation by -4 and adding the equations. Then we can solve for y.

$$\begin{array}{r} 4x^2 - 4y^2 = 36 \\ -4x^2 + (-4)y^2 = -4(9) \end{array}$$

$$\begin{array}{r} 4x^2 - 4y^2 = 36 \\ -4x^2 - 4y^2 = -36 \\ \hline 0 - 8y^2 = 0 \\ y = 0 \end{array}$$

STEP 2: Determine the value of x by substituting $y = 0$ into one of the given equations.

$x^2 + y^2 = 9$ Equation 2

$x^2 + 0^2 = 9$ substitute $y = 0$

$x^2 = 9$

$x = \pm 3$ Square Root Property

$x = 3$ and $x = -3$

So, this solution appears to have two solutions: $(3, 0)$ and $(-3, 0)$.

STEP 3: Check that the two solutions satisfy both original equations.

Equation 1:	Equation 2:
$4x^2 - 4y^2 = 36$	$x^2 + y^2 = 9$
solution: $(3, 0)$	solution: $(3, 0)$
$4(3)^2 - 2(0)^2 \stackrel{?}{=} 36$ $36 - 0 \stackrel{?}{=} 36$ $36 = 36$ ✔	$3^2 + 0^2 \stackrel{?}{=} 9$ $9 + 0 \stackrel{?}{=} 9$ $9 = 9$ ✔
solution: $(-3, 0)$	solution: $(-3, 0)$
$4(-3)^2 - 2(0)^2 \stackrel{?}{=} 36$ $36 - 0 \stackrel{?}{=} 36$ $36 = 36$ ✔	$(-3)^2 + 0^2 \stackrel{?}{=} 9$ $9 + 0 \stackrel{?}{=} 9$ $9 = 9$ ✔

So, the solutions to the system of equations are $(3, 0)$ and $(-3, 0)$.

SOLVE EACH OF THE FOLLOWING NONLINEAR SYSTEMS USING SUBSTITUTION.

1. $\begin{cases} -x - y = -11 \\ x^2 + y^2 = 73 \end{cases}$

2. $\begin{cases} y = -\dfrac{2}{5}x \\ x^2 - y^2 = 21 \end{cases}$

3. $\begin{cases} \dfrac{x^2}{49} + \dfrac{y^2}{16} = 1 \\ x^2 - y^2 = 49 \end{cases}$

LOOK AT THAT TEAMWORK!

4. $\begin{cases} x + y = 0 \\ 4x^2 + 2y^2 = 6 \end{cases}$

SOLVE EACH NONLINEAR SYSTEM USING ELIMINATION.

5. $\begin{cases} x^2 + y^2 = 4 \\ \dfrac{y^2}{4} - \dfrac{x^2}{4} = 1 \end{cases}$

6. $\begin{cases} -2y - x^2 = -12 \\ 2x + y = 6 \end{cases}$

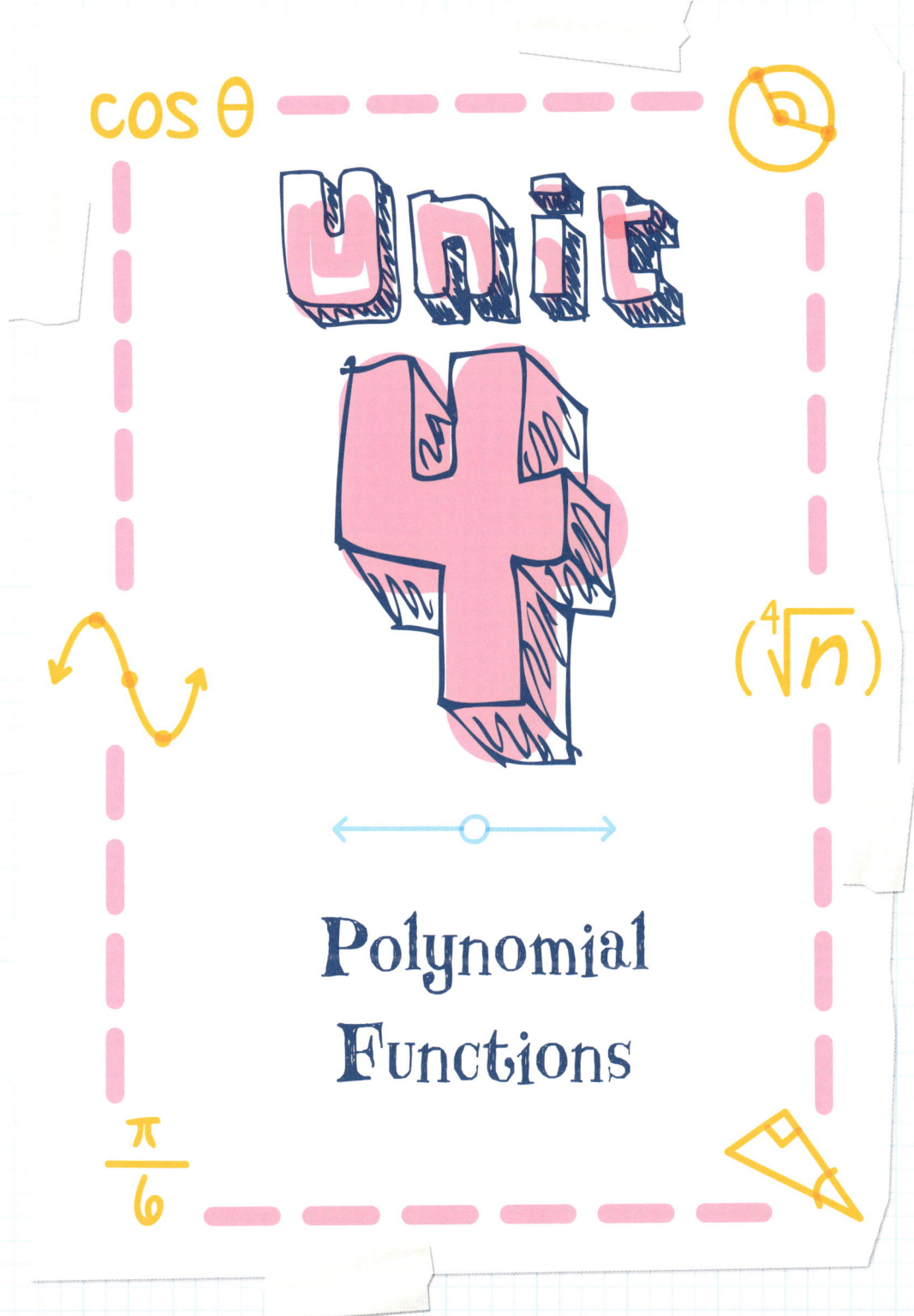

Unit 4

Polynomial Functions

$\cos \theta$

$(\sqrt[4]{n})$

$\dfrac{\pi}{6}$

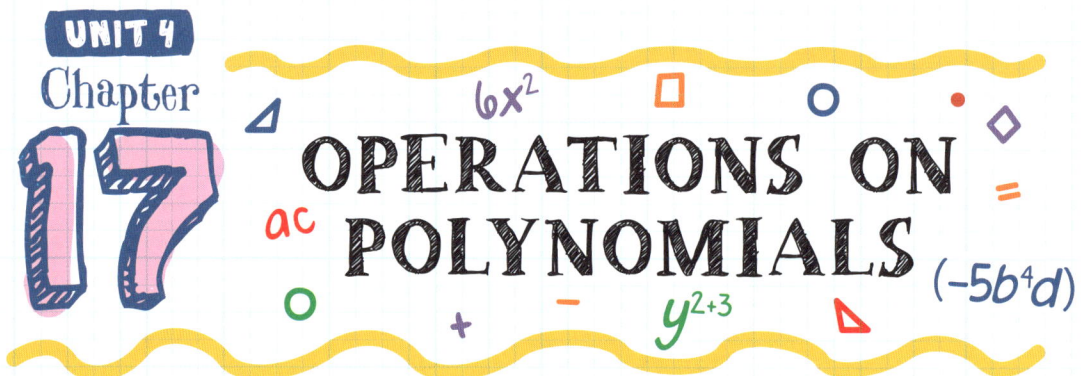

OPERATIONS ON POLYNOMIALS

POLYNOMIALS are expressions consisting of sums and products of constants and variables.

You can simplify polynomials by combining like terms.

EXAMPLE: Compute the following sum and simplify.

$(4x^3 - 6x^2 + 13x^4) + (-x^4 + 3x^3 - 8x^2)$

$4x^3 + (-6x^2) + 13x^4 + (-x^4) + 3x^3 + (-8x^2)$

$13x^4 + (-x^4) + 4x^3 + 3x^3 + (-6x^2) + (-8x^2)$ Combine like terms.

$12x^4 + 7x^3 + (-14x^2)$

So, $(4x^3 - 6x^2 + 13x^4) + (-x^4 + 3x^3 - 8x^2) = 12x^4 + 7x^3 - 14x^2$.

> For polynomials with just one variable, we often write the polynomial in descending powers of that variable.

To multiply polynomials, use the Distributive Property.

EXAMPLE: Compute the following product and simplify.

$-5a^3(a^4 - 7b)$ Distribute: Multiply each term inside the parentheses by the expression outside the parentheses.

$(-5a^3 \cdot a^4) - (-5a^3 \cdot 7b)$

$-5a^{3+4} - (-35a^3b)$

$= (-5a^7) + 35a^3b$

$= -5a^7 + 35a^3b$

So, $-5a^3(a^4 - 7b) = -5a^7 + 35a^3b$.

REMEMBER:

To multiply expressions with the same base:

1. Write the common base.

2. Add the exponents.

To multiply two binomials, use the **FOIL** method.

first, outer, inner, last

first   outer

$(a + b)(c + d) = ac + ad + bc + bd$

inner   last

Answer: $ac + ad + bc + bd$

EXAMPLE: Multiply: $(2x^4y^4 - 8x^3y^2)(9xy^3 + 10x^3y)$.

$(2x^4y^4 - 8x^3y^2)(9xy^3 + 10x^3y)$ FOIL

STEP 1: Multiply the **first** terms in each binomial.

$= 2 \cdot 9x^{4+1}y^{4+3} = 18x^5y^7$

STEP 2: Multiply the outer terms.

$= 2 \cdot 10x^{4+3}y^{4+1} = 20x^7y^5$

STEP 3: Multiply the inner terms.

$= -8 \cdot 9x^{3+1}y^{2+3} = -72x^4y^5$

STEP 4: Multiply the last terms.

$= -8 \cdot 10x^{3+3}y^{2+1} = -80x^6y^3$

STEP 5: Write all the products together as one polynomial.

$= 20x^7y^5 - 80x^6y^3 + 18x^5y^7 - 72x^4y^5$

So, $(2x^4y^4 - 8x^3y^2)(9xy^3 + 10x^3y) = 20x^7y^5 - 80x^6y^3 + 18x^5y^7 - 72x^4y^5$.

COMPUTE THE FOLLOWING AND SIMPLIFY YOUR ANSWER.

1. $(8x^7 - 3y^4 - 11x^5) + (2x^7 + 5x^5 - 9y^4)$

2. $(6m^8 + 2m^5 + m^2n) - (-7m^8 - 14m^5 + 4m^2n - 9)$

3. $(7ab^3 - 4b^6 - 12a^2) + (-5b^6 + 3a^2 + 2ab^3)$

4. $(2h^9 + 10g^4 + hg) + (hg - 21) - (16h^9 - 5g^4 - 6)$

5. $(18y^2 - 14y^7 + 7y^3) - (5y^7 - y^3 + 8y^2)$

6. $(k^6 - 4k^5 + 5k^4) + (16k^4 + 5) - (7k^6 - 3k^4 + 3)$

7. The binomial $5x + 8$ represents the width of a rectangle and the monomial $2x$ represents the length. What binomial represents the perimeter of the rectangle?

SIMPLIFY EACH POLYNOMIAL EXPRESSION.

8. $(a^7b^3 - a^9b^4)(a^9b^7)$

9. $5x^3(-8x^2 + 2xy)$

10. $(c^2d^8)(cd^5 - 9d + 2c^2)$

11. $(x^3y + 9)^2$

12. $h^2(6g^2 - 11g)$

13. $(m^7n + 4)^2$

14. The dimensions of Mira's rectangular vegetable garden are represented by the binomials $4x + 7$ and $x + 3$. What polynomial represents the area of the garden? Write the polynomial in descending powers of x.

FACTORING POLYNOMIALS

a^2

b^5

FACTORING is the process of "breaking down" expressions into their factors.

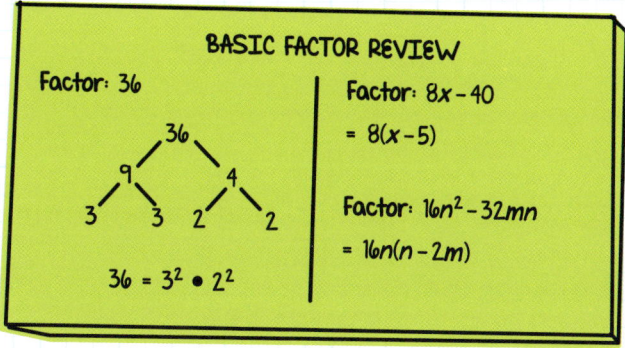

BASIC FACTOR REVIEW

Factor: 36

36
9   4
3   3   2   2

$36 = 3^2 \cdot 2^2$

Factor: $8x - 40$

$= 8(x - 5)$

Factor: $16n^2 - 32mn$

$= 16n(n - 2m)$

Some useful factoring methods are:

▶ Finding the greatest common factor (GCF)

▶ Grouping

▶ Trinomial factoring

▶ Using special formulas

We can factor by finding the **GREATEST COMMON FACTOR** of a polynomial.

EXAMPLE: Factor $14a^2b^5c^4 - 28ab^3c^5 + 42ab^3c^2$.

STEP 1: Find the greatest common factor of the constants and the lowest power of each variable.

GCF of 14, –28, 42: 14	GCF of b^5, b^3, and b^3: b^3
GCF of a^2, a, and a: a	GCF of c^4, c^5, and c^2: c^2

So, the GCF is $14ab^3c^2$.

STEP 2: Divide each term by $14ab^3c^2$ to find the remaining factor.

$14a^2b^5c^4 - 28ab^3c^5 + 42ab^3c^2$

$\dfrac{14a^2b^5c^4}{14ab^3c^2} = ab^2c^2$

$\dfrac{-28ab^3c^5}{14ab^3c^2} = -2c^3$

$\dfrac{42ab^3c^2}{14ab^3c^2} = 3$

> **REMEMBER:**
> Subtract the exponents when dividing expressions with the same base.
> $$\frac{a^m}{a^n} = a^{(m-n)}$$

STEP 3: Write your answer as the product of the GCF and the sum of the remaining factors.

$14ab^3c^2(ab^2c^2 - 2c^3 + 3)$

When we cannot factor using the GCF, we can try to **FACTOR BY GROUPING**: Break the polynomial into two or more groups that can be factored using the GCF.

EXAMPLE: Factor $n^3 - 3n^2 + 4n - 12$.

STEP 1: Break the polynomial into two simpler polynomials, each of which is factorable by GCF factoring.

$$n^3 - 3n^2 + 4n - 12 = (n^3 - 3n^2) + (4n - 12)$$

Group the terms $4n$ and -12. These have a GCF of 4.

Group the terms n^3 and $-3n^2$. These have a GCF of n^2.

STEP 2: Factor each of the groups separately, using the GCF of each group.

$$= (n^3 - 3n^2) + (4n - 12) = n^2(n - 3) + 4(n - 3)$$

STEP 3: Since the two terms $n^2(n - 3)$ and $4(n - 3)$ share the GCF $(n - 3)$, we can factor out $(n - 3)$.

$$= n^2(n - 3) + 4(n - 3)$$

$$= (n^2 + 4)(n - 3)$$

So, the polynomial $n^3 - 3n^2 + 4n - 12$ can be factored as $(n^2 + 4)(n - 3)$.

TRINOMIAL FACTORING involves rewriting a trinomial as the product of two binomials.

If the coefficient of the first term is 1, ask: What two numbers multiply to the coefficient of the third term and add up to the coefficient of the second term?

EXAMPLE: Factor $x^2 - 12x - 64$.

STEP 1: Ask: Which two numbers multiply to -64 and add up to -12?

$x^2 + (-12x) + (-64)$

$-16 \cdot 4 = -64$

$-16 + 4 = -12$

So, the numbers are -16 and 4.

STEP 2: Rewrite the expression with these factors.

$(x - 16)(x + 4)$

So, the polynomial $x^2 - 12x - 64$ can be factored as $(x - 16)(x + 4)$.

REMEMBER:
Multiplication is commutative. So, the product can also be written as $(x + 4)(x - 16)$.

If the coefficient of the first term is *not* 1, follow these steps.

EXAMPLE: Factor $3x^2 + 17x - 6$.

STEP 1: Multiply the coefficients from the first and last terms.

$3x^2 + 17x + (-6)$

$3 \cdot (-6) = -18$

STEP 2: List all the factors of that product. Then find the sum of each factor pair.

Product = −18	Sum of Factors
$1 \cdot (-18) = -18$	$1 + (-18) = -17$
$2 \cdot (-9) = -18$	$2 + (-9) = -7$
$3 \cdot (-6) = -18$	$3 + (-6) = -3$
$-1 \cdot 18 = -18$	$-1 + 18 = 17$
$-2 \cdot 9 = -18$	$-2 + 9 = 7$
$-3 \cdot 6 = -18$	$-3 + 6 = 3$

STEP 3: Identify the factor pair that multiplies to the product (−18) and adds up to the coefficient for the middle term (17).

STEP 4: Go back to the original trinomial and break the middle term (17x) into the sum of the two values in the factor pair (−1x and 18x).

$3x^2 + 17x - 6$

$3x^2 - 1x + 18x - 6$

STEP 5: Factor by grouping.

Break the polynomial into two simpler polynomials, each of which can be factored using the GCF.

$3x^2 - 1x + 18x - 6$

$(3x^2 - 1x) + (18x - 6)$

$x(3x - 1) + 6(3x - 1)$ Factor the GCF from each binomial.

STEP 6: Since the GCF of the two terms $x(3x - 1)$ and $6(3x - 1)$ is $(3x - 1)$, we can factor out $(3x - 1)$.

$= x(3x - 1) + 6(3x - 1)$

$= (x + 6)(3x - 1)$

Check the answer using FOIL to multiply the factors.

So, the polynomial $3x^2 + 17x - 6$ can be factored as $(x + 6)(3x - 1)$.

Using Special Formulas

Some polynomials can be factored using **SPECIAL FORMULAS**.

Difference of Two Squares	Sum of Two Cubes
$x^2 - y^2 = (x + y)(x - y)$	$x^3 + y^3 = (x + y)(x^2 - xy + y^2)$
Perfect Square Trinomial	**Difference of Two Cubes**
$x^2 + 2xy + y^2 = (x + y)^2$	$x^3 - y^3 = (x - y)(x^2 + xy + y^2)$
$x^2 - 2xy + y^2 = (x - y)^2$	

EXAMPLE: Factor $81m^8n^{12} - 49p^2h^{14}$.

STEP 1: Identify the special formula that can be used to factor.

Each term is a perfect square and we are finding the difference, so we can use the **Difference of Two Squares formula.**

STEP 2: Rewrite the polynomial in the form $x^2 - y^2$.

$81m^8n^{12} - 49p^2h^{14} = (9m^4n^6)^2 - (7ph^7)^2$ ← Difference of Two Squares

STEP 3: Apply the special formula.

Using the Difference of Two Squares formula, we can write this polynomial as $(x + y)(x - y)$.

$(9m^4n^6)^2 - (7ph^7)^2$

$= (9m^4n^6 + 7ph^7)(9m^4n^6 - 7ph^7)$

So, the polynomial $81m^8n^{12} - 49p^2h^{14}$ can be factored as $(9m^4n^6 + 7ph^7)(9m^4n^6 - 7ph^7)$.

EXAMPLE: Factor $25a^2 + 30ab + 9b^2$.

STEP 1: Identify the special formula that can be used to factor.

The first and last terms are perfect squares and the middle term is two times the product of the values being squared, so we can use the **Perfect Square Trinomial formula.**

STEP 2: Rewrite the polynomial in the form $x^2 + 2xy + y^2$.

$25a^2 + 30ab + 9b^2$

$= (5a)^2 + 2 \cdot 5a \cdot 3b + (3b)^2$ ← Perfect Square Trinomial!

STEP 3: Apply the special formula.

Using the Perfect Square Trinomial formula, we can rewrite this polynomial as $(x + y)^2$.

$(5a)^2 + 2 \cdot 5a \cdot 3b + (3b)^2 = (5a + 3b)^2$

So, the polynomial $25a^2 + 30ab + 9b^2$ can be factored as $(5a + 3b)^2$.

EXAMPLE: Factor $8y^{33} + 27z^9$.

STEP 1: Identify the special formula that can be used to factor.

Each term is a perfect cube and we are finding the sum, so we can use the **Sum of Two Cubes formula**.

STEP 2: Rewrite the polynomial in the form $x^3 + y^3$.

$8y^{33} + 27z^9 = (2y^{11})^3 + (3z^3)^3$ ← Sum of Two Cubes!

STEP 3: Apply the special formula.

Using the Sum of Two Cubes formula, we can rewrite this polynomial as $(x + y)(x^2 - xy + y^2)$.

$(2y^{11})^3 + (3z^3)^3$

$$= (2y^{11} + 3z^3)((2y^{11})^2 - 2y^{11} \cdot 3z^3 + (3z^3)^2)$$

$$= (2y^{11} + 3z^3)(4y^{22} - 6y^{11}z^3 + 9z^6)$$

So, the polynomial $8y^{33} + 27z^9$ can be factored as $(2y^{11} + 3z^3)(4y^{22} - 6y^{11}z^3 + 9z^6)$.

EXAMPLE: Factor $125c^3d^{12} - 343g^{21}$.

STEP 1: Identify the special formula that can be used to factor.

Each term is a perfect cube and we are finding the difference, so we can use the **Difference of Two Cubes formula**.

STEP 2: Rewrite the polynomial in the form $x^3 - y^3$.

$125c^3d^{12} - 343g^{21} = (5cd^4)^3 - (7g^7)^3$ ← Difference of Two Cubes

STEP 3: Apply the special formula.

Using the Difference of Two Cubes formula, we can rewrite this polynomial as $(x - y)(x^2 + xy + y^2)$.

$$(5cd^4)^3 - (7g^7)^3$$

$$= (5cd^4 - 7g^7)((5cd^4)^2 + 5cd^4 \cdot 7g^7 + (7g^7)^2)$$

$$= (5cd^4 - 7g^7)(25c^2d^8 + 35cd^4g^7 + 49g^{14})$$

So, the polynomial $125c^3d^{12} - 343g^{21}$ can be factored as $(5cd^4 - 7g^7)(25c^2d^8 + 35cd^4g^7 + 49g^{14})$.

USE THE GCF METHOD TO FACTOR COMPLETELY.

1. $24x^5y^3 + 36xy^2$

2. $8a^2b^6c^{18} + 32a^5b^{14}c^{25} - 64a^{17}b^{18}c^{29}$

3. $-11h^3j^4 - 33hj^6$

4. $2m^4n^7 + 2m^8n^8 + 4m^{10}n^9$

USE THE GROUPING METHOD TO FACTOR COMPLETELY.

5. $3c^6 + 9c^5 + 4c + 12$

6. $8x^3 - xy + 8x^2y - y^2$

7. $7d^2 + 14d^3 + 8d + 4$

USE TRINOMIAL FACTORING TO FACTOR COMPLETELY.

8. $a^2 + 2a - 3$

9. $d^2 - 12d + 36$

10. $6x^2 - 13x + 6$

STATE WHICH SPECIAL FORMULA IS NEEDED FOR FACTORING. THEN FACTOR COMPLETELY.

11. $121m^6 - 25n^6$

12. $49x^8 + 42x^4y^2 + 9y^4$

13. $125h^{24} + 512j^{36}$

14. $27c^9d^{18} - 343g^{24}$

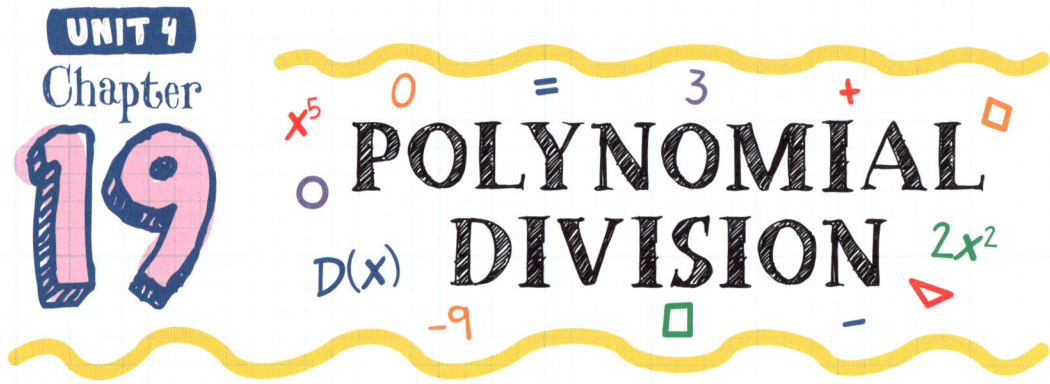

POLYNOMIAL DIVISION

POLYNOMIAL LONG DIVISION is similar to standard long division.

EXAMPLE: Divide $P(x) = x^5 + 3x^3 + 2x^2 - 5$ by $D(x) = x + 2$.

STEP 1: Write the division problem using the standard division bar.

> Insert **0** placeholders for the coefficients of x^4 and x.

$$x + 2 \overline{\smash{)}\, x^5 + 0x^4 + 3x^3 + 2x^2 + 0x - 5}$$

STEP 2: Divide. Ask: What can I multiply the divisor by so that the first term of the product matches the first term of the dividend?

Write the answer above the division bar.
This is the first term of the quotient.

$$\begin{array}{r} x^4 \\ x + 2 \overline{\smash{)}\, x^5 + 0x^4 + 3x^3 + 2x^2 + 0x - 5} \end{array}$$

STEP 3: Multiply the divisor by x^4. Write the product below the dividend.

$$x^4(x + 2) = x^5 + 2x^4$$

$$\begin{array}{r} x^4 \\ x + 2 \overline{\smash{)}\, x^5 + 0x^4 + 3x^3 + 2x^2 + 0x - 5} \\ \underline{x^5 + 2x^4} \end{array}$$

STEP 4: Subtract (or negate both terms in the expression and add). Then bring down the next term, $3x^3$.

$$
\begin{array}{r}
x^4 \\
x + 2 \overline{) x^5 + 0x^4 + 3x^3 + 2x^2 + 0x - 5} \\
\underline{-x^5 - 2x^4} \\
-2x^4 + 3x^3
\end{array}
$$

STEP 5: Repeat the previous steps. Divide. Multiply. Subtract. Then bring down the next term.

$$
\begin{array}{r}
x^4 - 2x^3 + 7x^2 - 12x + 24 \\
x + 2 \overline{) x^5 + 0x^4 + 3x^3 + 2x^2 + 0x - 5} \\
\underline{-x^5 - 2x^4} \\
-2x^4 + 3x^3 \\
\underline{2x^4 + 4x^3} \\
7x^3 + 2x^2 \\
\underline{-7x^3 - 14x^2} \\
-12x^2 + 0x \\
\underline{12x^2 + 24x} \\
24x - 5 \\
\underline{-24x - 48} \\
-53 \leftarrow \text{Remainder}
\end{array}
$$

Therefore, the **QUOTIENT** is $x^4 - 2x^3 + 7x^2 - 12x + 24$ and the **REMAINDER** is R $= -53$.

If we are dividing a polynomial by a linear polynomial of the form $x - a$, we can use **SYNTHETIC DIVISION**.

EXAMPLE: Use synthetic division to divide $P(x) = -5x^2 + 3x - 9 + 2x^3$ by $D(x) = x - 3$.

STEP 1: Rewrite the terms of the dividend in descending order of exponents. Then write the coefficients.

$$2x^3 - 5x^2 + 3x - 9$$

$$2 \quad -5 \quad 3 \quad -9 \leftarrow \text{coefficients}$$

STEP 2: Write the constant a to the left of the coefficients. Then bring down the first coefficient, 2, as shown.

$$
\begin{array}{c|cccc}
3 & 2 & -5 & 3 & -9 \\
  & \downarrow & & & \\
\hline
  & 2 & & &
\end{array}
$$

STEP 3: Multiply the first coefficient, 2, by $a = 3$, and then write the product under the second coefficient, -5.

$$
\begin{array}{c|cccc}
3 & 2 & -5 & 3 & -9 \\
  & \downarrow & 6 & & \quad (3 \cdot 2 = 6) \\
\hline
  & 2 & & &
\end{array}
$$

STEP 4: Add the second coefficient, -5, to the product we just found, 6, and write the sum.

$\boxed{3}$ 2 -5 3 -9

↓   6
_____

2   1 $(-5 + 6 = 1)$

STEP 5: Continue this procedure of multiplying and adding until you reach the last column.

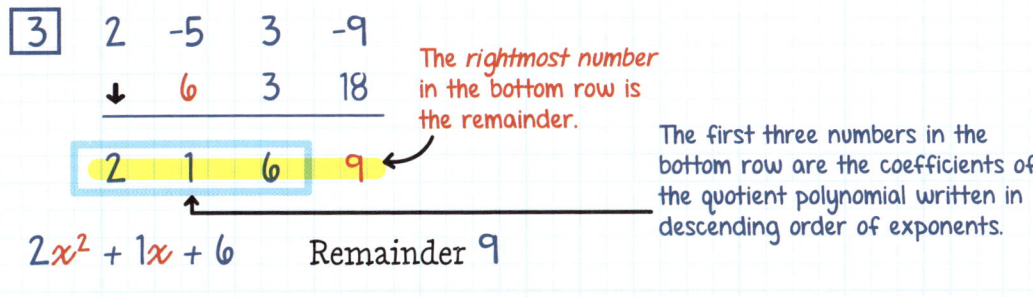

$\boxed{3}$ 2 -5 3 -9

↓   6   3   18   The *rightmost number*
_____   in the bottom row is
                      the remainder.
  2   1   6   9   The first three numbers in the
                      bottom row are the coefficients of
                      the quotient polynomial written in
$2x^2 + 1x + 6$ Remainder 9   descending order of exponents.

So, $(-5x^2 + 3x - 9 + 2x^3) \div (x - 3) = 2x^2 + x + 6 + \dfrac{9}{x-3}$.

The **REMAINDER THEOREM** says if the polynomial $P(x)$ is divided by $x - r$, then the remainder is $P(r)$.

EXAMPLE: Use the Remainder Theorem to find $P(-3)$ if $P(x) = 3x^3 + 2x^2 - 4x + 1$.

Divide $P(x) = 3x^3 + 2x^2 - 4x + 1$ by $D(x) = x + 3$.

$\boxed{-3}$ 3 2 -4 1   This is $x - (-3)$.

↓   -9   21   -51
_____

3   -7   17   -50

$3x^2 - 7x + 17$ Remainder -50

So, by the Remainder Theorem $P(-3) = -50$.

The **FACTOR THEOREM** says r is a zero of the polynomial P if and only if $x - r$ is a factor of $P(x)$.

EXAMPLE: Determine if $x - 5$ is a factor of $2x^2 - 7x - 15$. Then completely factor $2x^2 - 7x - 15$.

STEP 1: Use the Remainder Theorem to verify that $x - 5$ is a factor of $2x^2 - 7x - 15$.

Substitute $x = 5$ into $2x^2 - 7x - 15$.

$2(5)^2 - 7(5) - 15 = 50 - 35 - 15 = 0$

The remainder is 0. Therefore, by the Factor Theorem, $x - 5$ is a factor of $2x^2 - 7x - 15$.

STEP 2: Factor $2x^2 - 7x - 15$ completely.

We can use the factor we know, $(x - 5)$, to find the other factor. Use factoring or synthetic division.

$2x^2 - 7x - 15 = (2x + 3)(x - 5)$

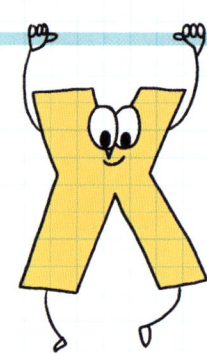

FOR QUESTIONS 1 THROUGH 3, DIVIDE USING POLYNOMIAL LONG DIVISION.

1. $(4x^4 + 2x^3 + 6x^2 + 4x + 5) \div (x + 7)$

2. $(-5x^3 - 10x + 75) \div (5x - 10)$

3. $(12x^5 + 6x^3 - 3x^2) \div (-x^2 - 1)$

FOR QUESTIONS 4 THROUGH 6, DIVIDE USING SYNTHETIC DIVISION.

4. $(x^3 - 7x + 9) \div (x - 2)$

5. $(12x^2 + 6x + 18) \div (3x + 12)$

6. $(4x^3 + 21x - 19) \div (x - 6)$

7. Find $P(8)$ if $P(x) = 2x^2 + 7x - 25$.

8. Find $P(-6)$ if $P(x) = 7x^3 - 10x + 13$.

9. Without performing division, find the remainder when
   $x^3 + 18x^2 - 33x + 169$ is divided by $x - 9$.

10. Without performing the division, find the remainder when $2x^3 + 4x^2 + 17x + 85$ is divided by $x + 3$.

11. Determine if $x + 4$ is a factor of $x^3 + 3x^2 + 3x + 28$. Then factor the polynomial completely.

12. Determine if $x - 2$ is a factor of $9x^3 + 8x^2 - 5x - 94$. Then factor the polynomial completely.

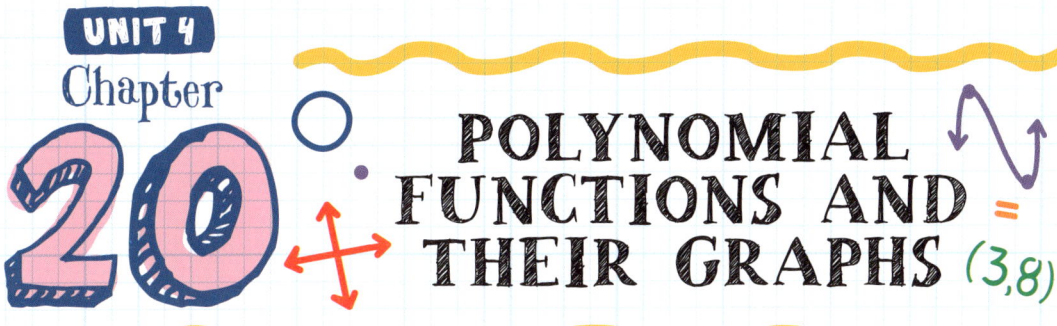

Chapter

20.

POLYNOMIAL FUNCTIONS AND THEIR GRAPHS (3,8)

Graphs of Common Polynomial Functions

CONSTANT FUNCTIONS are polynomials of degree 0.

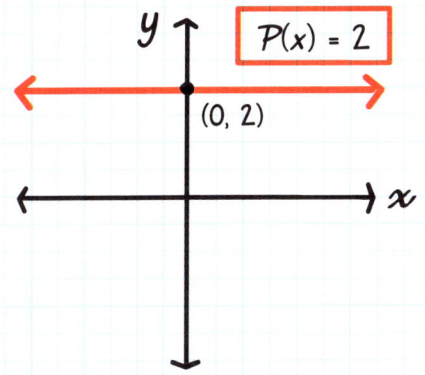

$P(x) = 2$

$(0, 2)$

LINEAR FUNCTIONS are polynomials of degree 1.

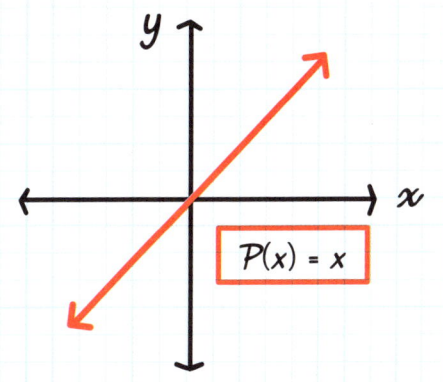

$P(x) = x$

QUADRATIC FUNCTIONS are polynomials of degree 2.

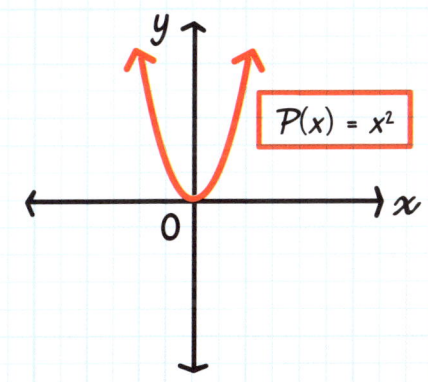

$P(x) = x^2$

CUBIC FUNCTIONS are polynomials of degree 3.

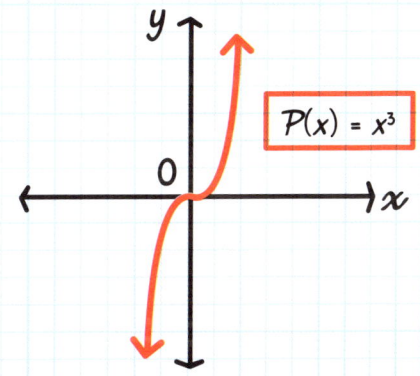

$P(x) = x^3$

The **END BEHAVIOR** of a polynomial function describes what the graph of the function looks like as it approaches positive infinity (∞) or negative infinity ($-\infty$).

We can determine the end behavior of a polynomial function's graph by whether the highest degree of the polynomial is **EVEN** or **ODD** and whether the leading coefficient is **POSITIVE** or **NEGATIVE**.

EXAMPLE: $x^4 - 10x^2 - 5$

▶ Highest degree: even

▶ Leading coefficient: positive

▶ Graph goes up at both ends.

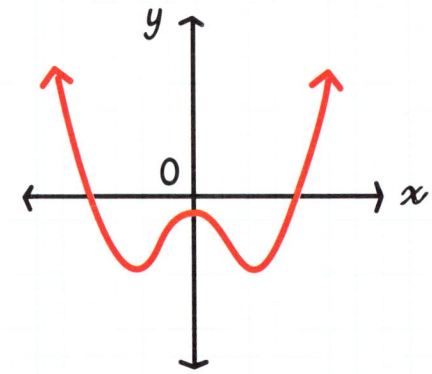

EXAMPLE: $-x^6 + 5x^3 - 4x$

▶ Highest degree: even

▶ Leading coefficient: negative

▶ Graph goes down at both ends.

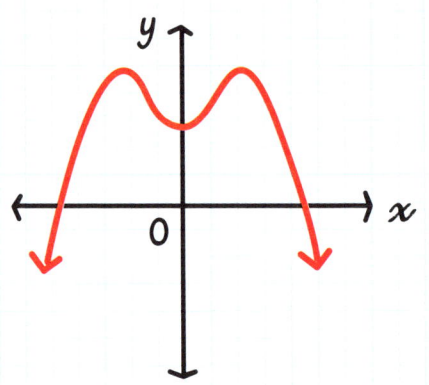

EXAMPLE: $x^5 - 8x^3 + 10x - 1$

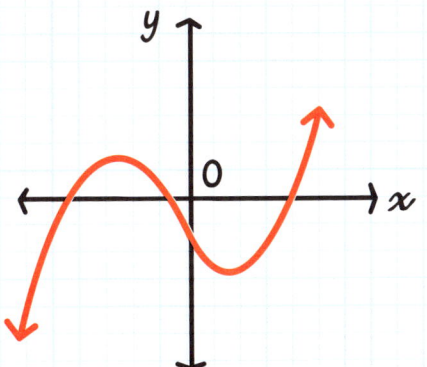

▶ Highest degree: odd

▶ Leading coefficient: positive

▶ Graph goes up to the right and down to the left.

EXAMPLE: $-x^5 - 2x^3 + 15x + 1$

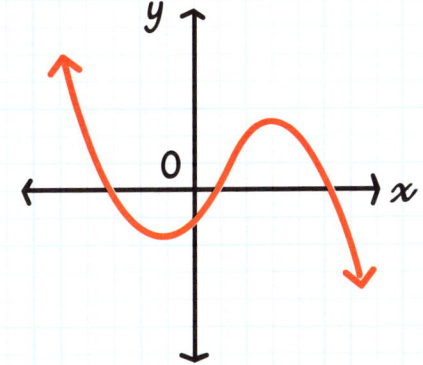

▶ Highest degree: odd

▶ Leading coefficient: negative

▶ Graph goes down to the right and up to the left.

THINK:

When the highest degree is *even*, the ends point in the *same* direction.

When the highest degree is *odd*, the ends point in *different* directions.

A **ZERO** (or **ROOT** or **SOLUTION**) of a polynomial function is an input that gives an output of zero.

Visually, the zeros of a polynomial function are where its graph crosses the x-axis.

EXAMPLE: Find the real zeros of the polynomial function $h(x) = (x^2 - 9)(x^2 - 16)$.

To find the zeros, determine when $h(x) = 0$.

We can do this by factoring the polynomial and then applying the Zero-Product Principle.

> Remember: The highest degree of a polynomial function tells you how many zeros it has.

$h(x) = (x^2 - 9)(x^2 - 16)$

$= (x + 3)(x - 3)(x + 4)(x - 4)$ Difference of Two Squares formula (twice)

$x + 3 = 0$	$x - 3 = 0$	$x + 4 = 0$	$x - 4 = 0$ Zero-Product Principle
$x = -3$	$x = 3$	$x = -4$	$x = 4$

Therefore, $h(-3) = 0$, $h(3) = 0$, $h(-4) = 0$, and $h(4) = 0$.

So, the zeros of $h(x) = (x^2 - 9)(x^2 - 16)$ are $x = -3$, $x = 3$, $x = -4$, and $x = 4$.

THINK:
The corresponding x-intercepts are the points $(-3, 0)$, $(3, 0)$, $(-4, 0)$, and $(4, 0)$.

Transformations of Polynomial Functions

We can graph polynomial functions using transformations of known graphs.

EXAMPLE: Graph $g(x) = (x + 5)^2 - 9$.

To graph this function, we can apply transformations to $f(x) = x^2$.

The $+ 5$ within the parentheses tells us to shift 5 units to the left. The -9 tells us to shift 9 units downward.

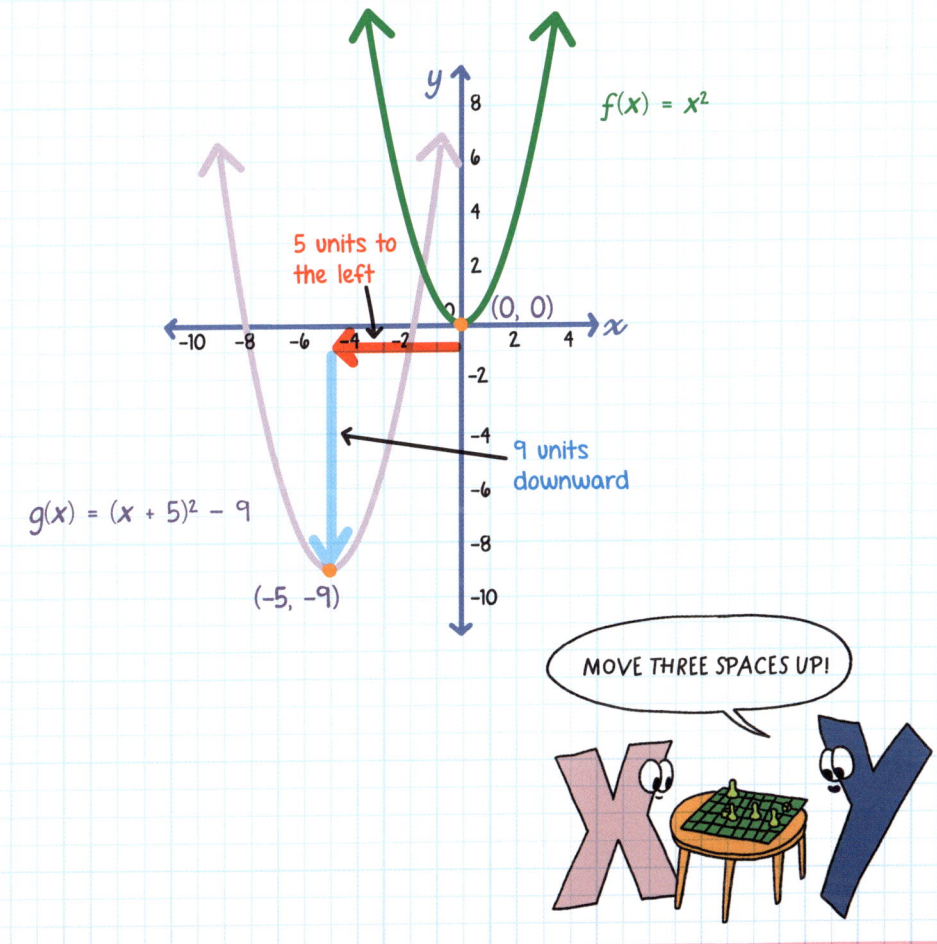

5 units to the left

$f(x) = x^2$

(0, 0)

9 units downward

$g(x) = (x + 5)^2 - 9$

(−5, −9)

MOVE THREE SPACES UP!

USE WHAT YOU KNOW ABOUT POLYNOMIAL FUNCTIONS AND THEIR GRAPHS TO ANSWER THE FOLLOWING QUESTIONS.

1. Find all real zeros of the polynomial function $g(x) = (x^2 - 9)(x + 6)$.

2. Find all real zeros of the polynomial function $h(x) = (x^2 - 16)(x^2 - 1)$.

3. Find all real zeros of the polynomial function $j(x) = x^3 - 8x^2 + 5x + 50$, given that 5 is a zero of the function.

DETERMINE THE END BEHAVIOR OF EACH FUNCTION'S GRAPH.

4. $f(x) = 9x^5 - 2x^2 + 7x - 3$

5. $h(x) = -14x^6 + 7x^5 - 8x + 4$

6. $g(x) = -7x^9 + 6x^2 - 12x + 22$

GRAPH THE POLYNOMIAL FUNCTION USING TRANSFORMATIONS.

7. $q(x) = -(x - 9)^3 + 2$

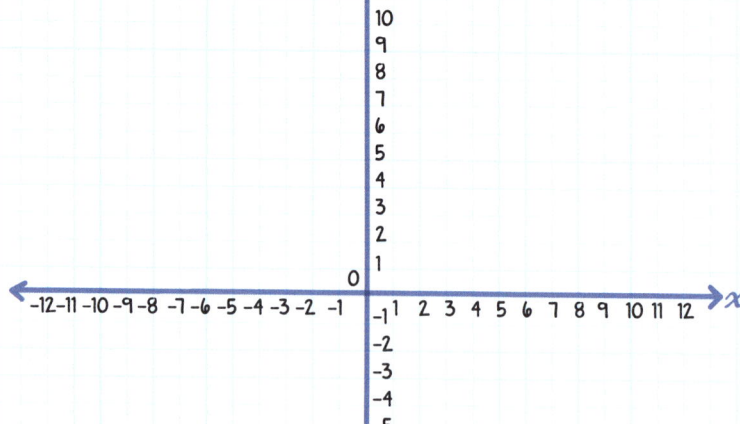

8. $p(x) = (x + 12)^4 - 1$

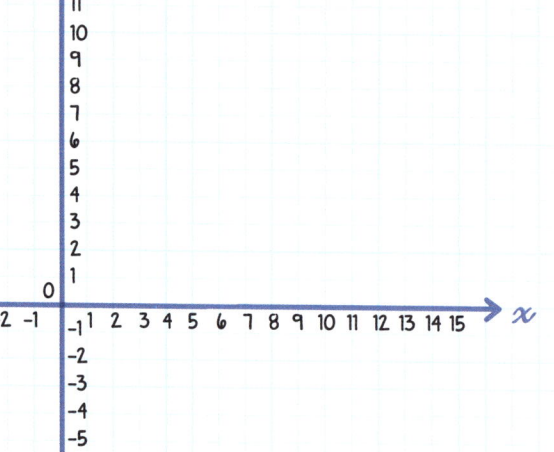

9. $j(x) = (x - 15)^3 + 4$

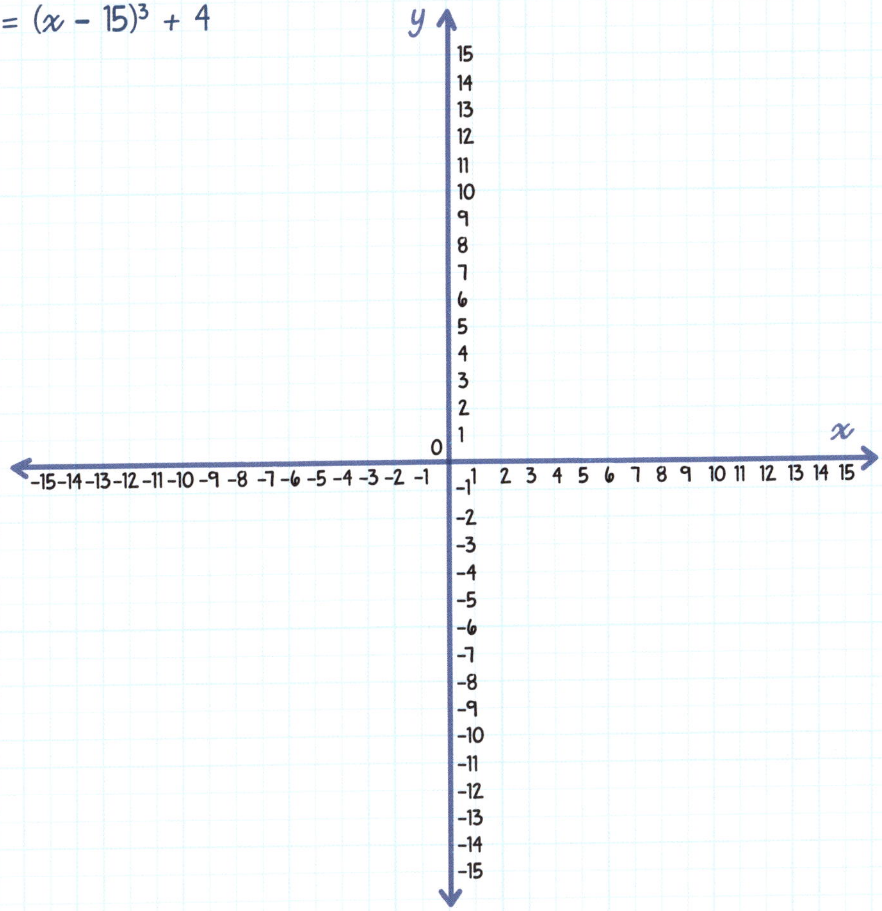
y
x
0
15 14 13 12 11 10 9 8 7 6 5 4 3 2 1
-1 -2 -3 -4 -5 -6 -7 -8 -9 -10 -11 -12 -13 -14 -15
-15 -14 -13 -12 -11 -10 -9 -8 -7 -6 -5 -4 -3 -2 -1
1 2 3 4 5 6 7 8 9 10 11 12 13 14 15

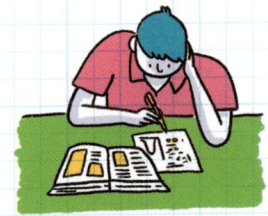

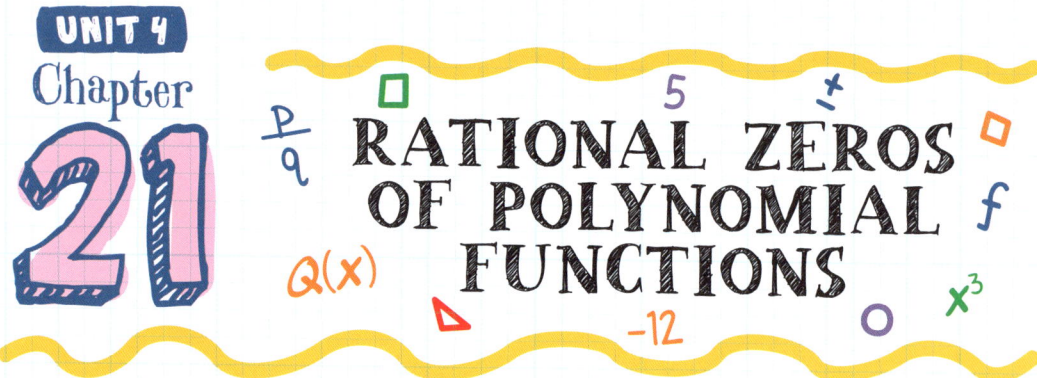

UNIT 4
Chapter 21
RATIONAL ZEROS OF POLYNOMIAL FUNCTIONS

The **RATIONAL ZEROS THEOREM** says that every rational zero of a polynomial with integer coefficients has the form $\frac{p}{q}$.

$$\frac{p}{q} = \frac{\text{factor of the constant term}}{\text{factor of the leading coefficient}}$$

We will refer to the fractions given by the Rational Zeros Theorem as **possible** rational zeros.

EXAMPLE: Find all the zeros of the polynomial function $Q(x) = x^3 - 3x^2 - 4x + 12$.

STEP 1: Identify all possible rational zeros using the Rational Zeros Theorem.

$Q(x) = 1x^3 - 3x^2 - 4x + 12$ p

q

Constant term: 12
Leading coefficient: 1

Factors of 12: ±1, ±2, ±3, ±4, ±6, ±12

Factors of 1: ±1

All possible rational zeros: $\pm\frac{1}{1}, \pm\frac{2}{1}, \pm\frac{3}{1}, \pm\frac{4}{1}, \pm\frac{6}{1}, \pm\frac{12}{1}$

We can rewrite these fractions: ±1, ±2, ±3, ±4, ±6, ±12

STEP 2: Find the actual rational zeros.

For this example, let's use synthetic division. Divide $x^3 - 3x^2 - 4x + 12$ by each of the possible rational zeros.

$\frac{p}{q}$	1	-3	-4	12	
1	1	-2	-6	6	
2	1	-1	-6	0	No remainder: $x - 2$ is a factor.
3	1	0	-4	0	No remainder: $x - 3$ is a factor.
4	1	1	0	12	
6	1	3	14	96	
12	1	9	104	1,260	
-1	1	-4	0	12	
-2	1	-5	6	0	No remainder: $x + 2$ is a factor.

By the Factor Theorem, 2, 3, and -2 are zeros of the polynomial. This means that $Q(2) = 0$, $Q(3) = 0$, and $Q(-2) = 0$.

THINK:
The dividend is a third-degree polynomial, so there are three zeros. Once you find three zeros, there is no need to check any further.

Therefore, the zeros of $Q(x) = x^3 - 3x^2 - 4x + 12$ are $x = 2$, $x = 3$, and $x = -2$.

Substitution can also be used to find the actual rational zeros. Substitute each possible zero into the polynomial.

FOR EACH OF THE FOLLOWING POLYNOMIAL FUNCTIONS, FIND ALL THE ZEROS. THEN FACTOR THE POLYNOMIAL COMPLETELY.

1. $h(x) = x^3 + 11x^2 + 10x - 72$

2. $q(x) = 2x^3 - 24x^2 + 70x - 48$

3. $f(x) = x^4 - 11x^3 + 17x^2 + 107x - 210$

FOUND YOU!

4. $j(x) = 3x^2 + 12x - 96$

5. $H(x) = x^3 - 9x^2 + 23x - 15$

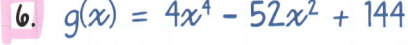

6. $g(x) = 4x^4 - 52x^2 + 144$

7. $Q(x) = x^4 - 16x^3 + 65x^2 - 38x - 120$

8. $R(x) = x^3 + 25x^2 + 178x + 264$

9. $b(x) = x^2 - 2x - 63$

10. $k(x) = x^3 + 15x^2 + 74x + 120$

WORK SPACE

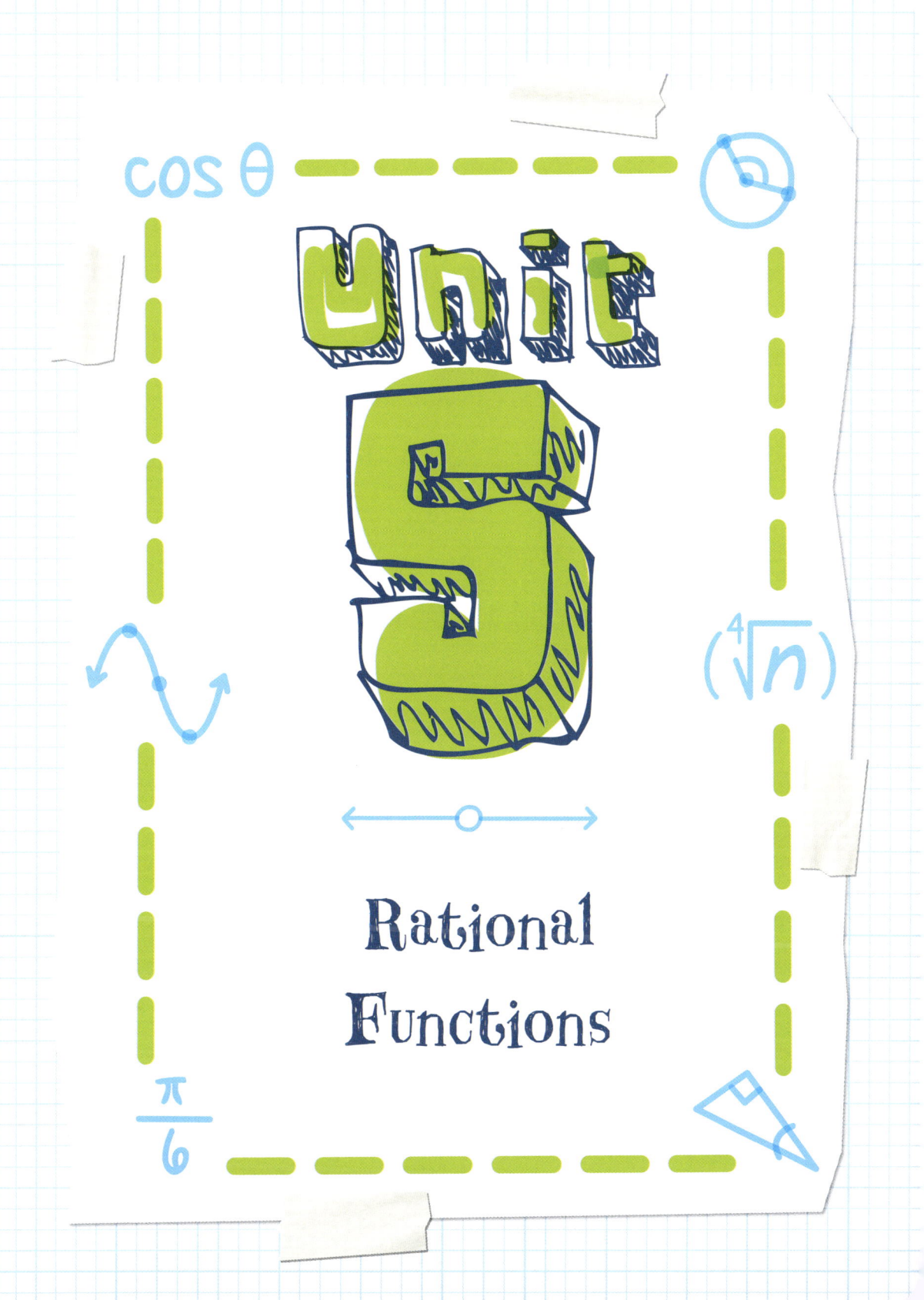

cos θ

Unit

5

Rational Functions

$\frac{\pi}{6}$

$(\sqrt[4]{n})$

Chapter 22 SIMPLIFYING RATIONAL EXPRESSIONS

$(4h^3)$
=
$6c^2$

A **RATIONAL EXPRESSION** is an expression that can be written as a quotient of polynomials. ← This means "as a fraction."

To simplify a rational expression:

1. Factor the numerator and denominator.

2. Cancel any factors that are common to both the numerator and the denominator. ↰ Factors ONLY! Not terms.

3. Identify any restrictions that must be made to the domain. Remember: We can't divide by zero!

THIS IS MY DOMAIN.

EXAMPLE: Simplify the rational expression $\dfrac{5m-30}{15n(m^2-9m+18)}$.

STEP 1: Factor the numerator and denominator.

$$\frac{5m-30}{15n(m^2-9m+18)}$$

$$\frac{5(m-6)}{15n(m-3)(m-6)}$$

STEP 2: Cancel all common factors.

$$\frac{5(\cancel{m-6})}{15n(m-3)(\cancel{m-6})} \quad m-6 \text{ can be canceled.}$$

$$\frac{\overset{1}{\cancel{5}}}{\underset{3}{\cancel{15}}n(m-3)} \quad \text{Reduce the fraction: } \frac{5}{15}=\frac{1\cdot 5}{3\cdot 5}=\frac{1}{3}$$

$$\frac{1}{3n(m-3)}$$

STEP 3: Identify the restrictions to the domain.

Ask: What is the domain of the original expression? All m, n except $n = 0$, $m = 3$, and $m = 6$.

The domain of the final expression is all m, n except $n = 0$ and $m = 3$. Since the restriction $m \neq 6$ is missing from the final expression, we must mention it explicitly.

So, $\dfrac{5m-30}{15n(m^2-9m+18)}$ simplifies to $\dfrac{1}{3n(m-3)}$, $m \neq 6$.

EXAMPLE: Simplify the rational expression $\dfrac{4x^4 - 4x^3 - x + 1}{x^2 - 1}$.

STEP 1: Factor the numerator and the denominator.

$$\dfrac{4x^4 - 4x^3 - x + 1}{x^2 - 1}$$

$$\dfrac{(4x^4 - 4x^3) + (-x + 1)}{x^2 - 1}$$ Factor the numerator by grouping.

$$\dfrac{4x^3(x - 1) - 1(x - 1)}{x^2 - 1}$$

$$\dfrac{(4x^3 - 1)(x - 1)}{x^2 - 1}$$

$$\dfrac{(4x^3 - 1)(x - 1)}{(x + 1)(x - 1)}$$ Factor the denominator as the difference of two squares.

STEP 2: Cancel all common factors.

$$\dfrac{(4x^3 - 1)\cancel{(x - 1)}}{(x + 1)\cancel{(x - 1)}}$$

$$\dfrac{4x^3 - 1}{x + 1}$$

STEP 3: Identify the restrictions to the domain.

The domain of the original expression is all x except $x = {-1}$ and $x = 1$. The domain of the final expression is all x except $x = {-1}$. Since the restriction $x \neq 1$ is missing from the final expression, we must mention it explicitly.

So, $\dfrac{4x^4 - 4x^3 - x + 1}{x^2 - 1}$ simplifies to $\dfrac{4x^3 - 1}{x + 1}$, $x \neq 1$.

EXAMPLE: Simplify the rational expression $\dfrac{24c^2d + 24cd^2}{6c^3 - 6cd^2}$.

STEP 1: Factor the numerator and denominator.

$$\dfrac{24c^2d + 24cd^2}{6c^3 - 6cd^2}$$

$\dfrac{24cd(c+d)}{6c(c^2-d^2)}$ Factor using the GCF.

$\dfrac{24cd(c+d)}{6c(c+d)(c-d)}$ Factor as the difference of two squares.

STEP 2: Cancel all common factors.

$\dfrac{4\;\,24cd(c+d)}{1\;\,6c(c+d)(c-d)}$

$\dfrac{4d}{c-d}$

STEP 3: Identify the restrictions to the domain.

The domain of the original expression is all c, d except $c = 0$, $c = d$, and $c = -d$. The domain of the final expression is all c, d except $c = d$. Since the restrictions $c \neq 0$ and $c \neq -d$ are missing from the final expression, we must mention them explicitly.

So, $\dfrac{24c^2d + 24cd^2}{6c^3 - 6cd^2}$ simplifies to $\dfrac{4d}{c-d}$, $c \neq 0$, $c \neq -d$.

SIMPLIFY THE RATIONAL EXPRESSION. IDENTIFY RESTRICTIONS TO THE DOMAIN.

1. $\dfrac{8g^5j^6}{-64g^{11}j^3}$

2. $\dfrac{25p^2 - 36}{6 + 5p}$

3. $\dfrac{7c - 56d}{6c^2d - 48cd^2}$

4. $\dfrac{x^2 - 6x - 27}{x^2 + 7x + 12}$

5. $\dfrac{2m - 4}{m^2 - 14m + 24}$

6. $\dfrac{d^7 - 2d^6}{d^{12} - 4d^{10}}$

7. $$\frac{5c^2 + 20c - 160}{20c^2 - 180c + 400}$$

8. $$\frac{2n^2 + 9n + 4}{14n^2 + 49n + 21}$$

9. $$\frac{35w^{17}v^5}{63w^{13}v^{16}}$$

10. $\dfrac{49y^2 - 81}{7y - 9}$

11. $\dfrac{3q - 9a}{11q^2a - 33qa^2}$

12. $\dfrac{x^2 - 14x + 48}{x^2 - 12x + 32}$

13. $\dfrac{5h-15}{h^2-12h+27}$

14. $\dfrac{7k^2+21k-70}{10k^2+110k+300}$

$16x$

(20) $\cdot$

$\square$

$=$

$\dfrac{5(h-3)}{h^2+7}$

OPERATIONS ON RATIONAL EXPRESSIONS

To find the **product** of rational expressions, multiply the numerators and multiply the denominators.

EXAMPLE: Multiply $\dfrac{h^2-25}{10h-30} \cdot \dfrac{8h-24}{h^2-6h+5}$. Write the product in simplest form.

STEP 1: Factor the numerators and denominators.

$$\frac{h^2-25}{10h-30} \cdot \frac{8h-24}{h^2-6h+5}$$

$$\frac{(h+5)(h-5)}{10(h-3)} \cdot \frac{8(h-3)}{(h-5)(h-1)}$$

STEP 2: Multiply the numerators and multiply the denominators.

$$\frac{8(h-3)(h+5)(h-5)}{10(h-3)(h-5)(h-1)}$$

STEP 3: Cancel all common factors.

$$\frac{\overset{4}{\cancel{8}}\cancel{(h-3)}(h+5)\cancel{(h-5)}}{\underset{5}{\cancel{10}}\cancel{(h-3)}\cancel{(h-5)}(h-1)}$$

$$\frac{4(h+5)}{5(h-1)}$$

Domain of the original expression: all h except $h = 1$, $h = 3$, and $h = 5$

Domain of the final expression: all h except $h = 1$

Since the restrictions $h \neq 3$ and $h \neq 5$ are missing from the final expression, we must mention them explicitly.

So, $\dfrac{h^2 - 25}{10h - 30} \cdot \dfrac{8h - 24}{h^2 - 6h + 5} = \dfrac{4(h+5)}{5(h-1)}$, $h \neq 3$, $h \neq 5$.

You can take a reciprocal to **divide** one rational expression by another.

EXAMPLE: Divide $\dfrac{x^2 - y^2}{4x^2 + 4xy} \div \dfrac{8x^2 - 8xy}{2x^2 - 2xy}$. Write the quotient in simplest form.

STEP 1: Factor the numerators and denominators.

$$\dfrac{x^2 - y^2}{4x^2 + 4xy} \div \dfrac{8x^2 - 8xy}{2x^2 - 2xy} = \dfrac{(x+y)(x-y)}{4x(x+y)} \div \dfrac{8x(x-y)}{2x(x-y)}$$

STEP 2: Divide.

$$\dfrac{(x+y)(x-y)}{4x(x+y)} \div \dfrac{8x(x-y)}{2x(x-y)}$$

$$\dfrac{(x+y)(x-y)}{4x(x+y)} \cdot \dfrac{2x(x-y)}{8x(x-y)}$$

THINK: To take the reciprocal, swap the numerator and denominator of the second rational expression. Then multiply.

STEP 3: Simplify.

$$\frac{\cancel{(x+y)}\cancel{(x-y)}\cdot 1\,\cancel{2x}\cancel{(x-y)}}{2\,\cancel{4x}\cancel{(x+y)}\cdot 8x\cancel{(x-y)}}$$

$$\frac{(x-y)}{16x}$$

STEP 4: Identify the restrictions to the domain.

Domain of the original expression: all x, y except $x = 0$, $y = 0$, $x = y$, and $x = {}^-y$

Domain of the final expression: all x except $x = 0$

Since the restrictions $y \neq 0$, $x \neq y$, and $x \neq {}^-y$ are missing from the final expression, we must mention them explicitly.

So, $\dfrac{x^2 - y^2}{4x^2 + 4xy} \div \dfrac{8x^2 - 8xy}{2x^2 - 2xy} = \dfrac{(x-y)}{16x}$, $y \neq 0$, $x \neq y$, $x \neq {}^-y$.

To find the **sum** or **difference** of two rational expressions, rewrite each expression with a common denominator and then add or subtract the numerators.

EXAMPLE: Subtract $\dfrac{6}{m^2 - 5m} - \dfrac{4}{5m - 25}$.

STEP 1: Rewrite each expression with a common denominator.

$\dfrac{6}{m^2 - 5m} - \dfrac{4}{5m - 25}$ Factor each denominator.

$= \dfrac{6}{m(m-5)} - \dfrac{4}{5(m-5)}$ Identify the least common denominator (LCD) for $m(m-5)$ and $5(m-5)$.

LCD: $5m(m - 5)$

Multiply each rational expression by a form of 1 to rewrite it with the LCD.

$$\frac{6}{m(m-5)} \cdot \frac{5}{5} - \frac{4}{5(m-5)} \cdot \frac{m}{m}$$

THINK:

To form the LCD, the first expression needs a 5 and the second needs an m.

$$\frac{30}{5m(m-5)} - \frac{4m}{5m(m-5)}$$

STEP 2: Subtract the numerators.

$$\frac{30}{5m(m-5)} - \frac{4m}{5m(m-5)} = \frac{30-4m}{5m(m-5)}$$

STEP 3: Factor the numerator and denominator.

$$\frac{30-4m}{5m(m-5)}$$

$$\frac{2(15-2m)}{5m(m-5)}$$

STEP 4: Identify the restrictions to the domain.

The initial expression and the final expression have the same domain, so there are no restrictions.

$$\frac{6m^2}{m^2-5m} - \frac{4}{5m-25} = \frac{2(15-2m)}{5m(m-5)}$$

also called a COMPLEX FRACTION

A **COMPOUND FRACTION** is a fraction in which the numerator, the denominator, or both are fractions.

EXAMPLE: Simplify the compound fraction $\dfrac{\dfrac{3}{x^2y} - \dfrac{1}{xy^2}}{\dfrac{8}{x^2y^2} + \dfrac{6}{xy}}$.

STEP 1: Simplify the numerator and the denominator.

$$\frac{\dfrac{3}{x^2y} - \dfrac{1}{xy^2}}{\dfrac{8}{x^2y^2} + \dfrac{6}{xy}} = \left(\frac{3}{x^2y} - \frac{1}{xy^2}\right) \div \left(\frac{8}{x^2y^2} + \frac{6}{xy}\right)$$

Simplify the numerator:

$$\frac{3}{x^2y} - \frac{1}{xy^2}$$

$$\frac{3}{x^2y} \cdot \frac{y}{y} - \frac{1}{xy^2} \cdot \frac{x}{x}$$

$$\frac{3y}{x^2y^2} - \frac{x}{x^2y^2}$$

$$\frac{3y - x}{x^2y^2}$$

Simplify the denominator:

$$\frac{8}{x^2y^2} + \frac{6}{xy}$$

$$\frac{8}{x^2y^2} + \frac{6}{xy} \cdot \frac{xy}{xy}$$

$$\frac{8}{x^2y^2} + \frac{6xy}{x^2y^2}$$

AS SIMPLE AS 1, 2, 3.

$$\frac{8+6xy}{x^2y^2}$$

So, $\left(\dfrac{3}{x^2y} - \dfrac{1}{xy^2}\right) \div \left(\dfrac{8}{x^2y^2} + \dfrac{6}{xy}\right) = \dfrac{3y-x}{x^2y^2} \div \dfrac{8+6xy}{x^2y^2}$.

STEP 2: Divide.

$$\frac{3y-x}{x^2y^2} \div \frac{8+6xy}{x^2y^2}$$

$$\frac{3y-x}{x^2y^2} \cdot \frac{x^2y^2}{8+6xy}$$

$$\frac{(3y-x) \cdot x^2y^2}{x^2y^2 \cdot (8+6xy)}$$

STEP 3: Simplify. Cancel all common factors.

$$\frac{(3y-x)\,x^2y^2}{x^2y^2 \cdot 2(4+3xy)}$$

$$\frac{3(y-x)}{2(4+3xy)}$$

STEP 4: Identify the restrictions to the domain.

The domain of the original expression is all x, y except $x = 0$, $y = 0$, and $xy = -\dfrac{4}{3}$. The domain of the final expression is all x, y except $xy = -\dfrac{4}{3}$. Since the restrictions $x \neq 0$ and $y \neq 0$ are missing from the final expression, we must mention them explicitly.

So, $\dfrac{\dfrac{3}{x^2y} - \dfrac{1}{xy^2}}{\dfrac{8}{x^2y^2} + \dfrac{6}{xy}} = \dfrac{3y-x}{2(4+3xy)}$, $x \neq 0$, $y \neq 0$.

MULTIPLY. WRITE THE PRODUCT IN SIMPLEST FORM.

1. $\dfrac{6a^3c^4}{12a^4bc^2} \cdot \dfrac{16a^2b^6}{32a^5bc^2}$

2. $\dfrac{7x+35}{x^2+2x-3} \cdot \dfrac{x^2-9}{x^2+3x-10}$

3. $\dfrac{3g^8j^9}{27h^6j^4} \cdot \dfrac{63h^5g^4}{9g^7hj^{12}}$

DIVIDE. WRITE THE QUOTIENT IN SIMPLEST FORM.

4. $(6y^2 - 36y) \div \dfrac{5y^2 - 20y}{y^2 - 10y + 24}$

5. $\dfrac{h^2 - 7h + 6}{h^5} \div \dfrac{h^2 - 4h - 12}{2h^2 + h^3}$

6. $\dfrac{m^2 - 4}{3m^2 - 28m + 32} \div \dfrac{4 - m^2}{3m^2 + 14m - 24}$

7. $\dfrac{2d^2-18}{3d^2-6d-9} \div \dfrac{3d^2-27}{3d^2-24d+45}$

ADD OR SUBTRACT. WRITE THE SUM OR DIFFERENCE IN SIMPLEST FORM.

8. $\dfrac{x^2-3x-8}{5x-35} - \dfrac{2x+6}{5x-35}$

9. $\dfrac{8d}{d-3} + \dfrac{9d}{d-4}$

10. $\dfrac{a^2 + 11a - 12}{a^2 + 13a + 12} + \dfrac{2a}{1+a}$

11. $\dfrac{2x}{x+6} - \dfrac{2x}{3}$

SIMPLIFY THE COMPOUND FRACTIONS.

12. $\dfrac{\dfrac{5x}{x^2 - 49}}{\dfrac{25x}{x+7}}$

13. $$\dfrac{\dfrac{c+4}{c+9}}{\dfrac{c-4}{2c+18}}$$

14. $$\dfrac{\dfrac{3m-7}{m-8}-\dfrac{m-5}{m-8}}{\dfrac{m-6}{m-4}+\dfrac{m-6}{m-4}}$$

RATIONAL FUNCTIONS AND THEIR GRAPHS

A **RATIONAL FUNCTION** is a ratio of polynomials (a fraction) where the denominator does not equal 0.

Consider the graph of the rational function $f(x) = \dfrac{1}{x}$.

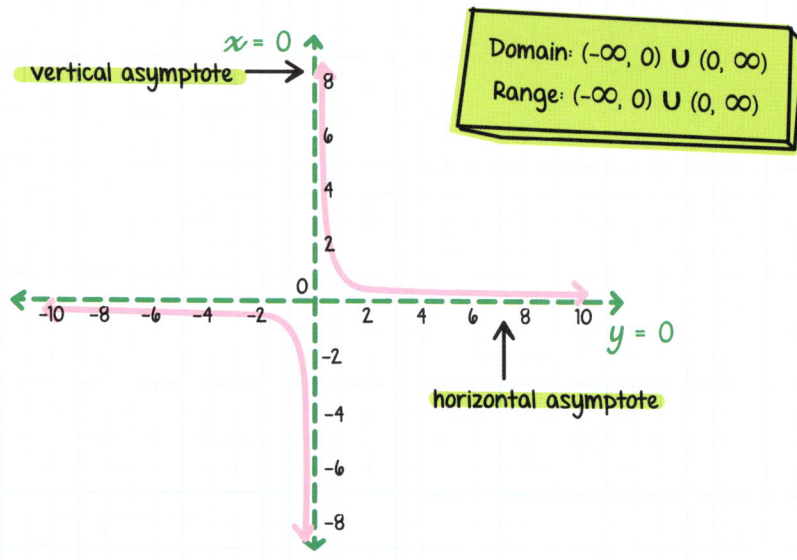

vertical asymptote → $x = 0$

Domain: $(-\infty, 0) \cup (0, \infty)$
Range: $(-\infty, 0) \cup (0, \infty)$

$y = 0$

horizontal asymptote

The graph has a **VERTICAL ASYMPTOTE** with the equation $x = 0$ (the y-axis). The graph of the function moves infinitely upward as it approaches 0 from the right, and it moves infinitely downward as it approaches 0 from the left.

There is also a **HORIZONTAL ASYMPTOTE** with the equation $y = 0$ (the x-axis). The graph of the function approaches the x-axis as it moves infinitely to the left and infinitely to the right.

The **domain** of a rational function is the set of all real numbers *except* the zeros of the denominator. To find the domain, ask: What x-values make the denominator zero?

Vertical Asymptote Test for a Rational Function

For the rational function $R(x) = \frac{P(x)}{Q(x)}$, if $Q(a) = 0$ and $P(a) \neq 0$, then $x = a$ is a vertical asymptote of R.

THINK: When you substitute a specific value for x into a rational function, if the denominator equals zero and the numerator does NOT equal zero, you know there is a vertical asymptote of x equal to that value.

Horizontal Asymptote Test for a Rational Function

▶ If the degree of the numerator is **less than** the degree of the denominator, then $y = 0$ is a horizontal asymptote.

▶ If the degree of the numerator is **equal to** the degree of the denominator, then a horizontal asymptote is:

$$y = \frac{\text{leading coefficient of numerator}}{\text{leading coefficient of denominator}}$$

▶ If the degree in the numerator is **greater than** the degree of the denominator, there is **NO** horizontal asymptote.

THINK: The function on page 218 has a degree of 0 numerator and a degree of 1 denominator. So $y=0$ is its horizontal asymptote.

EXAMPLE: Graph the rational function $f(x) = \frac{-3x}{x-5}$. Indicate the domain and range of f.

STEP 1: Find the domain of f.

Ask: What x-values make the denominator zero?

$x - 5 = 0$
$x - 5 + 5 = 0 + 5$
$x = 5$

The denominator is 0 when $x = 5$, so $x = 5$ is excluded from the domain.

Domain: $(-\infty, 5) \cup (5, \infty)$

STEP 2: Use the vertical asymptote test to check if $x = 5$ is a vertical asymptote.

$-3x$ numerator of the rational function

$-3(5)$ Substitute $x = 5$ into the numerator.

-15 -15 does not equal 0.

So, for $f(5)$, the denominator equals 0 but the numerator does not. This tell us that $x = 5$ is a vertical asymptote of $f(x)$.

STEP 3: Use the horizontal asymptote test to find any horizontal asymptotes of f.

The degree of the numerator *equals* the degree of the denominator. Therefore, the horizontal asymptote of f is

$$y = \frac{\text{leading coefficient of numerator}}{\text{leading coefficient of denominator}}.$$

$$f(x) = \frac{-3x}{1x-5} \qquad y = \frac{-3}{1} = -3$$

The degree of the numerator and denominator are both one. This tells us there is a horizontal asymptote of $y = -3$.

STEP 4: Locate the x- and y-intercepts of f.

x-intercept:

Set $y = f(x)$ equal to 0.

$$0 = \frac{-3x}{x-5}$$

$$0 = -3x$$

$$0 \div (-3) = -3x \div (-3)$$

$$0 = x$$

x-intercept: $(0, 0)$

y-intercept:

Substitute 0 for x in the function f.

$$f(0) = \frac{-3(0)}{0-5} = 0$$

y-intercept: $(0, 0)$

STEP 5: Graph the function $f(x) = \dfrac{-3x}{x-5}$ using the asymptotes and the intercepts.

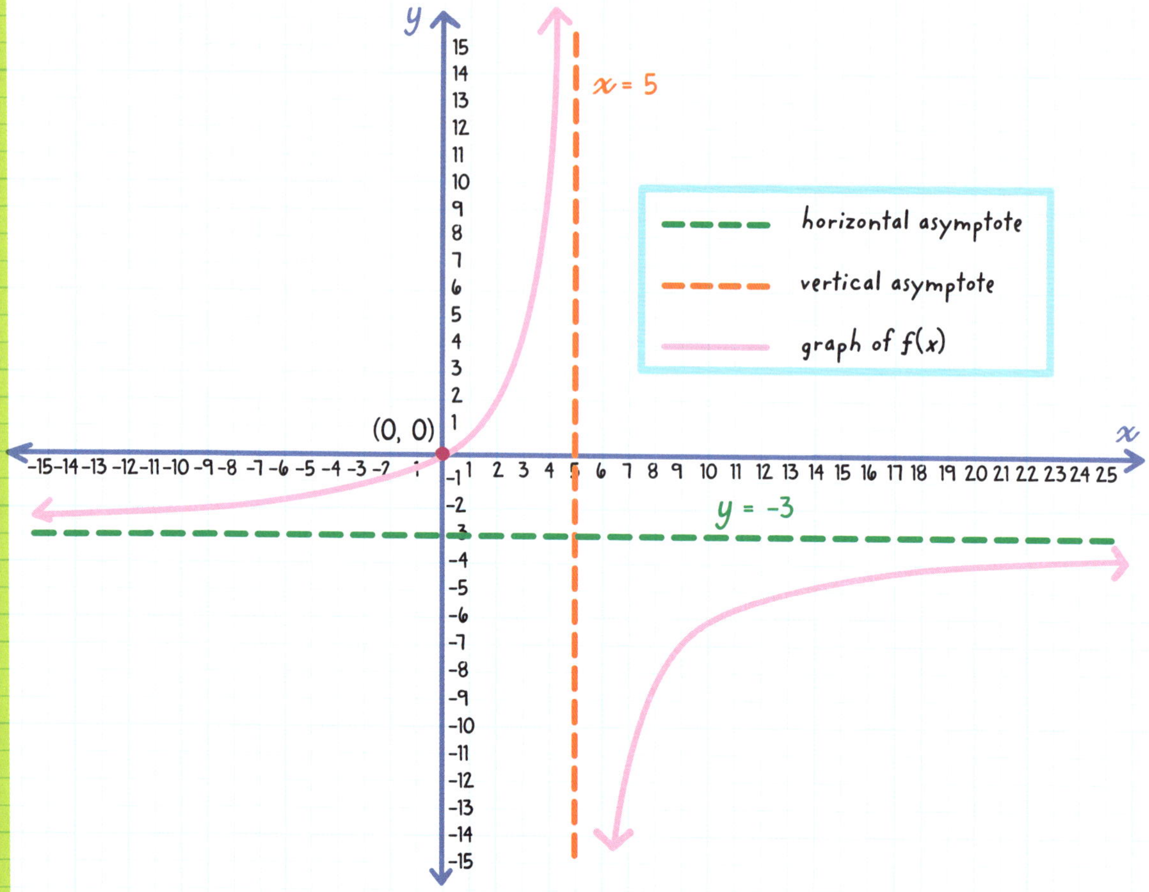

$x = 5$

– – – – horizontal asymptote

– – – – vertical asymptote

—— graph of $f(x)$

(0, 0)

$y = -3$

STEP 6: Determine the domain and range of the function.

Domain: $(-\infty, 5) \cup (5, \infty)$

Range: $(-\infty, -3) \cup (-3, \infty)$

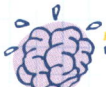

THINK:
Asymptotes tell us what values are excluded from the domain and range of a rational function.

IDENTIFY THE x- AND y-INTERCEPTS AND ANY VERTICAL AND HORIZONTAL ASYMPTOTES OF EACH FUNCTION.

1. $f(x) = \dfrac{2x}{x+7}$

2. $f(x) = \dfrac{3x+8}{x^2-49}$

3. $f(x) = \dfrac{x-10}{x^2+4x-5}$

4. $f(x) = \dfrac{6x+17}{x^2-25}$

MATCH EACH FUNCTION WITH ITS GRAPH.

5. $f(x) = \dfrac{x-6}{5x}$ _____

6. $f(x) = \dfrac{10}{2x+3}$ _____

7. $f(x) = \dfrac{x}{x^2-49}$ _____

8. $f(x) = \dfrac{3x}{x^2-4}$ _____

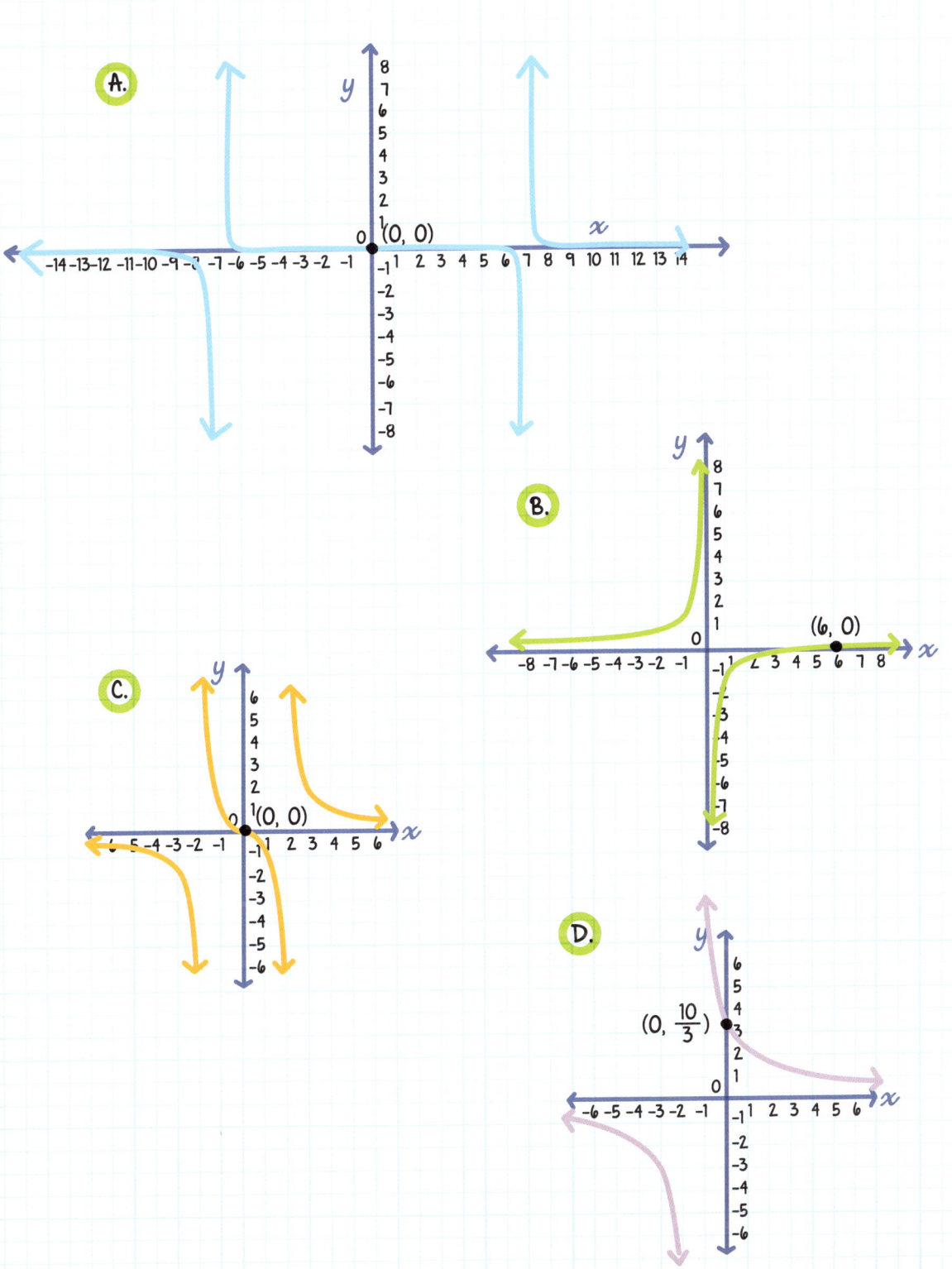

GRAPH THE FUNCTIONS.

9. $f(x) = \dfrac{4}{x-2} + 1$

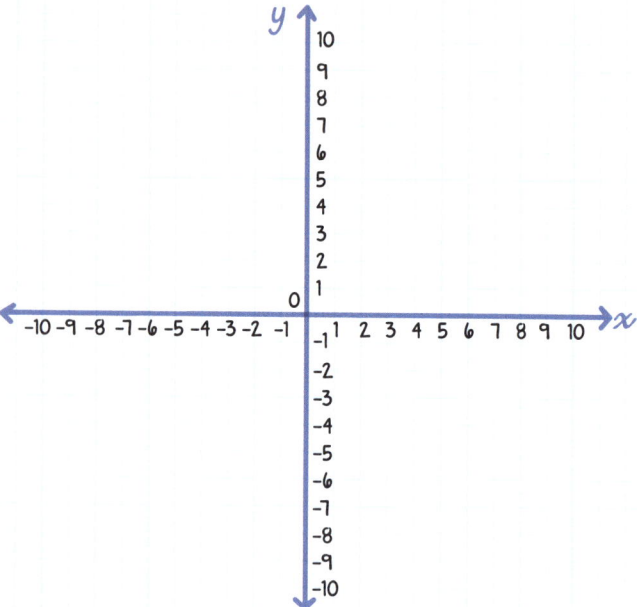

10. $f(x) = \dfrac{2x-1}{x+1}$

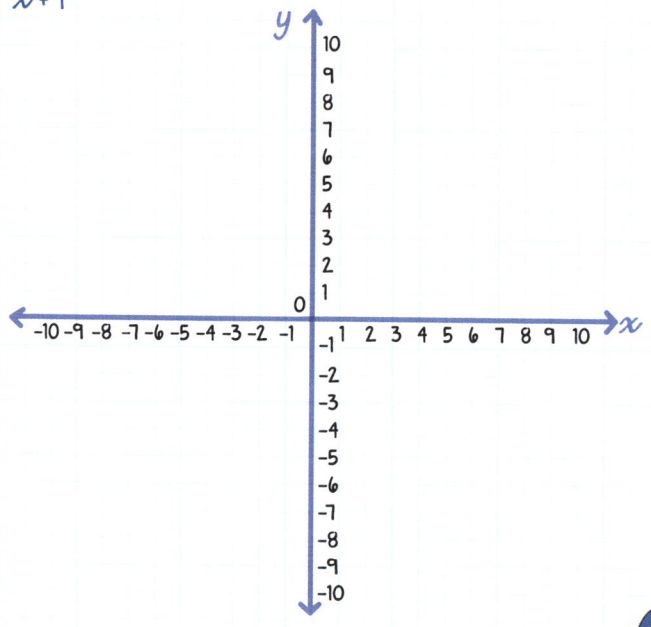

$\cos \theta$

$(\sqrt[4]{n})$

$\dfrac{\pi}{6}$

Unit 6

Radical Functions

UNIT 6
Chapter 25
OPERATIONS ON RADICALS

RADICALS are made up of two components: the index and the radicand.

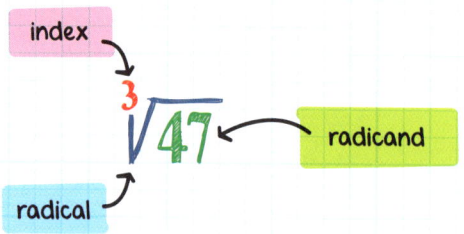

index

$\sqrt[3]{47}$

radicand

radical

> Remember: The index for square roots is 2, but we do not write it.

We can add or subtract radicals with the **same index** and the **same radicand** by adding or subtracting their coefficients.

EXAMPLE: Perform the indicated operations:

$$\sqrt{26} - 4\sqrt[3]{5} + 9\sqrt{26} - 14\sqrt[3]{5}.$$

> $\sqrt{26}$ and $9\sqrt{26}$ have the same index and radicand.

> $-4\sqrt[3]{5}$ and $-14\sqrt[3]{5}$ have the same index and radicand.

$$\sqrt{26} + (-4\sqrt[3]{5}) + 9\sqrt{26} + (-14\sqrt[3]{5})$$

$$(1\sqrt{26} + 9\sqrt{26}) + (-4\sqrt[3]{5} + (-14\sqrt[3]{5}))$$

$$(1 + 9)\sqrt{26} + (-4 - 14)\sqrt[3]{5}$$ Combine ONLY the coefficients.

$$10\sqrt{26} - 18\sqrt[3]{5}$$

If two radicals have different radicands, simplify them to get a common radicand.

EXAMPLE: Subtract $7\sqrt[3]{24x} - 3\sqrt[3]{81x}$.

STEP 1: Simplify each radical expression.

$7\sqrt[3]{24x}$ Greatest perfect cube factor of 24 is 8.

$7\sqrt[3]{8 \cdot 3x}$ Rewrite 24 as the product of 8 and 3. Then simplify.

$7 \cdot 2\sqrt[3]{3x}$

$14\sqrt[3]{3x}$

THINK:
To simplify these radicals, ask: "What is the greatest factor of the radicand that is a perfect power of the index?"

$3\sqrt[3]{81x}$ Greatest perfect cube factor of 81 is 27.

$3\sqrt[3]{27 \cdot 3x}$

$3 \cdot 3\sqrt[3]{3x}$

$9\sqrt[3]{3x}$ Now both the index and the radicand are the same.

STEP 2: Subtract the simplified radicals.

$14\sqrt[3]{3x} - 9\sqrt[3]{3x}$

$14\sqrt[3]{3x} - 9\sqrt[3]{3x}$ The radicals are the same, so you subtract the coefficents.

$(14 - 9)\sqrt[3]{3x}$

$5\sqrt[3]{3x}$

We can multiply and divide radicals only if they have the *same index*. Multiply or divide the radicands and place the result under a single radical symbol.

EXAMPLE: Simplify $\dfrac{35\sqrt{80}}{7\sqrt{2}} \cdot 4\sqrt{3}$.

THINK:
The index is the same, so these radicals can be multiplied and divided.

$\dfrac{35\sqrt{80}}{7\sqrt{2}} \cdot 4\sqrt{3}$

$\dfrac{35}{7} \cdot \sqrt{\dfrac{80}{2}} \cdot 4\sqrt{3}$ Separate the coefficients and the radicals.

$5 \cdot \sqrt{40} \cdot 4\sqrt{3}$ Simplify each radical.

$5 \cdot \sqrt{10 \cdot 4} \cdot 4\sqrt{3}$

$5 \cdot 2\sqrt{10} \cdot 4\sqrt{3}$

$(5 \cdot 2 \cdot 4)\sqrt{10} \cdot \sqrt{3}$ Multiply the coefficients together. Multiply the radicals together.

$40\sqrt{30}$

When we don't want to leave a radical in the dominator, we must **RATIONALIZE THE DENOMINATOR**.

One way to do this is to multiply both the numerator and denominator by the conjugate of the denominator.

EXAMPLE: Simplify $\dfrac{2\sqrt{3}}{8-\sqrt{5}}$.

$\dfrac{2\sqrt{3}}{8-\sqrt{5}} \cdot \dfrac{8+\sqrt{5}}{8+\sqrt{5}}$ Multiply by the conjugate of the denominator.

$\dfrac{2\sqrt{3}\,(8+\sqrt{5})}{(8-\sqrt{5})(8+\sqrt{5})}$

Distribute in the numerator.

Use FOIL in the denominator.

> The conjugate of $a+\sqrt{b}$ is $a-\sqrt{b}$.

$\dfrac{16\sqrt{3}+2\sqrt{15}}{64+8\sqrt{5}-8\sqrt{5}-\sqrt{25}}$ Factor.

$\dfrac{2(8\sqrt{3}+\sqrt{15})}{59}$

THAT WAS A NICE BREAK!

USE WHAT YOU KNOW ABOUT PERFORMING OPERATIONS
ON RADICALS TO SIMPLIFY EACH EXPRESSION.

1. $-9\sqrt[6]{h} + 5\sqrt[6]{h}$

2. $2\sqrt{17} + 19\sqrt[3]{45} + 7\sqrt{17} + 3\sqrt[3]{45}$

3. $4\sqrt{24} - \sqrt{54}$

4. $\sqrt{49} - 10\sqrt[3]{8} + \sqrt{48} + 8\sqrt[3]{27}$

5. $6\sqrt[3]{29} \cdot 9\sqrt[3]{7}$

6. $12\sqrt[3]{2} \cdot \sqrt[3]{3}$

7. $\dfrac{36\sqrt{64}}{6\sqrt{4}}$

8. $\dfrac{72\sqrt{96}}{9\sqrt{12}}$

9. $\dfrac{85\sqrt{66}}{5\sqrt{6}} \cdot \sqrt{18}$

10. $2\sqrt[3]{5}\,(6\sqrt[3]{200} + 9\sqrt[3]{25})$

11. $(\sqrt{7} + 8\sqrt{63})(2 - \sqrt{3}\,)$

12. $\dfrac{5x\sqrt{3}}{\sqrt{26}}$

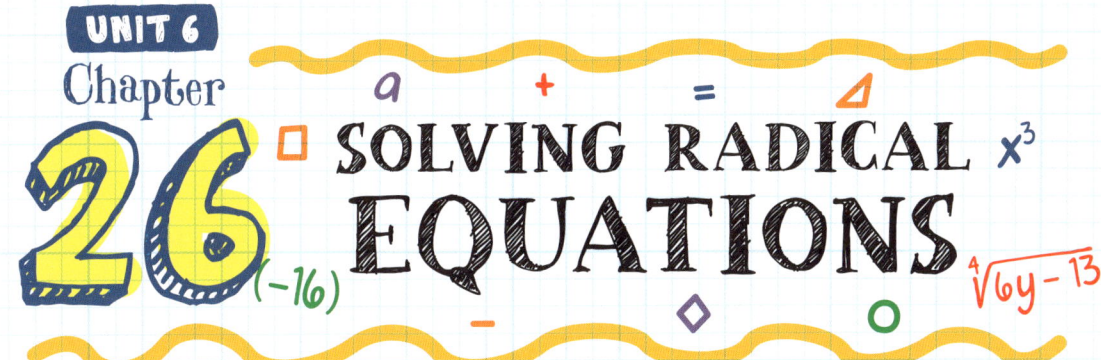

SOLVING RADICAL EQUATIONS

An equation containing at least one variable under a radical symbol is a **RADICAL EQUATION**. A radical equation can have one or more solutions or no solution. Be sure to check for extraneous solutions.

EXAMPLE: Solve for y in the equation $\sqrt[4]{6y - 26} - 2 = 0$.

STEP 1: Isolate the radical.

$$\sqrt[4]{6y - 26} - 2 = 0$$

$$\sqrt[4]{6y - 26} - 2 + 2 = 0 + 2$$

$$\sqrt[4]{6y - 26} = 2$$

STEP 2: Eliminate the radical by raising each side of the equation to the power of the index.

$$(\sqrt[4]{6y - 26})^4 = 2^4$$

$$6y - 26 = 16$$

STEP 3: Solve for the variable.

$6y - 26 + 26 = 16 + 26$

$6y = 42$

$6y \div 6 = 42 \div 6$

$y = 7$

There is one possible solution: $y = 7$.

STEP 4: Check to see if the possible solution satisfies the original equation.

Substitute the possible solution into the original equation.

$\sqrt[4]{6(7) - 26} - 2 = 0$

$\sqrt[4]{16} - 2 = 0$

$2 - 2 = 0$

$0 = 0$ ✓ True

So, the radical equation $\sqrt[4]{6y - 26} - 2 = 0$ has one solution: $y = 7$.

EXAMPLE: Solve for a in the equation $\sqrt{a} - 8 = \sqrt{a + 176}$.

STEP 1: Eliminate the radical on the right side of the equation by squaring both sides of the equation.

$(\sqrt{a} - 8)^2 = (\sqrt{a + 176})^2$

$(\sqrt{a} - 8)(\sqrt{a} - 8) = a + 176$

$(\sqrt{a})^2 - 8\sqrt{a} - 8\sqrt{a} + 64 = a + 176$

$a - 16\sqrt{a} + 64 = a + 176$

STEP 2: Isolate the radical $\sqrt{a}$.

$a - 16\sqrt{a} + 64 = a + 176$

$a - a - 16\sqrt{a} + 64 = a - a + 176$

$-16\sqrt{a} + 64 = 176$

$-16\sqrt{a} + 64 - 64 = 176 - 64$

$-16\sqrt{a} = 112$

$-16\sqrt{a} \div (-16) = 112 \div (-16)$

$\sqrt{a} = -7$

STEP 3: Eliminate the radical.

$(\sqrt{a})^2 = (-7)^2$

$a = 49$ There is one possible solution: $a = 49$.

STEP 4: Check to see if the possible solution satisfies the original equation.

Substitute the possible solution into the original equation.

$\sqrt{a} - 8 = \sqrt{a + 176}$

$\sqrt{49} - 8 = \sqrt{49 + 176}$

$-1 = 15$ ✗ False

Since the statement is false, $a = 49$ is an extraneous solution.

The radical equation $\sqrt{a} - 8 = \sqrt{a + 176}$ has no solution.

SOLVE EACH RADICAL EQUATION.

1. $\sqrt{\dfrac{2x}{7}} = 10$

2. $5\sqrt{y} - 9 = 21$

3. $\sqrt[3]{-d-2} - 8 = -12$

4. $4\sqrt{2w+13} - 1 = 11$

5. $\sqrt{a+4} = \sqrt{7a+3}$

6. $9 = \sqrt{4c+5}$

7. $10 + 2\sqrt{j} = 0$

8. $\sqrt[3]{l+9} = 1$

9. $\sqrt[3]{p+28} = \sqrt[3]{p^2+p-72}$

10. $7\sqrt{b} - 16 = 19$

WANNA BE
STUDY PARTNERS?

11. $\sqrt{-15f} - 6 = 24$

12. $\sqrt{g} + 5 = \sqrt{g + 45}$

13. $\sqrt{18k} = \sqrt{2k - 32}$

14. $\sqrt{m + 9} = \sqrt{m^2 + 2m - 3}$

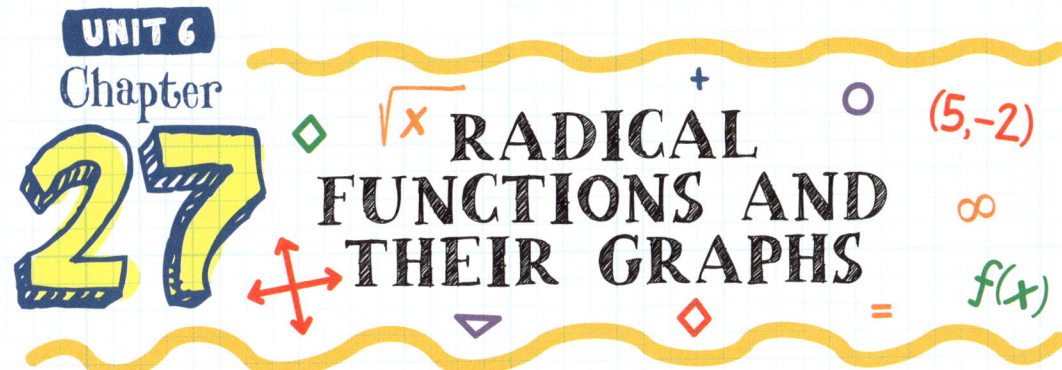

UNIT 6
Chapter 27 — RADICAL FUNCTIONS AND THEIR GRAPHS

A **RADICAL FUNCTION** is a function in which the independent variable appears under a radical symbol at least once.

The simplest radical function is $f(x) = \sqrt{x}$.

To graph it, follow these steps.

STEP 1: Make a table of values.

x	$f(x) = \sqrt{x}$	$f(x)$	$(x, f(x))$
0	$\sqrt{0}$	0	(0, 0)
1	$\sqrt{1}$	1	(1, 1)
4	$\sqrt{4}$	2	(4, 2)
9	$\sqrt{9}$	3	(9, 3)
16	$\sqrt{16}$	4	(16, 4)
25	$\sqrt{25}$	5	(25, 5)
36	$\sqrt{36}$	6	(36, 6)

Choose values for x that are positive *perfect squares* so that the values for y will be natural numbers.

STEP 2: Plot the points from the table. Then connect the points with a smooth curve.

> We can graph a cube root function in the same way. Just choose values for x that are perfect cubes so that the outputs will be integers.

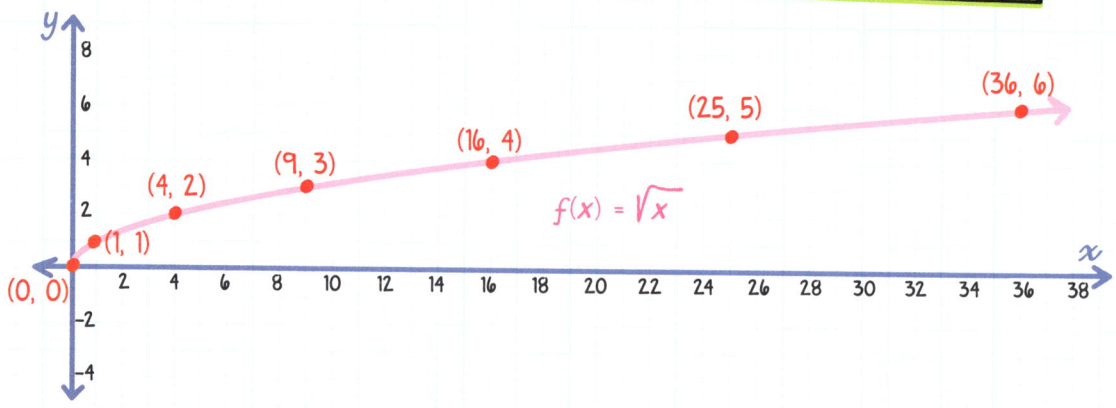

$f(x) = \sqrt{x}$

(0, 0) (1, 1) (4, 2) (9, 3) (16, 4) (25, 5) (36, 6)

We can use transformations to graph many radical functions.

The general form of a square root function is:

$$y = a\sqrt{x - h} + k$$

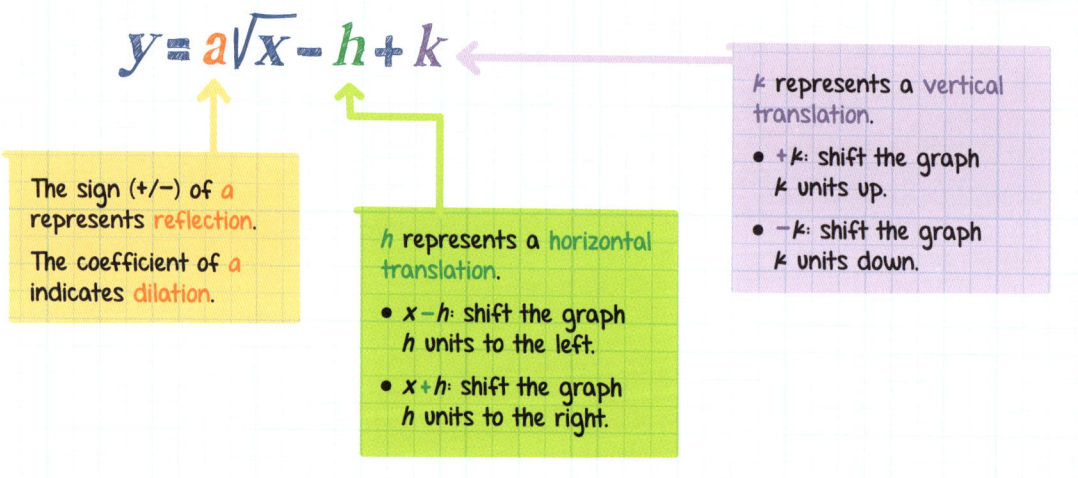

The sign (+/−) of *a* represents reflection.
The coefficient of *a* indicates dilation.

h represents a horizontal translation.
- *x − h*: shift the graph *h* units to the left.
- *x + h*: shift the graph *h* units to the right.

k represents a vertical translation.
- +*k*: shift the graph *k* units up.
- −*k*: shift the graph *k* units down.

We can use the general form of a radical function to graph many radical functions.

EXAMPLE: Graph $g(x) = 2\sqrt[3]{x} + 4$.

STEP 1: Graph the parent function $f(x) = \sqrt[3]{x}$.

STEP 2: Graph $h(x) = 2\sqrt[3]{x}$ by expanding the graph of $f(x) = \sqrt[3]{x}$ vertically by a factor of 2.

> The y-coordinate of each point is multiplied by 2.

STEP 3: Graph $g(x) = 2\sqrt[3]{x} + 4$ by shifting the graph of $h(x) = 2\sqrt[3]{x}$ up 4 units.

> We add 4 to the y-coordinate of each point.

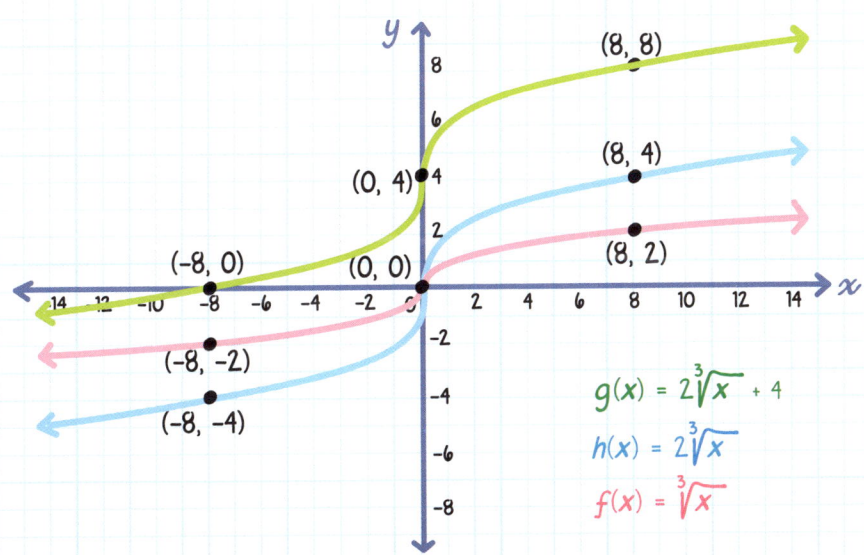

$g(x) = 2\sqrt[3]{x} + 4$

$h(x) = 2\sqrt[3]{x}$

$f(x) = \sqrt[3]{x}$

DESCRIBE IN WORDS HOW TO OBTAIN THE GIVEN GRAPH USING THE GRAPH OF $f(x) = \sqrt{x}$. DRAW THE GRAPH.

1. $h(x) = \sqrt{x-8} - 2$

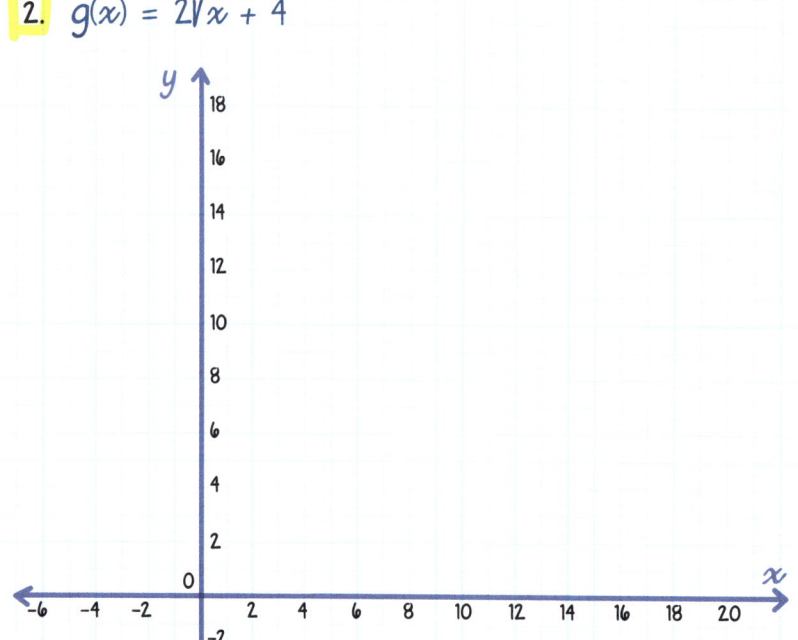

2. $g(x) = 2\sqrt{x} + 4$

3. $j(x) = \sqrt{x+7} - 1$

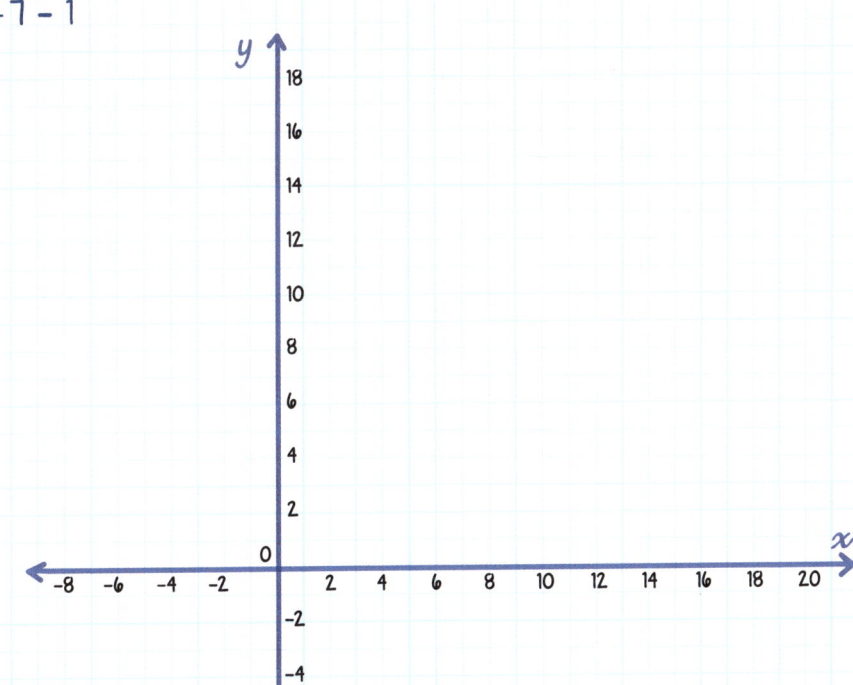

4. $k(x) = 5\sqrt{x} + 3$

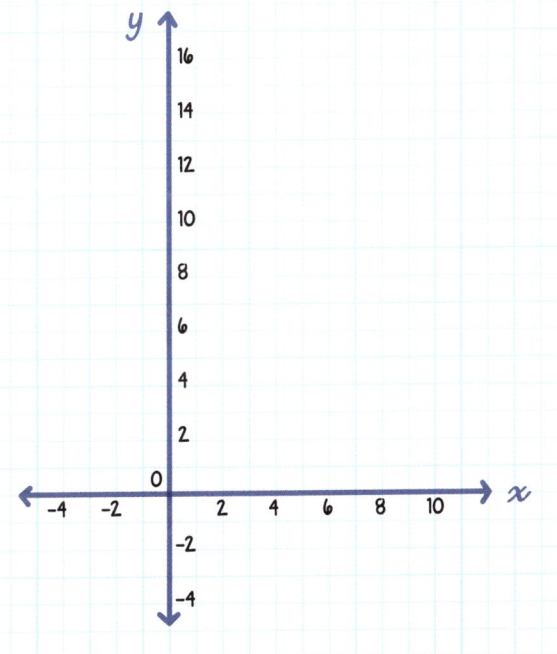

DESCRIBE IN WORDS HOW TO OBTAIN THE GIVEN GRAPH USING THE GRAPH OF $f(x) = \sqrt[3]{x}$. DRAW THE GRAPH.

5. $h(x) = \sqrt[3]{x-6}$

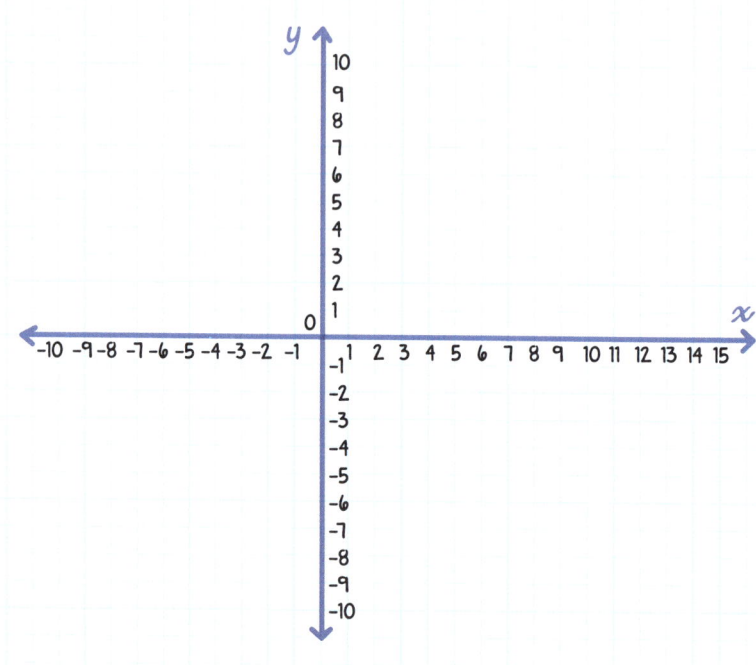

6. $g(x) = 4\sqrt[3]{x} + 12$

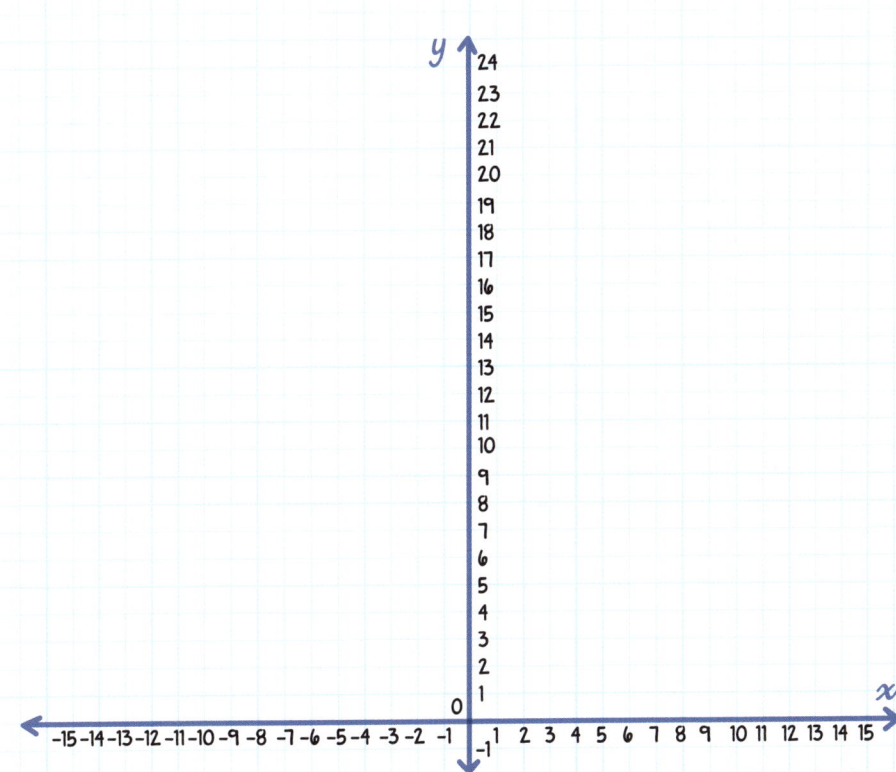

7. $j(x) = -8\sqrt[3]{x}$

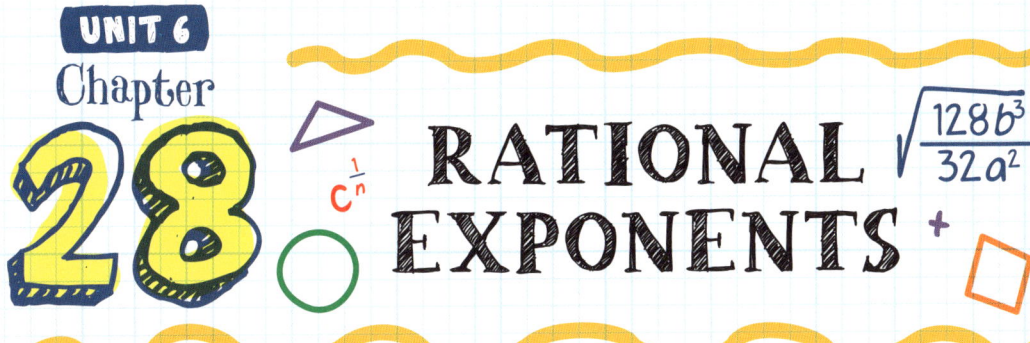

RATIONAL EXPONENTS

$\sqrt{\dfrac{128b^3}{32a^2}}$

RATIONAL EXPONENTS provide us with another way to write nth roots such as square roots and cube roots. They also allow us to express powers and roots at the same time.

CONVERSION RULES	
$\sqrt[1]{a} = a$	$a^{\frac{1}{n}} = \sqrt[n]{a}$
$\sqrt[n]{a} = a^{\frac{1}{n}}$	$a^{\frac{m}{n}} = (\sqrt[n]{a}\,)^m$

We can use conversion rules to rewrite rational expressions without rational exponents.

$16^{\frac{1}{2}} = \sqrt{16} = 4$

$8^{-\frac{1}{3}} = \dfrac{1}{8^{\frac{1}{3}}} = \dfrac{1}{\sqrt[3]{8}} = \dfrac{1}{2}$

$16^{\frac{3}{4}} = (\sqrt[4]{16}\,)^3 = 2^3 = 8$

$\left(\dfrac{9}{36}\right)^{-\frac{1}{2}} = \left(\dfrac{36}{9}\right)^{\frac{1}{2}} = \sqrt{\dfrac{36}{9}} = \dfrac{6}{3} = 2$

$(81)^{-\frac{3}{4}} = \dfrac{1}{81^{\frac{3}{4}}} = \dfrac{1}{\sqrt[4]{81^3}} = \dfrac{1}{3^3} = \dfrac{1}{27}$

REMEMBER:
Change a negative exponent to a positive exponent by taking a reciprocal.

$$15^{-\frac{1}{2}} = \frac{1}{15^{\frac{1}{2}}} = \frac{1}{\sqrt{15}} = \frac{1}{\sqrt{15}} \cdot \frac{\sqrt{15}}{\sqrt{15}} = \frac{\sqrt{15}}{15}$$ ← Rationalize the denominator!

Conversion rules can be used to rewrite rational expressions without radicals.

$$\sqrt{81} = 81^{\frac{1}{2}}$$

$$(\sqrt[5]{256})^3 = 256^{\frac{3}{5}}$$

$$-\sqrt[3]{\frac{27}{10}} = -\left(\frac{27}{10}\right)^{\frac{1}{3}}$$

WHEN I SING OFF-KEY, I TEND TO GET IRRATIONAL!

EXAMPLE: Evaluate the expression $135^{\frac{1}{2}} \cdot 60^{\frac{1}{2}}$.

$$135^{\frac{1}{2}} \cdot 60^{\frac{1}{2}}$$

$$\sqrt{135} \cdot \sqrt{60}$$ Write each factor as a square root.

$$\sqrt{9 \cdot 15} \cdot \sqrt{4 \cdot 15}$$ Simplify each radicand. (Find the greatest factor that is a perfect square.)

$$3\sqrt{15} \cdot 2\sqrt{15}$$ $\sqrt{15} \cdot \sqrt{15} = 15$

$$6 \cdot 15$$

$$90$$

EXAMPLE: Simplify the expression. Assume a and b are positive. First write the answer without any negative or fractional exponents. Then write the answer without any radical symbols and all exponents positive.

$$\left(\frac{32a^2}{128b^3}\right)^{-\frac{1}{2}}$$

$$\left(\frac{128b^3}{32a^2}\right)^{\frac{1}{2}} \quad \text{definition of negative exponent}$$

$$\sqrt{\frac{128b^3}{32a^2}} \quad \text{definition of rational exponent}$$

$$\frac{\sqrt{128b^3}}{\sqrt{32a^2}} \quad \text{square root quotient rule}$$

$$\frac{\sqrt{64 \cdot 2 \cdot b^2 \cdot b}}{\sqrt{16 \cdot 2 \cdot a^2}} \quad \text{Factor each radicand.}$$

$$\frac{8b\sqrt{2b}}{4a\sqrt{2}}$$

$$\frac{8b\sqrt{2b}}{4a\sqrt{2}} \cdot \frac{\sqrt{2}}{\sqrt{2}}$$

$$\frac{8b\sqrt{4b}}{2 \cdot 4a} = \frac{2 \cdot 8b\sqrt{b}}{2 \cdot 4a} = \frac{16b\sqrt{b}}{8a} = \frac{2b\sqrt{b}}{a}$$

So, the answer without any negative or fractional exponents is $\frac{2b\sqrt{b}}{a}$.

$$\frac{2b\sqrt{b}}{a} = \frac{2b(b)^{\frac{1}{2}}}{a} = \frac{2b(b)^{1+\frac{1}{2}}}{a} = \frac{2b^{\frac{3}{2}}}{a}$$

So, the answer without any radical symbols and all exponents positive is $\frac{2b^{\frac{3}{2}}}{a}$.

$$\left(\frac{32a^2}{128b^3}\right)^{-\frac{1}{2}} = \frac{2b\sqrt{b}}{a} = \frac{2b^{\frac{3}{2}}}{a}$$

EXAMPLE: Simplify the expression $(\sqrt[3]{d})^7 \cdot (\sqrt[3]{d})^2$.

STEP 1: Write each factor using a rational exponent.

$$(\sqrt[3]{d})^7 \cdot (\sqrt[3]{d})^2 = d^{\frac{7}{3}} \cdot d^{\frac{2}{3}}$$

STEP 2: Use the product rule for exponents: Add the exponents.

$$d^{\frac{7}{3}+\frac{2}{3}} = d^{\frac{9}{3}}$$

STEP 3: Simply the rational exponent.

$$d^{\frac{9}{3}} = d^3$$

EXAMPLE: Simplify the expression $\dfrac{\sqrt{y^3}}{(\sqrt[4]{y})^5}$.

STEP 1: Write the numerator and denominator using a rational exponent.

$$\frac{\sqrt{y^3}}{(\sqrt[4]{y})^5} = \frac{y^{\frac{3}{2}}}{y^{\frac{5}{4}}}$$

STEP 2: Use the quotient rule for exponents: Subtract the exponents.

$$y^{\frac{3}{2}-\frac{5}{4}}$$

$$y^{\frac{1}{4}}, \ y \neq 0 \qquad \frac{3}{2} - \frac{5}{4} = \frac{6}{4} - \frac{5}{4} = \frac{1}{4}$$

Note that we needed to restrict the domain to exclude 0 because the original expression $\dfrac{\sqrt{y^3}}{(\sqrt[4]{y})^5}$ is undefined when $y = 0$.

STEP 3: Rewrite the rational exponent as a 4th root.

$$\sqrt[4]{y}, \ y \neq 0$$

So, $\dfrac{\sqrt{y^3}}{(\sqrt[4]{y})^5}$ simplifies to $y^{\frac{1}{4}}, \ y \neq 0$ or $\sqrt[4]{y}, \ y \neq 0$.

REWRITE EACH EXPRESSION WITHOUT NEGATIVE OR FRACTIONAL EXPONENTS.

1. $32^{\frac{1}{2}}$

2. $1{,}296^{-\frac{4}{3}}$

3. $\left(\frac{16}{25}\right)^{-\frac{3}{2}}$

4. $256^{\frac{1}{4}}$

5. $\left(\frac{81}{36}\right)^{-\frac{1}{2}}$

REWRITE EACH EXPRESSION WITHOUT ANY RADICAL SYMBOLS AND ONLY POSITIVE EXPONENTS.

6. $\sqrt[3]{512}$

7. $\sqrt{28}$

8. $-\sqrt{\frac{16}{56}}$

9. $\sqrt[3]{96}$

FINALLY A BREAK!

EVALUATE AND SIMPLIFY EACH EXPRESSION. WRITE THE FINAL ANSWER WITHOUT ANY NEGATIVE OR FRACTIONAL EXPONENTS.

10. $27^{\frac{1}{2}} \cdot 75^{\frac{1}{2}}$

11. $(343a^7b^{12})^{-\frac{1}{3}}$

12. $3(40)^{\frac{1}{2}} - 6(160)^{\frac{1}{2}} + 5(28)^{\frac{1}{2}}$

13. $(\sqrt[4]{gh})^3 \cdot (\sqrt[4]{gh})^6$

14. $\dfrac{(\sqrt{c})^3}{(\sqrt[3]{c})^2}$

Unit 7

Exponential and Logarithmic Functions

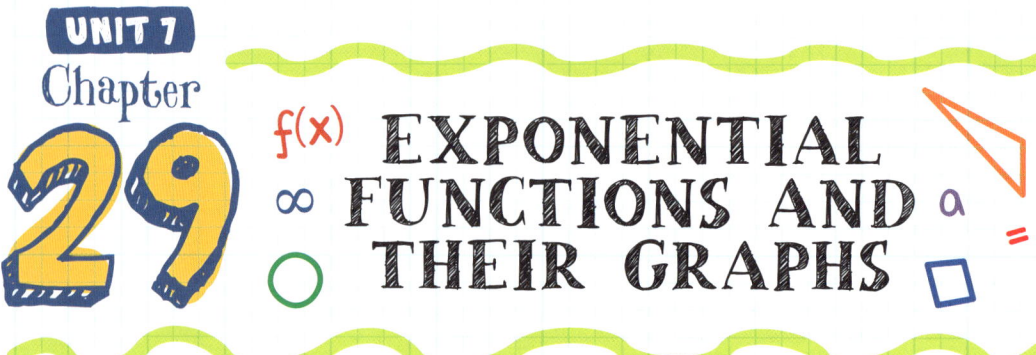

f(x)
∞
○

EXPONENTIAL FUNCTIONS AND THEIR GRAPHS

a
=
□

A simple **EXPONENTIAL FUNCTION** has the form:

$$f(x) = a^x$$

independent variable

constant

Two basic types of exponential functions are:

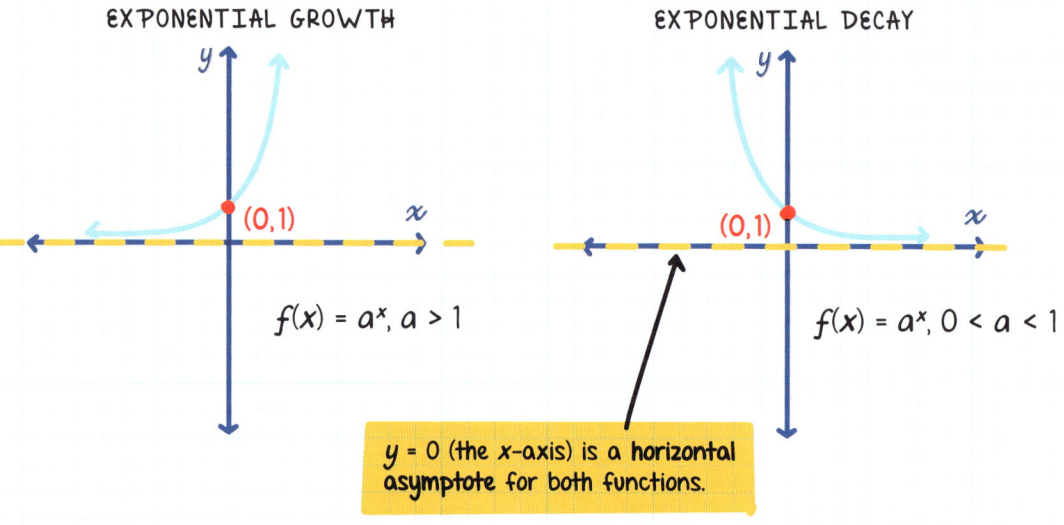

EXPONENTIAL GROWTH

y

(0,1)

x

$f(x) = a^x, a > 1$

EXPONENTIAL DECAY

y

(0,1)

x

$f(x) = a^x, 0 < a < 1$

$y = 0$ (the x-axis) is a **horizontal asymptote** for both functions.

Exponential growth: The function is increasing. The base, or constant, is greater than 1.

Exponential decay: The function is decreasing. The base is greater than zero but less than one. (A fraction!)

EXAMPLE: Compare the following graphs by indicating each function's key features: domain, range, y-intercept, and horizontal asymptote. Then indicate whether each function is increasing or decreasing and note each function's end behavior.

$f(x) = 5^x$ and $h(x) = 10^x$.

Both graphs share the same key features:

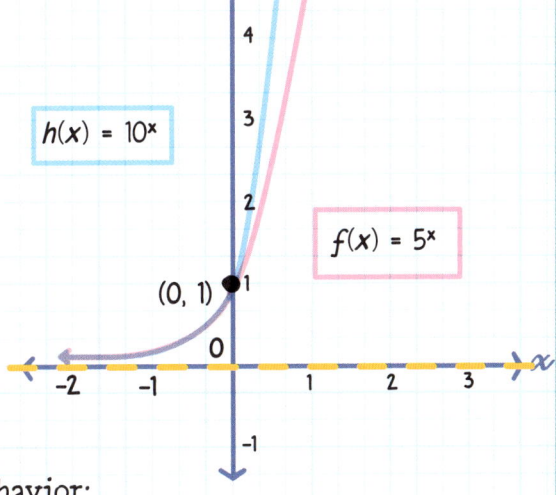

Domain: $(-\infty, \infty)$
Range: $(0, \infty)$
y-intercept: $(0, 1)$
Horizontal asymptote: $y = 0$

Both graphs have the same end behavior:

As x approaches $-\infty$, y approaches 0. (This is why there is a horizontal asymptote of $y = 0$.)

As x approaches ∞, y approaches ∞.

Both functions are increasing, but at different rates. The function $h(x) = 10^x$ is increasing *faster* than $f(x) = 5^x$.

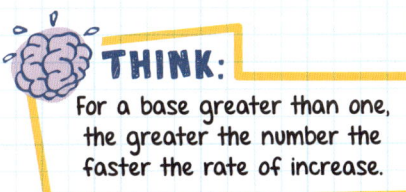

THINK:
For a base greater than one, the greater the number the faster the rate of increase.

TRANSFORMATIONS OF EXPONENTIAL FUNCTIONS

Translations

$y = a^x + k$	$y = a^x - k$
Shift *up* k units.	Shift *down* k units.
$y = a^{x+k}$	$y = a^{x-k}$
Shift *to the left* k units.	Shift *to the right* k units.

Reflections

$y = -a^x$	$y = a^{-x} = \left(\dfrac{1}{a}\right)^x$
Reflect across the *x-axis*.	Reflect across the *y-axis*.

Dilations

$y = ka^x, k > 1$	$y = ka^x, 0 < k < 1$
Vertically *stretch* by a factor of k.	Vertically *shrink* by a factor of k.
$y = a^{kx}, k > 1$	$y = a^{kx}, 0 < k < 1$
Horizontally *shrink* by a factor of k.	Horizontally *stretch* by a factor of k.

$0 < k < 1$ means k is greater than zero but less than one. So k is a fraction!

We can graph many exponential functions by applying transformations to $f(x) = a^x$.

EXAMPLE: Graph $h(x) = 5^{2x}$ using the graph of $f(x) = 5^x$.

STEP 1: Graph $f(x) = 5^x$.

STEP 2: Graph $h(x) = 5^{2x}$ by horizontally shrinking the graph of $f(x) = 5^x$.

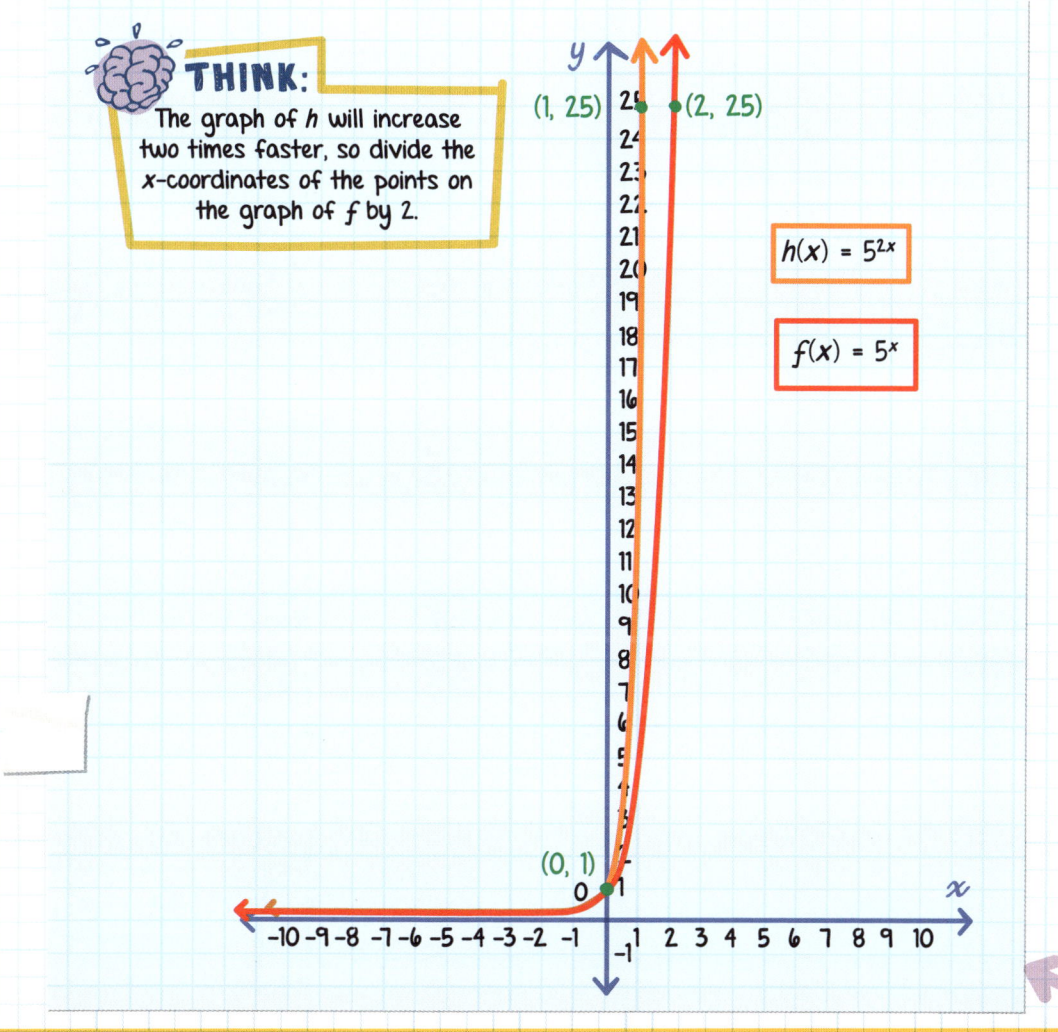

THINK:
The graph of h will increase two times faster, so divide the x-coordinates of the points on the graph of f by 2.

$(1, 25)$ $(2, 25)$

$h(x) = 5^{2x}$

$f(x) = 5^x$

$(0, 1)$

EULER'S NUMBER is an irrational number denoted by the symbol e.

> e is approximately equal to 2.71828.

The **NATURAL EXPONENTIAL FUNCTION** is the function $f(x) = e^x$.

> When graphing with a calculator, the points $(1, e)$ and $(1, \frac{1}{e})$ might be displayed as: $(1, 2.71828)$ and $(1, \frac{1}{2.71828})$.

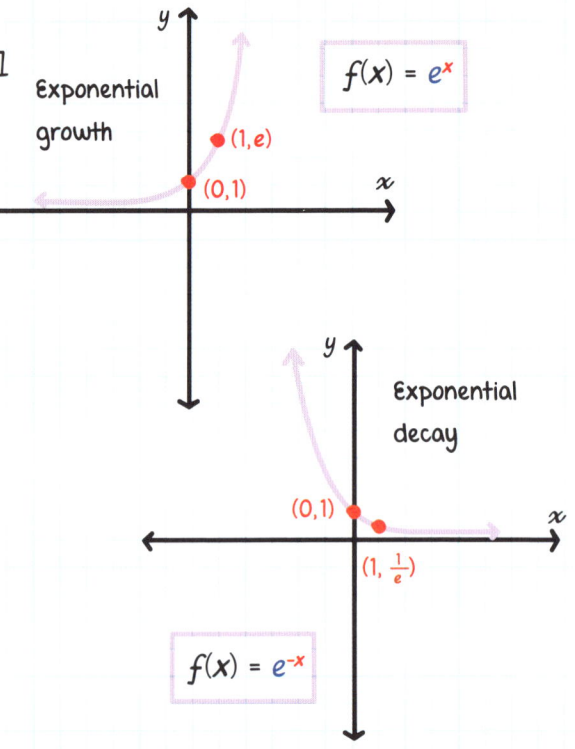

Exponential growth

$f(x) = e^x$

$(1, e)$
$(0, 1)$

Exponential decay

$(0, 1)$
$(1, \frac{1}{e})$

$f(x) = e^{-x}$

EXAMPLE: Graph $h(x) = -e^x + 5$ using $f(x) = e^x$.

STEP 1: Graph $f(x) = e^x$.

STEP 2: Graph $g(x) = -e^x$ by reflecting the graph of $f(x) = e^x$ across the y-axis.

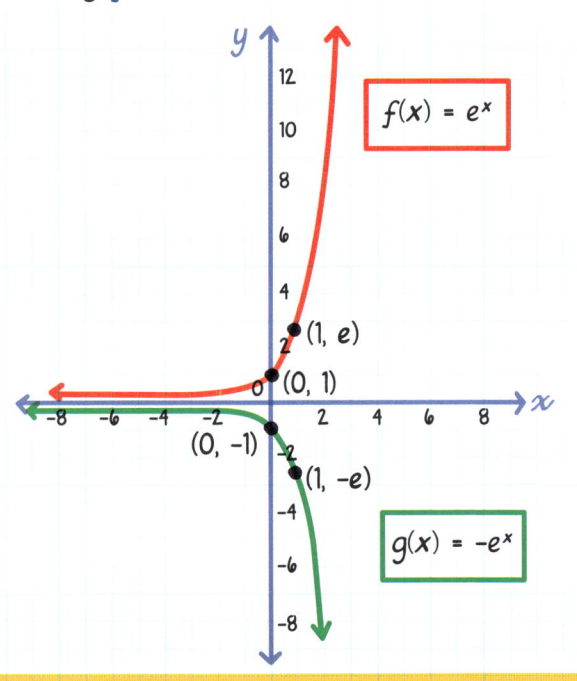

$f(x) = e^x$

$(1, e)$
$(0, 1)$
$(0, -1)$
$(1, -e)$

$g(x) = -e^x$

STEP 3: Graph $h(x) = -e^x + 5$ by shifting the graph of $g(x) = -e^x$ up 5 units.

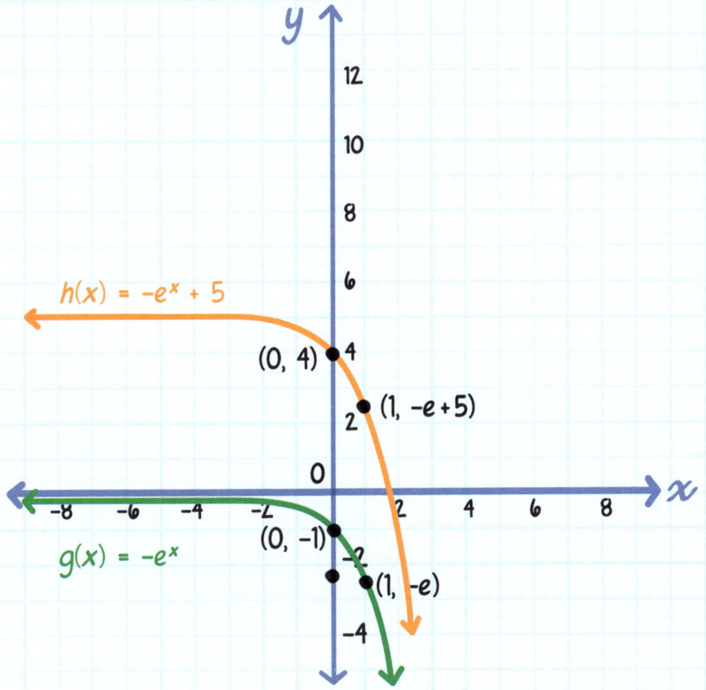

$h(x) = -e^x + 5$

$(0, 4)$

$(1, -e + 5)$

$(0, -1)$

$g(x) = -e^x$

$(1, -e)$

WHO KNEW
GRAPHS COULD BE
THIS FUN!

COMPARE THE GRAPHS BY IDENTIFYING EACH FUNCTION'S DOMAIN, RANGE, y-INTERCEPT, HORIZONTAL ASYMPTOTE, END BEHAVIOR, AND WHETHER EACH FUNCTION IS INCREASING OR DECREASING. STATE THE RELATIONSHIP BETWEEN THE GRAPHS.

1. $f(x) = 3^x$ and $g(x) = (\frac{1}{3})^x$

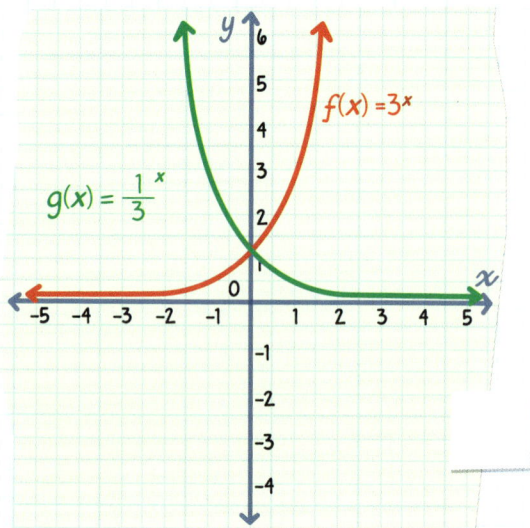

2. $p(x) = 5e^x$
   and $q(x) = -5e^{-x}$

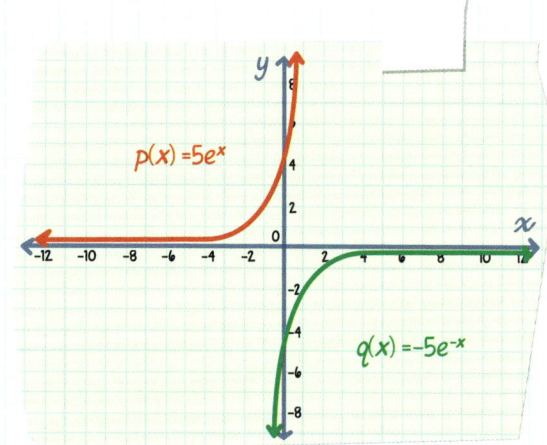

3. $h(x) = (\frac{2}{5})^x$ and $j(x) = (\frac{5}{2})^x$

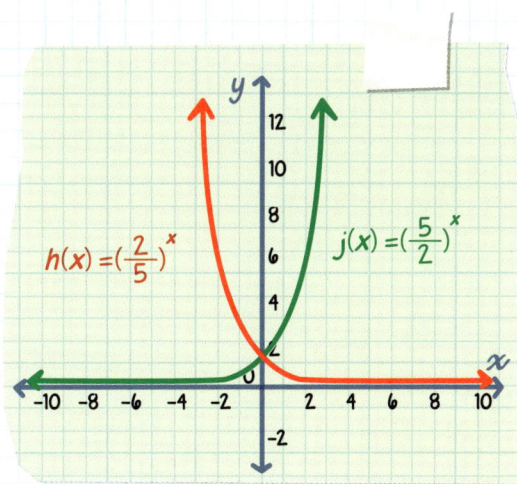

4. $k(x) = \frac{1}{2}e^x$ and $m(x) = -\frac{1}{2}e^{-x}$

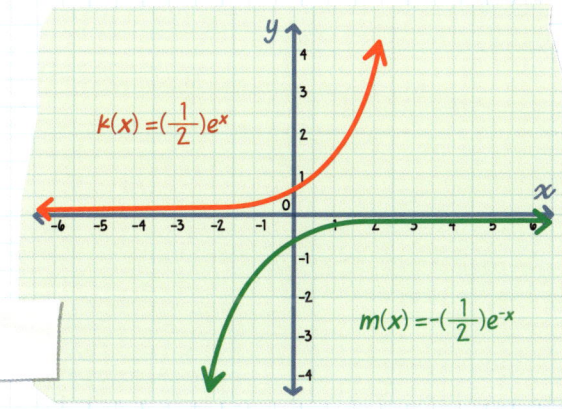

DESCRIBE IN WORDS HOW TO OBTAIN THE GRAPH OF THE GIVEN FUNCTION USING THE GRAPH OF THE PARENT FUNCTION.

5. $w(x) = -6^{5x}$

6. $j(x) = 7^{x-3} + 9$

7. $v(x) = 3^{8x}$

DESCRIBE IN WORDS HOW TO OBTAIN THE GRAPH OF THE GIVEN FUNCTION USING ITS PARENT FUNCTION. DRAW THE GRAPH.

8. $h(x) = 4^{x+8} - 2$

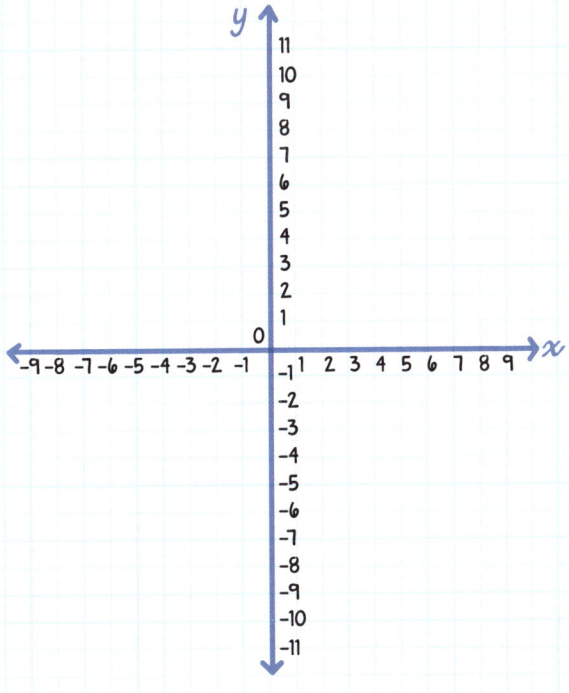

LOGARITHMIC FUNCTIONS AND THEIR GRAPHS

The inverse of the exponential function $f(x) = a^x$ is the **LOGARITHMIC FUNCTION** with base a, written as $g(x) = \log_a x$.

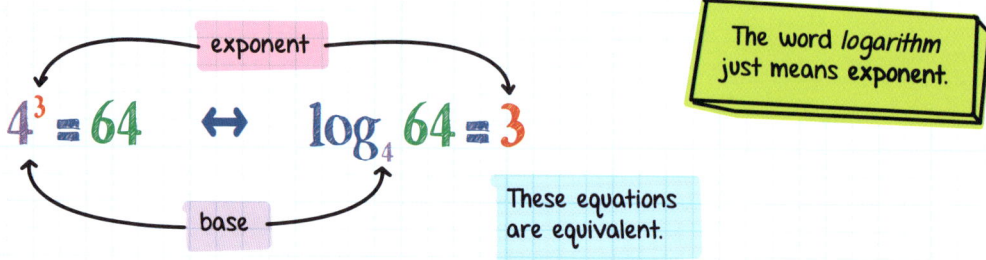

exponent

$$4^3 = 64 \quad \leftrightarrow \quad \log_4 64 = 3$$

base

> The word *logarithm* just means exponent.

> These equations are equivalent.

Since a logarithmic function is the **inverse** of an exponential function:

▶ We can graph $y = \log_a x$ by reflecting the graph of $y = a^x$ across the line $y = x$.

▶ The domain of a logarithmic function is the range of the corresponding exponential function.

▶ The range of a logarithmic function is the domain of the corresponding exponential function.

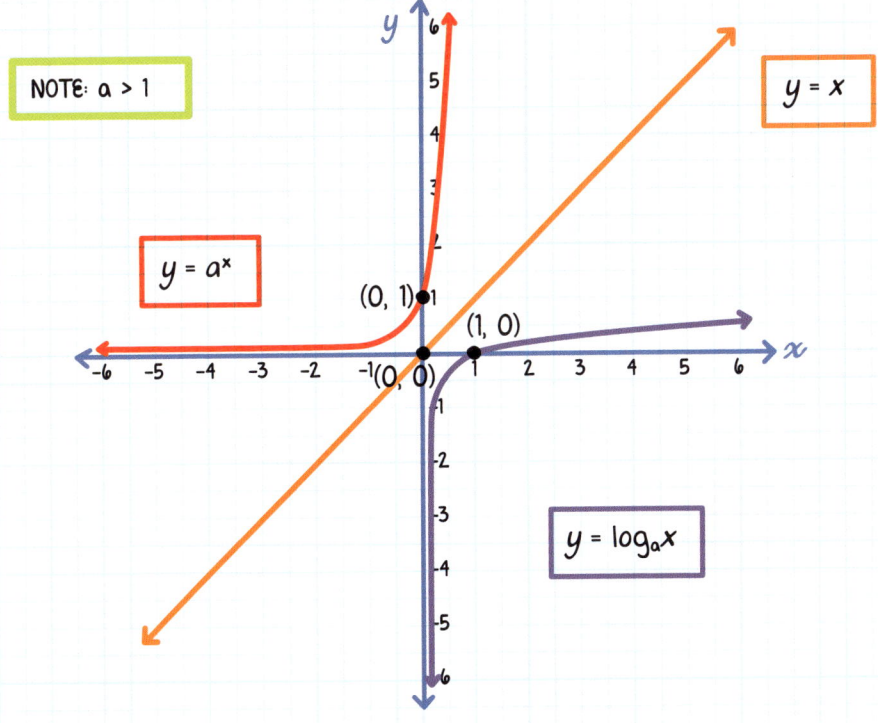

NOTE: $a > 1$

$y = x$

$y = a^x$

$(0, 1)$

$(1, 0)$

$(0, 0)$

$y = \log_a x$

The inverse of the exponential function with base 10, $f(x) = 10^x$, is called the **COMMON LOGARITHMIC FUNCTION**, and it is written as $g(x) = \log x$.

The inverse of the natural exponential function, $f(x) = e^x$, is called the **NATURAL LOGARITHMIC FUNCTION**, and it is written as $g(x) = \ln x$.

THINK:

$\log x = \log_{10} x$.

$\ln x = \log_e x$.

We can graph many other logarithmic functions by applying transformations to $f(x) = \log_a x$.

TRANSFORMATIONS OF LOGARITHMIC FUNCTIONS

Translations

$y = \log_a x + k$	$\log_a x - k$
Shift *up* k units.	Shift *down* k units.
$y = \log_a(x + h)$	$y = \log_a(x - h)$
Shift *to the left* h units.	Shift *to the right* h units.

Reflections

$y = -\log_a x$	$y = \log_a(-x)$
Reflect across the x-axis.	Reflect across the y-axis.

Dilations

$y = b\log_a x$	$y = \log_a cx$
Vertically stretch by a factor of b if $b > 1$. Vertically shrink by a factor of b if $0 < b < 1$.	Horizontally shrink by a factor of c if $c > 1$. Horizontally stretch by a factor of c if $0 < c < 1$.

EXAMPLE: Graph $w(x) = 4\log_2(-x)$ using $f(x) = \log_2 x$. State the domain, range, and vertical asymptote of w.

STEP 1: Graph $f(x) = \log_2 x$.

STEP 2: Graph $s(x) = \log_2(-x)$ by reflecting the graph of $f(x) = \log_2 x$ across the y-axis.

STEP 3: Graph $w(x) = 4\log_2(-x)$ by vertically stretching the graph of $s(x) = \log_2(-x)$ by a factor of 4.

THINK:
The graph of w will increase four times faster, so multiply the y-coordinates of the points on the graph of s by 4.

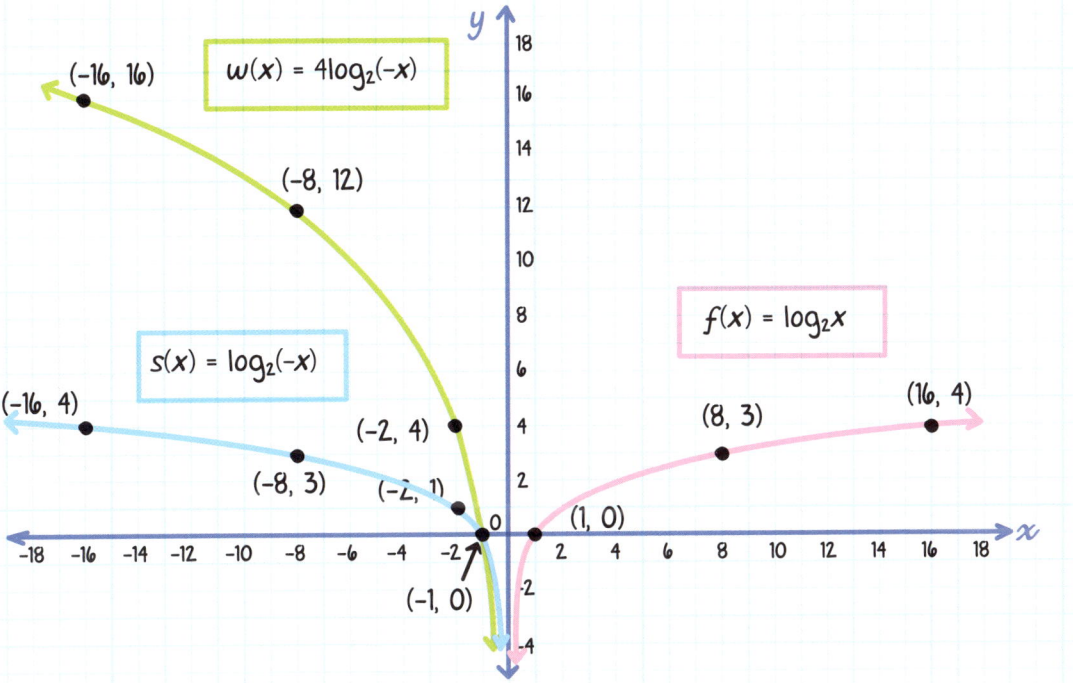

Domain: $(-\infty, 0)$

Range: $(-\infty, \infty)$

Vertical asymptote: $x = 0$

PROPERTIES OF LOGARITHMS		
PROPERTY	**DEFINITION**	**EXAMPLE**
Zero Property	$\log_b 1 = 0$	$\log_2 1 = 0$
Identity Property	$\log_b b = 1$	$\log_6 6 = 1$
Product Property	$\log_b mn = \log_b m + \log_b n$	$\log_5 14 = \log_5 (7 \cdot 2)$ $= \log_5 7 + \log_5 2$
Quotient Property	$\log_b \dfrac{m}{n} = \log_b m - \log_b n$	$\log_3 \dfrac{22}{7} =$ $\log_3 22 - \log_3 7$
Power Property	$\log_b m^n = n \log_b m$	$\log_8 3^5 = 5 \log_8 3$
One-to-One Property	If $\log_b m = \log_b n$, then $m = n$.	Given $\log_8 (3x) = \log_8 (x - 2)$, then $3x = x - 2$.

EXAMPLES: Expand each logarithm using the Properties of Logarithms.

▶ $\log_5 \sqrt{13a^9}$

$\log_5 (13a^9)^{\frac{1}{2}}$ Rewrite the radical as an exponent.

$\dfrac{1}{2}(\log_5 13a^9)$ Power Property

$\dfrac{1}{2}(\log_5 13 + \log_5 a^9)$ Product Property

$\dfrac{1}{2}(\log_5 13 + 9\log_5 a)$ Power Property

▶ $\log_2\left(\dfrac{x^3 y}{z}\right)$

$\log_2 x^3 y - \log_2 z$ Quotient Property

$\log_2 x^3 + \log_2 y - \log_2 z$ Product Property

$3\log_2 x + \log_2 y - \log_2 z$ Power Property

WE WORK SO WELL TOGETHER!

REWRITE EACH EXPONENTIAL EQUATION IN ITS EQUIVALENT LOGARITHMIC FORM.

1. $4^3 = 64$

2. $7^2 = 49$

3. $2^{-5} = \dfrac{1}{32}$

REWRITE EACH LOGARITHMIC EQUATION IN ITS EQUIVALENT EXPONENTIAL FORM.

4. $\log_3 81 = 4$

5. $\log_5 \dfrac{1}{25} = -2$

6. $\log_9 \dfrac{f}{h} = j$

DESCRIBE IN WORDS HOW TO GRAPH THE GIVEN FUNCTION, USING THE GRAPH OF $f(x) = \log_2 x$. THEN DRAW IT.

7. $h(x) = \log_2(x + 8) - 5$

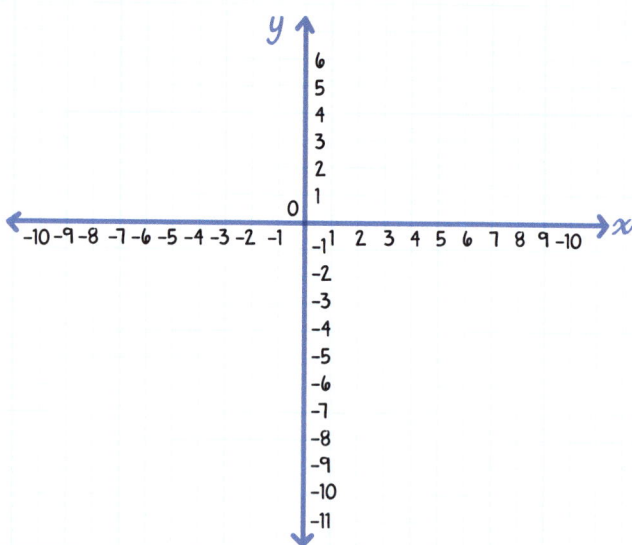

8. Following is the graph of the function $f(x) = \log_a x - 8$. What is the value of a?

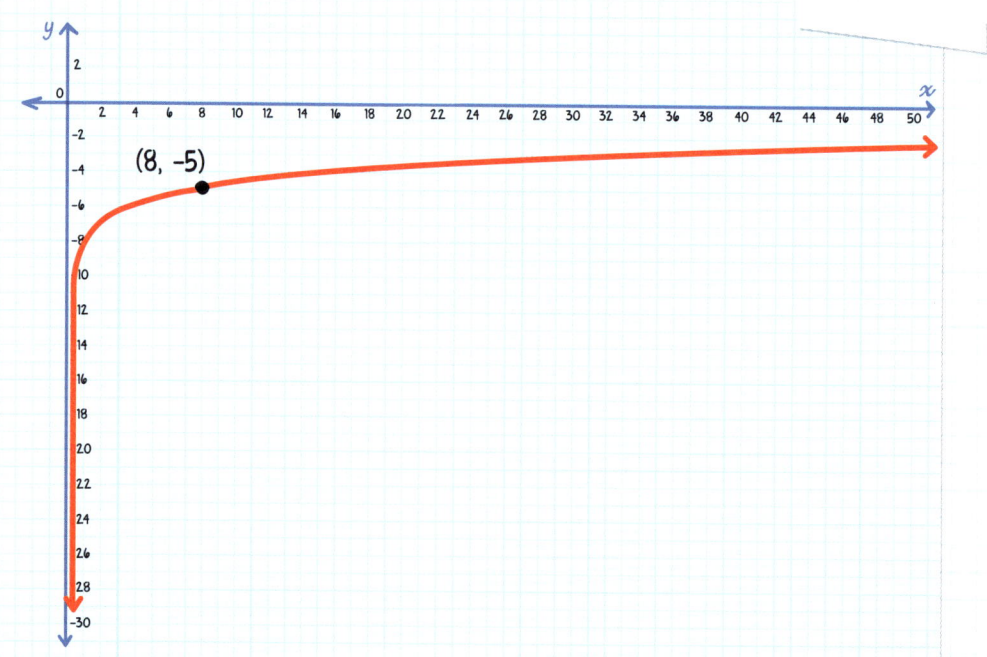

(8, −5)

EXPAND EACH OF THE FOLLOWING LOGARITHMS.

9. $\log_5 75$

10. $\log_3 \sqrt{23g^7}$

11. $\log_2 \left(\dfrac{jk^4}{h} \right)$

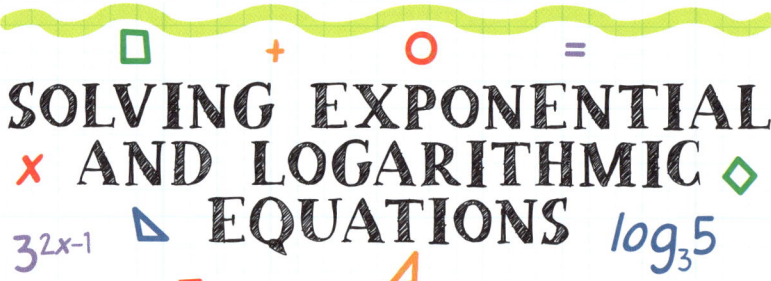

UNIT 7

Chapter 31

$\square$ $+$ $\bigcirc$ $=$

SOLVING EXPONENTIAL AND LOGARITHMIC EQUATIONS

x $\diamond$

3^{2x-1} $\triangle$ $-$ $\triangle$ $\log_3 5$

An **EXPONENTIAL EQUATION** is an equation in which a variable appears in an exponent.

We can solve an exponential equation by getting *equal bases* on each side.

EXAMPLE: Solve $5^x = 625$.

$5^x = 5^4$ Rewrite 625 as a power of 5.

$x = 4$

CHECK YOUR ANSWER

$5^x = 625$

$5^4 = 625$ Substitute $x = 4$.

$625 = 625$ ✓

We can solve exponential equations by taking a logarithm of each side.

EXAMPLE: Solve $3^{2x-1} = 5$.

THINK: We can use any base, but for the quickest solution let's use a base of 3.

$\log_3 3^{2x-1} = \log_3 5$

$(2x - 1)\log_3 3 = \log_3 5$ Power Property

$2x - 1 = \log_3 5 \qquad \log_3 3 = 1$

$2x = \log_3 5 + 1$

$x = \dfrac{1}{2}(\log_3 5 + 1)$

CHECK YOUR ANSWER

$3^{2x-1} = 5$

$3^{2(\frac{1}{2}(\log_3 5 + 1)) - 1} = 5$

$3^{(\log_3 5 + 1) - 1} = 5$

$3^{\log_3 5} = 5$

THINK: 3^x and $\log_3 x$ are inverses of each other.

$5 = 5$ ✓

EXAMPLE: Solve $3e^5 x = 10$.

$3e^5 x = 10$

$\dfrac{3e^{5x}}{3} = \dfrac{10}{3}$

$e^{5x} = \dfrac{10}{3}$

$\ln e^{5x} = \ln \frac{10}{3}$ Take the natural logarithm of both sides.

$5x \ln e = \ln \frac{10}{3}$ Power Property

$5x = \ln \frac{10}{3}$ $\ln e = 1$

$x = \frac{1}{5} \ln \frac{10}{3}$

A **LOGARITHMIC EQUATION** is an equation that involves the logarithm of an expression containing a variable.

EXAMPLE: Solve $\log_4(7x - 2) = \log_4(x + 10)$.

STEP 1: "Cancel" the logs and simplify.

$\cancel{\log_4}(7x - 2) = \cancel{\log_4}(x + 10)$
$7x - 2 = x + 10$
$7x = x + 12$
$6x = 12$
$x = 2$

 **THINK:**
If logs on either side of the equal sign have the same base, the One-to-One Property of logarithms says we can cancel them.

STEP 2: Check to see if the solution is extraneous.

$\log_4(7x - 2) = \log_4(x + 10)$

$\log_4(7 \cdot 2 - 2) = \log_4(2 + 10)$

$\log_4(14 - 2) = \log_4(12)$

$\log_4(12) = \log_4(12)$ ✓

EXAMPLE: Solve $\log_2 x + \log_2(x + 3) = 2$.

STEP 1: Rewrite the two logarithms as a single logarithm.

$\log_2 x + \log_2(x + 3) = 2$

$\log_2[x(x + 3)] = 2$ Product Property

$\log_2(x^2 + 3x) = 2$ Distributive Property

$x^2 + 3x = 2^2$ Rewrite in exponential form.

$x^2 + 3x - 4 = 0$

$(x + 4)(x - 1) = 0$ Factor

THINK:
The Product Property says that the sum of two logarithms is the same as the product under a single logarithm.

STEP 2: Use the Zero-Product Principle to solve for x.

$x + 4 = 0 \qquad x - 1 = 0$

$x = -4 \qquad x = 1$

STEP 3: Check to see if the solutions are extraneous.

$x = 1$

$\log_2 x + \log_2(x + 3) = 2$

$\log_2 1 + \log_2(1 + 3) = 2$

$\log_2 1 + \log_2 4 = 2$

$0 + 2 = 2$ Evaluate each addend: $2^0 = 1$; $2^2 = 4$

$2 = 2$ ✓

$x = -4$

$\log_2 x + \log_2(x + 3) = 2$

$\log_2(-4) + \log_2(-4 + 3) = 2$

$\log_2(-4) + \log_2(-1) = 2$ ✗

Negative numbers are not in the domain of $f(x) = \log_2 x$, so the left-hand side is undefined. This means $x = -4$ is an extraneous solution.

$x = 1$ is the only solution.

YOU'RE THE ONLY ONE FOR ME.

SOLVE EACH EXPONENTIAL EQUATION.

1. $8^{6x} = 32^{3x-9}$

2. $5^{x+9} = 125$

3. $4e^{3x} = 57$

4. $e^{2x} + 6e^x + 16 = 11$

5. $7^{12x} = 49^{x-15}$

6. $2e^{13x} = 29$

7. $6x^2e^x + 18xe^x = 0$

SOLVE EACH LOGARITHMIC EQUATION.

8. $\log_4(9x - 13) = \log_4(-2x + 20)$

9. $\log_3(x + 8) = 4$

10. $\log_4(x + 6) + \log_4 x = 2$

11. $\ln x = 7$

12. $\ln x - \ln(6 - x) = 0$

13. $\log_2(x - 12) = 7$

14. $\log_6(7x - 10) = \log_6(12x - 45)$

WORK SPACE

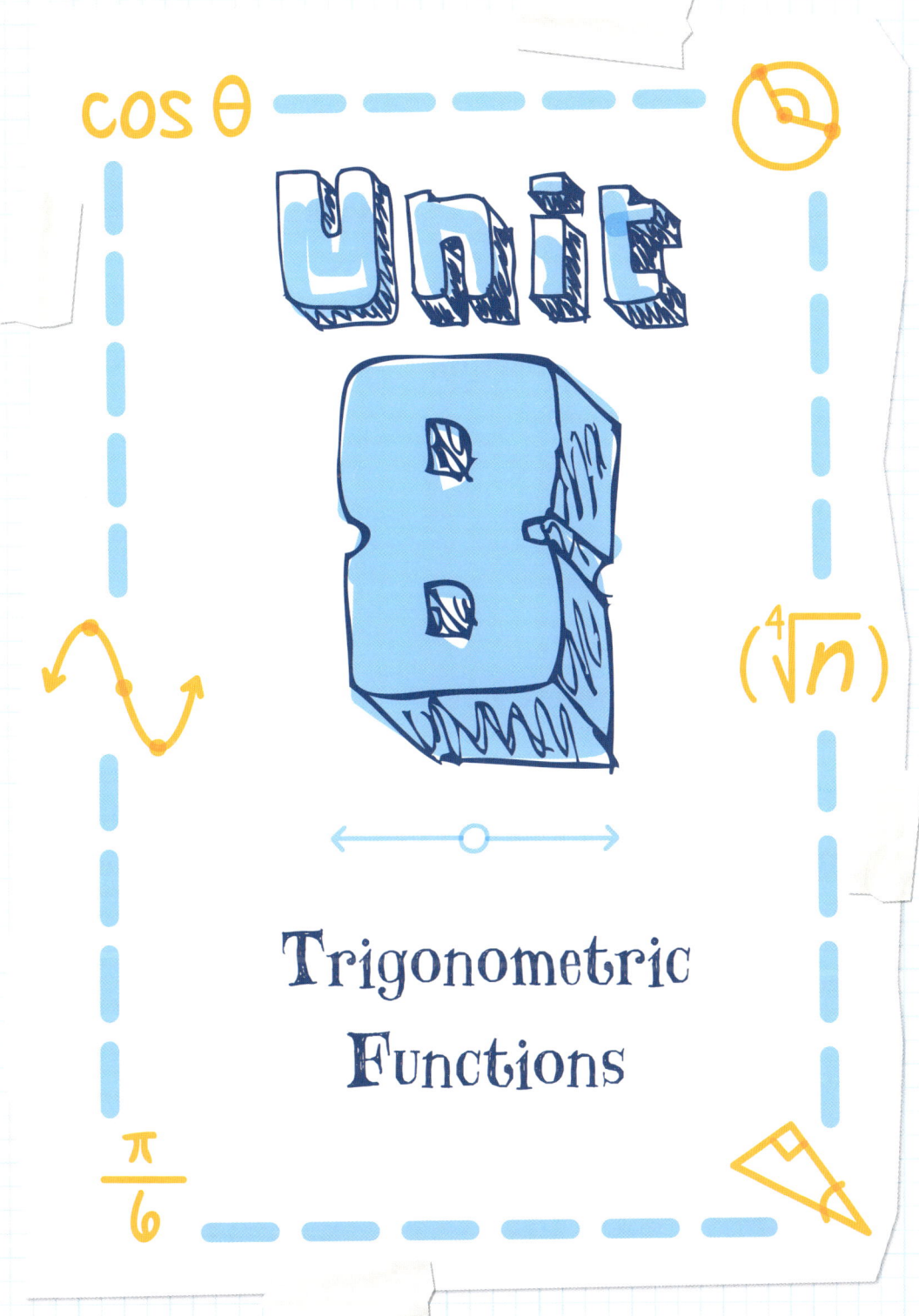

cos θ

Unit

8

Trigonometric Functions

$\frac{\pi}{6}$

$(\sqrt[4]{n})$

ANGLES AND THEIR MEASURE

An angle is in **STANDARD POSITION** when its vertex lies at the origin (0, 0) and one of its sides lies on the positive x-axis.

The ray on the positive x-axis is the **INITIAL SIDE**.

The other ray is the **TERMINAL SIDE**.

Two angles in standard position are **COTERMINAL** if their terminal sides are in the same place.

The rotation of an angle is measured in **DEGREES** (°). One full rotation is equal to 360°.

THINK:
A 135° angle is coterminal with a 495° angle.

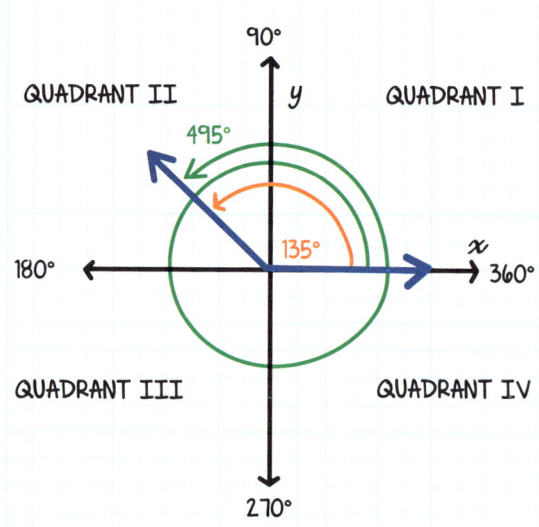

Angles of rotation can be **POSITIVE** or **NEGATIVE** depending on the direction of rotation.

Positive angle of rotation = counterclockwise rotation

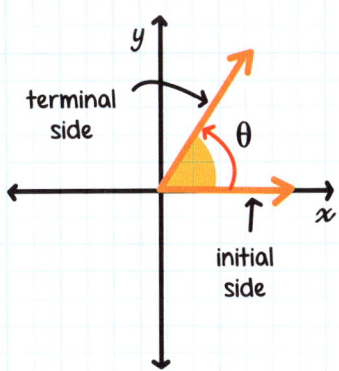

Negative angle of rotation = clockwise rotation

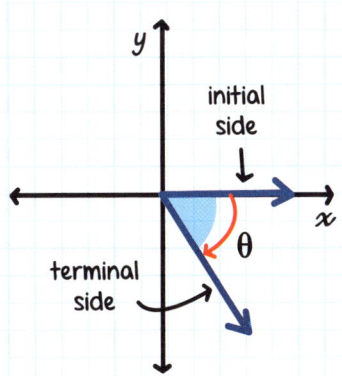

EXAMPLE: Draw coterminal angles 90° and -270° in standard position.

Then indicate in which quadrant or on which axis the terminal side lies.

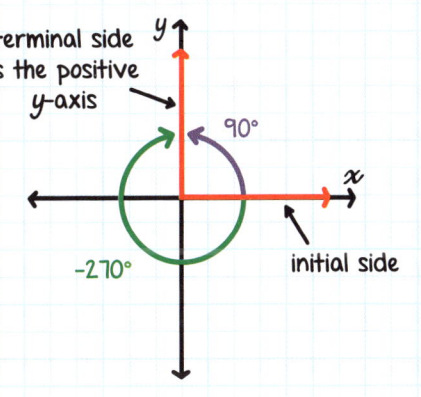

A **CENTRAL ANGLE** is an angle whose vertex lies in the center of a circle.

ARC LENGTH is the distance from endpoint to endpoint of a central angle. It is equal to the measure of the central angle.

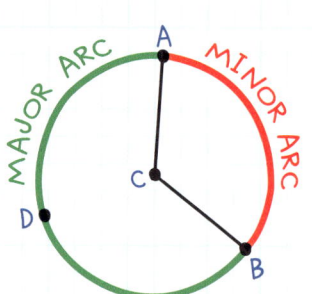

A **MINOR ARC** has measure less than **180°**.

A **MAJOR ARC** has measure greater than **180°**.

The measure of a major arc and a minor arc in the same circle will add up to **360°**.

Arcs can have the same measure but different lengths or the same length but different measures.

CONGRUENT arcs have the same measure *and* the same length.

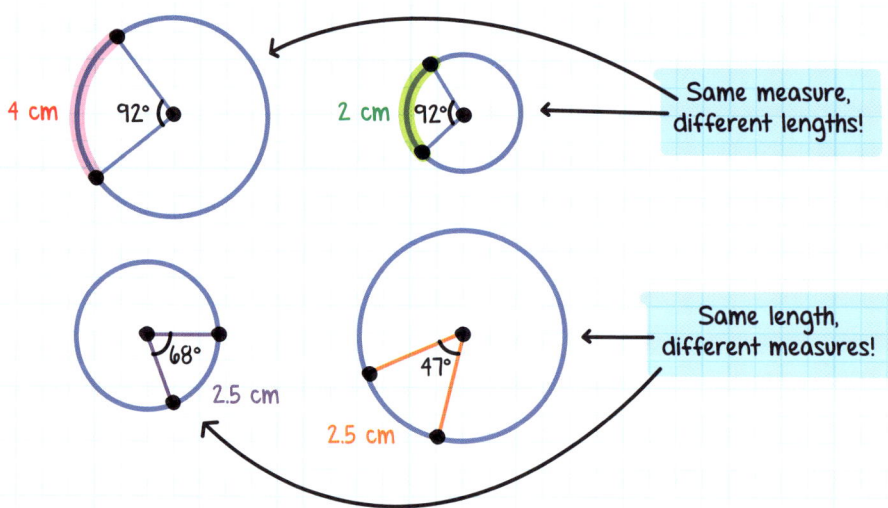

EXAMPLE: Find the measure of $\overset{\frown}{PRS}$.

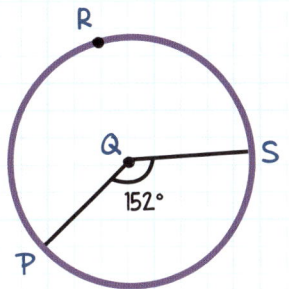

$m\overset{\frown}{PRS} + m\overset{\frown}{PS} = 360°$

$m\overset{\frown}{PRS} + 152° = 360°$

$m\overset{\frown}{PRS} + 152° - 152° = 360° - 152°$

$m\overset{\frown}{PRS} = 208°$

Angles can also be measured with **RADIANS**.

We can convert from degrees to radians or from radians to degrees using the proportion shown.

$$\frac{\angle \text{ in degrees}}{180} = \frac{\angle \text{ in radians}}{\pi}$$

EXAMPLE: Convert $\frac{5\pi}{3}$ to degrees.

$\frac{\angle \text{ in degrees}}{180°} = \frac{\frac{5\pi}{3}}{\pi}$ Substitute $\frac{5\pi}{3}$ into the proportion.

Divide: $\frac{5\pi}{3} \div \pi = \frac{5\pi}{3} \cdot \frac{1}{\pi} = \frac{5}{3}$.

$\frac{\angle \text{ in degrees}}{180°} = \frac{5}{3}$

$\angle \text{ in degrees} = \frac{5}{3} \cdot 180$

$\angle \text{ in degrees} = \frac{900}{3}$

$\angle \text{ in degrees} = 300$

So, $\frac{5\pi}{3}$ radians is 300°.

Shortcuts!

To convert radians to degrees, multiply by $\frac{180}{\pi}$.

$\frac{4\pi}{5} \cdot \frac{180}{\pi}$

$\frac{720\pi}{5\pi}$

144

So, $\frac{4\pi}{5}$ radians is $144°$.

To convert degrees to radians, multiply by $\frac{\pi}{180}$.

$175° \cdot \frac{\pi}{180}$

$\frac{175\pi}{180}$

$\frac{35\pi}{36}$

So, $175°$ is $\frac{35\pi}{36}$ radians.

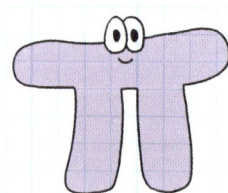

DRAW THE COTERMINAL ANGLES WITH THE GIVEN DEGREE MEASURES IN STANDARD POSITION. THEN INDICATE IN WHICH QUADRANT OR ON WHICH AXIS THE TERMINAL SIDE RESIDES.

1. 78° and −282°

2. 198° and −162°

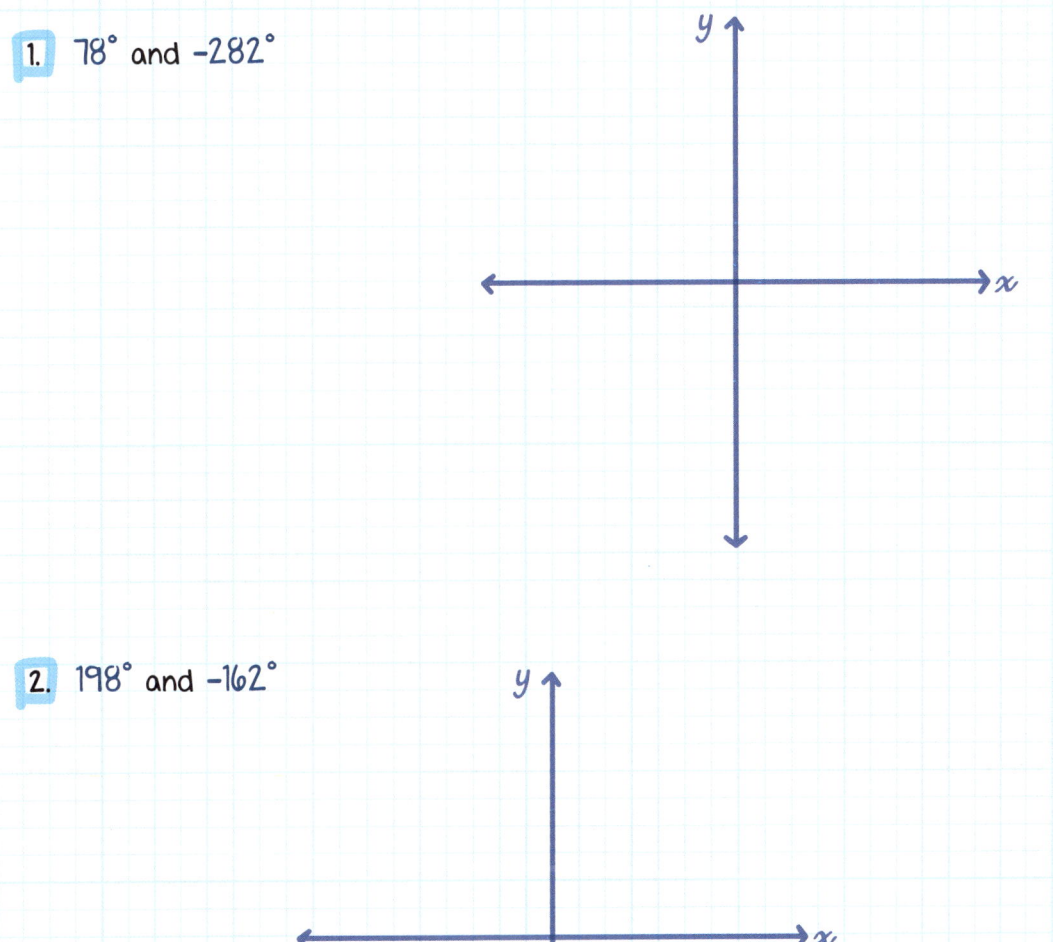

3. 295° and 655°

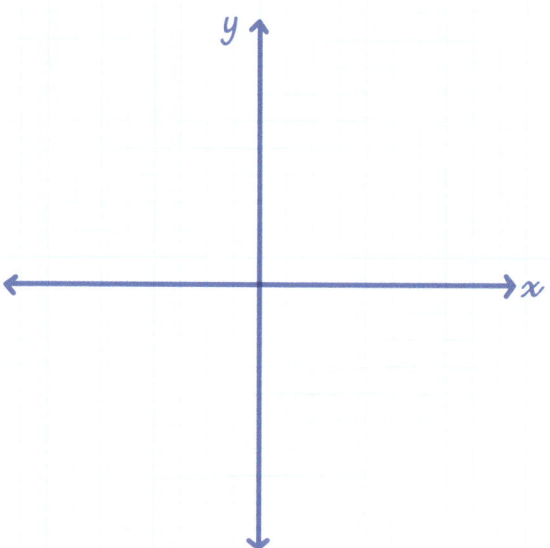

4. Name one positive and one negative angle that is coterminal with the given angle.

A. 55°

B. 90°

C. 640°

5. If the measure of major arc $\overset{\frown}{HJK}$ is 212°, what is the measure of minor arc $\overset{\frown}{HK}$?

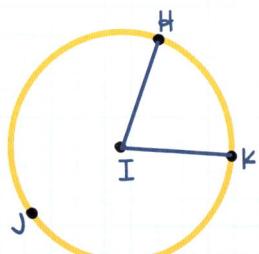

6. Given the measurements below, find m$\widehat{WX}$ and m$\widehat{WZY}$.

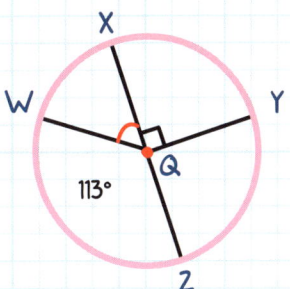

7. Indicate whether each statement is true or false.

A. Two arcs with the same measure can have different lengths.

B. Two arcs cannot have different lengths and the same measure.

CONVERT THE GIVEN DEGREE MEASURE TO RADIANS.

8. 47°

9. −126°

10. $335°$

CONVERT THE GIVEN RADIAN MEASURE TO DEGREES.

11. $\dfrac{\pi}{15}$

12. $-\dfrac{5\pi}{2}$

13. $\dfrac{8\pi}{15}$

Chapter 33

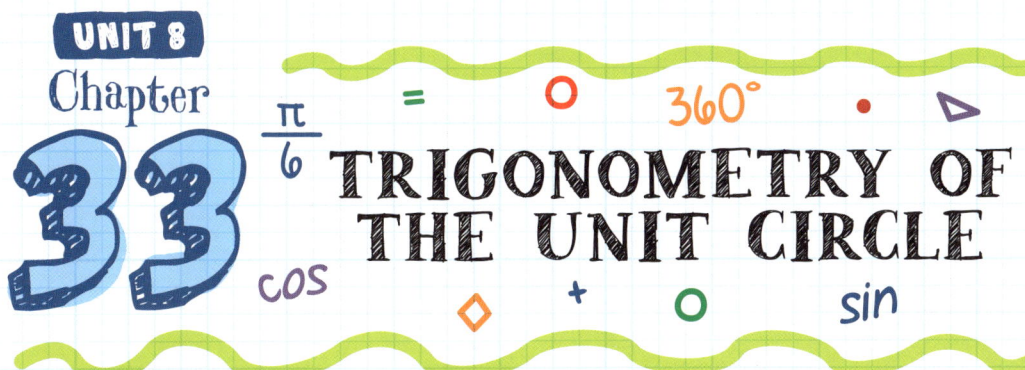

$\frac{\pi}{6}$ = ○ 360° • ▷

cos ◇ + ○ sin

TRIGONOMETRY OF THE UNIT CIRCLE

The **UNIT CIRCLE** is the circle with **radius** 1 and **center** (0, 0).

> Unit circle in the Cartesian plane

The **equation** of the unit circle is $x^2 + y^2 = 1$.

The **circumference** of the unit circle is $2\pi \cdot 1 = 2\pi$.

TRIGONOMETRIC FUNCTIONS are specific functions that are defined in terms of points on the unit circle.

THINK:
> The range of the wrapping function is the unit circle.

We can use the **WRAPPING FUNCTION** to help identify trigonometric functions.

The wrapping function shows all the trigonometric functions by identifying angles with points on the unit circle.

> The angle measures in radians are the inputs.

> The points are the outputs.

EXAMPLE: Find $W(-\frac{13\pi}{6})$.

$W(-\frac{13\pi}{6}) = (\frac{\sqrt{3}}{2}, -\frac{1}{2})$

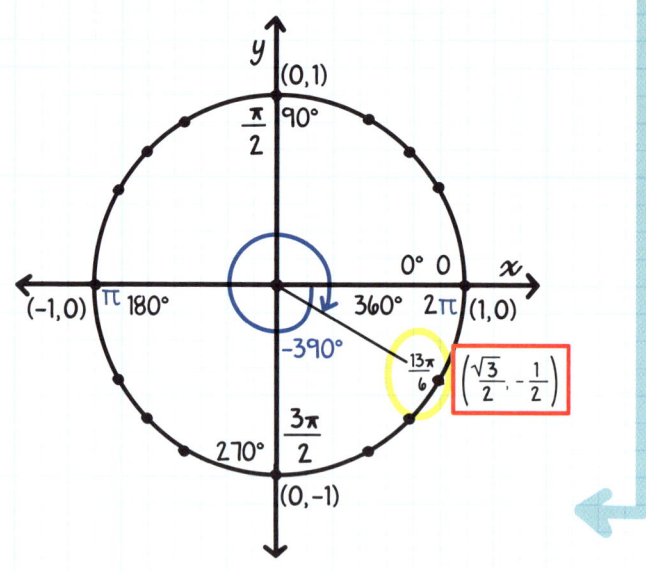

We can use the unit circle to evaluate the **SINE**, **COSINE**, **TANGENT**, **COTANGENT**, **SECANT**, and **COSECANT** of an angle (θ) via the wrapping function:

$\sin\theta = y$	$\cos\theta = x$	$\tan\theta = \dfrac{\sin\theta}{\cos\theta} = \dfrac{y}{x}$
$\csc\theta = \dfrac{1}{\sin\theta} = \dfrac{1}{y}$	$\sec\theta = \dfrac{1}{\cos\theta} = \dfrac{1}{x}$	$\cot\theta = \dfrac{\cos\theta}{\sin\theta} = \dfrac{x}{y}$

These are types of trigonometric functions.

EXAMPLES: Compute each of the following using the unit circle..

▶ $\cos\left(\frac{7\pi}{6}\right)$

$W\left(\frac{7\pi}{6}\right) = \left(-\frac{\sqrt{3}}{2}, -\frac{1}{2}\right)$

So, $\cos\frac{7\pi}{6} = -\frac{\sqrt{3}}{2}$.

▶ $\sin\left(-\frac{\pi}{2}\right)$

$W\left(-\frac{\pi}{2}\right) = (0, -1)$

So, $\sin\left(-\frac{\pi}{2}\right) = -1$.

▶ $\cot\left(-\frac{5\pi}{3}\right)$

$W\left(-\frac{5\pi}{3}\right) = \left(\frac{1}{2}, \frac{\sqrt{3}}{2}\right)$

So, $\cot\left(-\frac{5\pi}{3}\right) = \dfrac{\frac{1}{2}}{\frac{\sqrt{3}}{2}} = \left(\frac{1}{2} \div \frac{\sqrt{3}}{2}\right) = \left(\frac{1}{2} \cdot \frac{2}{\sqrt{3}}\right) = \frac{2}{2\sqrt{3}} = \frac{1}{\sqrt{3}}$.

FIND EACH POINT ON THE UNIT CIRCLE.

1. $W(\frac{9\pi}{2})$

2. $W(\frac{14\pi}{3})$

3. $W(-\frac{7\pi}{4})$

EVALUATE EACH FUNCTION AT THE GIVEN VALUE.

4. $\cos\dfrac{3\pi}{4}$

5. $\sin\dfrac{\pi}{3}$

6. $\sin(-4\pi)$

7. $\cot \frac{2\pi}{3}$

8. $\sec \frac{\pi}{4}$

9. $W\left(\frac{7\pi}{6}\right)$

10. $\sin\left(-\frac{5\pi}{2}\right)$

Chapter

34

RIGHT TRIANGLE TRIGONOMETRY

25 - △ tan 45° 2x

SOH □ HYP $\sqrt{3}$ △

TRIGONOMETRY can be used to find measures in right triangles.

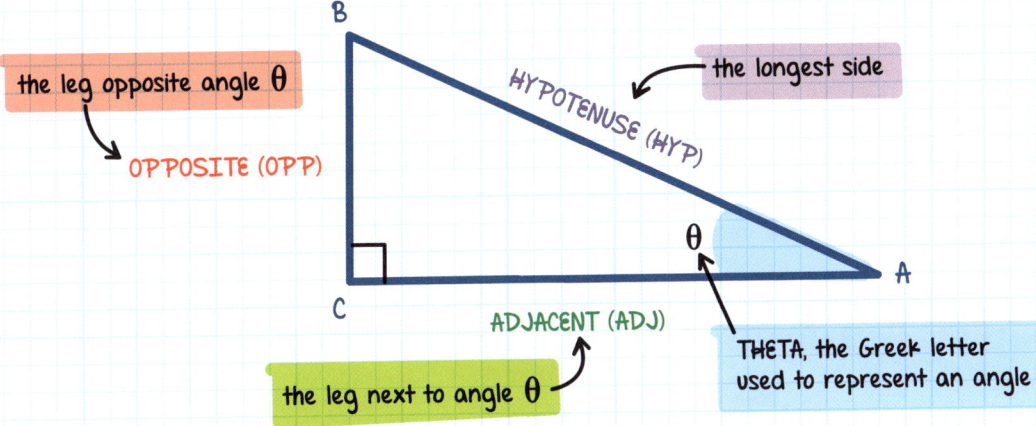

the leg opposite angle θ

OPPOSITE (OPP)

HYPOTENUSE (HYP)

the longest side

ADJACENT (ADJ)

the leg next to angle θ

θ

THETA, the Greek letter used to represent an angle

The trigonometric functions SINE (SIN), COSINE (COS), and TANGENT (TAN) are each a ratio of side lengths of a right triangle. They are often used to find unknown angle measures or side lengths of a right triangle.

$$\sin \theta = \frac{OPP}{HYP} \qquad \cos \theta = \frac{ADJ}{HYP} \qquad \tan \theta = \frac{OPP}{ADJ}$$

COSECANT (CSC), SECANT (SEC), and COTANGENT (COT) are also ratios of the side lengths of right triangles. They are the reciprocals of sine, cosine, and tangent, respectively.

$$\csc A = \frac{HYP}{OPP} \qquad \sec A = \frac{HYP}{ADJ} \qquad \cot A = \frac{ADJ}{OPP}$$

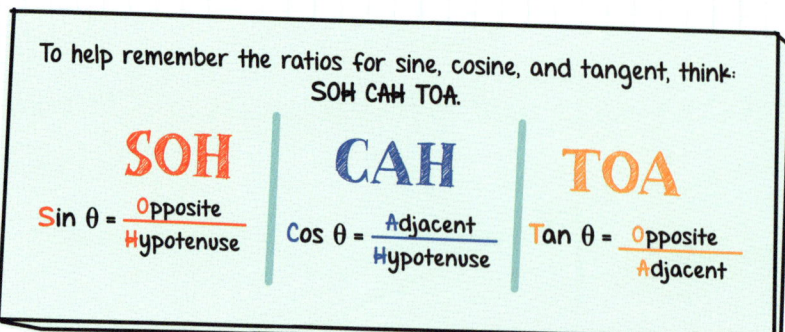

To help remember the ratios for sine, cosine, and tangent, think: SOH CAH TOA.

SOH $\quad$ **CAH** $\quad$ **TOA**

$$\text{Sin } \theta = \frac{\text{Opposite}}{\text{Hypotenuse}} \quad \Big| \quad \text{Cos } \theta = \frac{\text{Adjacent}}{\text{Hypotenuse}} \quad \Big| \quad \text{Tan } \theta = \frac{\text{Opposite}}{\text{Adjacent}}$$

EXAMPLE: Compute all six trigonometric functions for angle R in △NMR.

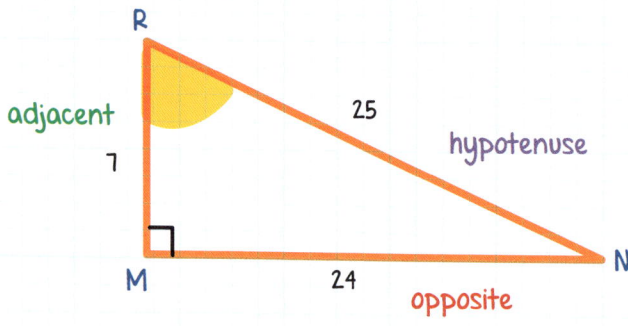

$$\sin R = \frac{OPP}{HYP} = \frac{24}{25} \qquad \csc R = \frac{HYP}{OPP} = \frac{25}{24}$$

$$\cos R = \frac{ADJ}{HYP} = \frac{7}{25} \qquad \sec R = \frac{HYP}{ADJ} = \frac{25}{7}$$

$$\tan R = \frac{OPP}{ADJ} = \frac{24}{7} \qquad \cot R = \frac{ADJ}{OPP} = \frac{7}{24}$$

A **SPECIAL RIGHT TRIANGLE** is a triangle with a feature (angle or side) that makes calculations of its side lengths or angle measures easier or for which formulas exist.

The two most common special right triangles are:

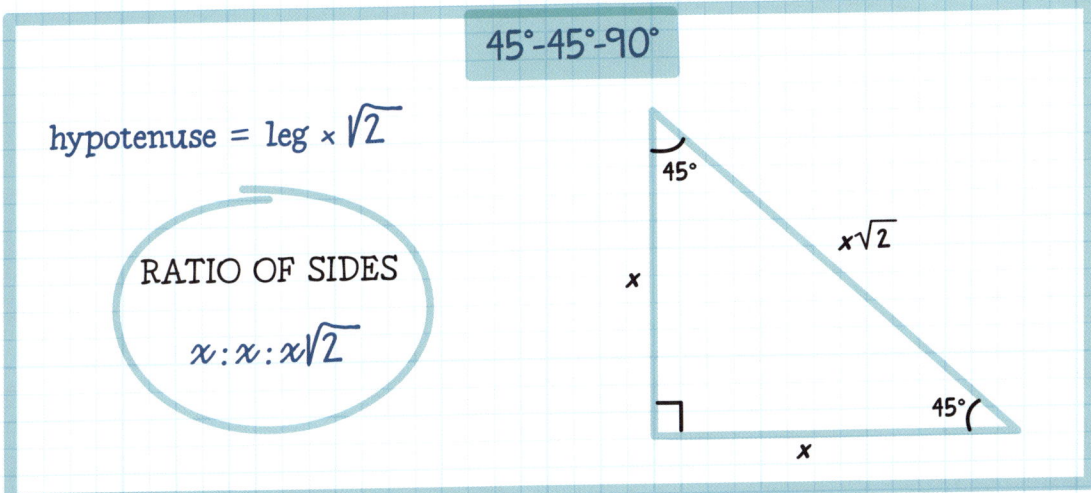

45°-45°-90°

hypotenuse = leg × $\sqrt{2}$

RATIO OF SIDES

$x : x : x\sqrt{2}$

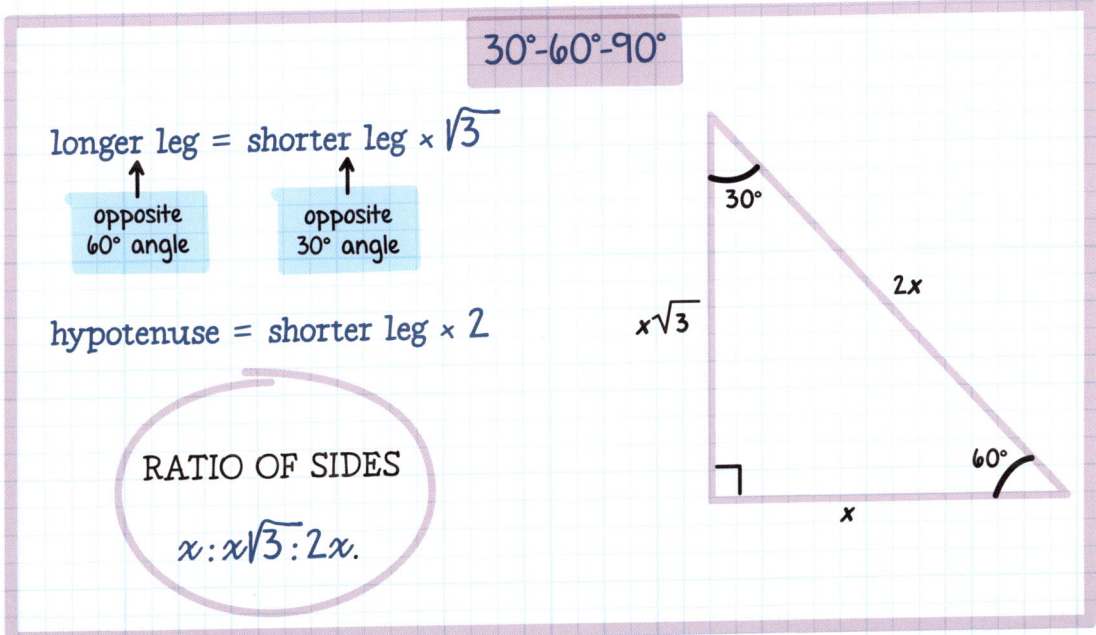

30°-60°-90°

longer leg = shorter leg × $\sqrt{3}$

↑ opposite 60° angle

↑ opposite 30° angle

hypotenuse = shorter leg × 2

RATIO OF SIDES

$x : x\sqrt{3} : 2x$.

EXAMPLE: Given △PQR, find the length of the leg $\overline{QR}$ and the hypotenuse.

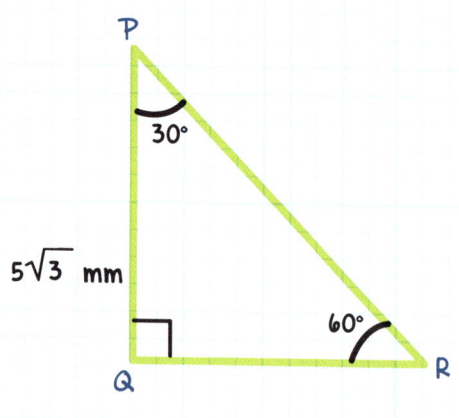

The length of $\overline{PQ}$ is $x\sqrt{3} = 5\sqrt{3}$ mm.

The length of $\overline{QR}$ is x.

The length of the hypotenuse is $2x$.

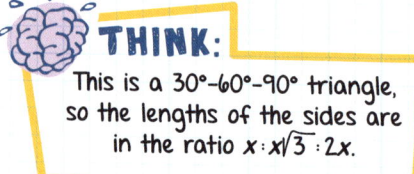

THINK:
This is a 30°-60°-90° triangle, so the lengths of the sides are in the ratio $x : x\sqrt{3} : 2x$.

Solve for x.

$$x\sqrt{3} = 5\sqrt{3}$$

$$\frac{x\sqrt{3}}{\sqrt{3}} = \frac{5\sqrt{3}}{\sqrt{3}}$$

$$x = 5$$

The length of $\overline{QR}$ is $x = 5$ mm.

The length of the hypotenuse is $2x = 2(5) = 10$ mm.

We can replace x by any nonzero real number we want. The simplest choice is $x = 1$. That leaves us with the triangles below.

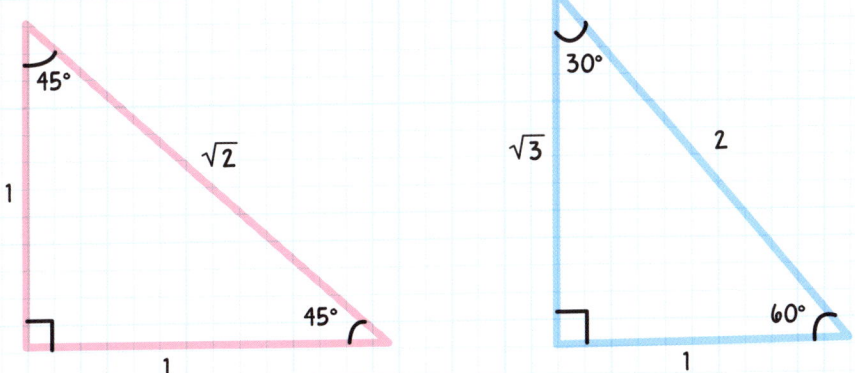

The values of the six trigonometric functions for these angles are given in the table.

θ	30°	45°	60°
$\sin \theta = \dfrac{OPP}{HYP}$	$\dfrac{1}{2}$	$\dfrac{1}{\sqrt{2}}$	$\dfrac{\sqrt{3}}{2}$
$\cos \theta = \dfrac{ADJ}{HYP}$	$\dfrac{\sqrt{3}}{2}$	$\dfrac{1}{\sqrt{2}}$	$\dfrac{1}{2}$
$\tan \theta = \dfrac{OPP}{ADJ}$	$\dfrac{1}{\sqrt{3}}$	1	$\sqrt{3}$
$\cot \theta = \dfrac{ADJ}{OPP}$	$\sqrt{3}$	1	$\dfrac{1}{\sqrt{3}}$
$\sec \theta = \dfrac{HYP}{ADJ}$	$\dfrac{2}{\sqrt{3}}$	$\sqrt{2}$	2
$\csc \theta = \dfrac{HYP}{OPP}$	2	$\sqrt{2}$	$\dfrac{2}{\sqrt{3}}$

A **REFERENCE ANGLE** is the acute angle formed by the terminal side of an angle θ and the x-axis.

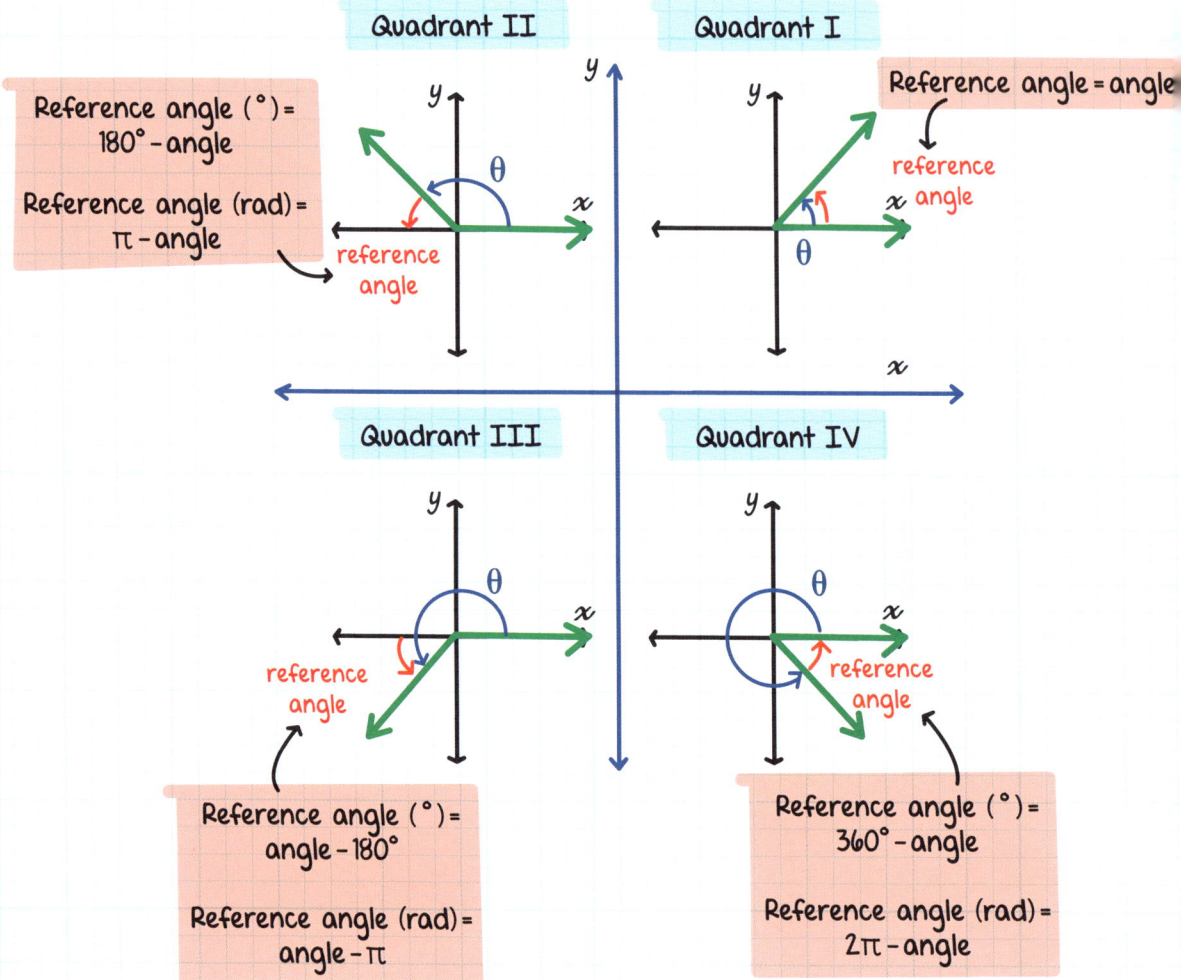

Reference angle (°) =
180° – angle

Reference angle (rad) =
π – angle

Quadrant II

reference
angle

Quadrant I

Reference angle = angle

reference
angle

Quadrant III

reference
angle

Reference angle (°) =
angle – 180°

Reference angle (rad) =
angle – π

Quadrant IV

reference
angle

Reference angle (°) =
360° – angle

Reference angle (rad) =
2π – angle

EXAMPLE: Find the measure of the reference angle.

Since the given angle, $\frac{19\pi}{6}$, is NOT between 0 and 2π, we must first find an angle coterminal with the given angle that is between 0 and 2π. We can start by subtracting the measure of one rotation (2π) from the given angle.

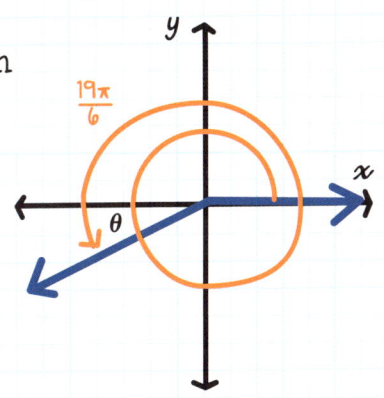

$$\frac{19\pi}{6} - 2\pi = \frac{19\pi}{6} - \frac{12\pi}{6} = \frac{7\pi}{6}$$

The given angle is in Quadrant III, and $\frac{7\pi}{6}$ is between 0 and 2π. So, we can subtract π from $\frac{7\pi}{6}$ to find the reference angle.

$$\frac{7\pi}{6} - \pi = \frac{7\pi}{6} - \frac{6\pi}{6} = \frac{\pi}{6}$$

So, the measure of the reference angle θ is $\frac{\pi}{6}$.

We can use reference angles to help us evaluate trigonometric functions.

I'M READY TO EVALUATE TRIG FUNCTIONS.

STEP 1: Find the reference angle.

STEP 2: Evaluate the trigonometric function using the reference angle.

STEP 3: Determine the sign (positive or negative) of the trigonometric function by looking at the quadrant in which the *given* angle sits.

To know which functions are positive in which quadrants, just remember:

"All Students Take Calculus."

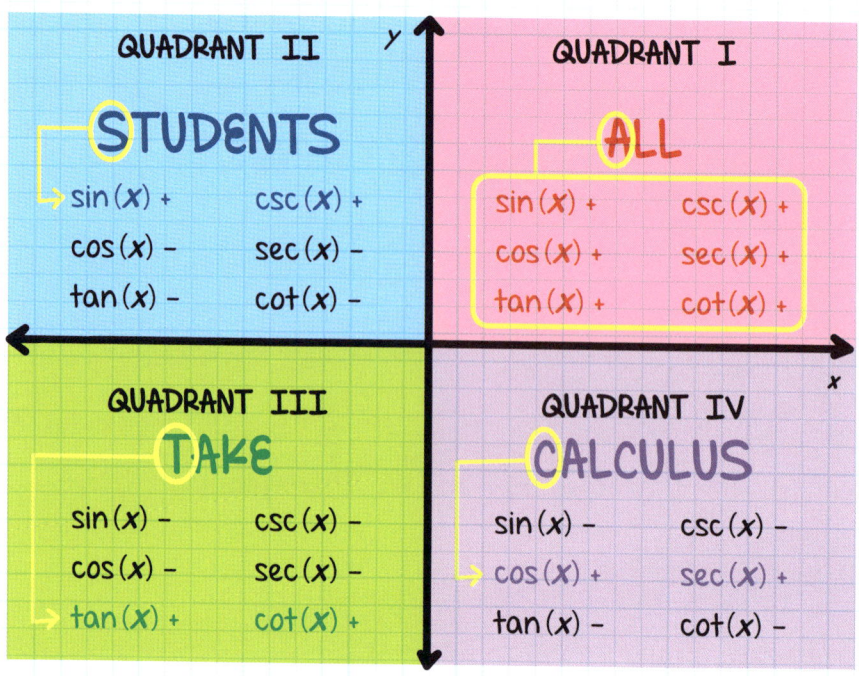

QUADRANT II

STUDENTS

$\sin(x)$ + $\csc(x)$ +
$\cos(x)$ − $\sec(x)$ −
$\tan(x)$ − $\cot(x)$ −

QUADRANT I

ALL

$\sin(x)$ + $\csc(x)$ +
$\cos(x)$ + $\sec(x)$ +
$\tan(x)$ + $\cot(x)$ +

QUADRANT III

TAKE

$\sin(x)$ − $\csc(x)$ −
$\cos(x)$ − $\sec(x)$ −
$\tan(x)$ + $\cot(x)$ +

QUADRANT IV

CALCULUS

$\sin(x)$ − $\csc(x)$ −
$\cos(x)$ + $\sec(x)$ +
$\tan(x)$ − $\cot(x)$ −

EXAMPLE: Evaluate $\csc \dfrac{11\pi}{3}$ without using a calculator.

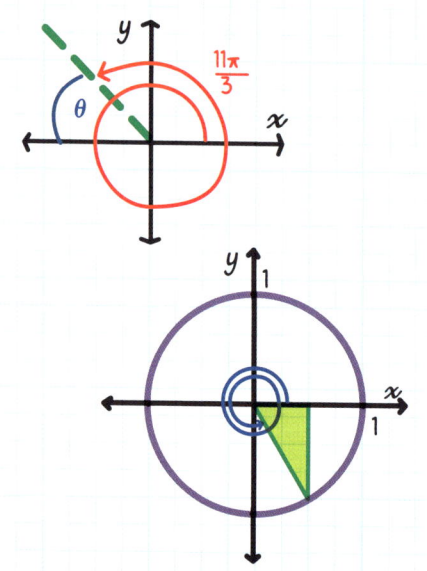

STEP 1: Find the reference angle.

Since the angle $\dfrac{11\pi}{3}$ is *greater than* 2π, first find an angle that is coterminal with $\dfrac{11\pi}{3}$ and whose measure is between 0 and 2π.

$$\frac{11\pi}{3} - 2\pi = \frac{11\pi}{3} - \frac{6\pi}{3} = \frac{5\pi}{3}$$

Since the given angle is in Quadrant IV and is coterminal with the angle measuring $\frac{5\pi}{3}$, and $\frac{5\pi}{3}$ is between 0 and 2π, we can subtract $\frac{5\pi}{3}$ from 2π to find the reference angle for the given angle.

$$2\pi - \frac{5\pi}{3} = \frac{6\pi}{3} - \frac{5\pi}{3} = \frac{\pi}{3} \longleftarrow \text{reference angle}$$

STEP 2: Evaluate the function using the reference angle.

$$\csc \frac{\pi}{3} = \frac{2}{\sqrt{3}}$$

STEP 3: Determine whether the answer is positive or negative.

Since the given angle is in Quadrant IV, cosecant is negative.

Therefore, $\csc \frac{11\pi}{3} = -\frac{2}{\sqrt{3}}$.

Right triangle trigonometry can be used to solve real-world problems.

EXAMPLE: An airplane is stationed 226 feet from an air traffic control tower. The angle of elevation from the nose of the plane to the top of the tower is 60°. What is the height of the tower to the nearest tenth of a foot?

To solve this problem, we can use a 30°-60°-90° triangle and a trigonometric ratio.

The **angle of elevation** is the angle from the horizontal line of the runway to the top of the tower. In this problem, we are told that it is 60°.

We can sketch the situation to help us evaluate it. Since we need to determine the height of the tower, we label the height x.

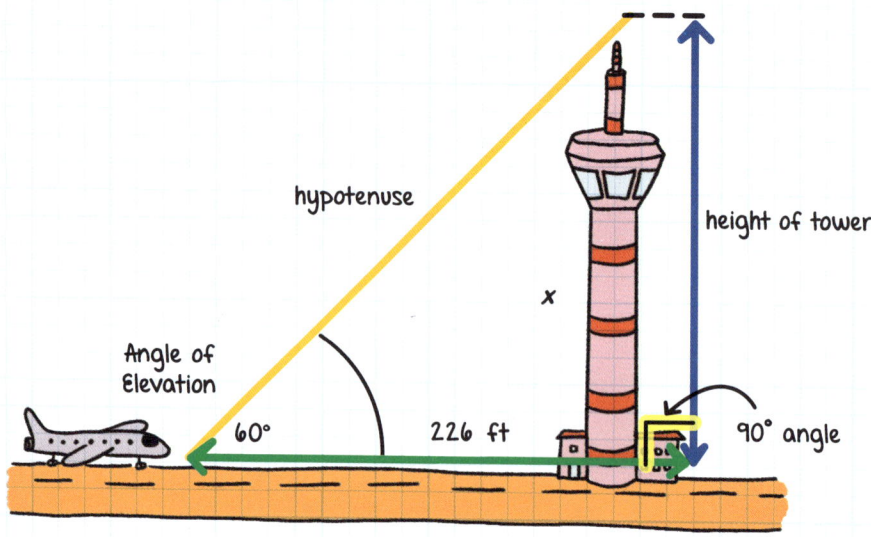

To find the height of the tower, we can write a trigonometric ratio using the tangent function and solve for x.

$$\tan 60° = \frac{OPP}{ADJ} = \frac{x}{226}$$

$$226 \cdot \tan 60° = \frac{x}{226} \cdot 226$$

$$226\sqrt{3} = x \qquad \tan 60° = \sqrt{3}$$

$391.4 \approx x$ Use a scientific calculator to approximate the result to the nearest tenth.

So, the height of the air traffic control tower to the nearest tenth of a foot is 391.4 feet.

1. Compute the six trigonometric functions of the angle θ.

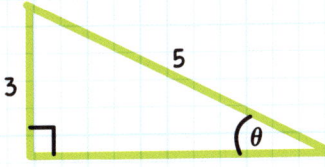

2. Find the values of the given angles.

sin 45°	cot 60°
sec 60°	csc 30°
tan 30°	tan 45°

3. Given △RST, find the length of each leg.

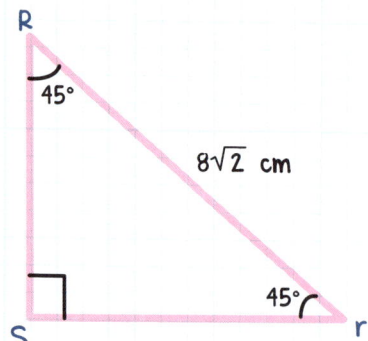

4. Given △GHK, find the length of the shorter leg and the length of the hypotenuse.

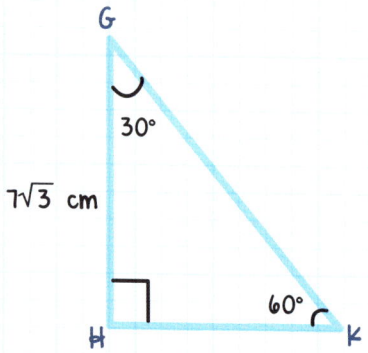

FIND THE MEASURE OF THE REFERENCE ANGLE FOR EACH OF THE GIVEN ANGLES.

5. 215°

6. $\dfrac{7\pi}{6}$

7. $\dfrac{3\pi}{5}$

8. $78°$

EVALUATE THE GIVEN TRIGONOMETRIC FUNCTION WITHOUT USING A CALCULATOR.

9. $\csc \dfrac{5\pi}{3}$

10. $\cot \dfrac{9\pi}{4}$

11. $\cos \dfrac{4\pi}{3}$

12. $\sec \dfrac{\pi}{4}$

13. The Cortez family installs a 12-foot slide in their backyard. The base of the slide forms a 30° angle with the ground. How tall is the slide's ladder?

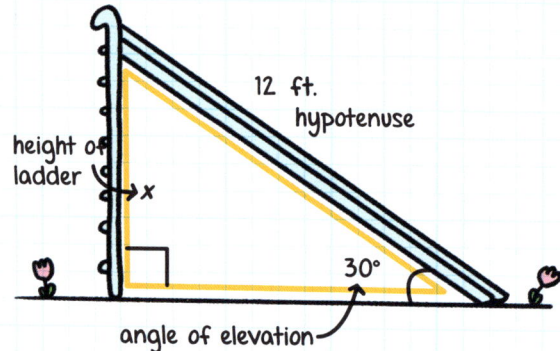

12 ft. hypotenuse

height of ladder ↳ →x

30°

angle of elevation

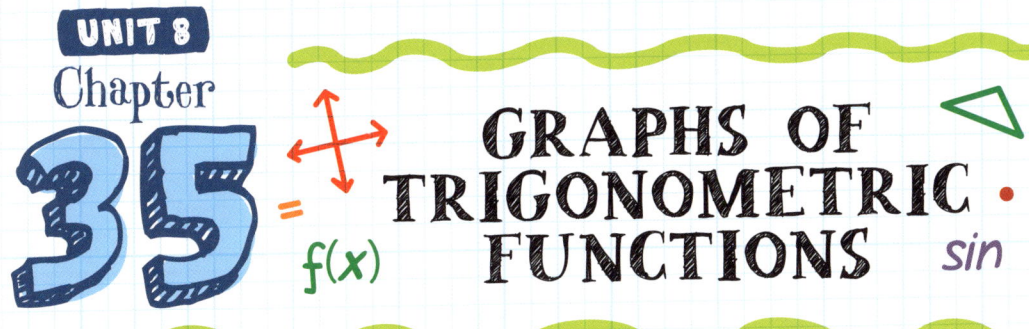

GRAPHS OF TRIGONOMETRIC FUNCTIONS

$f(x)$ = sin

Trigonometric functions are **PERIODIC**. Periodic functions repeat at regular intervals. One complete interval is called a **CYCLE**. The length of a cycle is called a **PERIOD**.

$f(x) = \sin x$ is periodic with period 2π. It is an **odd** function. It is symmetrical about the origin.

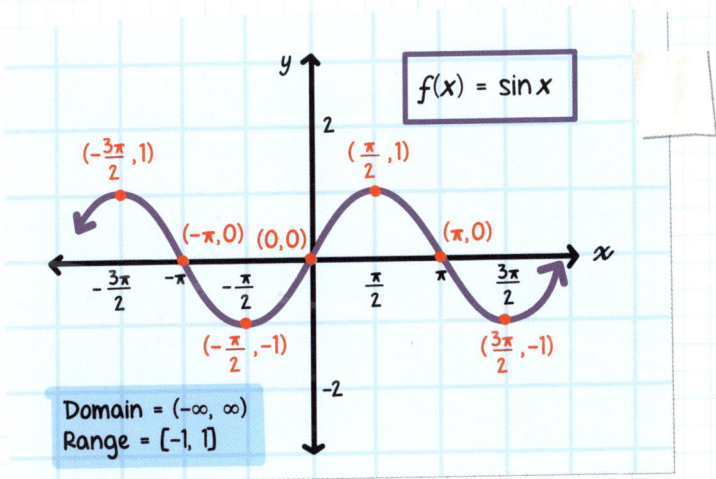

$f(x) = \sin x$

$\left(-\frac{3\pi}{2}, 1\right)$ $\left(\frac{\pi}{2}, 1\right)$

$(-\pi, 0)$ $(0, 0)$ $(\pi, 0)$

$\left(-\frac{\pi}{2}, -1\right)$ $\left(\frac{3\pi}{2}, -1\right)$

Domain = $(-\infty, \infty)$
Range = $[-1, 1]$

$f(x) = \cos x$ is also periodic with period 2π. It is an **even** function and symmetrical across the y-axis.

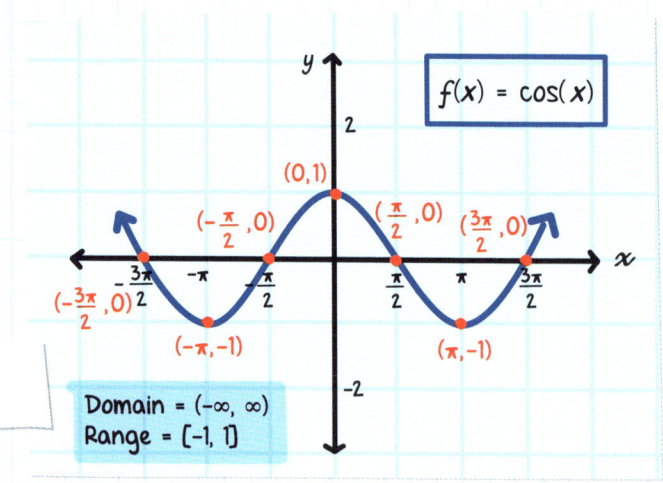

$f(x) = \tan x$ **is periodic with period** π. Also, it is an **odd** function.

When we extend the graph infinitely in both directions, it looks like this:

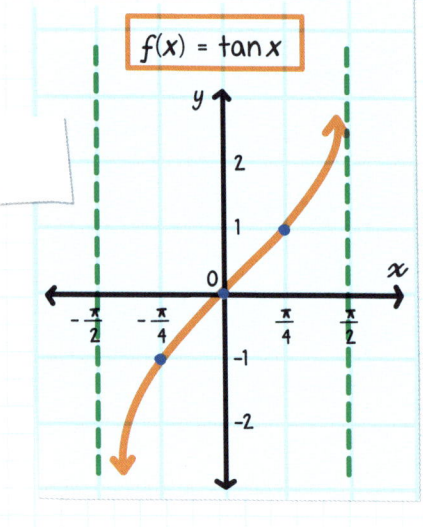

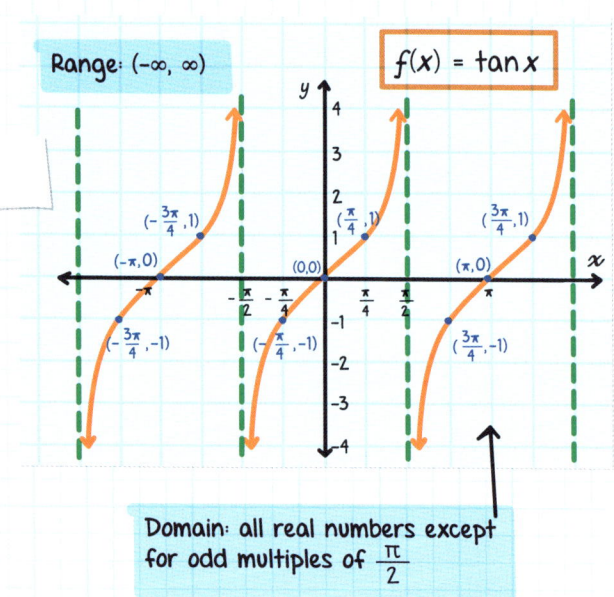

Domain: all real numbers except for odd multiples of $\frac{\pi}{2}$

Here is a formula for more general sine and cosine functions.

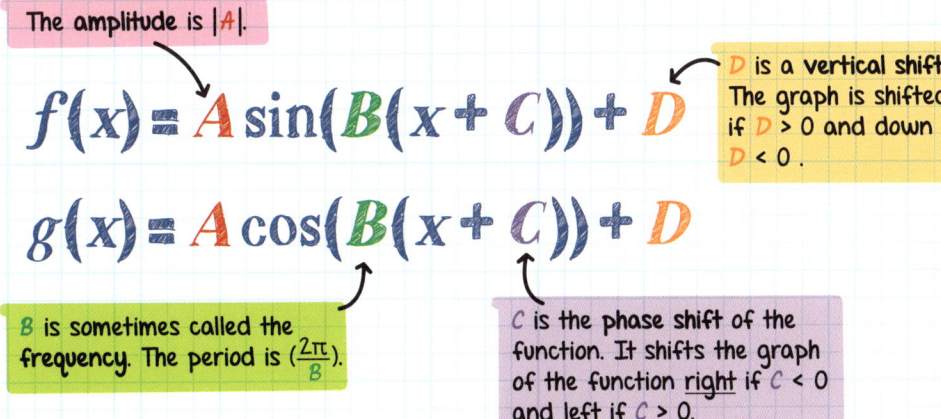

The amplitude is $|A|$.

$$f(x) = A \sin(B(x + C)) + D$$

$$g(x) = A \cos(B(x + C)) + D$$

D is a vertical shift. The graph is shifted up if $D > 0$ and down if $D < 0$.

B is sometimes called the frequency. The period is $\left(\frac{2\pi}{B}\right)$.

C is the phase shift of the function. It shifts the graph of the function <u>right</u> if $C < 0$ and <u>left</u> if $C > 0$.

EXAMPLE: Graph $w(x) = 2\cos(x - \pi) + 1$.

STEP 1: Identify the amplitude, frequency, phase shift, and vertical shift.

$w(x) = 2\cos(1x - \pi) + 1$

The amplitude of this cosine function is 2.

The frequency is 1.

Therefore, the period of the function is 2π.

$$\frac{2\pi}{B} = \frac{2\pi}{1} = 2\pi$$

The phase shift is $^-\pi$. Since $^-\pi < 0$, the graph shifts π units to the right.

The vertical shift is $+1$. Therefore, the graph shifts up 1 unit.

Now we are ready to graph the function.

STEP 2: The amplitude of this cosine function is 2. So, vertically stretch $f(x) = \cos x$, by a factor of 2 to get the graph of $g(x) = 2\cos x$. The range of g is [-2, 2].

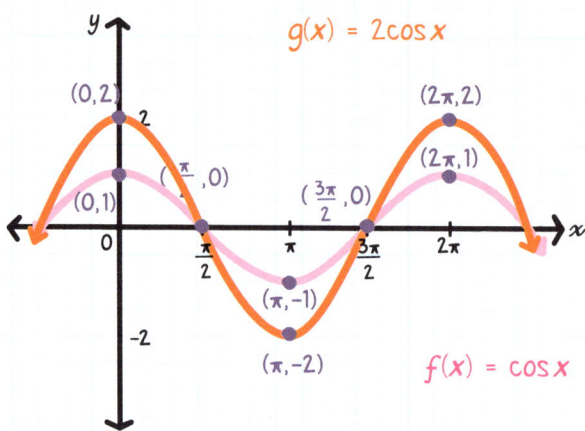

STEP 3: The phase shift is $^-\pi$. Therefore, shift the graph of $g(x) = 2\cos x$ to the right π units to get the graph of $h(x) = 2\cos(1x - \pi)$.

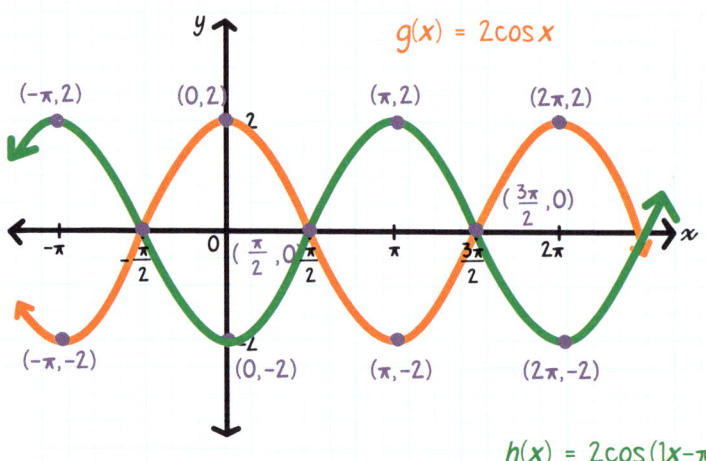

STEP 4: The vertical shift is $+1$. Shift the graph of $h(x) = 2\cos(x - \pi)$ up 1 unit to get the graph of $w(x) = 2\cos(x - \pi) + 1$. The range of w is $[-1, 3]$.

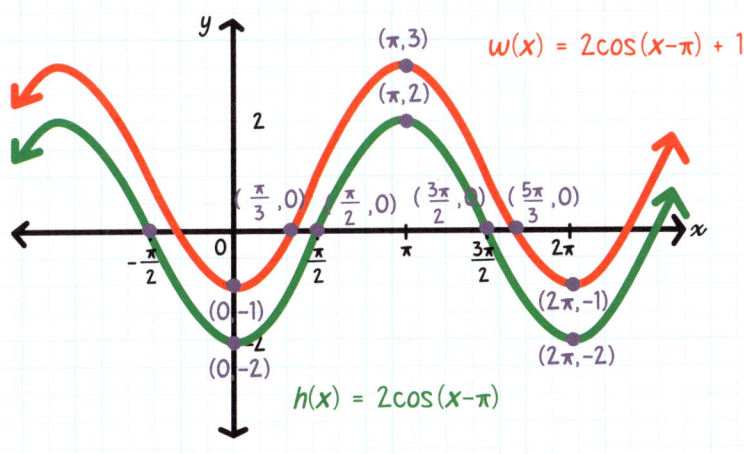

MATCH THE FUNCTION WITH ITS GRAPH.

1. $f(x) = \sin 5x$ _____

2. $g(x) = 3\cos\dfrac{3}{4}x$ _____

3. $h(x) = 2\sin(x - 2\pi) - 1$ _____

4. $q(x) = \cos(x + \dfrac{\pi}{6})$ _____

5. $j(x) = 4\cos(x + \dfrac{\pi}{6})$ _____

A.

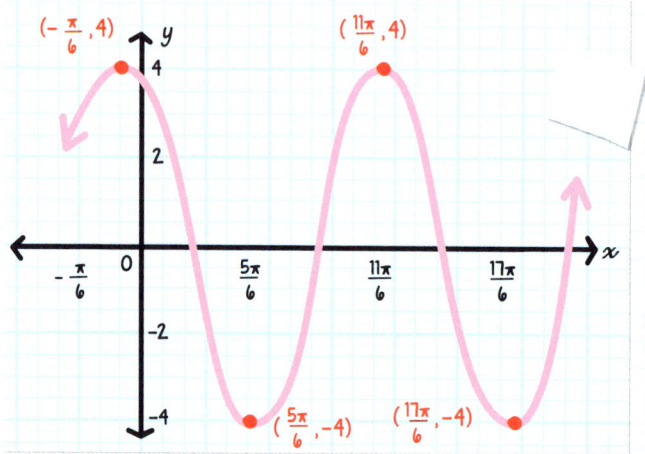

B.

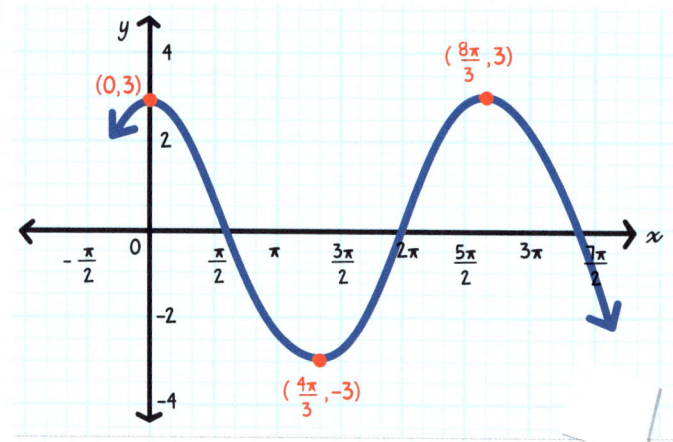

C.

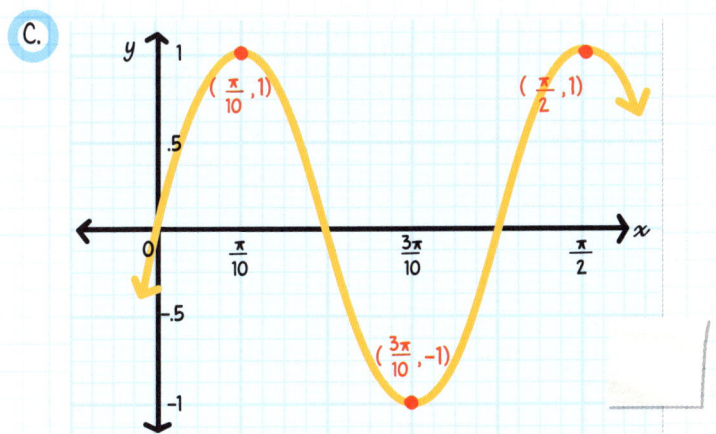

D.

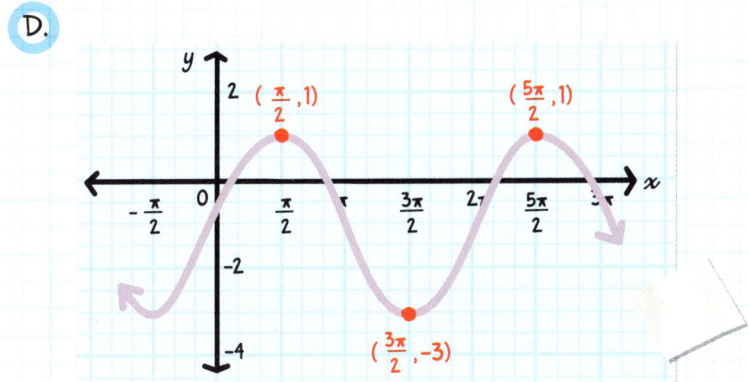

E.

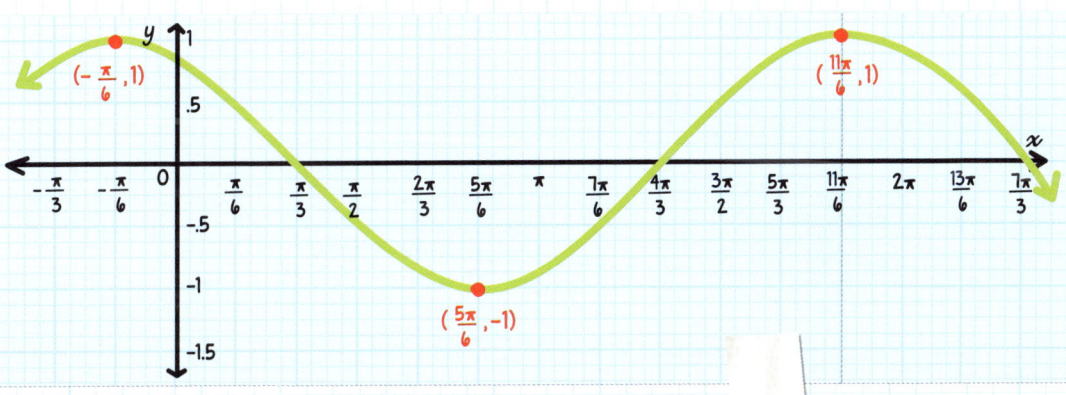

DRAW ONE CYCLE OF THE FUNCTION'S GRAPH.

6. $f(x) = \frac{1}{4}\cos 2x$

7. $h(x) = \sin(3x) + 4$

8. $w(x) = \cos(x - \pi)$

9. $g(x) = 2\sin(x - \frac{\pi}{2}) + 1$

10. $j(x) = \sin 2x - 2$

11. $v(x) = \cos(x + \frac{\pi}{2})$

12. $d(x) = 3\sin(x - \pi) - 2$

sin x ○ INVERSE $^{-1}$ f(x)
TRIGONOMETRIC
△ FUNCTIONS ≤ $\frac{\pi}{2}$
y = □

The graph of the function $f(x) = \sin x$ *fails* the horizontal line test, and therefore it is *not* invertible.

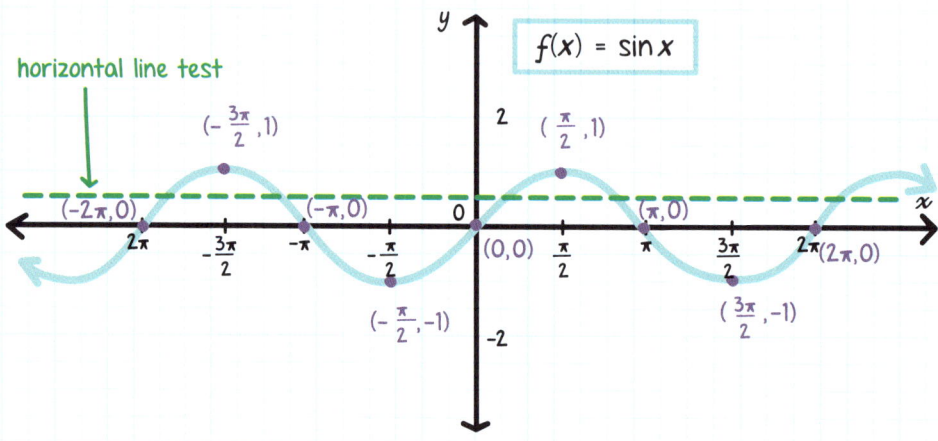

horizontal line test

$f(x) = \sin x$

$(-\frac{3\pi}{2}, 1)$ $(\frac{\pi}{2}, 1)$

$(-2\pi, 0)$ $(-\pi, 0)$ $(\pi, 0)$ $(2\pi, 0)$

2π $-\frac{3\pi}{2}$ $-\pi$ $-\frac{\pi}{2}$ $(0,0)$ $\frac{\pi}{2}$ π $\frac{3\pi}{2}$ 2π

$(-\frac{\pi}{2}, -1)$ $(\frac{3\pi}{2}, -1)$

However, if we restrict the domain of $f(x) = \sin x$ so that $-\frac{\pi}{2} \leq x \leq \frac{\pi}{2}$, then the resulting function *is* invertible.

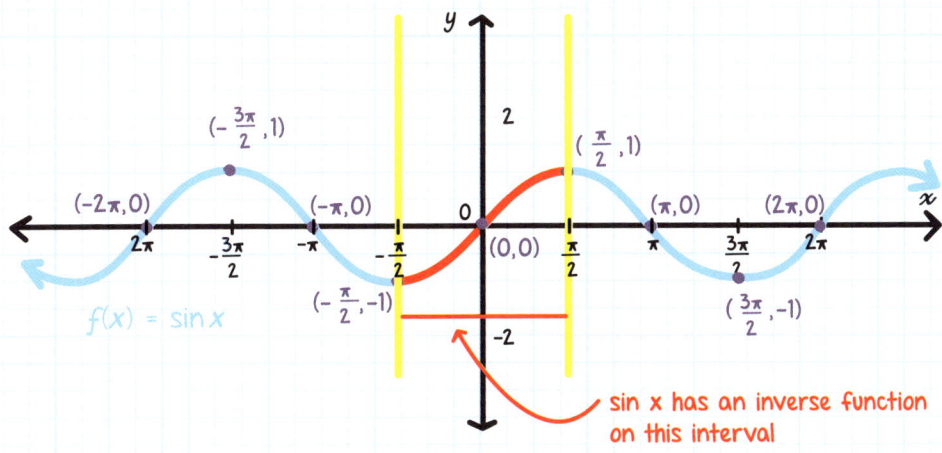

sin x has an inverse function on this interval

We call the inverse of this restricted sine function the **ARCSINE FUNCTION** (or **INVERSE SINE FUNCTION**), and we write it as $f^{-1}(x) = \arcsin x$ or $f^{-1}(x) = \sin^{-1} x$.

The function $g(x) = \arcsin x$ has the following properties:

▶ Domain: $[-1, 1]$ ▶ Range: $\left[-\frac{\pi}{2}, \frac{\pi}{2}\right]$

▶ $y = \arcsin x$ *if and only if* $x = \sin y$ and $-\frac{\pi}{2} \leq y \leq \frac{\pi}{2}$.

▶ $\arcsin(\sin x) = x$ as long as $-\frac{\pi}{2} \leq x \leq \frac{\pi}{2}$.

▶ $\sin(\arcsin x) = x$ as long as $-1 \leq x \leq 1$.

▶ $\arcsin(-x) = -\arcsin x$

The graph of the function $f(x) = \cos x$ also *fails* the horizontal line test, and therefore it is *not* invertible.

However, if we restrict the domain of $f(x) = \cos x$ so that $0 \leq x \leq \pi$, then the resulting function *is* invertible.

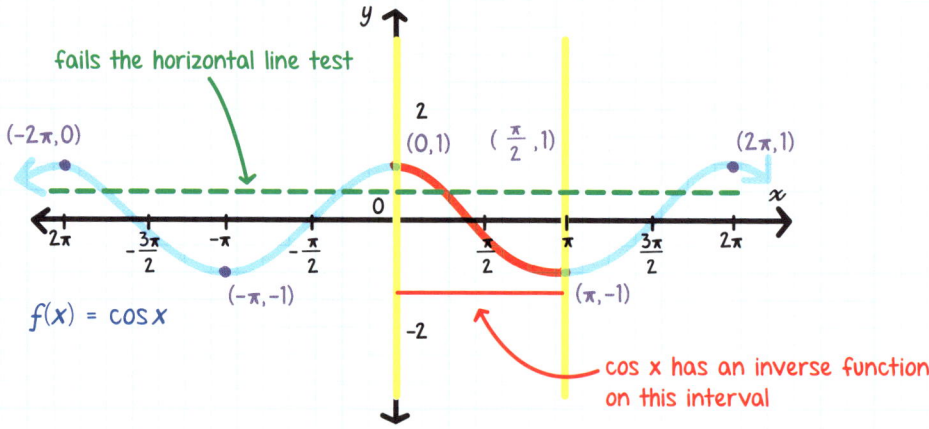

We call this function the **ARCCOSINE FUNCTION** (or **INVERSE COSINE FUNCTION**), and we write it as $f^{-1}(x) = \arccos x$ or $f^{-1}(x) = \cos^{-1} x$.

The function $g(x) = \arccos x$ has the following properties:

▶ Domain: $[-1, 1]$ ▶ Range: $[0, \pi]$

▶ $y = \arccos x$ *if and only if* $x = \cos y$ and $0 \leq y \leq \pi$.

▶ $\arccos(\cos x) = x$ as long as $0 \leq x \leq \pi$.

▶ $\cos(\arccos x) = x$ as long as $-1 \leq x \leq 1$.

▶ $\arccos(-x) = \pi - \arccos x$

The graph of $f(x) = \tan x$ also *fails* the horizontal line test, and therefore it is *not* invertible.

However, if we restrict the domain of $f(x) = \tan x$ so that $-\frac{\pi}{2} < x < \frac{\pi}{2}$, then the resulting function *is* invertible.

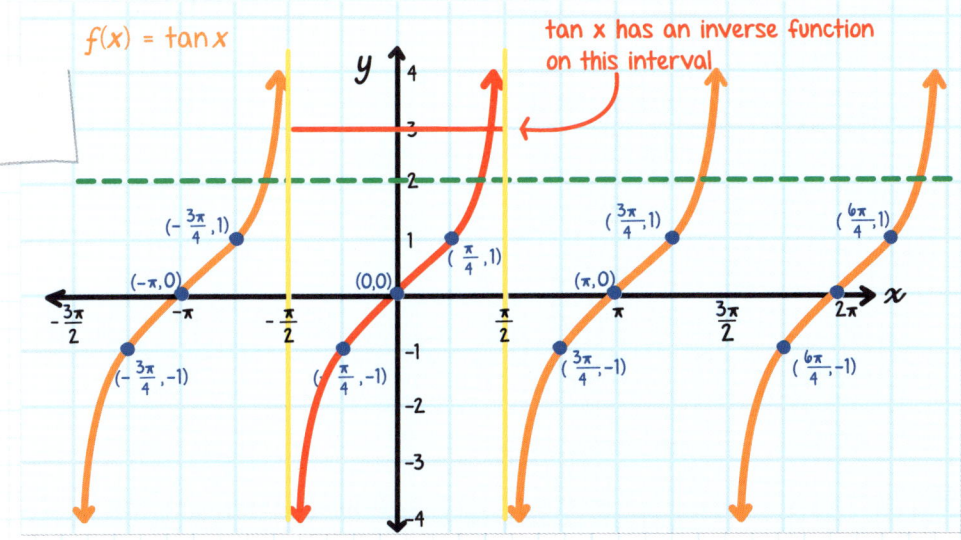

We call this function the **ARCTAN FUNCTION** (or **INVERSE TANGENT FUNCTION**), and we write it as $f^{-1}(x) = \arctan x$ or $f^{-1}(x) = \tan^{-1} x$.

The function $g(x) = \arctan x$ has the following properties:

▶ Domain: $(-\infty, \infty)$　　▶ Range: $\left(-\frac{\pi}{2}, \frac{\pi}{2}\right)$

▶ $y = \arctan x$ if *and only if* $x = \tan y$ and $-\frac{\pi}{2} < y < \frac{\pi}{2}$.

▶ $\arctan(\tan x) = x$ as long as $-\frac{\pi}{2} < x < \frac{\pi}{2}$.

▶ $\tan(\arctan x) = x$ for all real x.

▶ $\arctan(-x) = -\arctan x$

EXAMPLE: Evaluate the inverse trigonometric expression $\arcsin(-\frac{\sqrt{2}}{2})$ without using a calculator.

$\theta = \arcsin(-\frac{\sqrt{2}}{2})$ *if and only if* $\sin\theta = -\frac{\sqrt{2}}{2}$ and $-\frac{\pi}{2} \leq \theta \leq \frac{\pi}{2}$.

 **THINK:**

We are looking for an angle in radians whose sine is $-\frac{\sqrt{2}}{2}$, and this angle must be between $-\frac{\pi}{2}$ and $\frac{\pi}{2}$.

Since $\sin(-\frac{\pi}{4}) = -\frac{\sqrt{2}}{2}$ and $-\frac{\pi}{2} \leq -\frac{\pi}{4} \leq \frac{\pi}{2}$, $\arcsin(-\frac{\sqrt{2}}{2}) = -\frac{\pi}{4}$.

EXAMPLE: Find the measure of the angle shown. Then approximate the answer to the nearest degree.

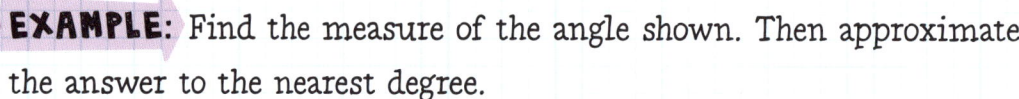

To find θ, first write a trigonometric ratio.

$\cos\theta = \frac{ADJ}{HYP} = \frac{5}{12}$

Use the inverse cosine to solve for θ.

$\theta = \cos^{-1}\frac{5}{12}$

Next, use a scientific or graphing calculator to find the approximate degree measure of θ. You should get: 65.38 . . .

Round this measurement to the nearest degree: 65°.

So, θ ≈ 65°.

EXAMPLE: Evaluate $\cos(\arctan \frac{17}{11})$.

STEP 1: Recall the arctan $\frac{17}{11}$ is an angle. If we call this angle θ, then, θ = arctan $\frac{17}{11}$. So, tan θ = $\frac{17}{11}$.

STEP 2: Draw a right triangle and label one of the acute angles θ.

tan θ = $\frac{17}{11}$ = $\frac{OPP}{ADJ}$, so label the side opposite this angle 17, and the side adjacent to this angle 11.

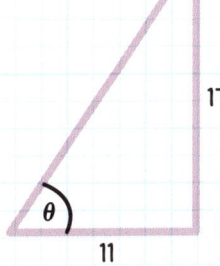

STEP 3: Use the Pythagorean Theorem to find the length of the hypotenuse of this triangle.

Let's let the length of the hypotenuse be equal to c.

$17^2 + 11^2 = c^2$

$410 = c^2$

$\sqrt{410} = c$

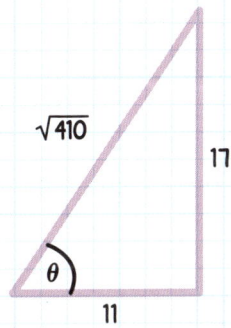

Use the triangle to find cos θ.

$$\cos\theta = \frac{ADJ}{HYP} = \frac{11}{\sqrt{410}}$$

Therefore, $\cos\left(\arctan\dfrac{17}{11}\right) = \dfrac{11}{\sqrt{410}}$. This can also be written as $\dfrac{11\sqrt{410}}{410}$.
(To see that these two expressions are equivalent, we can rationalize the denominator of the first expression.)

I SURE AM WORKING HARD! RIGHT?

EVALUATE THE GIVEN INVERSE TRIGONOMETRIC EXPRESSION WITHOUT USING A CALCULATOR.

1. $\sin^{-1}\dfrac{\sqrt{3}}{2}$

2. $\arccos\left(-\dfrac{\sqrt{2}}{2}\right)$

3. $\arcsin 2$

4. $\arctan(-1)$

5. $\cos^{-1}(\frac{\sqrt{3}}{2})$

6. $\tan^{-1}(\frac{1}{\sqrt{3}})$

FIND THE MEASURE OF THE ANGLE SHOWN. THEN APPROXIMATE YOUR ANSWER TO THE NEAREST DEGREE.

7.

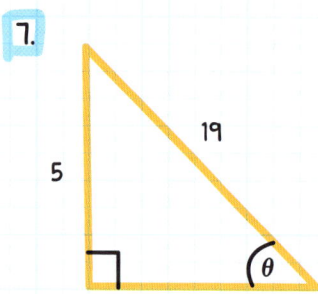

5

19

θ

8.

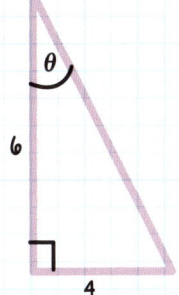

9.

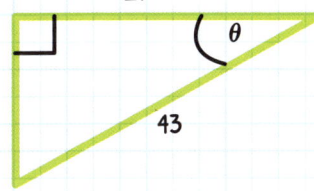

10.

EVALUATE THE GIVEN EXPRESSION.

11. $\cos(\sin^{-1}\frac{1}{4})$

12. $\sin(\tan^{-1}\frac{7}{2})$

13. $\tan(\cos^{-1}\frac{1}{2})$

14. $\tan(\sin^{-1}\frac{5}{8})$

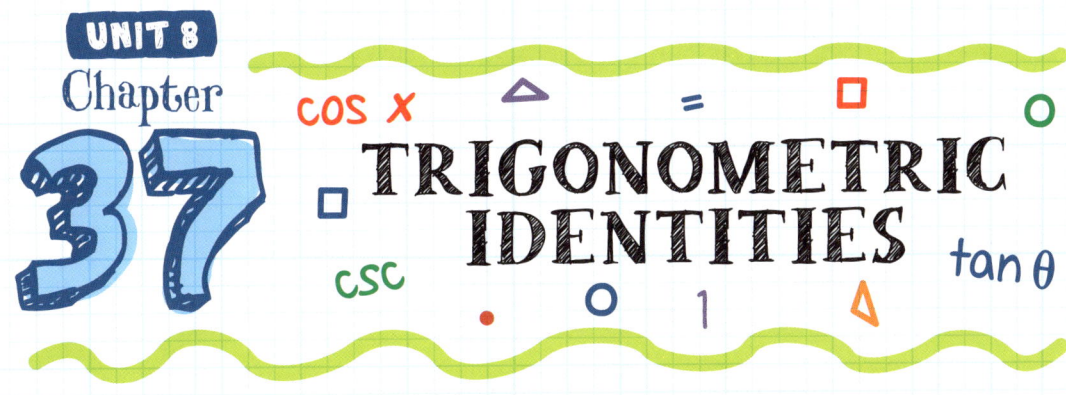

UNIT 8
Chapter
37
cos x
TRIGONOMETRIC
IDENTITIES
csc
tan θ

An **IDENTITY** is an equation that is ALWAYS true.

A **TRIGONOMETRIC IDENTITY** is an identity that contains at least one trigonometric function.

Reciprocal Identities:

$$\sin \theta = \frac{1}{\csc \theta} \qquad \csc \theta = \frac{1}{\sin \theta}$$

$$\cos \theta = \frac{1}{\sec \theta} \qquad \sec \theta = \frac{1}{\cos \theta}$$

$$\tan \theta = \frac{1}{\cot \theta} \qquad \cot \theta = \frac{1}{\tan \theta}$$

Quotient Identities:

$$\tan \theta = \frac{\sin \theta}{\cos \theta}$$

$$\cot \theta = \frac{\cos \theta}{\sin \theta}$$

Negative Identities:

$$\sin(-\theta) = -\sin \theta \qquad \csc(-\theta) = -\csc \theta$$

$$\tan(-\theta) = -\tan \theta \qquad \cot(-\theta) = -\cot \theta$$

$$\cos(-\theta) = \cos \theta \qquad \sec(-\theta) = \sec \theta$$

Trigonometric identities can be used to simplify trigonometric expressions.

EXAMPLE: Simplify $\dfrac{\csc x}{\sec x}$.

STEP 1: Rewrite the expression using the Reciprocal Identities $\csc\theta = \dfrac{1}{\sin\theta}$ and $\sec\theta = \dfrac{1}{\cos\theta}$.

$$\frac{\csc x}{\sec x} = \frac{\dfrac{1}{\sin x}}{\dfrac{1}{\cos x}}$$

STEP 2: Rewrite the expression with a division symbol instead of the fraction bar. Then flip and multiply.

$$\frac{1}{\sin x} \div \frac{1}{\cos x} = \frac{1}{\sin x} \cdot \frac{\cos x}{1} = \frac{\cos x}{\sin x}$$

STEP 3: Rewrite the expression using the appropriate Quotient Identity $\cot\theta = \dfrac{\cos\theta}{\sin\theta}$.

$$\frac{\cos x}{\sin x} = \cot x$$

So, $\dfrac{\csc x}{\sec x} = \cot x$.

We can verify (or prove) that a trigonometric identity is true by rewriting one side of the identity with a series of equivalent expressions until we get an expression that is equal to the other side.

EXAMPLE: Verify the identity: $\dfrac{1}{\sin x \cdot \cot x} = \dfrac{1}{\cos x}$.

STEP 1: Rewrite the left-hand side in terms of sines and/or cosines. Use the Quotient Identity $\cot \theta = \dfrac{\cos \theta}{\sin \theta}$.

$$\frac{1}{\sin x \cdot \cot x} = \frac{1}{\cos x}$$

$$\frac{1}{\sin x \cdot \dfrac{\cos x}{\sin x}} = \frac{1}{\cos x}$$

NICE!

STEP 2: Simplify the left-hand side.

$$\frac{1}{\sin x \cdot \dfrac{\cos x}{\sin x}} = \frac{1}{\cos x}$$

$$\frac{1}{\cos x} = \frac{1}{\cos x} \quad \checkmark$$

Helpful Tips for Verifying Identities

1. Try rewriting all trigonometric expressions in terms of sines and cosines.

2. Add and reduce any fractions. Simplify compound fractions. Factor when possible.

3. When a trigonometric expression appears on one side of the equal sign but not the other, attempt to substitute it with another expression by using a trigonometric identity, or attempt to eliminate it with algebraic manipulation.

Let's look at a few more advanced trigonometric identities.

Pythagorean Identities:

$\sin^2\theta + \cos^2\theta = 1$

$1 + \tan^2\theta = \sec^2\theta$

$1 + \cot^2\theta = \csc^2\theta$

Cofunction Identities:

$\sin\theta = \cos(\frac{\pi}{2} - \theta)$ $\cos\theta = \sin(\frac{\pi}{2} - \theta)$

$\sec\theta = \csc(\frac{\pi}{2} - \theta)$ $\csc\theta = \sec(\frac{\pi}{2} - \theta)$

$\tan\theta = \cot(\frac{\pi}{2} - \theta)$ $\cot\theta = \tan(\frac{\pi}{2} - \theta)$

EXAMPLE: Simplify: $\sin(\frac{\pi}{2} - x)\csc x$.

STEP 1: Rewrite the expression using a **COFUNCTION IDENTITY** and a **RECIPROCAL IDENTITY**.

Cofunction Identity: $\cos\theta = \sin(\frac{\pi}{2} - \theta)$

Reciprocal Identity: $\csc\theta = \dfrac{1}{\sin\theta}$

$\sin(\frac{\pi}{2} - x)\csc x = \cos x \cdot \dfrac{1}{\sin x}$

STEP 2: Multiply. Then use the Quotient Identity: $\cot\theta = \dfrac{\cos\theta}{\sin\theta}$.

$\cos x \cdot \dfrac{1}{\sin x} = \dfrac{\cos x}{\sin x} = \cot x$

So, $\sin(\frac{\pi}{2} - x)\csc x = \cot x$.

SIMPLIFY EACH TRIGONOMETRIC EXPRESSION.

1. $\dfrac{\sin(-x)}{\cos(-x)}$

2. $\dfrac{\sec x}{\tan x}$

3. $\dfrac{\tan\left(\dfrac{\pi}{2} - \theta\right)}{\sec \theta}$

4. $\dfrac{\cos^2(-x)}{\cot^2 x}$

CHAPTER 37

VERIFY EACH IDENTITY.

5. $\csc x \tan x = \sec x$

6. $\dfrac{\cos^2 \theta}{1 + \sin \theta} = 1 - \sin \theta$

7. $\sin(\dfrac{\pi}{2} - x) \tan x = \sin x$

8. $\dfrac{\cos^2(-x)}{\cot^2 x} = \sin^2 x$

9. $\dfrac{\tan\theta - \cot\theta}{\sec\theta + \csc\theta} = \sin\theta - \cos\theta$

10. $\dfrac{1+\sin x}{\cos x} = \dfrac{\cos x}{1-\sin x}$

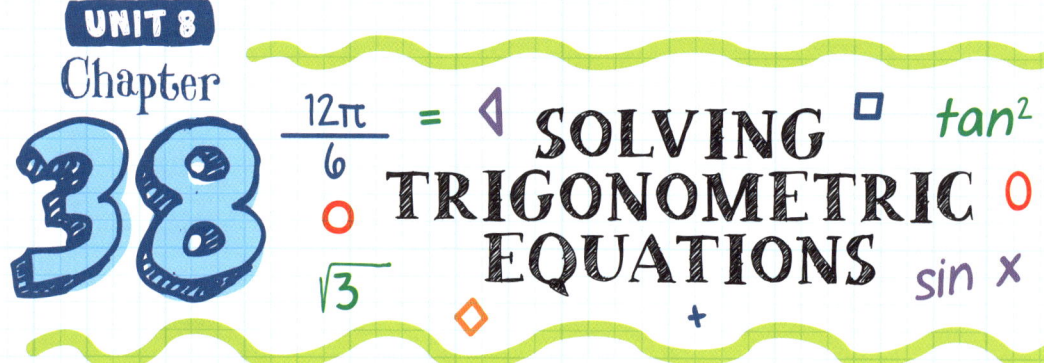

SOLVING TRIGONOMETRIC EQUATIONS

A **TRIGONOMETRIC EQUATION** is an equation in which a variable appears inside a trigonometric function.

EXAMPLE: Solve each equation on the interval $[0, 2\pi]$.

▶ $\cos x - \dfrac{\sqrt{3}}{2} = 0$

$\cos x - \dfrac{\sqrt{3}}{2} + \dfrac{\sqrt{3}}{2} = 0 + \dfrac{\sqrt{3}}{2}$

$\cos x = \dfrac{\sqrt{3}}{2}$

Since $\dfrac{\sqrt{3}}{2} > 0$ and cosine is positive in the first and fourth quadrants, we need to find two solutions: one between 0 and $\dfrac{\pi}{2}$ (the Quadrant I solution) and another between $\dfrac{3\pi}{2}$ and 2π (the Quadrant IV solution).

The Quadrant I solution is simply $x = \cos^{-1}(\dfrac{\sqrt{3}}{2}) = \dfrac{\pi}{6}$.

The Quadrant IV solution is $x = 2\pi - \dfrac{\pi}{6} = \dfrac{12\pi}{6} - \dfrac{\pi}{6} = \dfrac{11\pi}{6}$.

So, on the interval $[0, 2\pi]$, the solutions are $\dfrac{\pi}{6}$ and $\dfrac{11\pi}{6}$.

▶ $2\tan x = \sec x$

Rewrite the expression on the left using the Quotient Identity $\tan x = \dfrac{\sin x}{\cos x}$ and the expression on the right using the Reciprocal Identity $\sec x = \dfrac{1}{\cos x}$.

$$2\,\frac{\sin x}{\cos x} = \frac{1}{\cos x}$$

To remove the denominators, multiply both sides of the equation by $\cos x$.

$$\cos x \left(2\,\frac{\sin x}{\cos x}\right) = \left(\frac{1}{\cos x}\right)\cos x$$

$$2\sin x = 1$$

$$\frac{2\sin x}{2} = \frac{1}{2}$$

$$\sin x = \frac{1}{2}$$

THINK:

Since we eliminated the denominator $\cos x$, it is possible that **extraneous solutions** can appear.

Check any possible solutions at the end to make sure they are not extraneous.

Since $\dfrac{1}{2} > 0$ and sine is positive in the first and second quadrants, we need to find two solutions: one between 0 and $\dfrac{\pi}{2}$ (the Quadrant I solution) and another between $\dfrac{\pi}{2}$ and π (the Quadrant II solution).

The Quadrant I solution is simply $x = \sin^{-1}\left(\dfrac{1}{2}\right) = \dfrac{\pi}{6}$.

The Quadrant II solution is $x = \pi - \dfrac{\pi}{6} = \dfrac{6\pi}{6} - \dfrac{\pi}{6} = \dfrac{5\pi}{6}$.

Since neither of these solutions would make $\cos x = 0$, they are *not* extraneous.

So, on the interval $[0, 2\pi]$, the solutions are $\dfrac{\pi}{6}$ and $\dfrac{5\pi}{6}$.

▶ $\sec^2 x + \tan^2 x = 3$

To solve this trigonometric equation, we can use the Pythagorean Identity $\sec^2 x = \tan^2 x + 1$.

$\sec^2 x + \tan^2 x = 3$

$(\tan^2 x + 1) + \tan^2 x = 3$

$\tan^2 x + \tan^2 x = 2$

$2\tan^2 x = 2$

$\tan^2 x = 1$

$\tan x = \pm 1$ Square Root Property

Between 0 and 2π, $\tan x = 1$ when $x = \frac{\pi}{4}$ or $x = \frac{5\pi}{4}$.

Similarly, between 0 and 2π, $\tan x = -1$ when $x = \frac{3\pi}{4}$ or $x = \frac{7\pi}{4}$.

So, on the interval $[0, 2\pi]$, the solutions are $\frac{\pi}{4}$, $\frac{3\pi}{4}$, $\frac{5\pi}{4}$, and $\frac{7\pi}{4}$.

LOOK AT ME GO!

SOLVE EACH EQUATION ON THE INTERVAL $[0, 2\pi]$.

1. $2\cos x - 1 = 0$

2. $3\sin x - 3 = 0$

3. $8\sin^2 x - 6 = 0$

4. $\sin x = \sqrt{2} - \sin x$

5. $\sin^2 x + 1 = 2\sin x$

6. $4\sin^2 x \cos x - 2\cos x = 0$

7. $2\sin x + \sin^2 x - 3 = 0$

8. $2\cot x + 2\cos x = \cot x$

9. $\cos^2 x = 2\sin x + 2$

10. $2\cos x + 1 = \sec x$

11. $4\cos^2 x - 3 = 0$

12. $2\sin x = \tan x$

WORK SPACE

YOU DID IT!

$\cos \theta$

SOLUTIONS

$(\sqrt[4]{n})$

$\dfrac{\pi}{6}$

Answer Key

UNIT 1

Fundamentals of Algebra

CHAPTER 1

LINEAR EQUATIONS AND INEQUALITIES

1 $\frac{3x}{4} + 25 = 9 - y$ Substitute
$x = -8$ and
$y = -10$.

$\frac{3(-8)}{4} + 25 \overset{?}{=} 9 - (-10)$

$-\frac{24}{4} + 25 \overset{?}{=} 9 + 10$

$-6 + 25 \overset{?}{=} 9 + 10$

$19 = 19$ ✓ Both sides of the
equation are equal.

$x = -8$, $y = -10$ is a solution
to the linear equation.

2 $7(13r + 2) = 40r - 88$

$7(13(-2) + 2) \overset{?}{=} 40(-2) - 88$ Substitute
$r = -2$.

$7(-24) \overset{?}{=} 40(-2) - 88$

$-168 \overset{?}{=} -80 - 88$

$-168 = -168$ ✓ Both sides of the
equation are equal.

$r = -2$ is a solution to
the linear equation.

3 $\frac{2mn}{mn} + 5 = 8m - 8n$ Substitute
$m = 5$ and
$n = 4$.

$\frac{2(5)(4)}{(5)(4)} + 5 \overset{?}{=} 8(5) - 8(4)$

$\frac{40}{20} + 5 \overset{?}{=} 40 - 32$

$2 + 5 \overset{?}{=} 40 - 32$

$7 \neq 8$ ✗ Both sides of the
equation are **not** equal.

$m = 5$, $n = 4$ is **not** a solution
to the linear equation.

4 $116 = 71 - 5g$

$116 - 71 = 71 - 71 - 5g$

$45 = -5g$

$45 \div (-5) = -5g \div (-5)$

$-9 = g$

5 $11x - 3 = 6(x + 12)$

$11x - 3 = 6x + 72$

$11x - 3 + 3 = 6x + 72 + 3$

$11x = 6x + 75$

$11x - 6x = 6x - 6x + 75$

$5x = 75$

$5x \div 5 = 75 \div 5$

$x = 15$

6 $\frac{10y - 4}{8} = -32$

$\frac{10y - 4}{8} \cdot 8 = -32 \cdot 8$

$10y - 4 = -256$

$10y - 4 + 4 = -256 + 4$

$10y = -252$

$10y \div 10 = -252 \div 10$

$y = -25.2$

7 $V = \frac{1}{3}bh$

$V \cdot 3 = \frac{1}{3}bh \cdot 3$

$3V = bh$

$3V \div b = bh \div b$

$\frac{3V}{b} = h$

8 $a = \frac{4}{5}c(b-d)$

$a \bullet \frac{5}{4} = \frac{4}{5}c(b-d) \bullet \frac{5}{4}$

$\frac{5}{4}a = c(b-d)$

$\frac{5}{4}a \div (b-d) = c(b-d) \div (b-d)$

$\frac{5a}{4(b-d)} = c$

9 Let r equal the revenue the owner received in the app's first month.

$\frac{r}{381,000} = \frac{45}{3000}$

$r = \frac{45}{3000} \bullet 381,000$

$r = 45 \bullet 127$

$r = 5,715$

The owner earned $5,715 in revenue in the first month.

10 $-15 - 9s \le 30$

$-15 + 15 - 9s \le 30 + 15$

$-9s \le 45$

$-9s \div (-9) \le 45 \div (-9)$

$s \ge -5$

Inequality Notation	Graphical Notation	Interval Notation
$s \ge -5$	-7 -5 -3 -1 0 1 2 3	$[-5, \infty)$

11 $3(2-w) - 4 > 17$

$6 - 3w - 4 > 17$

$2 - 3w > 17$

$2 - 2 - 3w > 17 - 2$

$-3w > 15$

$-3w \div (-3) > 15 \div (-3)$

$w < -5$

Inequality Notation	Graphical Notation	Interval Notation
$w < -5$	-11 -9 -7 -5 -3 -1 0 1	$(-\infty, -5]$

12 $\frac{3}{8} \ge 1\frac{1}{4}d - \frac{1}{2}$

$\frac{3}{8} + \frac{1}{2} \ge 1\frac{1}{4}d - \frac{1}{2} + \frac{1}{2}$

$\frac{3}{8} + \frac{1}{2} \ge 1\frac{1}{4}d$

$\frac{3}{8} + \frac{4}{8} \ge \frac{5}{4}d$

$\frac{7}{8} \ge \frac{5}{4}d$

$\frac{7}{8} \div \frac{5}{4} \ge \frac{5}{4}d \div \frac{5}{4}$

$\frac{7}{8} \bullet \frac{4}{5} \ge d$

$\frac{7}{10} \ge d$

Inequality Notation	Interval Notation
$d \le \frac{7}{10}$	$(-\infty, \frac{7}{10}]$

13 Let m = the total dollars that Ms. Dana started with.

$67 \le m - (548 + 213)$

$67 \le m - 761$

$67 + 761 \le m - 761 + 761$

$828 \le m$

$m \ge 828$

The least amount of money that Ms. Dana could have started with is $828.

CHAPTER 2

GRAPHING LINEAR EQUATIONS AND INEQUALITIES

1 Use any two points on the line. The points (–5, 0) and (0, 3) lie on the line. Substitute the values into the slope formula.

$$m = \frac{y_2 - y_1}{x_2 - x_1} = \frac{3 - 0}{0 - (-5)} = \frac{3}{5}$$

$$m = \frac{3}{5}$$

2 Plot the point (0, –4). Use the given slope of $\frac{4}{7}$ to draw the line. Rise 4 and run 7 from the starting point.

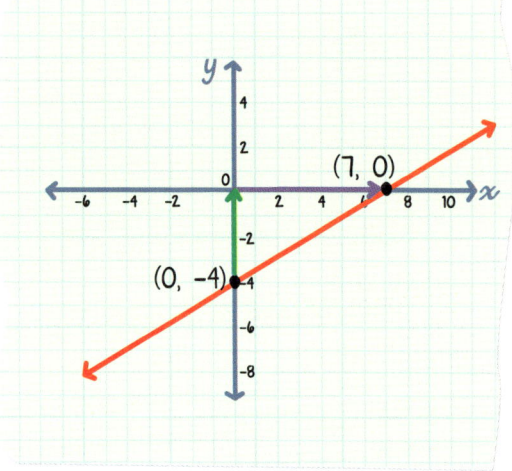

3 $m = \frac{y_2 - y_1}{x_2 - x_1} = \frac{4 - (-6)}{2 - 4} = \frac{10}{-2} = -5$

4 $m = \frac{y_2 - y_1}{x_2 - x_1} = \frac{-3 - (-5)}{9 - 7} = \frac{2}{2} = 1$

5 The equation $y = 7x - 3$ is in the slope-intercept form $y = mx + b$. So, we have $b = -3$, and know the y-intercept is (0, –3).

The x-intercept is where the line intersects the x-axis and the y-coordinate is 0, so we can find the x-intercept by substituting $y = 0$ into the equation.

$y = 7x - 3$
$0 = 7x - 3$
$0 + 3 = 7x - 3 + 3$
$3 = 7x$
$x = \frac{3}{7}$

The x-intercept is $(\frac{3}{7}, 0)$ and the y-intercept is (0, –3).

6 Solve for y to write the equation in slope-intercept form.

$y - 6 = 8(x - 2)$
$y - 6 = 8x - 16$
$y = 8x - 10$

The slope is $m = 8$.
Substitute any value of x to find a point on the line.

If $x = 2$, $y = 8(2) - 10 = 6$. The line passes through the point $(2, 6)$.

7 Substitute the values of the given coordinate points into the slope formula to find the slope.

$$m = \frac{27 - 9}{19 - (-5)} = \frac{18}{24} = \frac{3}{4}$$

Write the equation of the line in point-slope form.

$$y - y_1 = m(x - x_1)$$
$$y - 27 = \frac{3}{4}(x - 19)$$

Write the equation of the line in slope-intercept form by isolating y.

$$y - 27 = \frac{3}{4}x - 14.25$$
$$y - 27 + 27 = \frac{3}{4}x - 14.25 + 27$$
$$y = \frac{3}{4}x + 12.75$$

8 Use the slope formula to find the slope of each line.

$$m_j = \frac{15 - (-12)}{5 - (-4)} = \frac{27}{9} = 3$$
$$m_p = \frac{(-2) - 3}{6 - (-9)} = \frac{-5}{15} = -\frac{1}{3}$$

9 The slopes are negative reciprocals, so line j and line p are **perpendicular**.

10 We know the slope and a point on each line. So, we can write the equation of each line in point-slope form and then solve for y to convert each equation to slope-intercept form.

Line j:
$$y - y_1 = m(x - x_1)$$
$$y - 15 = 3(x - 5) \longleftarrow \text{point-slope form}$$
$$y - 15 = 3x - 15$$
$$y - 15 + 15 = 3x - 15 + 15$$
$$y = 3x \longleftarrow \text{slope-intercept form}$$

Line p:
$$y - y_1 = m(x - x_1)$$
$$y - 3 = -\frac{1}{3}(x - (-9)) \longleftarrow \text{point-slope form}$$
$$y - 3 = -\frac{1}{3}(x + 9)$$
$$y - 3 = -\frac{1}{3}x - 3$$
$$y - 3 + 3 = -\frac{1}{3}x - 3 + 3$$
$$y = -\frac{1}{3}x \longleftarrow \text{slope-intercept form}$$

11 Rewrite the inequality as an equation: $y = \frac{1}{2}x + 4$.

This linear equation is in slope-intercept form, so we know that the y-intercept is $(0, 4)$ and the slope is $\frac{1}{2}$. Graph this line. Use a solid line because $\geq$ includes solutions on the line.

Test the point (0, 0).

$$0 \overset{?}{\geq} \frac{1}{2}(0) + 4$$

$0 \geq 4$ ✗ False

Since this statement is false, shade the side of the line that does not include (0, 0).

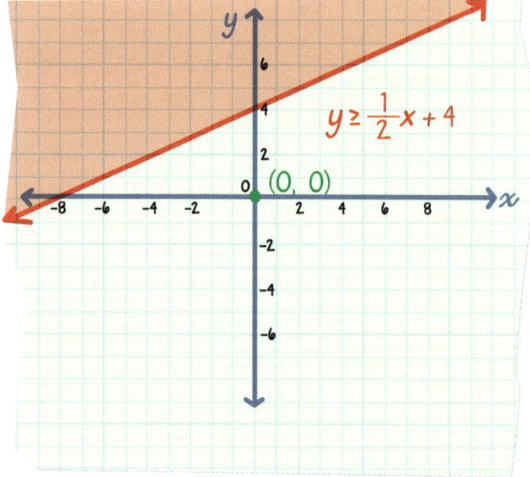

$$y \geq \frac{1}{2}x + 4$$

(0, 0)

12 Rewrite the inequality as an equation: $-9x - 3y = 6$.

Rewrite the equation in slope-intercept form.

$$-9x - 3y = 6$$
$$-3y = 9x + 6$$
$$y = -3x - 2$$

The y-intercept is (0, -2) and the slope is -3. Graph this line. Use a dashed line because < does not include solutions on the line.

Test the point (0, 0).

$$-9(0) - 3(0) \overset{?}{<} 6$$

$0 < 6$ ✓ True

Since this statement is true, shade the side of the line that includes (0, 0).

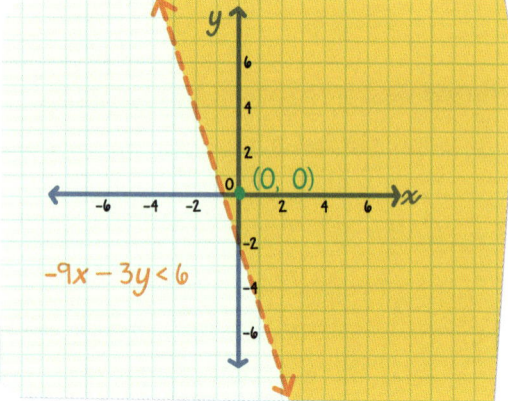

(0, 0)

$$-9x - 3y < 6$$

13 Rewrite the inequality as an equation: $y + \frac{1}{3}x = 4$.

Rewrite the equation in slope-intercept form.

$$y + \frac{1}{3}x = 4$$
$$y = -\frac{1}{3}x + 4$$

The y-intercept is (0, 4) and the slope is $-\frac{1}{3}$. Graph this line. Use a solid line because ≤ includes solutions on the line.

Test the point (0, 0).

$$(0) + \frac{1}{3}(0) \overset{?}{\leq} 4$$

$$0 \leq 4 \quad \checkmark \quad \text{True}$$

Since this statement is true, shade the side of the line that includes (0, 0).

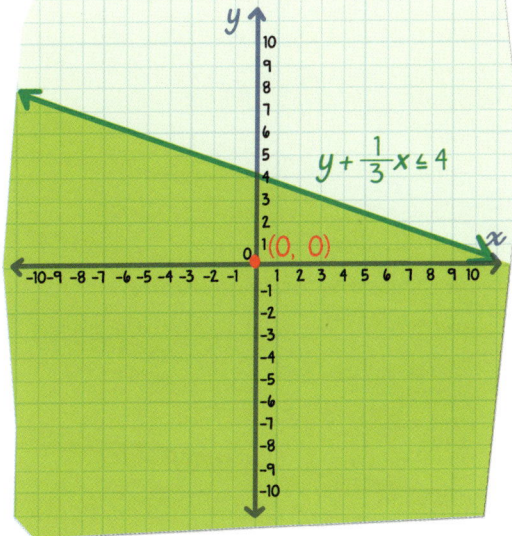

CHAPTER 3

SOLVING ABSOLUTE VALUE EQUATIONS AND INEQUALITIES

① $|x - 6| = 4$
The distance between x and 6 is 4.

So, x is <u>4 less than 6</u> or <u>4 more than 6</u>.

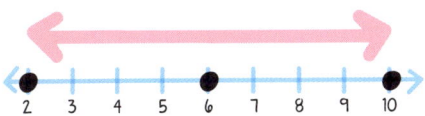

$$|x - 6| = 4$$
$$|2 - 6| = |10 - 6| = 4$$

The solutions to the absolute value equation are $x = 2$ and $x = 10$.

② $|x - 3| = 12$
The distance between x and 3 is 12.

So, x is <u>12 less than 3</u> or <u>12 more than 3</u>.

$$|x - 3| = 12$$
$$|-9 - 3| = |15 - 3| = 12$$

The solutions to the absolute value equation are $x = -9$ and $x = 15$.

③ $|x - 7| = 9$
The distance between x and 7 is 9.

So, x is <u>9 less than 7</u> or <u>9 more than 7</u>.

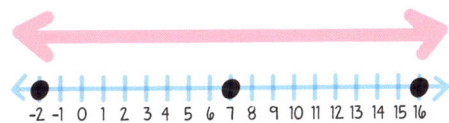

$$|x - 7| = 9$$
$$|-2 - 7| = |16 - 7| = 9$$

The solutions to the absolute value equation are $x = -2$ and $x = 16$.

4 Isolate the absolute value.
$$9|x + 2| = 27$$
$$(9|x + 2|) \div 9 = 27 \div 9$$
$$|x + 2| = 3$$

Rewrite the absolute value inequality as two linear equations. Then solve.

$x + 2 = 3$	$x + 2 = -3$
$x + 2 - 2 = 3 - 2$	$x + 2 - 2 = -3 - 2$
$x = 1$	$x = -5$

Solutions: $x = 1$ and $x = -5$

5 Isolate the absolute value.
$$2 + 5|x - 6| = 12$$
$$2 - 2 + 5|x - 6| = 12 - 2$$
$$(5|x - 6|) \div 5 = 10 \div 5$$
$$|x - 6| = 2$$

Rewrite the absolute value inequality as two linear equations. Then solve.

$x - 6 = 2$	$x - 6 = -2$
$x - 6 + 6 = 2 + 6$	$x - 6 + 6 = -2 + 6$
$x = 8$	$x = 4$

Solutions: $x = 8$ and $x = 4$

6 Isolate the absolute value.
$$|x - 3| - 9 = 17$$

$$|x - 3| - 9 + 9 = 17 + 9$$
$$|x - 3| = 26$$

Rewrite the absolute value inequality as two linear equations. Then solve.

$x - 3 = 26$	$x - 3 = -26$
$x - 3 + 3 = 26 + 3$	$x - 3 + 3 = -26 + 3$
$x = 29$	$x = -23$

Solutions: $x = 29$ and $x = -23$

7 $|x - 8| = |-x + 3|$
Rewrite the absolute value inequality as two linear equations. Then solve.

$x - 8 = -x + 3$	$x - 8 = -(-x + 3)$
$x - 8 + 8 = -x + 3 + 8$	$x - 8 + 8 = x - 3 + 8$
$x + x = -x + x + 11$	$x - x = x - x + 5$
$2x \div 2 = 11 \div 2$	$0 = 5$
$x = \dfrac{11}{2}$	False

Solution: $x = \dfrac{11}{2}$

8 $|x| > 6$
Rewrite the absolute value inequality as two linear inequalities.

$x < -6$	$x > 6$

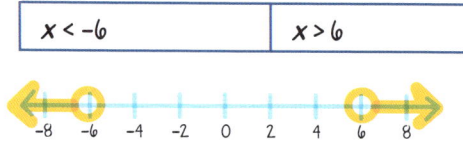

Interval notation: $(-\infty, -6) \cup (6, \infty)$

358

9 $|x| < 12$

Rewrite the absolute value inequality as two linear inequalities.

| $x > -12$ | $x < 12$ |

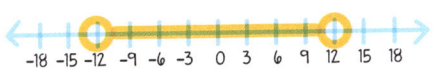

Interval notation: $(-12, 12)$

10 $|x| \geq 5$

Rewrite the absolute value inequality as two linear inequalities.

| $x \leq -5$ | $x \geq 5$ |

Interval notation: $(-\infty, -5] \cup [5, \infty)$

11 Isolate the absolute value.

$|8x - 1| - 7 \geq 18$

$|8x - 1| - 7 + 7 \geq 18 + 7$

$|8x - 1| \geq 25$

Rewrite the absolute value inequality as two linear inequalities. Then solve.

$8x - 1 \leq -25$	$8x - 1 \geq 25$
$8x - 1 + 1 \leq -25 + 1$	$8x - 1 + 1 \geq 25 + 1$
$8x \div 8 \leq -24 \div 8$	$8x \div 8 \geq 26 \div 8$
$x \leq -3$	$x \geq \frac{13}{4}$

Interval notation:

$(-\infty, -3] \cup [\frac{13}{4}, \infty)$

12 $|x + 1| \leq 3$

Rewrite the absolute value inequality as two linear inequalities. Then solve.

$x + 1 \geq -3$	$x + 1 \leq 3$
$x + 1 - 1 \geq -3 - 1$	$x + 1 - 1 \leq 3 - 1$
$x \geq -4$	$x \leq 2$

$-4 \leq x \leq 2$

Interval notation: $[-4, 2]$

13 $|12x - 4| < 18$

Rewrite the absolute value inequality as two linear inequalities. Then solve.

$12x - 4 > -18$	$12x - 4 < 18$
$12x - 4 + 4 > -18 + 4$	$12x - 4 + 4 < 18 + 4$
$12x \div 12 > -14 \div 12$	$12x \div 12 < 22 \div 12$
$x > -\frac{7}{6}$	$x < \frac{11}{6}$

$-\frac{7}{6} < x < \frac{11}{6}$

Interval notation: $(-\frac{7}{6}, \frac{11}{6})$

14 Isolate the absolute value.

$7|3x - 5| + 14 > 21$

$7|3x - 5| + 14 - 14 > 21 - 14$

$7|3x - 5| \div 7 > 7 \div 7$

$|3x - 5| > 1$

Rewrite the absolute value inequality as two linear inequalities. Then solve.

$$3x - 5 < -1 \qquad \bigg| \qquad 3x - 5 > 1$$
$$3x - 5 + 5 < -1 + 5 \quad \bigg| \quad 3x - 5 + 5 > 1 + 5$$
$$3x \div 3 < 4 \div 3 \qquad \bigg| \qquad 3x \div 3 > 6 \div 3$$
$$x < \frac{4}{3} \qquad\qquad \bigg| \qquad x > 2$$

Interval notation:
$(-\infty, \frac{4}{3}) \cup (2, \infty)$

CHAPTER 4

GRAPHING ABSOLUTE VALUE EQUATIONS AND INEQUALITIES

1 $y = |x + 4|$
standard form: $y = 1|x + 4| + 0$
$a = 1$: graph opens upward
vertex: $(h, k) = (-4, 0)$

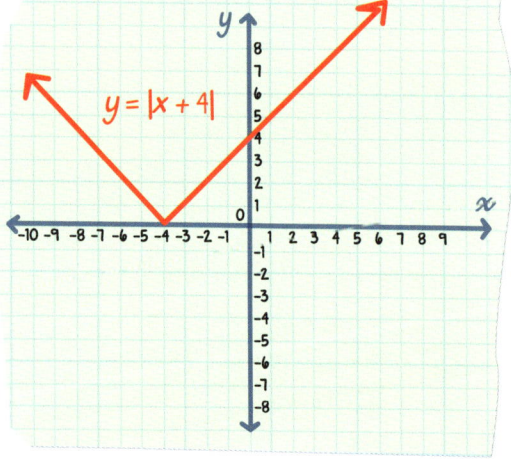

2 $y = -|x| + 7$
standard form: $y = -1|x - 0| + 7$
$a = -1$: graph opens downward
vertex: $(h, k) = (0, 7)$

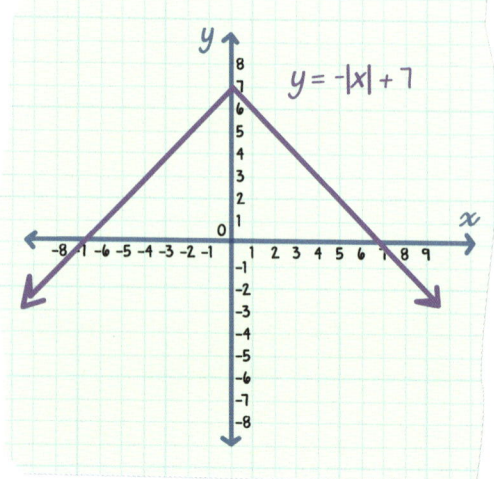

3 $y = |x - 2| - 1$
standard form: $y = 1|x - 2| - 1$
$a = 1$: graph opens upward
vertex: $(h, k) = (2, -1)$

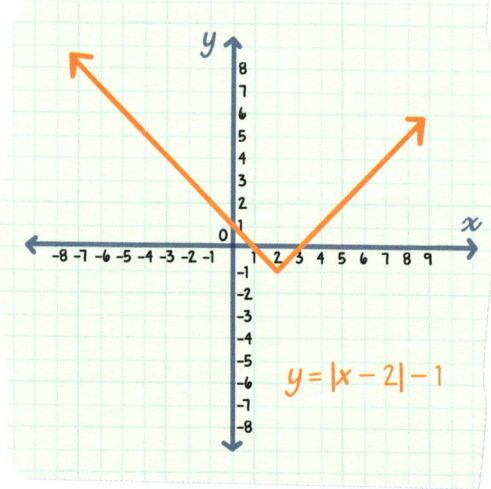

4 $y = -|x + 3| - 4$

standard form: $y = -1|x + 3| - 4$

$a = -1$: graph opens downward

vertex: $(h, k) = (-3, -4)$

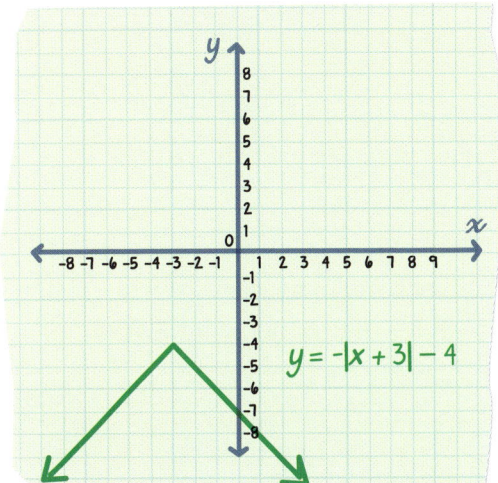

$y = -|x + 3| - 4$

5 $y > |x| + 3$

boundary line: $y = |x| + 3$

inequality symbol: $>$, so boundary line is dashed

$a = 1$: graph opens upward

vertex: $(h, k) = (0, 3)$

Test the point $(0, 0)$.

$0 \overset{?}{>} |(0)| + 3$

$0 \overset{?}{>} 3$ False

Since the inequality is false, shade the region that does NOT contain $(0, 0)$.

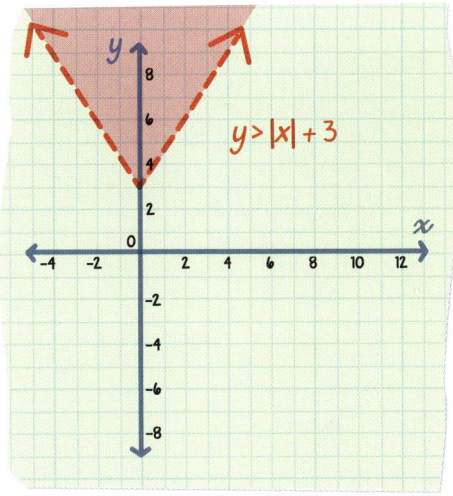

$y > |x| + 3$

6 $y \le |x - 6|$

boundary line: $y = |x - 6|$

inequality symbol: $\le$, so boundary line is solid

$a = 1$: graph opens upward

vertex: $(h, k) = (6, 0)$

Test the point $(0, 0)$.

$0 \overset{?}{\le} |(0) - 6|$

$0 \overset{?}{\le} 6$ True

Since the inequality is true, shade the region that DOES contain $(0, 0)$.

The graph is on the next page!

361

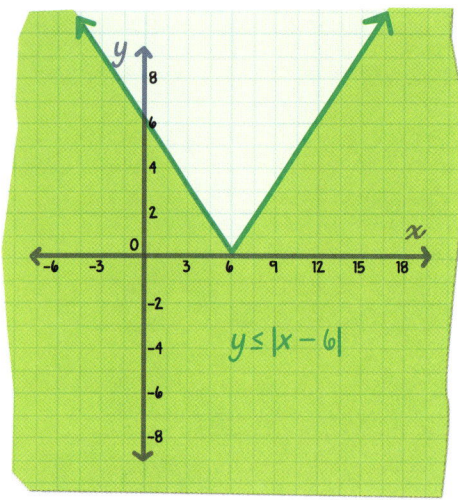

$y \le |x - 6|$

7 $y \ge |x + 8| - 1$
boundary line: $y = |x + 8| - 1$
inequality symbol: ≥, so boundary
line is solid
$a = 1$: graph opens upward
vertex: $(h, k) = (-8, -1)$

Test the point $(0, 0)$.
$0 \overset{?}{\ge} |(0) + 8| - 1$
$0 \overset{?}{\ge} 7$ False

Since the inequality is false,
shade the region that does NOT
contain $(0, 0)$.

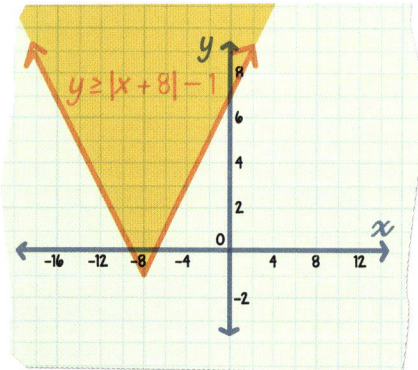

$y \ge |x + 8| - 1$

8 $y < |x - 7| + 2$
boundary line: $y = |x - 7| + 2$
inequality symbol: <, so boundary
line is dashed
$a = 1$: graph opens upward
vertex: $(h, k) = (7, 2)$

Test the point $(0, 0)$.
$0 \overset{?}{<} |(0) - 7| + 2$
$0 \overset{?}{<} 9$ True

Since the inequality is true,
shade the region that DOES
contain $(0, 0)$.

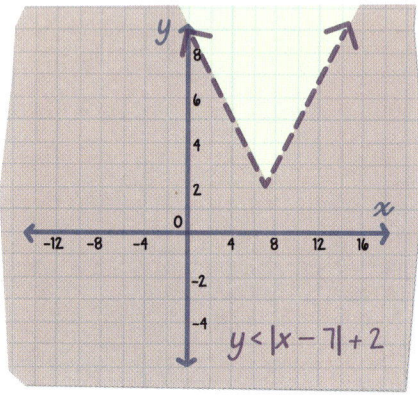

$y < |x - 7| + 2$

9 The graph of $y = |x| - 2$ opens
upward. Its vertex is at $(0, -2)$.

The graph of $y = -|x - 2|$ opens
downward. Its vertex is at $(2, 0)$.

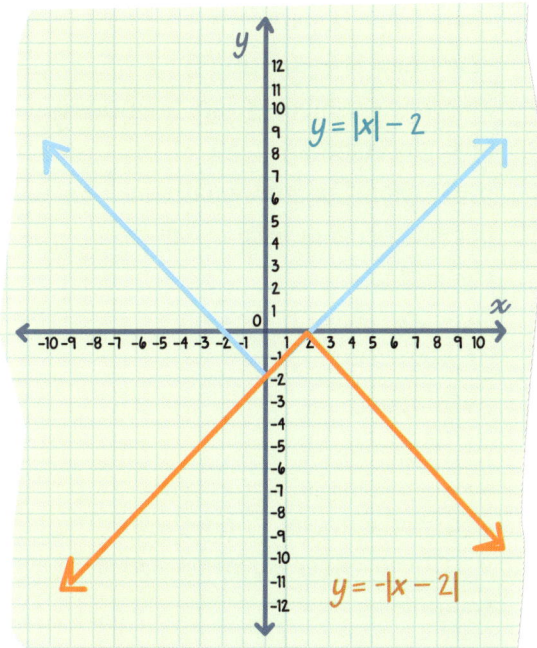

The graphs are similar because they are both absolute value graphs. They are different because they open in opposite directions, and one has a vertex on the x-axis and the other has a vertex on the y-axis.

CHAPTER 5

SOLVING LINEAR SYSTEMS

1 $\begin{cases} 8x - y = 13 \\ 4y = 12 \end{cases}$

Solve the second equation for y.
$4y = 12$
$y = 3$

Substitute $y = 3$ into the first equation and solve for x.
$8x - (3) = 13$
$8x = 16$
$x = 2$

There is exactly one solution:
$x = 2$ and $y = 3$, or $(x, y) = (2, 3)$.

2 $\begin{cases} 3x + 5y = 5 \\ 6x + 2y = 34 \end{cases}$

Solve Equation 2 for y.
$6x + 2y = 34$
$6x - 6x + 2y = -6x + 34$
$2y = -6x + 34$
$2y \div 2 = (-6x + 34) \div 2$
$y = -3x + 17$

Substitute $y = -3x + 17$ into Equation 1.
$3x + 5y = 5$
$3x + 5(-3x + 17) = 5$
$3x - 15x + 85 = 5$
$-12x + 85 = 5$
$-12x + 85 - 85 = 5 - 85$
$-12x = -80$
$x = \dfrac{20}{3}$

Substitute $x = \dfrac{20}{3}$ into Equation 1 and solve for y.
$3x + 5y = 5$
$3(\dfrac{20}{3}) + 5y = 5$
$20 + 5y = 5$
$20 - 20 + 5y = 5 - 20$

$5y \div 5 = -15 \div 5$

$5y = -15$

$y = -3$

There is exactly one solution:
$x = \frac{20}{3}$ and $y = -3$ or $(x, y) = (\frac{20}{3}, -3)$.

3 $\begin{cases} x + 7y = 21 \\ 2x - 4y = -12 \end{cases}$

Solve the first equation for x.

$x + 7y = 21$

$x = 21 - 7y$

Substitute $x = 21 - 7y$ into the second equation and solve for y.

$2(21 - 7y) - 4y = -12$

$42 - 14y - 4y = -12$

$42 - 18y = -12$

$-18y = -54$

$y = 3$

Substitute $y = 3$ into the first equation and solve for x.

$x + 7(3) = 21$

$x + 21 = 21$

$x = 0$

There is exactly one solution:
$x = 0$ and $y = 3$, or $(x, y) = (0, 3)$.

4 $\begin{cases} -6x + 2y = 5 \quad \text{Equation 1} \\ -2x + 2y = 5 \quad \text{Equation 2} \end{cases}$

Multiply Equation 2 by -1, so that when the two equations are added together y will be eliminated.

$-6x + 2y = 5$

$\underline{2x - 2y = -5}$

$-4x + 0 = 0$

$\qquad x = 0$

Find the value of y by substituting $x = 0$ into either equation. Let's use Equation 2.

$-2x + 2y = 5$

$-2(0) + 2y = 5$

$2y = 5$

$y = \frac{5}{2}$

This system has exactly one solution: $(x, y) = (0, \frac{5}{2})$.

5 $\begin{cases} 4x + y = 3 \quad \text{Equation 1} \\ -4x - y = 14 \quad \text{Equation 2} \end{cases}$

Notice that when we add the equations x and y are both eliminated.

$4x + y = 3$

$\underline{-4x - y = 14}$

$0 + 0 = 17$

Since $0 = 17$ is false, this system has no solutions. The graphs of the two equations are parallel lines (they do not intersect).

6 $\begin{cases} -\frac{1}{2}x + 2y = 8 & \text{Equation 1} \\ 5x + 6y = 24 & \text{Equation 2} \end{cases}$

Multiply Equation 1 by 10, so that when the two equations are added together x will be eliminated.

$$-5x + 20y = 80$$
$$\underline{5x + 6y = 24}$$
$$26y = 104$$
$$y = 4$$

Find the value of x by substituting $y = 4$ into either equation. Let's use Equation 2.

$$5x + 6y = 24$$
$$5x + 6(4) = 24$$
$$5x + 24 = 24$$
$$5x = 0$$
$$x = 0$$

Both equations are satisfied, so this system has exactly one solution: $(x, y) = (0, 4)$.

7 $\begin{cases} 6x + 7y > 9 & \text{Inequality 1} \\ x - 5y < 14 & \text{Inequality 2} \end{cases}$

Graph each inequality on the same coordinate plane to identify the region of overlap.

For Inequality 1:

Rewrite $6x + 7y > 9$ as an equation in slope-intercept form. (Solve for y.)
$$6x + 7y = 9$$
$$7y = -6x + 9$$
$$y = -\frac{6}{7}x + \frac{9}{7}$$

Graph $y = -\frac{6}{7}x + \frac{9}{7}$. Use a dashed line (>).

Test the point $(0, 0)$.
$$6(0) + 7(0) \overset{?}{>} 9$$
$$0 > 9 \text{ False}$$

Since the statement is false, shade the region that does NOT include $(0, 0)$.

For Inequality 2:

Rewrite $x - 5y < 14$ as an equation in slope-intercept form.
$$x - 5y = 14$$
$$-5y = -x + 14$$
$$y = \frac{1}{5}x - \frac{14}{5}$$

Graph $y = \frac{1}{5}x - \frac{14}{5}$. Use a dashed line (<).

Test the point (0, 0).
$(0) - 5(0) \overset{?}{<} 14$
$0 < 14$ True

Since the statement is true, shade the region that DOES include (0, 0)

The region of overlap is the solution.

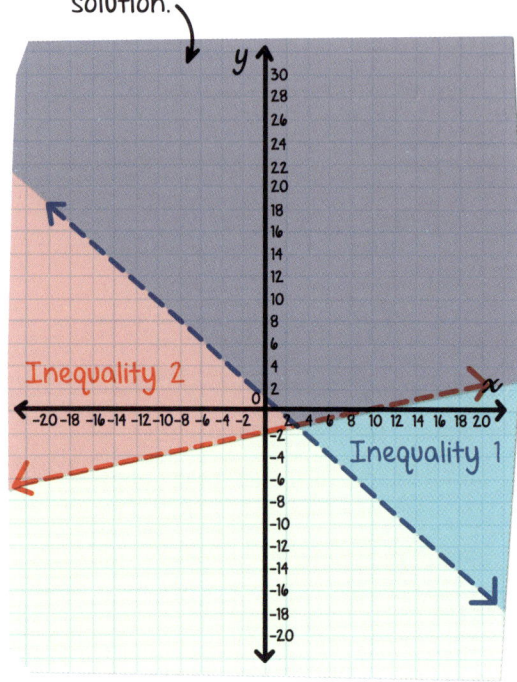

8 $\begin{cases} -x + 6y < 11 & \text{Inequality 1} \\ y \geq 5 & \text{Inequality 2} \end{cases}$

Graph each inequality on the same coordinate plane to identify the region of overlap.

For Inequality 1:

Rewrite $-x + 6y < 11$ as an equation in slope-intercept form.
(Solve for y.)
$-x + 6y = 11$
$6y = x + 11$
$y = \frac{1}{6}x + \frac{11}{6}$

Graph $y = \frac{1}{6}x + \frac{11}{6}$. Use a dashed line (<).

Test the point (0, 0).
$-(0) + 6(0) \overset{?}{<} 11$
$0 < 11$ True

Since the statement is true, shade the region that DOES include (0, 0).

For Inequality 2:

Rewrite $y \geq 5$ as an equation: $y = 5$.

Graph $y = 5$. Use a solid line (≥).

Test the point (0, 0).
$0 \overset{?}{\geq} 5$ False

Since the statement is false, shade the region that does NOT include (0, 0).

The region of overlap is the solution.

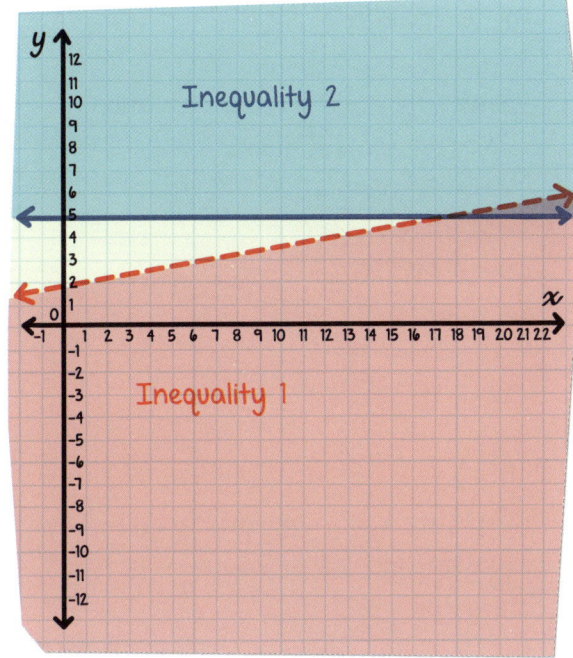

Since the statement is true, shade the region that DOES include (0, 0).

For Inequality 2:

Rewrite $11x + 9y > -13$ as an equation. (Solve for y.)
$$11x + 9y = -13$$
$$\frac{11}{9}x + y = -\frac{13}{9}$$
$$y = -\frac{11}{9}x - \frac{13}{9}$$

Graph $y = -\frac{11}{9}x - \frac{13}{9}$. Use a dashed line (>).

Test the point (0, 0).
$11(0) + 9(0) \overset{?}{>} -13$
$0 > -13$ True

Since the statement is true, shade the region that DOES include (0, 0).

The region of overlap is the solution.

9. $\begin{cases} 2y < 8 & \text{Inequality 1} \\ 11x + 9y > -13 & \text{Inequality 2} \end{cases}$

Graph each inequality on the same coordinate plane to identify the region of overlap.

For Inequality 1:

Rewrite $2y < 8$ as an equation. (Solve for y.)
$$2y = 8$$
$$y = 4$$

Graph $y = 4$. Use a dashed line (<).

Test the point (0, 0).
$2(0) \overset{?}{<} 8$
$0 < 8$ True

The graph is on the next page!

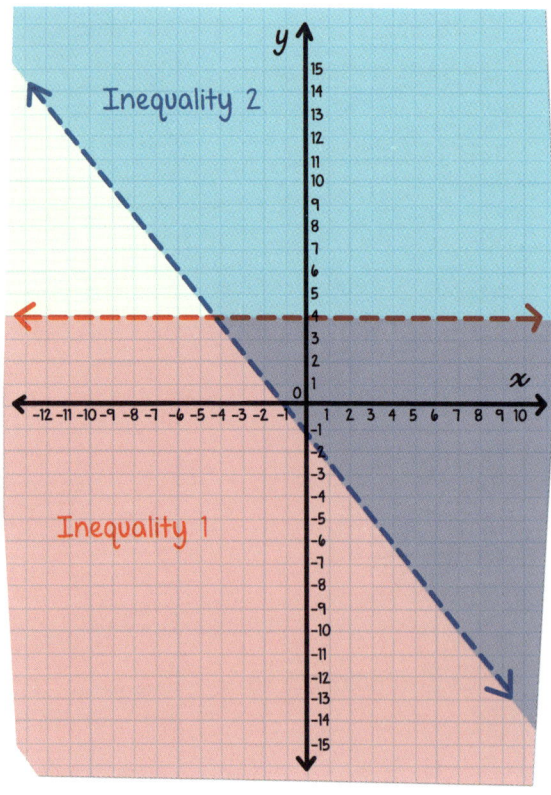

Inequality 2

Inequality 1

10 Let the number of cheese pizzas equal x.

Let the number of pepperoni pizzas equal y.

Write two equations, one that equals the total cost, one that equals the total number of pizzas.

$$\begin{cases} 16x + 19y = 971 \text{ Equation for} \\ \qquad\qquad\qquad \text{total cost} \\ \\ x + y = 56 \text{ Equation for total} \\ \qquad\qquad \text{number of pizzas} \end{cases}$$

Solve the second equation for y.

$x + y = 56$

$y = 56 - x$

Substitute $y = 56 - x$ into the first equation and solve for x.

$16x + 19(56 - x) = 971$

$16x + 1,064 - 19x = 971$

$-3x + 1,064 = 971$

$-3x = -93$

$x = 31$

Substitute $x = 31$ into the second equation and solve for y.

$31 + y = 56$

$y = 25$

Principal Johnson ordered 31 cheese pizzas and 25 pepperoni pizzas.

> You could also solve problem 10 with the elimination method.

CHAPTER 6

EXPONENTS AND ROOTS

1 $(-4)^3$

$(-4)(-4)(-4)$

-64

2 $(3x^3y^2)^2$

$3^2 \cdot x^6 \cdot y^4$

$9x^6y^4$

3 $(-\sqrt{16})^0 + \frac{6^{-2}}{3}$

$1 + \frac{6^{-2}}{3}$

$1 + \frac{1}{3 \cdot 6^2}$

$1 + \frac{1}{108}$

$\frac{109}{108}$

4 $-(\frac{5}{8})^{-2}$

$-(\frac{8}{5})^2$

$-\frac{64}{25}$

5 $\sqrt{49} = 7$

6 $\sqrt[4]{-256}$

There is no value that can be multiplied by itself four times to get −256. So, $\sqrt[4]{-256}$ is **undefined**.

7 $\sqrt[3]{512} = 8$

8 $\sqrt{84}$
$\sqrt{4 \cdot 21}$
$\sqrt{2^2 \cdot 21}$
$\sqrt{2^2} \sqrt{21}$
$2\sqrt{21}$

9 $\sqrt{18}$
$\sqrt{9 \cdot 2}$
$\sqrt{3^2 \cdot 2}$
$3\sqrt{2}$

10 $\frac{24b^3h^4}{8bh^2}$

Divide the coefficients and subtract the exponents.

$3b^2h^2$

11 $\sqrt{121x^4y^5}$

$\sqrt{121x^2 \cdot x^2 \cdot y^2 \cdot y^2 \cdot y^1}$
$11x \cdot x \cdot y \cdot y\sqrt{y}$
$11x^2y^2\sqrt{y}$

12 $\sqrt{36x^6y^7}$

$\sqrt{36x^3 \cdot x^3 \cdot y^3 \cdot y^3 \cdot y^1}$
$6|x^3y^3|\sqrt{y}$

CHAPTER 7

COMPLEX NUMBERS

1 i^{158}

Divide the exponent by 4:
$158 \div 4 = 39$ R2.
So, $i^{158} = i^2 = -1$.

2 i^{227}

Divide the exponent by 4:
$227 \div 4 = 56$ R3.
So, $i^{227} = i^3 = -i$

3 i^{469}

Divide the exponent by 4:
$469 \div 4 = 117$ R1
So, $i^{469} = i^1 = i$

4 $3i\sqrt{-49}$
$3i\sqrt{49 \cdot (-1)}$
$3i \cdot 7i$
$21i^2$
$21 \cdot (-1) = -21$

5 $4\sqrt{-76}$

$4\sqrt{4 \cdot 19 \cdot (-1)}$

$4 \cdot 2\sqrt{19}\ i$

$8i\sqrt{19}$

6 $-5i^9 + 7i^9$

$2i^9$

$2i$

7 $16i^{18} - 5i^{18}$

$11i^{18}$

$11i^2$

$11 \cdot (-1)$

-11

8 $(4 + 2i) + (8 + 7i)$

$(4 + 8) + (2 + 7)i$

$12 + 9i$

9 $(13 + 3i) - (9 + 11i)$

$(13 - 9) + (3 - 11)i$

$4 - 8i$

10 $(2 - 4i)(6 + 7i)$

$(2 \cdot 6 - (-4) \cdot 7) + (2 \cdot 7 + (-4) \cdot 6)i$

$(12 + 28) + (14 - 24)i$

$40 - 10i$

11 $\dfrac{8 - 6i}{2 + 7i}$

$\dfrac{(8 - 6i)}{(2 + 7i)} \cdot \dfrac{(2 - 7i)}{(2 - 7i)}$

$\dfrac{(16 - 42) + (-56 - 12)i}{2^2 + 7^2}$

$\dfrac{-26 - 68i}{4 + 49}$

$\dfrac{-26 - 68i}{53}$

$-\dfrac{26}{53} - \dfrac{68}{53}i$

12 $\dfrac{3 + 4i}{10 - 5i}$

$\dfrac{(3 + 4i)}{(10 - 5i)} \cdot \dfrac{(10 + 5i)}{(10 + 5i)}$

$\dfrac{30 + 15i + 40i + 20i^2}{10^2 + 5^2}$

$\dfrac{30 + 15i + 40i - 20}{100 + 25}$

$\dfrac{10 + 55i}{125}$

$\dfrac{10}{125} + \dfrac{55}{125}i$

$\dfrac{2}{25} + \dfrac{11}{25}i$

UNIT 2

Functions

CHAPTER 8

RELATIONS AND FUNCTIONS

1 Domain: {−9, −5, 7, 14}
Range: {0, 1, 2, 8, 15}

The relation **is not** a function because the input −9 has two outputs (0 and 1).

2 Domain: {−14, 6, 19, 45, 63}
Range: {−13, −12, −8, 1, 54}

The relation **is** a function

because there is exactly one output for each input.

3 The relation **is** a function. Any vertical line drawn on the coordinate plane would touch at most one point of the graph, so the graph passes the vertical line test.

4 The relation **is NOT** a function. There are vertical lines that would pass through more than one point on the graph, so the graph fails the vertical line test.

5

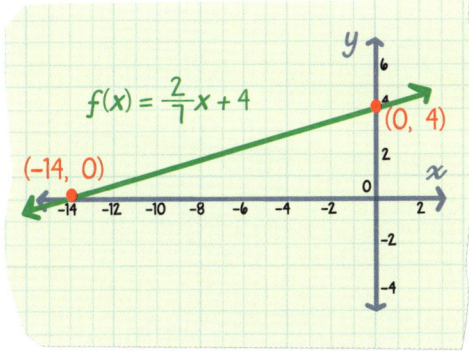

$f(x) = \frac{2}{7}x + 4$

$(0, 4)$

$(-14, 0)$

f has an x-intercept of (–14, 0) and a y-intercept of (0, 4).

6 $k(g) = \frac{9g + 7}{5} - 1$; $g = 2$

$k(2) = \frac{9(2) + 7}{5} - 1$

$k(2) = \frac{25}{5} - 1$

$k(2) = 5 - 1$

$k(2) = 4$

7 $p(k) = k - 6m$; $k = m - 3d$

$p(m - 3d) = (m - 3d) - 6m$

$p(m - 3d) = -3d - 5m$

8 $p(x) = \frac{1}{3}x + 12$; $p(x) = 9$

$9 = \frac{1}{3}x + 12$

$-3 = \frac{1}{3}x$

$-9 = x$

$x = -9$

9 $d(k) = -4 + \frac{1}{4}k$; $d(k) = 24$

$24 = -4 + \frac{1}{4}k$

$28 = \frac{1}{4}k$

$112 = k$

$k = 112$

10 Domain: [–5, 5]
Range: [–4, 3]

The function is decreasing over the interval (–5, –2).

The function is increasing over the interval (–2, 1).

The function is constant over the interval (1, 5).

CHAPTER 9

LINEAR FUNCTIONS AND THEIR GRAPHS

1 Pick any two points on the line to plug into the slope formula. Using the points $(0, -6)$ and $(9, 0)$, we find the slope is:

$$m = \frac{y_2 - y_1}{x_2 - x_1} = \frac{0 - (-6)}{9 - 0} = \frac{6}{9} = \frac{2}{3}$$

The y-intercept is $(0, -6)$. For the slope-intercept form: $b = -6$.

The equation of the line is $y = \frac{2}{3}x - 6$.

So, $f(x) = \frac{2}{3}x - 6$.

2 Pick any two points on the line to plug into the slope formula. Using the points $(-2, 4)$ and $(0, -2)$, we find the slope is:

$$m = \frac{y_2 - y_1}{x_2 - x_1} = \frac{-2 - 4}{0 - (-2)} = \frac{-6}{2} = -3$$

The y-intercept is $(0, -2)$. For the slope-intercept form: $b = -2$.

The equation of the line is $y = -3x - 2$.

So, $f(x) = -3x - 2$.

3 $f(x) = g(x)$ at $x = 2$ (point of intersection)

$f(x) > g(x)$ on $(2, \infty)$ (where $f(x)$ is above $g(x)$)

$f(x) < g(x)$ on $(-\infty, 2)$ (where $f(x)$ is below $g(x)$)

4 $f(x) = g(x)$ at $x = -2$ (point of intersection is $(-2, 0)$.)

$f(x) > g(x)$ on $(-\infty, -2)$

$f(x) < g(x)$ on $(-2, \infty)$

5 Substitute $x = 4$ and $y = 7$ to find p.

$$y = px - 1$$
$$7 = 4p - 1$$
$$8 = 4p$$
$$2 = p$$

Use the value of p to find y when $x = 16$.

$$y = px - 1$$
$$y = (2)(16) - 1$$
$$y = 32 - 1$$
$$y = 31$$

6 Substitute $x = 3$ and $y = 15$ to find d.
$$y = dx$$
$$15 = 3d$$
$$5 = d$$

Use the value of d to find y when $x = 9$.
$$y = (5)(9)$$
$$y = 45$$

7 Let x represent the number of hours worked. Let y represent the amount earned, in dollars. The amount of money earned varies directly with the number of hours worked: $y = kx$.

Substitute $x = 21$ and $y = 273$ to find k.

$273 = 21k$

$13 = k$

Use the value of k to find x when $y = 455$.

$455 = 13x$

$35 = x$

The cashier worked 35 hours the following week.

8 Let x represent the number of stops. Let y represent the price of a ticket, in dollars. The price of the ticket varies directly with the number of stops: $y = kx$.

Substitute $x = 6$ and $y = 4.50$ to find k.

$4.50 = 6k$

$0.75 = k$

Use the value of k to find y when $x = 17$.

$y = (0.75)(17)$

$y = 12.75$

The price of the bus ticket would be $12.75.

CHAPTER 10

ABSOLUTE VALUE FUNCTIONS AND THEIR GRAPHS

1 $f(x) = -|x - 9| + 2$

Write the standard form: $f(x) = -|x - 9| + 2$. We see the vertex is $(h, k) = (9, 2)$ and $a = -1$. Since a is negative, the graph is facing downward.

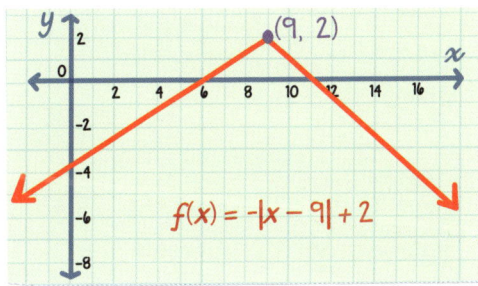

$f(x) = -|x - 9| + 2$

2 $f(x) = |6x + 3|$

First, factor to get the function in standard form:

$f(x) = |6x + 3|$

$f(x) = |6(x + \frac{1}{2})|$

373

$f(x) = 6|(x + \frac{1}{2})|$

$f(x) = 6|x + \frac{1}{2}|$

Standard form: $f(x) = 6|x - \frac{1}{2}| + 0$.

In standard form we see the vertex is $(h, k) = (-\frac{1}{2}, 0)$ and $a = 6$. Since a is not equal to 1, plot one more point to determine the width of the V. Since $f(0) = 3$, the y-intercept is $(0, 3)$. Since a is positive, the graph opens upward.

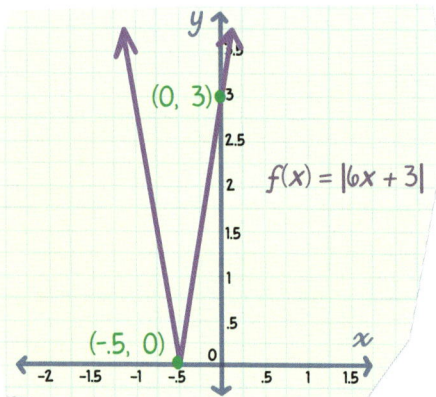

3 $f(x) = -|\frac{3}{4}x|$

First, take $\frac{3}{4}$ outside the absolute value to get the function into standard form.

$f(x) = -|\frac{3}{4}x|$

$f(x) = -\frac{3}{4}|x|$

Standard form: $f(x) = -1|\frac{3}{4}x - 0| + 0$. In standard form we see the vertex is $(h, k) = (0, 0)$ and $a = -\frac{3}{4}$.

Since a is not equal to 1, plot one more point to determine the width of the V. $f(1) = -\frac{3}{4}$, so plot the point $(1, -\frac{3}{4})$. Since a is negative, the graph opens downward..

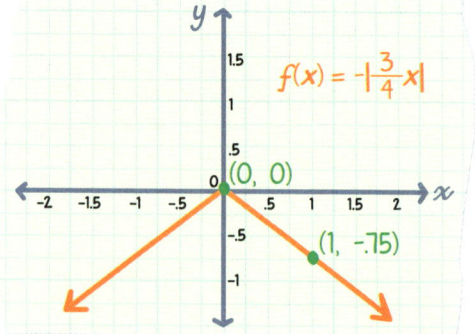

4 $f(x) = |\frac{1}{3}x| + 2$

Write the standard form of the function: $f(x) = \frac{1}{3}|x - 0| + 0$. We see the vertex is $(h, k) = (0, 2)$ and $a = \frac{1}{3}$. Since a is not equal to 1, plot one more point to determine the width of the V. $f(3) = 3$, so, plot point $(3, 3)$. Plot the point. Since a is positive, the graph opens facing upward.

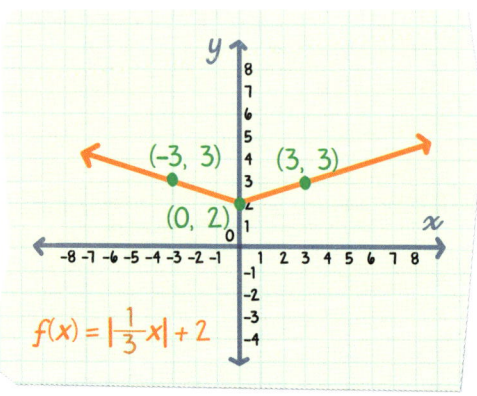

5 $f(x) = 2|x - 6|$

Write the standard form of the function: $f(x) = 2|x - 6| + 0$.

So, the vertex is $(h, k) = (6, 0)$ and $a = 2$. Since a *is not equal* to 1, plot one more point to determine the width of the V. $f(5) = 2$, so plot point $(5, 2)$. Since a is positive, the graph opens upward.

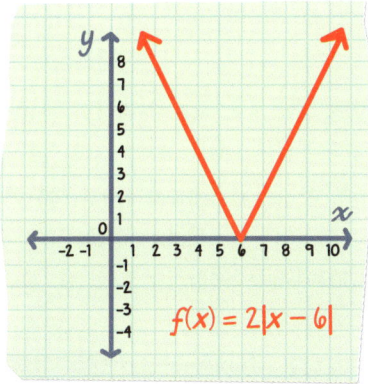

6 $f(x) = |-\frac{3}{5}x|$

Write the standard form of the function: $f(x) = \frac{3}{5}|x - 0| + 0$. The vertex is $(h, k) = (0, 0)$ and $a = \frac{3}{5}$. Since a *is not equal* to 1, plot one more point to determine the width of the V. $f(5) = 3$, so plot point $(5, 3)$. Plot the point. Since a is positive, the graph opens upward.

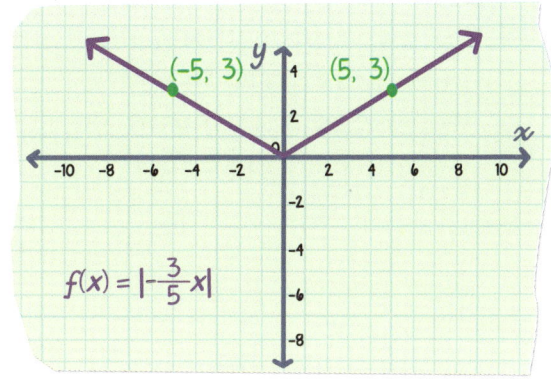

$f(x) = |-\frac{3}{5}x|$

7 Use the vertex and any other point on the graph to find the value of a. Then write the standard form.

Vertex: $(h, k) = (0, -3)$
Other point: $(x, f(x)) = (1, 5)$

Standard form: $f(x) = a|x - h| + k$

Substitute the vertex and the other point into the standard form. Solve for a.

$f(x) = a|x - h| + k$
$5 = a|1 - 0| - 3$
$5 = a|1| - 3$
$5 = a - 3$
$8 = a$

So, the absolute value function in standard form is $f(x) = 8|x| - 3$.

375

8 Use the vertex and any other point on the graph to find the value of a. Then write the function in standard form.

Vertex: $(h, k) = (8, 2)$
Other point: $(x, f(x)) = (9, 3)$

Standard form: $f(x) = a|x - h| + k$

Substitute the vertex and the other point into the standard form. Solve for a.

$f(x) = a|x - h| + k$
$3 = a|9 - 8| + 2$
$3 = a|1| + 2$
$3 = a + 2$
$1 = a$

So, the absolute value function in standard form is $f(x) = |x - 8| + 2$.

9 Use the vertex and any other point on the graph to find the value of a. Then write the function in standard form.

Vertex: $(h, k) = (0, -7)$
Other point: $(x, f(x)) = (4, 6)$

Standard form: $f(x) = a|x - h| + k$

Substitute the vertex and the other point into the standard form. Solve for a.

$f(x) = a|x - h| + k$
$-6 = a|4 - 0| - 7$
$-6 = a|4| - 7$
$-6 = 4a - 7$
$1 = 4a$
$\dfrac{1}{4} = a$

So, the absolute value function in standard form is $f(x) = \dfrac{1}{4}|x| - 7$.

10 A. Use the vertex (the turning point of path) and any other point on the path to find the value of a. Then write the standard form.

Vertex: $(8, 0)$
Other point: $(18, 10)$

Standard form: $f(x) = a|x - h| + k$

Substitute the vertex and the other point into the standard form. Solve for a.

$f(x) = a|x - h| + k$
$10 = a|18 - 8| + 0$
$10 = a|10| + 0$
$10 = 10a$
$1 = a$

So, the absolute value function in standard form that represents the race path is $f(x) = |x - 8|$.

B. Substitute the coordinates of the path into the standard form of the function.

$f(x) = |x - 8|$
$f(10) = |10 - 8|$
$f(10) = 2$

That exact location is possible because $f(10) = 2$, which means $(10, 2)$ is on the path.

CHAPTER 11

TRANSFORMATIONS OF FUNCTIONS

1. $f(x) = x - 3$

2. $g(x) = \sqrt{x - 2} + 7$

3. $p(x) = x + 11$

4. $d(x) = -|x + 2|$

5. $f(x) = 4x^2$

6. $f(x) = \frac{2}{7}x^2$

7. The graph of $g(x) = |x + 4| + 1$ is a transformation of the graph of $f(x) = |x|$ translated 4 units to the left and 1 unit up.

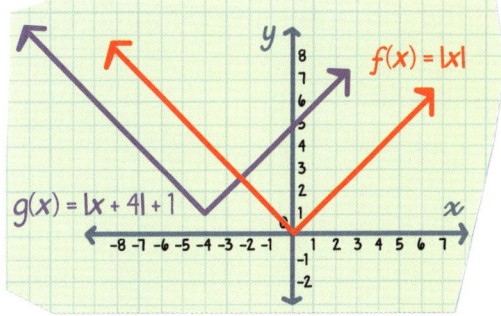

8. The graph of $p(x) = -|x - 11|$ is a transformation of the graph of $d(x) = |x|$ reflected across the x-axis and translated 11 units to the right.

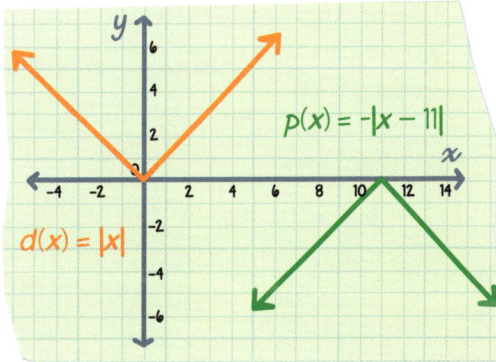

9 The graph of $h(x) = (x-6)^2 + 4$ is a transformation of the graph of $j(x) = x^2$ translated 6 units to the right and 4 units up.

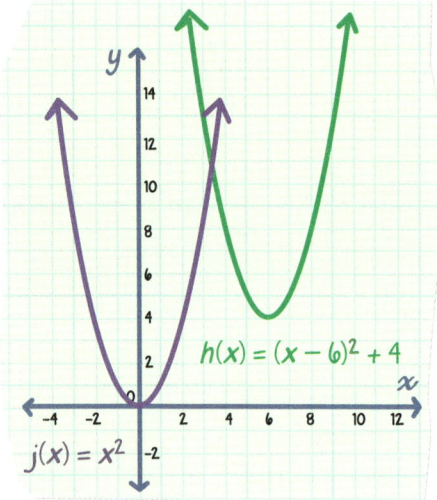

$h(x) = (x-6)^2 + 4$

$j(x) = x^2$

10 The graph $k(x) = \frac{1}{2}\sqrt{x}$ is a transformation of the graph of $f(x) = \sqrt{x}$ vertically shrunk by a factor of $\frac{1}{2}$.

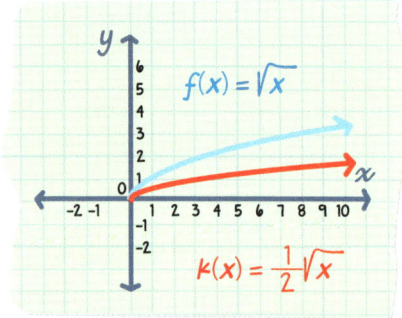

$f(x) = \sqrt{x}$

$k(x) = \frac{1}{2}\sqrt{x}$

11 The graph of the parent function is translated 8 units to the right and vertically stretched

by a factor of 2 to produce the graph. So, the equation of the graph is $f(x) = 2\sqrt{x-8}$.

12 The graph of the parent function is translated 3 units down to produce the graph. So, the equation of the graph is $f(x) = x^2 - 3$.

13 A. Odd: This graph is symmetrical across the origin. If you rotate it 180°, it looks identical to the original.

B. Even: This graph is symmetrical across the y-axis.

C. Even: This graph is symmetrical across the y-axis.

D. Neither: The graph is not symmetrical across the y-axis or the origin.

CHAPTER 12

OPERATIONS ON FUNCTIONS

1 $(f+g)(x) = (2x+9) + (x^2-3)$
$= 2x + 6 + x^2$
$= x^2 + 2x + 6$
Domain: $(-\infty, \infty)$

2 $(f-g)(x) = (2x+9) - (x^2-3)$
$= 2x + 12 - x^2$

$= -x^2 + 2x + 12$

Domain: $(-\infty, \infty)$

3. $(fg)(x) = (2x + 9)(x^2 - 3)$

$= 2x^3 - 6x + 9x^2 - 27$

$= 2x^3 + 9x^2 - 6x - 27$

Domain: $(-\infty, \infty)$

4. $(\frac{f}{g})(x) = \frac{2x + 9}{x^2 - 3}$

For the domain, $x^2 - 3 \neq 0$,

so $x \neq \pm\sqrt{3}$.

Domain: $(-\infty, -\sqrt{3}) \cup (-\sqrt{3}, \sqrt{3}) \cup (\sqrt{3}, \infty)$

5. $(f + g)(x) = -4\sqrt{x + 2} + 7x$

$= 7x - 4\sqrt{x + 2}$

Domain: $[-2, \infty)$

6. $(f - g)(x) = -4\sqrt{x + 2} - 7x$

$= -7x - 4\sqrt{x + 2}$

Domain: $[-2, \infty)$

7. $(fg)(x) = (-4\sqrt{x + 2}) \cdot (7x)$

$= -28x\sqrt{x + 2}$

Domain: $[-2, \infty)$

8. $(\frac{f}{g})(x) = \frac{-4\sqrt{x + 2}}{7x}$

For the domain, $x \neq 0$.

Domain: $(-2, 0) \cup (0, \infty)$

9. $(f \circ g)(x) = f(g(x)) = f(6x^2)$

$= \sqrt{6x^2 + 1}$

Domain of g: $(-\infty, \infty)$

Domain of $f \circ g$: $(-\infty, \infty)$

10. $(f \circ h)(x) = f(h(x)) = f(-5x^2)$

$= \sqrt{-5x^2 + 1}$

For the domain, $-5x^2 + 1 \geq 0$ because we cannot take the square of a negative number.

So, $x^2 \leq \frac{1}{5}$, or $x \leq \sqrt{\frac{1}{5}}$

and $x \geq -\sqrt{\frac{1}{5}}$.

Domain of h: $(-\infty, \infty)$

Domain of $f \circ h$: $[-\frac{1}{\sqrt{5}}, \frac{1}{\sqrt{5}}]$

11. $(g \circ f)(x) = g(f(x))$

$= g(\sqrt{x + 1}) = 6(\sqrt{x + 1})^2$

$= 6(x + 1)$

$= 6x + 6$

Domain of f: $[-1, \infty)$

Domain of $f \circ g$: $(-\infty, \infty)$

12. $(g \circ h)(x) = g(h(x)) = g(-5x^2)$

$= 6(-5x^2)^2 = 6(25x^4) = 150x^4$

Domain of h: $(-\infty, \infty)$

Domain of $g \circ h$: $(-\infty, \infty)$

13. A. $(f \circ g)(4) = f(g(4)) = f(12(4))$

$= f(48) = -48^2 - 4$

$= -2304 - 4 = -2308$

B. $(g \circ f)(\frac{1}{2}) = g(f(\frac{1}{2}))$

$= g(-(\frac{1}{2})^2 - 4) = g(-\frac{1}{4} - 4)$

$= g(-\frac{17}{4}) = 12(-\frac{17}{4}) = 3(-17) = -51$

14. Solution 1: Let the "outside" function be $g(x) = \frac{x}{3}$. Then the "inside" function is $h(x) = \sqrt{2x - 8}$.

Solution 2: Let the "outside" function be $g(x) = \frac{\sqrt{2x}}{3}$. Then the "inside" function is $h(x) = x - 4$.

CHAPTER 13

INVERSE FUNCTIONS

1. The relation is a one-to-one function. Each input has a unique output (so it's a function), and each output has a unique input (so it's one-to-one).

2. The relation is NOT a function. The input 18 has two outputs: 2 and 19.

3. Graph A is the graph of a one-to-one function. Every horizontal line would hit at most one point on the graph. Therefore, this graph passes the horizontal line test.

   Graph B is NOT the graph of a one-to-one function. There are horizontal lines that will hit more than one point on the graph. Therefore, this graph fails the horizontal line test.

4. Domain of g^{-1}: {5, 18, 21, 34}
   Range of g^{-1}: {4, 10, 17, 24}

5. Since $f^{-1}(3) = 15$, $f(15) = 3$.

6. Since $f^{-1}(-8.5) = 4$, $f(4) = -8.5$.

7. $(f \circ g)(x) = f(g(x)) = f(\frac{x-9}{7})$
   $= 7(\frac{x-9}{7}) + 9 = (x-9) + 9 = x$
   $(g \circ f)(x) = g(f(x)) = g(7x + 9)$
   $= \frac{(7x+9) - 9}{7} = \frac{7x}{7} = x$

   Since $(f \circ g)(x) = x$ and $(g \circ f)(x) = x$, f and g are inverses of each other, and we can write $g = f^{-1}$ or $f = g^{-1}$.

8. Write the original function: $f(x) = 2x + 15$

   Replace $f(x)$ with y: $y = 2x + 15$
   Interchange x and y: $x = 2y + 15$

   Solve for y.
   $x - 15 = 2y$
   $\frac{x-15}{2} = \frac{2y}{2}$
   $y = \frac{x-15}{2}$
   $f^{-1}(x) = \frac{x-15}{2}$
   Domain: $(-\infty, \infty)$

9. Write the original function: $f(x) = x^3 - 8$

   Replace $f(x)$ with y: $y = x^3 - 8$
   Interchange x and y: $x = y^3 - 8$

   Solve for y.
   $x + 8 = y^3$

$\sqrt[3]{x + 8} = \sqrt[3]{y^3}$

$\sqrt[3]{x + 8} = y$

$f^{-1}(x) = \sqrt[3]{x + 8}$

Domain: $(-\infty, \infty)$

10 To graph f^{-1}, graph f and reflect it across the line $y = x$.
To find the rule for f^{-1}:
Write the original function:
$f(x) = -2x + 14$

Replace $f(x)$ with y: $y = -2x + 14$
Interchange x and y: $x = -2y + 14$

Solve for y.
$x - 14 = -2y$

$\dfrac{x - 14}{-2} = \dfrac{-2y}{-2}$

$-\dfrac{x}{2} + 7 = y$

$f^{-1}(x) = -\dfrac{x}{2} + 7$

Domain: $(-\infty, \infty)$

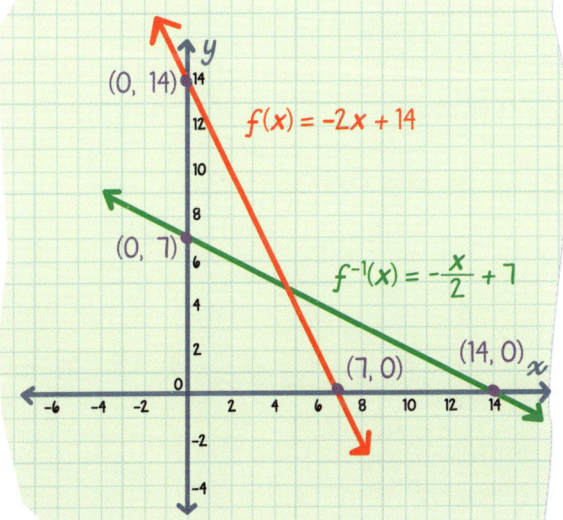

11 To graph f^{-1}, graph f and reflect it across the line $y = x$.

To find the rule for f^{-1}:

Write the original function:
$f(x) = 12x - 6$

Replace $f(x)$ with y: $y = 12x - 6$
Interchange x and y: $x = 12y - 6$

Solve for y.
$x + 6 = 12y$

$\dfrac{x + 6}{12} = \dfrac{12y}{12}$

$\dfrac{x}{12} + \dfrac{1}{2} = y$

$f^{-1}(x) = \dfrac{x}{12} + \dfrac{1}{2}$

Domain: $(-\infty, \infty)$

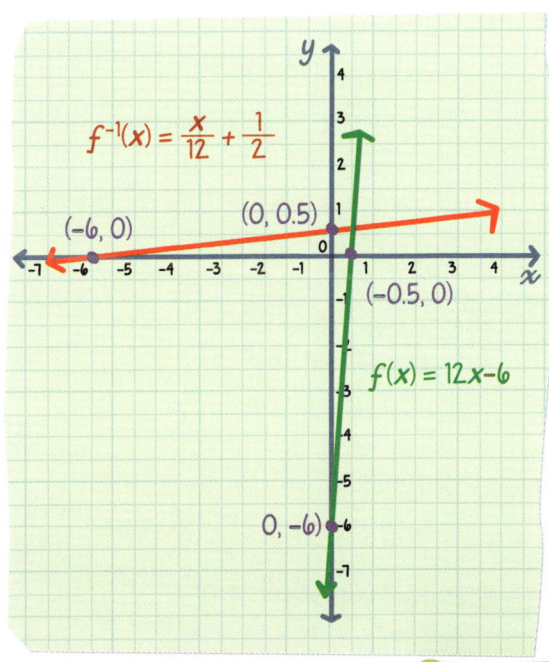

UNIT 3

Quadratic Functions

CHAPTER 14

SOLVING QUADRATIC EQUATIONS

1 $x^2 - 2x = 3$
$x^2 - 2x - 3 = 0$
$(x + 1)(x - 3) = 0$
$x = -1, x = 3$

2 $12 = x^2 - 4x$
$x^2 - 4x - 12 = 0$
$(x + 2)(x - 6) = 0$
$x = -2, x = 6$

3 $x^2 - 11x + 28 = 0$
$(x - 4)(x - 7) = 0$
$x = 4, x = 7$

4 $2x^2 + 21x = -40$
$2x^2 + 21x + 40 = 0$
$2x^2 + 16x + 5x + 40 = 0$
$2x(x + 8) + 5(x + 8) = 0$
$(2x + 5)(x + 8) = 0$
$x = -\dfrac{5}{2}, x = -8$

5 $2(x + 6)^2 - 10 = 8$
$2(x + 6)^2 = 18$
$(x + 6)^2 = 9$
$x + 6 = \pm\sqrt{9}$
$x + 6 = \pm 3$
$x = -6 \pm 3$
$x = -9, x = -3$

6 $4x^2 = 324$
$x^2 = 81$
$x = \pm\sqrt{81}$
$x = -9 \text{ or } x = 9$

7 $x^2 + 4x = 12$
$x^2 + 4x + (\dfrac{4}{2})^2 = 12 + (\dfrac{4}{2})^2$
$x^2 + 4x + 4 = 12 + 4$
$(x + 2)^2 = 16$
$x + 2 = \pm 4$
$x + 2 = 4 \text{ or } x + 2 = -4$
$x = 2 \text{ or } x = -6$

8 $x^2 - 20x - 21 = 0$
$x^2 - 20x = 21$
$x^2 - 20x + (-\dfrac{20}{2})^2 = 21 + (-\dfrac{20}{2})^2$
$x^2 - 20x + 100 = 21 + 100$
$(x - 10)^2 = 121$
$x - 10 = \pm 11$
$x - 10 = 11 \text{ or } x - 10 = -11$
$x = 21 \text{ or } x = -1$

9 $x^2 - 8x = 20$
$x^2 - 8x + (-\dfrac{8}{2})^2 = 20 + (-\dfrac{8}{2})^2$
$x^2 - 8x + 16 = 20 + 16$
$(x - 4)^2 = 36$
$x - 4 = \pm 6$
$x - 4 = 6 \text{ or } x - 4 = -6$
$x = 10 \text{ or } x = -2$

10 $\dfrac{1}{2}x^2 - 5x = 9$
$\dfrac{1}{2}x^2 - 5x - 9 = 0$
$a = \dfrac{1}{2}, b = -5, c = -9$
$x = \dfrac{-b \pm \sqrt{b^2 - 4ac}}{2a}$

$$x = \frac{-(-5) \pm \sqrt{(-5)^2 - 4(\frac{1}{2})(-9)}}{2(\frac{1}{2})}$$

$$x = \frac{5 \pm \sqrt{25 + 18}}{1}$$

$$x = 5 \pm \sqrt{43}$$

$$x = 5 + \sqrt{43} \text{ and } x = 5 - \sqrt{43}$$

11 $-6x^2 + 4x + 16 = 0$

$a = -6, \ b = 4, \ c = 16$

$$x = \frac{-b \pm \sqrt{b^2 - 4ac}}{2a}$$

$$x = \frac{-4 \pm \sqrt{4^2 - 4(-6)(16)}}{2(-6)}$$

$$x = \frac{-4 \pm \sqrt{400}}{-12}$$

$$x = \frac{-4 \pm 20}{-12}$$

$$x = \frac{-4 + 20}{-12} \text{ and } x = \frac{-4 - 20}{-12}$$

$$x = \frac{16}{-12} \text{ and } x = \frac{-24}{-12}$$

$$x = -\frac{4}{3} \text{ and } x = 2$$

12 $3x^2 + 6x = -15$

$3x^2 + 6x + 15 = 0$

$a = 3, \ b = 6, \ c = 15$

$D = b^2 - 4ac$

$D = 6^2 - 4(3)(15)$

$D = 36 - 180$

$D = -144$

D is less than zero, so we know there are zero real solutions (the two solutions are complex).

13 $x^2 + 7x + 2 = 0$

$a = 1, \ b = 7, \ c = 2$

$D = b^2 - 4ac$

$D = 7^2 - 4(1)(2)$

$D = 49 - 8$

$D = 41$

D is greater than 0, so there are two distinct real solutions.

14 $-2x^2 - 4x + 10 = 0$

$a = -2, \ b = -4, \ c = 10$

$D = b^2 - 4ac$

$D = (-4)^2 - 4(-2)(10)$

$D = 16 + 80$

$D = 96$

D is greater than 0, so there two distinct real solutions.

CHAPTER 15

QUADRATIC FUNCTIONS AND THEIR GRAPHS

1 Complete the square to write the function in vertex form.

$f(x) = 3x^2 + 12x - 12$

$3(x^2 + 4x) - 12$

$3(x^2 + 4x + (\frac{4}{2})^2) - 12 - 3(\frac{4}{2})^2$

$3(x^2 + 4x + 4) - 12 - 12$

$3(x^2 + 4x + 4) - 24$

$3(x + 2)^2 - 24$

vertex: $(-2, -24)$

axis of symmetry: $x = -2$

Since $a = 3 > 0$, the graph is a parabola that opens upward.

2 Complete the square to write the function in vertex form.

$g(x) = -x^2 - 18x + 3$
$-(x^2 + 18x) + 3$
$-(x^2 + 18x + (\frac{18}{2})^2) + 3 + (\frac{18}{2})^2$
$-(x^2 + 18x + 81) + 84$
$-(x + 9)^2 + 84$

vertex: $(-9, 84)$
axis of symmetry: $x = -9$

Since $a = -1 < 0$, the graph is a parabola that opens downward.

3 Complete the square to write the function in vertex form.

$h(x) = 2x^2 - 4x + 8$
$2(x^2 - 2x) + 8$
$2(x^2 - 2x + (\frac{2}{2})^2) + 8 - 2(\frac{2}{2})^2$
$2(x^2 - 2x + 1) + 8 - 2$
$2(x - 1)^2 + 6$

vertex: $(1, 6)$
axis of symmetry: $x = 1$

Since $a = 2 > 0$, the graph is a parabola that opens upward.

4 Complete the square to write the function in vertex form.

$f(x) = 2x^2 + 8x + 10$
$2(x^2 + 4x) + 10$
$2(x^2 + 4x + (\frac{4}{2})^2) + 10 - 2(\frac{4}{2})^2$
$2(x^2 + 4x + 4) + 10 - 2(4)$
$2(x + 2)^2 + 2$

vertex: $(-2, 2)$
orientation: opens upward
y-intercept: $(0, 10)$

This parabola does not intersect the x-axis.

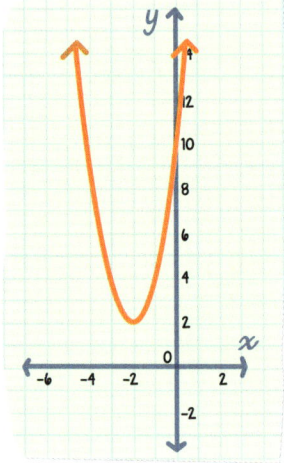

5 Complete the square to write the function in vertex form.

$p(x) = x^2 - 7x - 8$

$(x^2 - 7x + (\frac{7}{2})^2) - 8 - (\frac{7}{2})^2$

$(x^2 - 7x + (\frac{7}{2})^2) - 8 - (\frac{49}{4})$

$(x - \frac{7}{2})^2 - \frac{81}{4}$

vertex: $(\frac{7}{2}, \frac{81}{4})$
orientation: opens upward
y-intercept: $(0, -8)$

The x-intercepts are $(-1, 0)$ and $(8, 0)$.

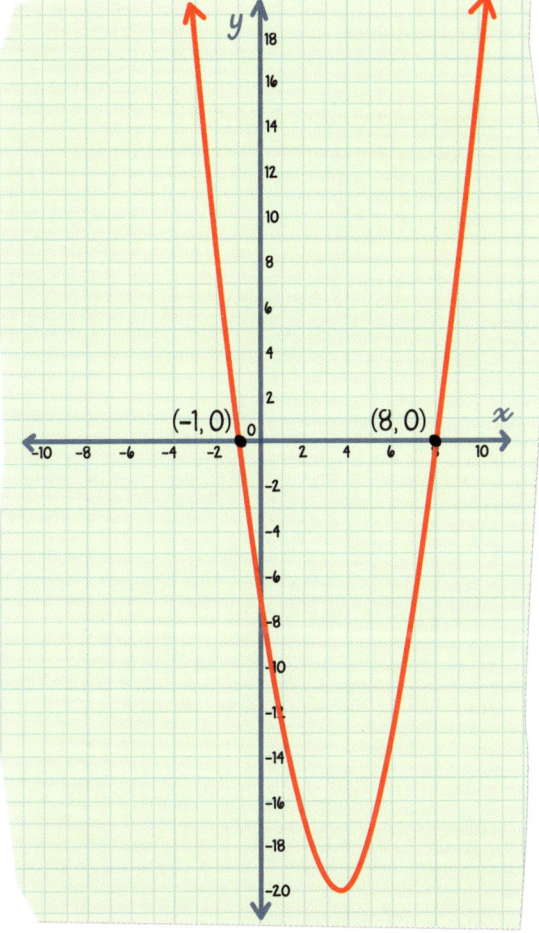

CHAPTER 16

SOLVING NONLINEAR SYSTEMS OF EQUATIONS

1. $\begin{cases} -x - y = -11 \\ x^2 + y^2 = 73 \end{cases}$

Solve the first equation for x. Then substitute the value of x from the first equation into the second equation and solve for y.

First equation:
$-x - y = -11$
$x = 11 - y$

Second equation:
$x^2 + y^2 = 73$
$(11 - y)^2 + y^2 = 73$
$121 - 22y + y^2 + y^2 = 73$
$121 - 22y + 2y^2 = 73$
$2y^2 - 22y + 121 = 73$
$2y^2 - 22y + 48 = 0$
$2(y^2 - 11y + 24) = 0$
$(y - 8)(y - 3) = 0$
$y - 8 = 0$ or $y - 3 = 0$
$y = 8$ or $y = 3$

Substitute the values of y into the first equation to find the corresponding values of x.
$x = 11 - y$
$x = 11 - (8)$
$x = 3$
$x = 11 - y$

$x = 11 - (3)$

$x = 8$

Solutions: (3, 8) and (8, 3)

2 $\begin{cases} y = -\frac{2}{5}x \\ x^2 - y^2 = 21 \end{cases}$

Substitute the value of y from the first equation into the second equation and solve for x.

$x^2 - y^2 = 21$

$x^2 - (-\frac{2}{5}x)^2 = 21$

$x^2 - \frac{4}{25}x^2 = 21$

$\frac{21}{25}x^2 = 21$

$x^2 = 25$

$x = \pm 5$

$x = 5$ or $x = -5$

Substitute the values of x into the first equation to find the corresponding values of y.

$y = -\frac{2}{5}x$

$y = -\frac{2}{5}(5)$

$y = -2$

$y = -\frac{2}{5}x$

$y = -\frac{2}{5}(-5)$

$y = 2$

Solutions: (5, –2) and (–5, 2)

3 $\begin{cases} \frac{x^2}{49} + \frac{y^2}{16} = 1 \\ x^2 - y^2 = 49 \end{cases}$

Solve the second equation for x^2. Then substitute that value for x^2 into the first equation and solve for y.

Second equation:

$x^2 - y^2 = 49$

$x^2 = 49 + y^2$

First equation:

$\frac{x^2}{49} + \frac{y^2}{16} = 1$

$\frac{(49 + y^2)}{49} + \frac{y^2}{16} = 1$

$784 \bullet (\frac{(49 + y^2)}{49} + \frac{y^2}{16}) = 784 \bullet 1$

$16(49 + y^2) + 49y^2 = 784$

$784 + 16y^2 + 49y^2 = 784$

$65y^2 = 0$

$y^2 = 0$

$y = 0$

Substitute the value of y into the second equation to find the corresponding values of x.

$x^2 = 49 + y^2$

$x^2 = 49 + (0)^2$

$x^2 = 49$

$x = \pm 7$

$x = 7$ or $x = -7$

Solutions: (–7, 0) and (7, 0)

4
$$\begin{cases} x + y = 0 \\ 4x^2 + 2y^2 = 6 \end{cases}$$

Solve the first equation for x. Then substitute the value of x from the first equation into the second equation and solve for y.

First equation:
$x + y = 0$
$x = -y$

Second equation:
$4x^2 + 2y^2 = 6$
$4(-y)^2 + 2y^2 = 6$
$4y^2 + 2y^2 = 6$
$6y^2 = 6$
$y^2 = 1$
$y = \pm 1$
$y = 1$ or $y = -1$

Substitute the values of y into the first equation to find the corresponding values of x.
$x + y = 0$
$x + (1) = 0$
$x + 1 - 1 = 0 - 1$
$x = -1$

$x + y = 0$
$x + (-1) = 0$
$x - 1 + 1 = 0 + 1$
$x = 1$

Solutions: (1, –1) and (–1, 1)

5
$$\begin{cases} x^2 + y^2 = 4 \\ \dfrac{y^2}{4} - \dfrac{x^2}{4} = 1 \end{cases}$$

Eliminate x by multiplying the first equation by $-\frac{1}{4}$.
$-\frac{1}{4}(x^2 + y^2 = 4)$
$-\frac{x^2}{4} - \frac{y^2}{4} = -1$

Add the equations. Then solve for y.
$$-\frac{x^2}{4} - \frac{y^2}{4} = -1$$
$$+\;\frac{x^2}{4} - \frac{y^2}{4} = 1$$
$$\overline{}$$
$$-\frac{y^2}{4} = 0$$
$$y = 0$$

Find x by substituting $y = 0$ into one of the original equations.
$x^2 + y^2 = 4$
$x^2 + 0^2 = 4$
$x^2 = 4$
$x = \pm 2$

So, the solutions to the system of equations are (2, 0) and (–2, 0).

6 $\begin{cases} -2y - x^2 = -12 \\ 2x + y = 6 \end{cases}$

Eliminate y by multiplying the second equation by 2.

$2(2x + y = 6)$

$4x + 2y = 12$

Add the equations. Then solve for x.

$-2y - x^2 = -12$

$+ 2y + 4x = 12$

$\overline{}$

$4x - x^2 = 0$

$x(4 - x) = 0$

$x = 0$ and $x = 4$

Find y by substituting both $x = 0$ and $x = 4$ into one of the original equations.

$2x + y = 6 \qquad 2x + y = 6$

$2(0) + y = 6 \qquad 2(4) + y = 6$

$y = 6 \qquad\qquad y = -2$

So, the solutions to the system of equations are $(0, 6)$ and $(4, -2)$.

UNIT 4

Polynomial Functions

CHAPTER 17

OPERATIONS ON POLYNOMIALS

1 $(8x^7 - 3y^4 - 11x^5) + (2x^7 + 5x^5 - 9y^4)$

$8x^7 - 3y^4 - 11x^5 + 2x^7 + 5x^5 - 9y^4$

$8x^7 + 2x^7 - 3y^4 - 9y^4 - 11x^5 + 5x^5$

$10x^7 - 12y^4 - 6x^5$

$10x^7 - 6x^5 - 12y^4$

2 $(6m^8 + 2m^5 + m^2n) - (-7m^8 - 14m^5 + 4m^2n - 9)$

$6m^8 + 2m^5 + m^2n + 7m^8 + 14m^5 - 4m^2n + 9$

$6m^8 + 7m^8 + 2m^5 + 14m^5 + m^2n - 4m^2n + 9$

$13m^8 + 16m^5 - 3m^2n + 9$

3 $(7ab^3 - 4b^6 - 12a^2) + (-5b^6 + 3a^2 + 2ab^3)$

$7ab^3 - 4b^6 - 12a^2 - 5b^6 + 3a^2 + 2ab^3$

$7ab^3 + 2ab^3 - 4b^6 - 5b^6 - 12a^2 + 3a^2$

$9ab^3 - 9b^6 - 9a^2$

$-9b^6 + 9ab^3 - 9a^2$

4 $(2h^9 + 10g^4 + hg) + (hg - 21) - (16h^9 - 5g^4 - 6)$

$2h^9 + 10g^4 + hg + hg - 21 - 16h^9 + 5g^4 + 6$

$2h^9 - 16h^9 + 10g^4 + 5g^4 + hg + hg - 21 + 6$

$-14h^9 + 15g^4 + 2hg - 15$

5. $(18y^2 - 14y^7 + 7y^3) - (5y^7 - y^3 + 8y^2)$
$18y^2 - 14y^7 + 7y^3 - 5y^7 + y^3 - 8y^2$
$18y^2 - 8y^2 - 14y^7 - 5y^7 + 7y^3 + y^3$
$10y^2 - 19y^7 + 8y^3$
$-19y^7 + 8y^3 + 10y^2$

6. $(k^6 - 4k^5 + 5k^4) + (16k^4 + 5) - (7k^6 - 3k^4 + 3)$

$k^6 - 4k^5 + 5k^4 + 16k^4 + 5 - 7k^6 + 3k^4 - 3$

$k^6 - 7k^6 - 4k^5 + 5k^4 + 16k^4 + 3k^4 + 5 - 3$

$-6k^6 - 4k^5 + 24k^4 + 2$

7. Perimeter $= 2(l + w)$
$2(2x + 5x + 8)$
$2(7x + 8)$
$14x + 16$

8. $(a^7b^3 - a^9b^4)(a^9b^7)$
$a^7b^3(a^9b^7) - a^9b^4(a^9b^7)$
$a^{16}b^{10} - a^{18}b^{11}$

9. $5x^3(-8x^2 + 2xy)$
$5x^3(-8x^2) + 5x^3(2xy)$
$-40x^5 + 10x^4y$

10. $(c^2d^8)(cd^5 - 9d + 2c^2)$
$(c^2d^8)(cd^5) - (c^2d^8)(9d) + (c^2d^8)(2c^2)$
$c^3d^{13} - 9c^2d^9 + 2c^4d^8$

11. $(x^3y + 9)^2$
$(x^3y + 9)(x^3y + 9)$
$(x^3y)(x^3y) + (x^3y)(9) + (9)(x^3y) + (9)(9)$
$x^6y^2 + 9x^3y + 9x^3y + 81$
$x^6y^2 + 18x^3y + 81$

12. $h^2(6g^2 - 11g)$
$h^2(6g^2) - h^2(11g)$
$6g^2h^2 - 11gh^2$

13. $(m^7n + 4)^2$
$(m^7n + 4)(m^7n + 4)$
$(m^7n)(m^7n) + (m^7n)(4) + (4)(m^7n) + (4)(4)$
$m^{14}n^2 + 4m^7n + 4m^7n + 16$
$m^{14}n^2 + 8m^7n + 16$

14. Area $= lw$
$(4x + 7)(x + 3)$
$(4x)(x) + (4x)(3) + (7)(x) + (7)(3)$
$4x^2 + 12x + 7x + 21$
$4x^2 + 19x + 21$

CHAPTER 18

FACTORING POLYNOMIALS

1. $24x^5y^3 + 36xy^2$

GCF of 24 and 36: 12
GCF of x^5 and x: x
GCF of y^3 and y^2: y^2

Therefore, the GCF is $12xy^2$.

Divide each term by the GCF.

$\dfrac{24x^5y^3}{12xy^2} = 2x^4y$

$\dfrac{36xy^2}{12xy^2} = 3$

$12xy^2(2x^4y + 3)$

2 $8a^2b^6c^{18} + 32a^5b^{14}c^{25} - 64a^{17}b^{18}c^{29}$

GCF of 8, 32, and −64: 8
GCF of a^2, a^5, and a^{17}: a^2
GCF of b^6, b^{14}, and b^{18}: b^6
GCF of c^{18}, c^{25}, and c^{29}: c^{18}

Therefore, the GCF is $8a^2b^6c^{18}$.

Divide each term by the GCF.

$\dfrac{8a^2b^6c^{18}}{8a^2b^6c^{18}} = 1$

$\dfrac{32a^5b^{14}c^{25}}{8a^2b^6c^{18}} = 4a^3b^8c^7$

$\dfrac{-64a^{17}b^{18}c^{29}}{8a^2b^6c^{18}} = -8a^{15}b^{12}c^{11}$

$8a^2b^6c^{18}(1 + 4a^3b^8c^7 - 8a^{15}b^{12}c^{11})$

3 $-11h^3j^4 - 33hj^6$

GCF of −11 and −33: 11
GCF of h^3 and h: h
GCF of j^4 and j^6: j^4

Therefore, the GCF is $11hj^4$.

Divide each term by the GCF.

$\dfrac{-11h^3j^4}{11hj^4} = -h^2$

$\dfrac{-33hj^6}{11hj^4} = -3j^2$

$11hj^4(-h^2 - 3j^2)$ **Factor −1**
$-11hj^4(h^2 + 3j^2)$

4 $2m^4n^7 + 2m^8n^8 + 4m^{10}n^9$

GCF of 2, 2, and 4: 2
GCF of m^4, m^8, and m^{10}: m^4
GCF of n^7, n^8, and n^9: n^7

Therefore, the GCF is $2m^4n^7$.

Divide each term by the GCF.

$\dfrac{2m^4n^7}{2m^4n^7} = 1$

$\dfrac{2m^8n^8}{2m^4n^7} = m^4n$

$\dfrac{4m^{10}n^9}{2m^4n^7} = 2m^6n^2$

$2m^4n^7(1 + m^4n + 2m^6n^2)$

5 $3c^6 + 9c^5 + 4c + 12$
$(3c^6 + 9c^5) + (4c + 12)$
$3c^5(c + 3) + 4(c + 3)$
$(3c^5 + 4)(c + 3)$

6 $8x^3 - xy + 8x^2y - y^2$
$(8x^3 - xy) + (8x^2y - y^2)$
$x(8x^2 - y) + y(8x^2 - y)$
$(x + y)(8x^2 - y)$

7 $7d^2 + 14d^3 + 8d + 4$
$(7d^2 + 14d^3) + (8d + 4)$
$7d^2(1 + 2d) + 4(2d + 1)$
$(7d^2 + 4)(2d + 1)$

8 $a^2 + 2a - 3$
$-1 \cdot 3 = -3$ and $-1 + 3 = 2$
$(a - 1)(a + 3)$

9 $d^2 - 12d + 36$
$-6 \cdot (-6) = 36$ and $-6 + (-6) = -12$
$(d - 6)(d - 6) = (d - 6)^2$

10 $6x^2 - 13x + 6$
$6 \cdot 6 = 36$ and $-4 + (-9) = -13$
$6x^2 - 4x - 9x + 6$
$(6x^2 - 4x) + (-9x + 6)$
$2x(3x - 2) - 3(3x - 2)$
$(2x - 3)(3x - 2)$

11 $121m^6 - 25n^6$

Rewrite the polynomial in the
form $x^2 - y^2$.

$(11m^3)^2 - (5n^3)^2$

Using the Difference of Two
Squares formula, rewrite this
polynomial as $(x + y)(x - y)$.

$(11m^3 + 5n^3)(11m^3 - 5n^3)$

12 $49x^8 + 42x^4y^2 + 9y^4$

Rewrite the polynomial in the
form $x^2 + 2xy + y^2$.

$(7x^4)^2 + 2 \cdot 7x^4 \cdot 3y^2 + (3y^2)^2$

Using the Perfect Square
Trinomial formula, rewrite this
polynomial as $(x + y)^2$.

$(7x^4 + 3y^2)^2$

13 $125h^{24} + 512j^{36}$

Rewrite the polynomial in the
form $x^3 + y^3$.

$(5h^8)^3 + (8j^{12})^3$

Using the Sum of Two Cubes
formula, rewrite this polynomial as
$(x + y)(x^2 - xy + y^2)$.

$(5h^8 + 8j^{12})((5h^8)^2 - 5h^8 \cdot 8j^{12} + (8j^{12})^2)$
$(5h^8 + 8j^{12})(25h^{16} - 40h^8j^{12} + 64j^{24})$

14 $27c^9d^{18} - 343g^{24}$

Rewrite the polynomial in the
form $x^3 - y^3$.

$(3c^3d^6)^3 - (7g^8)^3$

Using the Difference of Two Cubes
formula, rewrite this polynomial as
$(x - y)(x^2 + xy + y^2)$.

$(3c^3d^6 - 7g^8)((3c^3d^6)^2 + 3c^3d^6 \cdot 7g^8 + (7g^8)^2)$
$(3c^3d^6 - 7g^8)(9c^6d^{12} + 21c^3d^6g^8 + 49g^{16})$

CHAPTER 19

POLYNOMIAL DIVISION

1 $(4x^4 + 2x^3 + 6x^2 + 4x + 5) \div (x + 7)$

$$
\begin{array}{r}
4x^3 - 26x^2 + 188x - 1312 \\
x + 7 \overline{\smash{\big)}\ 4x^4 + 2x^3 + 6x^2 + 4x + 5} \\
\underline{-4x^4 - 28x^3} \\
-26x^3 + 6x^2 \\
\underline{+26x^3 + 182x^2} \\
+188x^2 + 4x \\
\underline{-188x^2 - 1316x} \\
-1312x + 5 \\
\underline{+1312x + 9184} \\
9189
\end{array}
$$

$(4x^4 + 2x^3 + 6x^2 + 4x + 5) \div (x + 7) =$
$4x^3 - 26x^2 + 188x - 1,312 + \dfrac{9189}{x + 7}$

2 $(-5x^3 - 10x + 75) \div (5x - 10)$

$$
\begin{array}{r}
-x^2 - 2x - 6 \\
5x - 10 \overline{\smash{\big)}\ -5x^3 + 0x^2 - 10x + 75} \\
\underline{+5x^3 - 10x^2} \\
-10x^2 - 10x \\
\underline{+10x^2 - 20x} \\
-30x + 75 \\
\underline{+30x - 60} \\
15
\end{array}
$$

$(-5x^3 - 10x + 75) \div (5x - 10)$
$= -x^2 - 2x - 6 + \dfrac{15}{5x - 10}$

3 $(12x^5 + 6x^3 - 3x^2) \div (-x^2 - 1)$

$$
\begin{array}{r}
-12x^3 + 0x^2 + 6x + 3 \\
-x^2 + 0x - 1 \overline{\smash{\big)}\ 12x^5 + 0x^4 + 6x^3 - 3x^2 + 0x + 0} \\
\underline{-12x^5 - 0x^4 - 12x^3} \\
-6x^3 - 3x^2 + 0x \\
\underline{+6x^3 - 0x^2 + 6x} \\
-3x^2 + 6x + 0 \\
\underline{+3x^2 - 0 + 3} \\
6x + 3
\end{array}
$$

$(12x^5 + 6x^3 - 3x^2) \div (-x^2 - 1)$
$= -12x^3 + 6x + 3 + \dfrac{6x + 3}{-x^2 - 1}$

4 $(x^3 - 7x + 9) \div (x - 2)$

2	1	0	-7	9
		2	4	-6
	1	2	-3	3

$(x^3 - 7x + 9) \div (x - 2)$
$= x^2 + 2x - 3 + \dfrac{3}{x - 2}$

5 $(12x^2 + 6x + 18) \div (3x + 12)$
$3x + 12 = 3(\mathbf{x} + 4)$

-4	12	6	18
		-48	168
	12	-42	186

So, $(12x^2 + 6x + 18) \div (x + 4)$
$= 12x - 42 + \dfrac{186}{x + 4}$.

$(12x^2 + 6x + 18) \div 3(x + 4)$

$$= \frac{1}{3}(12x - 42 + \frac{186}{x+4})$$

$$= 4x - 14 + \frac{62}{x+4}$$

6 $(4x^3 + 21x - 19) \div (x - 6)$

$$
\begin{array}{r|rrrr}
6 & 4 & 0 & 21 & -19 \\
  &   & 24 & 144 & 990 \\
\hline
  & 4 & 24 & 165 & 971
\end{array}
$$

$(4x^3 + 21x - 19) \div (x - 6)$
$$= 4x^2 + 24x + 165 + \frac{971}{x-6}$$

7 Find $P(8)$ if $P(x) = 2x^2 + 7x - 25$.

Divide $P(x) = 2x^2 + 7x - 25$ by
$D(x) = x - 8$.

$$
\begin{array}{r|rrr}
8 & 2 & 7 & -25 \\
  &   & 16 & 184 \\
\hline
  & 2 & 23 & 159
\end{array}
$$

So, by the Remainder Theorem
$P(8) = 159$.

8 Find $P(-6)$ if $P(x) = 7x^3 - 10x + 13$.

Divide $P(x) = 7x^3 - 10x + 13$ by
$D(x) = x + 6$.

$$
\begin{array}{r|rrrr}
-6 & 7 & 0 & -10 & 13 \\
   &   & -42 & 252 & -1452 \\
\hline
   & 7 & -42 & 242 & -1439
\end{array}
$$

So, by the Remainder Theorem
$P(-6) = -1,439$.

9 Find the value of the dividend
when $x = 9$ to find the remainder.

$x^3 + 18x^2 - 33x + 169$
$(9)^3 + 18(9)^2 - 33(9) + 16$
$729 + 1458 - 297 + 16$
$1,906$ remainder

10 Find the value of the dividend
when $x = -3$ to find the remainder.

$2x^3 + 4x^2 + 17x + 85$
$2(-3)^3 + 4(-3)^2 + 17(-3) + 85$
$-54 + 36 - 51 + 85$
16 remainder

11 Find the remainder to determine if
$x + 4$ is a factor.

$x^3 + 3x^2 + 3x + 28$
$(-4)^3 + 3(-4)^2 + 3(-4) + 28$
$-64 + 3 \bullet 16 - 12 + 28$
$-64 + 48 - 12 + 28$
0

The remainder is 0, so $x + 4$ i
s a factor.

Use synthetic division to
find the other factor.

$$
\begin{array}{r|rrrr}
-4 & 1 & 3 & 3 & 28 \\
   &   & -4 & 4 & -28 \\
\hline
   & 1 & -1 & 7 & 0
\end{array}
$$

$x^2 - x + 7$

This is a quadratic equation. Use the discriminant ($b^2 - 4ac$) to determine if you can factor further.

Since $(-1)^2 - 4 \cdot 1 \cdot 7 = 1 - 28 = -27 < 0$

So, $x^3 + 3x^2 + 3x + 28$ factors as $(x + 4)(x^2 - x + 7)$.

12 Find the remainder to determine if $x - 2$ is a factor.

$9x^3 + 8x^2 - 5x - 94$
$9(2)^3 + 8(2)^2 - 5(2) - 94$
$9 \cdot 8 + 8 \cdot 4 - 10 - 94$
$72 + 32 - 10 - 94$
0

The remainder is 0 so, $x - 2$ is a factor.

Use synthetic division to find the other factor.

2	9	8	-5	-94
		18	52	94
	9	26	47	0

$9x^2 + 26x + 47$

This is a quadratic equation. Use the discriminant ($b^2 - 4ac$) to determine if you can factor further.

Since $26^2 - 4 \cdot 9 \cdot 47 = -1016 < 0$, the expression $9x^2 + 26x + 47$ has complex roots, and therefore the polynomial is factored completely in the real numbers.

So, $9x^3 + 8x^2 - 5x - 94$ factors as $(x - 2)(9x^2 + 26x + 47)$.

CHAPTER 20

POLYNOMIAL FUNCTIONS AND THEIR GRAPHS

1 Factor $g(x)$ and apply the Zero-Product Principle to find the zeros.

$g(x) = (x^2 - 9)(x + 6)$
$g(x) = (x + 3)(x - 3)(x + 6)$

$x + 3 = 0$	$x - 3 = 0$	$x + 6 = 0$
$x = -3$	$x = 3$	$x = -6$

Therefore, $g(-3) = 0$, $g(3) = 0$, and $g(-6) = 0$.

So, the zeros are:
$x = -3$, $x = 3$, and $x = -6$.

2 Factor $h(x)$ and apply the Zero-Product Principle to find the zeros.

$h(x) = (x^2 - 16)(x^2 - 1)$

$h(x) = (x + 4)(x - 4)(x + 1)(x - 1)$

$x + 4 = 0$	$x - 4 = 0$	$x + 1 = 0$	$x - 1 = 0$
$x = -4$	$x = 4$	$x = -1$	$x = 1$

Therefore, $h(-4) = 0$, $h(4) = 0$, $h(-1) = 0$, and $h(1) = 0$.

So, the zeros are:
$x = -4$, $x = 4$, $x = -1$, and $x = 1$.

3 Use synthetic division to find the factors of $j(x)$ and apply the Zero-Product Principle to find the zeros.

$$\begin{array}{r|rrrr} 5 & 1 & -8 & 5 & 50 \\ & & 5 & -15 & -50 \\ \hline & 1 & -3 & -10 & 0 \end{array}$$

$x^2 - 3x - 10$

$j(x) = x^3 - 8x^2 + 5x + 50$

$j(x) = (x - 5)(x^2 - 3x - 10)$

$j(x) = (x - 5)(x - 5)(x + 2)$

$x - 5 = 0$	$x + 2 = 0$
$x = 5$	$x = -2$

Therefore, $j(5) = 0$ and $j(-2) = 0$.

So, the zeros are:
$x = 5$ and $x = -2$.

4 $f(x) = 9x^5 - 2x^2 + 7x - 3$

Highest degree: 5

Leading coefficient: 9

Since the degree of the function is odd and the leading coefficient is positive, the graph of the function goes up at the right end and down at the left end.

5 $h(x) = -14x^6 + 7x^5 - 8x + 4$

Highest degree: 6

Leading coefficient: −14

Since the degree of the function is even and the leading coefficient is negative, the graph of the function goes down at both ends.

6 $g(x) = -7x^9 + 6x^2 - 12x + 22$

Highest degree: 9

Leading coefficient: −7

Since the degree of the function is odd and the leading coefficient is negative, the graph of the function goes down at the right end and up at the left end.

7 Graph the function $f(x) = x^3$ reflected across the x-axis and shifted 9 units to the right and 2 units up.

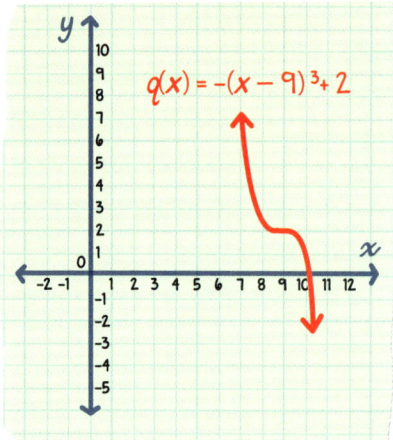

$q(x) = -(x - 9)^3 + 2$

8 Graph the function $f(x) = x^4$ shifted 12 units to the left and 1 unit down.

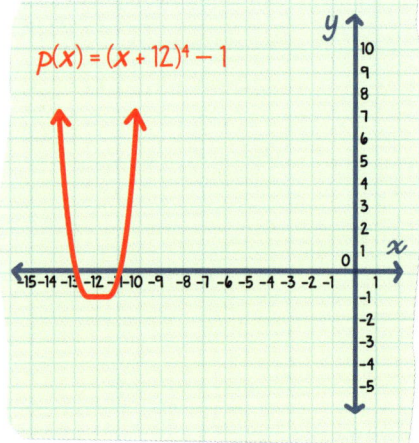

$p(x) = (x + 12)^4 - 1$

9 Graph the function $f(x) = x^3$ shifted 15 units to the right and 4 units up.

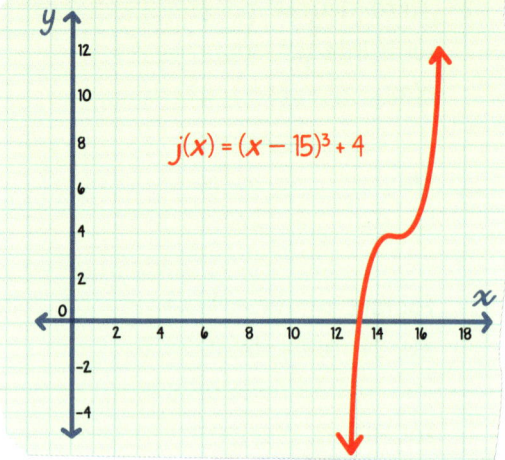

$j(x) = (x - 15)^3 + 4$

CHAPTER 21

RATIONAL ZEROS OF POLYNOMIAL FUNCTIONS

1 Third-degree polynomial with integer coefficients:
$h(x) = x^3 + 11x^2 + 10x - 72$

Constant term: -72
Leading coefficient: 1

Factors of -72: ±1, ±2, ±3, ±4, ±6, ±8, ±9, ±12, ±18, ±24, ±36, ±72

Factors of 1: ±1

All possible rational zeros: ±1, ±2, ±3, ±4, ±6, ±8, ±9, ±12, ±18, ±24, ±36, ±72

$\dfrac{p}{q}$	1	11	10	-72
1	1	12	22	-50
-1	1	10	0	-72
2	1	13	36	0

So, $x - 2$ is a factor. By the Factor Theorem, $h(2) = 0$. Therefore, 2 is a zero of h.

The quotient is $x^2 + 13x + 36$. We can use quadratic factoring techniques to find the other zeros.

$x^2 + 13x + 36 = 0$
$(x + 4)(x + 9) = 0$
$x + 4 = 0 \quad x + 9 = 0$
$x = -4 \quad x = -9$

So, the zeros of h are 2, -4, and -9.

By the Factor Theorem, the factors of h are $x - 2$, $x + 4$, and $x + 9$.

So, $h(x) = (x - 2)(x + 4)(x + 9)$.

2 Third-degree polynomial with integer coefficients:
$q(x) = 2x^3 - 24x^2 + 70x - 48$

Constant term: -48
Leading coefficient: 2

Factors of -48: ±1, ±2, ±3, ±4, ±6, ±8, ±12, ±16, ±24, ±48

Factors of 2: ±1, ±2

All possible rational zeros: ±1, ±$\dfrac{1}{2}$, ±2, ±3, ±$\dfrac{3}{2}$, ±4, ±6, ±8, ±12, ±16, ±24, ±48

$\dfrac{p}{q}$	2	-24	70	-48
1	2	-22	48	0

So, $x - 1$ is a factor. By the Factor Theorem, $q(1) = 0$. Therefore, 1 is a zero of q.

The quotient is $2x^2 - 22x + 48$. We can use quadratic factoring techniques to find the other zeros.

$2x^2 - 22x + 48 = 0$
$2(x^2 - 11x + 24) = 0$
$2(x - 8)(x - 3) = 0$
$x - 8 = 0 \quad x - 3 = 0$
$x = 8 \quad x = 3$

So, the zeros of q are 1, 3, and 8.

By the Factor Theorem, the factors of q are $x - 1$, $x - 3$, and $x - 8$.

So, $q(x) = 2(x - 1)(x - 3)(x - 8)$.

3 Fourth-degree polynomial with integer coefficients:
$f(x) = x^4 - 11x^3 + 17x^2 + 107x - 210$

Constant term: −210
Leading coefficient: 1

Factors of −210: ±1, ±2, ±3, ±5, ±6, ±7, ±10, ±14, ±15, ±21, ±30, ±35, ±42, ±70, ±105, ±210

Factors of 1: ±1

All possible rational zeros: ±1, ±2, ±3, ±5, ±6, ±7, ±10, ±14, ±15, ±21, ±30, ±35, ±42, ±70, ±105, ±210

$\frac{p}{q}$	1	−11	17	107	−210
1	1	−10	7	114	−96
−1	1	−12	29	78	−288
2	1	−9	−1	105	0

So, $x - 2$ is a factor. By the Factor Theorem, $f(2) = 0$. Therefore, 2 is a zero of f.

The quotient is $x^3 - 9x^2 - x + 105$. We can use synthetic division on this new polynomial to continue finding zeros.

Third-degree polynomial with integer coefficients:
$x^3 - 9x^2 - x + 105$

Constant term: 105
Leading coefficient: 1

Factors of 105: ±1, ±3, ±5, ±7, ±15, ±21, ±35, ±105

Factors of 1: ±1

All possible rational zeros in reduced form: ±1, ±3, ±5, ±7, ±15, ±21, ±35, ±105

$\frac{p}{q}$	1	-9	-1	105
1	1	-8	-9	96
-1	1	-10	9	96
3	1	-6	-19	48
-3	1	-12	35	0

So, $x + 3$ is a factor. By the Factor Theorem, $f(-3) = 0$. Therefore, -3 is a zero of the polynomial f.

The quotient is $x^2 - 12x + 35$. We can use quadratic factoring techniques to find the other zeros.

$x^2 - 12x + 35 = 0$
$(x - 7)(x - 5) = 0$
$x - 7 = 0 \quad x - 5 = 0$
$x = 7 \quad x = 5$

So, the zeros of f are -3, 2, 5, and 7.

By the Factor Theorem, the factors of f are $x + 3$, $x - 2$, $x - 5$, and $x - 7$.

So, $f(x) = (x + 3)(x - 2)(x - 5)(x - 7)$.

4 $j(x) = 3x^2 + 12x - 96$

Factor: $j(x) = 3(x - 4)(x + 8)$

$x - 4 = 0$	$x + 8 = 0$	Zero-Product
$x = 4$	$x = -8$	Principle

So, $j(x) = 3(x - 4)(x + 8)$, and the zeros of j are 4 and -8.

5 Third-degree polynomial with integer coefficients:
$H(x) = x^3 - 9x^2 + 23x - 15$

Constant term: -15
Leading coefficient: 1

Factors of -15: ±1, ±3, ±5, ±15

Factors of 1: ±1

All possible rational zeros: ±1, ±3, ±5, ±15

$\frac{p}{q}$	1	-9	23	-15
1	1	-8	15	0

So, $x - 1$ is a factor. By the Factor Theorem, $H(1) = 0$. Therefore, 1 is a zero of H.

The quotient is $x^2 - 8x + 15$. We can use quadratic factoring techniques to find the other zeros.

$x^2 - 8x + 15 = 0$
$(x - 3)(x - 5) = 0$
$x - 3 = 0 \quad x - 5 = 0$
$x = 3 \quad x = 5$

So, the zeros of H are 1, 3, and 5.

By the Factor Theorem, the factors of H are $x - 1$, $x - 3$, and $x - 5$.

So, $H(x) = (x - 1)(x - 3)(x - 5)$.

6 Fourth-degree polynomial with integer coefficients:
$g(x) = 4x^4 - 52x^2 + 144$

Constant term: 144
Leading coefficient: 4

Factors of 144: ±1, ±2, ±3, ±4, ±6, ±8, ±9, ±12, ±16, ±18, ±24, ±36, ±48, ±72, ±144

Factors of 4: ±1, ±2, ±4

All possible rational zeros: ±1, $\pm\dfrac{1}{2}$, $\pm\dfrac{1}{4}$, ±2, ±3, $\pm\dfrac{3}{2}$, $\pm\dfrac{3}{4}$, ±4, ±6, ±8, ±9, $\pm\dfrac{9}{2}$, $\pm\dfrac{9}{4}$, ±12, ±16, ±18, ±24, ±36, ±48, ±72, ±144

$\dfrac{p}{q}$	4	0	-52	0	144
1	4	4	-48	-48	96
-1	4	-4	-48	48	96
$\dfrac{1}{2}$	4	2	-51	$-\dfrac{51}{2}$	$\dfrac{525}{4}$
$-\dfrac{1}{2}$	4	-2	-51	$\dfrac{51}{2}$	$\dfrac{525}{4}$
$\dfrac{1}{4}$	4	1	$-\dfrac{207}{4}$	$-\dfrac{207}{16}$	$\dfrac{9009}{64}$

$\dfrac{p}{q}$	4	0	-52	0	144
$-\dfrac{1}{4}$	4	-1	$-\dfrac{207}{4}$	$\dfrac{207}{16}$	$\dfrac{9009}{64}$
2	4	8	-36	-72	0

So, $x - 2$ is a factor. By the Factor Theorem, $g(2) = 0$. Therefore, 2 is a zero of g.

The quotient is $4x^3 + 8x^2 - 36x - 72$. We can use synthetic division on this new polynomial to continue finding zeros.

Third-degree polynomial with integer coefficients: $4x^3 + 8x^2 - 36x - 72$

Constant term: -72
Leading coefficient: 4

Factors of -72: ±1, ±2, ±3, ±4, ±6, ±8, ±9, ±12, ±18, ±24, ±36, ±72

Factors of 4: ±1, ±2, ±4

All possible rational zeros in reduced form: ±1, $\pm\dfrac{1}{2}$, $\pm\dfrac{1}{4}$, ±2, ±3, $\pm\dfrac{3}{2}$, $\pm\dfrac{3}{4}$, ±4, ±6, ±8, ±9, $\pm\dfrac{9}{2}$, $\pm\dfrac{9}{4}$, ±12, ±16, ±18, ±24, ±36, ±48, ±72

$\frac{p}{q}$	4	8	-36	-72
2	4	16	-4	-80
-2	4	0	-36	0

So, $x + 2$ is a factor. By the Factor Theorem, $g(-2) = 0$. Therefore, -2 is a zero of the polynomial g.

The quotient is $4x^2 - 36$. We can use quadratic factoring techniques to find the other zeros.

$4x^2 - 36 = 0$
$4(x^2 - 9) = 0$
$4(x - 3)(x + 3) = 0$
$x - 3 = 0 \quad x + 3 = 0$
$x = 3 \quad x = -3$

So, the zeros of g are -3, -2, 2, and 3.

By the Factor Theorem, the factors of g are $x + 3$, $x + 2$, $x - 2$, and $x - 3$.

So, $g(x) = (x + 3)(x + 2)(x - 2)(x - 3)$.

7 Fourth-degree polynomial with integer coefficients:
$Q(x) = x^4 - 16x^3 + 65x^2 - 38x - 120$

Constant term: -120
Leading coefficient: 1

Factors of -120: ± 1, ± 2, ± 3, ± 4, ± 5, ± 6, ± 8, ± 10, ± 12, ± 15, ± 20, ± 24, ± 30, ± 40, ± 60, ± 120

Factors of 1: ± 1

All possible rational zeros: ± 1, ± 2, ± 3, ± 4, ± 5, ± 6, ± 8, ± 10, ± 12, ± 15, ± 20, ± 24, ± 30, ± 40, ± 60, ± 120

$\frac{p}{q}$	1	-16	65	-38	-120
1	1	-15	50	12	-108
-1	1	-17	82	-120	0

So, $x + 1$ is a factor. By the Factor Theorem, $Q(-1) = 0$. Therefore, -1 is a zero of Q.

The quotient is $x^3 - 17x^2 + 82x - 120$. We can use synthetic division on this new polynomial to continue finding zeros.

Third-degree polynomial with integer coefficients:
$x^3 - 17x^2 + 82x - 120$

Constant term: -120
Leading coefficient: 1

Factors of -120: ± 1, ± 2, ± 3, ± 4, ± 5, ± 6, ± 8, ± 10, ± 12, ± 15, ± 20, ± 24, ± 30, ± 40, ± 60, ± 120

Factors of 1: ±1

All possible rational zeros in reduced form: ±1, ±2, ±3, ±4, ±5, ±6, ±8, ±10, ±12, ±15, ±20, ±24, ±30, ±40, ±60, ±120

$\frac{p}{q}$	1	-17	82	-120
-1	1	-18	100	-220
2	1	-15	52	-16
-2	1	-19	120	-360
3	1	-14	40	0

So, $x - 3$ is a factor. By the Factor Theorem, $Q(3) = 0$. Therefore, 3 is a zero of the polynomial Q.

The quotient is $x^2 - 14x + 40$. We can use quadratic factoring techniques to find the other zeros.

$x^2 - 14x + 40 = 0$
$(x - 4)(x - 10) = 0$
$x - 4 = 0 \quad x - 10 = 0$
$x = 4 \quad x = 10$

So, the zeros of Q are -1, 3, 4, and 10.

By the Factor Theorem, the factors of Q are $x + 1$, $x - 3$, $x - 4$, and $x - 10$.

So, $Q(x) = (x + 1)(x - 3)(x - 4)(x - 10)$.

8 Third-degree polynomial with integer coefficients:
$R(x) = x^3 + 25x^2 + 178x + 264$

Constant term: 264
Leading coefficient: 1

Factors of 264: ±1, ±2, ±3, ±4, ±6, ±8, ±11, ±12, ±22, ±24, ±33, ±44, ±66, ±88, ±132, ±264

Factors of 1: ±1

All possible rational zeros: ±1, ±2, ±3, ±4, ±6, ±8, ±11, ±12, ±22, ±24, ±33, ±44, ±66, ±88, ±132, ±264

$\frac{p}{q}$	1	25	178	264
1	1	26	204	468
-1	1	24	154	110
2	1	27	232	728
-2	1	23	132	0

So, $x + 2$ is a factor. By the Factor Theorem, $R(-2) = 0$. Therefore, -2 is a zero of R.

The quotient is $x^2 + 23x + 132$. We can use quadratic factoring techniques to find the other zeros.

$x^2 + 23x + 132 = 0$
$(x + 11)(x + 12) = 0$
$x + 11 = 0 \quad x + 12 = 0$
$x = -11 \quad x = -12$

So, the zeros of R are -2, -11, and -12

By the Factor Theorem, the factors of R are $x + 2$, $x + 11$, and $x + 12$.

So, $R(x) = (x + 2)(x + 11)(x + 12)$.

9 $b(x) = x^2 - 2x - 63$

Factor: $b(x) = (x - 9)(x + 7)$

$x - 9 = 0$ $x = 9$	$x + 7 = 0$ $x = -7$	Zero-Product Principle

So, $b(x) = (x - 9)(x + 7)$, and the zeros of b are 9 and -7.

10 Third-degree polynomial with integer coefficients:
$k(x) = x^3 + 15x^2 + 74x + 120$

Constant term: 120
Leading coefficient: 1

Factors of 120: ± 1, ± 2, ± 3, ± 4, ± 5, ± 6, ± 8, ± 10, ± 12, ± 15, ± 20, ± 24, ± 30, ± 40, ± 60, ± 120

Factors of 1: ± 1

All possible rational zeros: ± 1, ± 2, ± 3, ± 4, ± 5, ± 6, ± 8, ± 10, ± 12, ± 15, ± 20, ± 24, ± 30, ± 40, ± 60, ± 120

$\frac{p}{q}$	1	15	74	120
1	1	16	90	210
-1	1	14	60	60
2	1	17	108	336
-2	1	13	48	24
3	1	18	128	504
-3	1	12	38	6
4	1	19	150	720
-4	1	11	30	0

So, $x + 4$ is a factor. By the Factor Theorem, $k(-4) = 0$. Therefore, -4 is a zero of k.

The quotient is $x^2 + 11x + 30$. We can use quadratic factoring techniques to find the other zeros.

$x^2 + 11x + 30 = 0$
$(x + 5)(x + 6) = 0$
$x + 5 = 0 \quad x + 6 = 0$
$x = -5 \quad x = -6$

So, the zeros of k are -4, -5, and -6.

By the Factor Theorem, the factors of k are $x + 4$, $x + 5$, and $x + 6$.

So, $k(x) = (x + 4)(x + 5)(x + 6)$.

403

UNIT 5

Rational Functions

CHAPTER 22

SIMPLIFYING RATIONAL EXPRESSIONS

1 $\dfrac{8g^5j^6}{-64g^{11}j^3}$

$\dfrac{g^5j^6}{-8g^{11}j^3}$

$\dfrac{j^3}{-8g^6}$

$-\dfrac{j^3}{-8g^6}$, $j \neq 0$

2 $\dfrac{25p^2 - 36}{6 + 5p}$

$\dfrac{(5p+6)(5p-6)}{6+5p}$

$5p - 6$, $p \neq -\dfrac{6}{5}$

3 $\dfrac{7c - 56d}{6c^2d - 48cd^2}$

$\dfrac{7(c-8d)}{6cd(c-8d)}$

$\dfrac{7}{6cd}$, $c \neq 8d$

4 $\dfrac{x^2 - 6x - 27}{x^2 + 7x + 12}$

$\dfrac{(x+3)(x-9)}{(x+3)(x+4)}$

$\dfrac{x-9}{x+4}$, $x \neq -3$

5 $\dfrac{2m-4}{m^2 - 14m + 24}$

$\dfrac{2(m-2)}{(m-2)(m-12)}$

$\dfrac{2}{m-12}$, $m \neq 2$

6 $\dfrac{d^7 - 2d^6}{d^{12} - 4d^{10}}$

$\dfrac{d^6(d-2)}{d^{10}(d^2 - 4)}$

$\dfrac{d^6(d-2)}{d^{10}(d+2)(d-2)}$

$\dfrac{(d-2)}{d^4(d+2)(d-2)}$

$\dfrac{1}{d^4(d+2)}$, $d \neq 2$

7 $\dfrac{5c^2 + 20c - 160}{20c^2 - 180c + 400}$

$\dfrac{5(c^2 + 4c - 32)}{20(c^2 - 9c + 20)}$

$\dfrac{5(c-4)(c+8)}{20(c-5)(c-4)}$

$\dfrac{c+8}{4(c-5)}$, $c \neq 4$

8 $\dfrac{2n^2 + 9n + 4}{14n^2 + 49n + 21}$

$\dfrac{2n^2 + n + 8n + 4}{7(2n^2 + 7n + 3)}$

$\dfrac{(2n^2 + n) + (8n + 4)}{7(2n^2 + 7n + 3)}$

$\dfrac{n(2n+1) + 4(2n+1)}{7(2n+1)(n+3)}$

$\dfrac{(2n+1)(n+4)}{7(2n+1)(n+3)}$

$\dfrac{n+4}{7(n+3)}$, $n \neq -\dfrac{1}{2}$

9 $\dfrac{35w^{17}v^5}{63w^{13}v^{16}}$

$\dfrac{5w^{17}v^5}{9w^{13}v^{16}}$

$\dfrac{5w^4}{9v^{11}}$, $w \neq 0$

10 $\dfrac{49y^2 - 81}{7y - 9}$

$\dfrac{(7y+9)(7y-9)}{7y-9}$

$7y + 9,\ y \neq \dfrac{9}{7}$

11 $\dfrac{3q - 9a}{11q^2 a - 33qa^2}$

$\dfrac{3(q - 3a)}{11qa(q - 3a)}$

$\dfrac{3}{11qa},\ q \neq 3a$

12 $\dfrac{x^2 - 14x + 48}{x^2 - 12x + 32}$

$\dfrac{(x - 6)(x - 8)}{(x - 4)(x - 8)}$

$\dfrac{x - 6}{x - 4},\ x \neq 8$

13 $\dfrac{5h - 15}{h^2 - 12h + 27}$

$\dfrac{5(h - 3)}{(h - 3)(h - 9)}$

$\dfrac{5}{(h - 9)},\ h \neq 3$

14 $\dfrac{7k^2 + 21k - 70}{10k^2 + 110k + 300}$

$\dfrac{7(k^2 + 3k - 10)}{10(k^2 + 11k + 30)}$

$\dfrac{7(k - 2)(k + 5)}{10(k + 5)(k + 6)}$

$\dfrac{7(k - 2)}{10(k + 6)},\ k \neq -5$

CHAPTER 23

OPERATIONS ON RATIONAL EXPRESSIONS

1 $\dfrac{6a^3 c^4}{12a^4 bc^2} \cdot \dfrac{16a^2 b^6}{32a^5 bc^2}$

$\dfrac{(6a^3 c^4)(16a^2 b^6)}{(12a^4 bc^2)(32a^5 bc^2)}$

$\dfrac{a^5 b^6 c^4}{4a^9 b^2 c^4}$

$\dfrac{b^4}{4a^4},\ b \neq 0,\ c \neq 0$

2 $\dfrac{7x + 35}{x^2 + 2x - 3} \cdot \dfrac{x^2 - 9}{x^2 + 3x - 10}$

$\dfrac{7(x + 5)}{(x - 1)(x + 3)} \cdot \dfrac{(x + 3)(x - 3)}{(x - 2)(x + 5)}$

$\dfrac{7(x + 5)(x + 3)(x - 3)}{(x - 1)(x + 3)(x - 2)(x + 5)}$

$\dfrac{7(x - 3)}{(x - 1)(x - 2)},\ x \neq -3,\ x \neq -5$

3 $\dfrac{3g^8 j^9}{27h^6 j^4} \cdot \dfrac{63h^5 g^4}{9g^7 hj^{12}}$

$\dfrac{(3g^8 j^9)(63h^5 g^4)}{(27h^6 j^4)(9g^7 hj^{12})}$

$\dfrac{(7g^{12} j^9 h^5)}{9h^7 j^{16} g^7}$

$\dfrac{7g^5}{9h^2 j^7},\ g \neq 0$

4 $(6y^2 - 36y) \div \dfrac{5y^2 - 20y}{y^2 - 10y + 24}$

$\dfrac{6y^2 - 36y}{1} \div \dfrac{5y^2 - 20y}{y^2 - 10y + 24}$

$\dfrac{6y^2 - 36y}{1} \cdot \dfrac{y^2 - 10y + 24}{5y^2 - 20y}$

$\dfrac{6y(y - 6)}{1} \cdot \dfrac{(y - 4)(y - 6)}{5y(y - 4)}$

$\dfrac{6y(y - 6)(y - 4)(y - 6)}{5y(y - 4)}$

$$\frac{6(y-6)(y-6)}{5}$$

$$\frac{6(y-6)^2}{5}, \; y \neq 0, \; y \neq 4, \; y \neq 6$$

5 $\quad \dfrac{h^2-7h+6}{h^5} \div \dfrac{h^2-4h-12}{2h^2+h^3}$

$$\frac{h^2-7h+6}{h^5} \bullet \frac{2h^2+h^3}{h^2-4h-12}$$

$$\frac{(h-6)(h-1)}{h^5} \bullet \frac{h^2(2+h)}{(h-6)(h+2)}$$

$$\frac{\cancel{(h-6)}(h-1)\,h^2\cancel{(2+h)}}{h^5\cancel{(h-6)}(h+2)}$$

$$\frac{h^2(h-1)}{h^5}, \; h \neq -2, \; h \neq 6$$

$$\frac{(h-1)}{h^3}, \; h \neq -2, \; h \neq 6$$

6 $\quad \dfrac{m^2-4}{3m^2-28m+32} \div \dfrac{4-m^2}{3m^2+14m-24}$

$$\frac{m^2-4}{3m^2-28m+32} \bullet \frac{3m^2+14m-24}{4-m^2}$$

$$\frac{(m+2)(m-2)}{(3m-4)(m-8)} \bullet \frac{(3m-4)(m+6)}{(2+m)(2-m)}$$

$$\frac{(m+2)(m-2)\cancel{(3m-4)}(m+6)}{\cancel{(3m-4)}(m-8)\cancel{(2+m)}\cancel{(2-m)}}$$

Note: $(2-m) = -1(m-2)$

$$\frac{(m+6)}{-(m-8)}, \; m \neq -2, \; m \neq -6, \; m \neq \frac{4}{3}, \; m \neq 2$$

7 $\quad \dfrac{2d^2-18}{3d^2-6d-9} \div \dfrac{3d^2-27}{3d^2-24d+45}$

$$\frac{2d^2-18}{3d^2-6d-9} \bullet \frac{3d^2-24d+45}{3d^2-27}$$

$$\frac{2(d^2-9)}{3(d^2-2d-3)} \bullet \frac{3(d^2-8d+15)}{3(d^2-9)}$$

$$\frac{2\cancel{(d+3)}\cancel{(d-3)}}{3\cancel{(d-3)}(d+1)} \bullet \frac{1}{1} \frac{3(d-5)\cancel{(d-3)}}{3\cancel{(d+3)}\cancel{(d-3)}}$$

$$\frac{2(d-5)}{3(d+1)}, \; d \neq -3, \; d \neq 3, \; d \neq 5$$

8 $\quad \dfrac{x^2-3x-8}{5x-35} - \dfrac{2x+6}{5x-35}$

$$\frac{x^2-3x-8-(2x+6)}{5x-35}$$

$$\frac{x^2-5x-14}{5x-35}$$

$$\frac{\cancel{(x-7)}(x+2)}{5\cancel{(x-7)}}$$

$$\frac{x+2}{5}, \; x \neq 7$$

9 $\quad \dfrac{8d}{d-3} + \dfrac{9d}{d-4}$

$$\frac{8d}{d-3} \bullet \frac{d-4}{d-4} + \frac{9d}{d-4} \bullet \frac{d-3}{d-3}$$

$$\frac{8d(d-4)}{(d-3)(d-4)} + \frac{9d(d-3)}{(d-4)(d-3)}$$

$$\frac{8d(d-4)+9d(d-3)}{(d-3)(d-4)}$$

$$\frac{8d^2-32d+9d^2-27d}{(d-3)(d-4)}$$

$$\frac{17d^2-59d}{(d-3)(d-4)}$$

$$\frac{d(17d-59)}{(d-3)(d-4)}$$

10 $\quad \dfrac{a^2+11a-12}{a^2+13a+12} + \dfrac{2a}{1+a}$

$$\frac{a^2+11a-12}{(a+1)(a+12)} + \frac{2a}{1+a}$$

$$\frac{a^2+11a-12}{(a+1)(a+12)} + \frac{2a}{1+a} \bullet \frac{a+12}{a+12}$$

$$\frac{a^2+11a-12}{(a+1)(a+12)} + \frac{2a(a+12)}{(1+a)(a+12)}$$

$$\frac{a^2+11a-12}{(a+1)(a+12)} + \frac{2a^2+24a}{(1+a)(a+12)}$$

$$\frac{a^2+11a-12+2a^2+24a}{(a+1)(a+12)}$$

$$\frac{3a^2+35a-12}{(a+1)(a+12)}$$

$$\frac{(3a-1)\cancel{(a+12)}}{(a+1)\cancel{(a+12)}}$$

$$\frac{3a-1}{a+1}, \; a \neq -12$$

11 $\quad \dfrac{2x}{x+6} - \dfrac{2x}{3}$

$$\frac{2x}{x+6} \cdot \frac{3}{3} - \frac{2x}{3} \cdot \frac{x+6}{x+6}$$

$$\frac{2x(3)}{3(x+6)} - \frac{2x(x+6)}{3(x+6)}$$

$$\frac{6x}{3(x+6)} - \frac{2x^2+12x}{3(x+6)}$$

$$\frac{6x-(2x^2+12x)}{3(x+6)}$$

$$\frac{-2x^2-6x}{3(x+6)}$$

$$\frac{-2x(x+3)}{3(x+6)}$$

12 $\quad \dfrac{\dfrac{5x}{x^2-49}}{\dfrac{25x}{x+7}}$

$$\frac{5x}{x^2-49} \div \frac{25x}{x+7}$$

$$\frac{5x}{(x-7)(x+7)} \div \frac{25x}{x+7}$$

$$\frac{5x}{(x-7)(x+7)} \cdot \frac{x+7}{25x}$$

$$\frac{5x\cancel{(x+7)}}{(x-7)\cancel{(x+7)}(25x)}$$

$$\frac{5x}{25\cancel{x}(x-7)}$$

$$\frac{1}{5(x-7)}, \; x \neq 0, \; x \neq -7$$

13 $\quad \dfrac{\dfrac{c+4}{c+9}}{\dfrac{c-4}{2c+18}}$

$$\frac{c+4}{c+9} \div \frac{c-4}{2c+18}$$

$$\frac{c+4}{c+9} \div \frac{c-4}{2(c+9)}$$

$$\frac{c+4}{c+9} \cdot \frac{2(c+9)}{c-4}$$

$$\frac{(c+4) \cdot 2 \cdot \cancel{(c+9)}}{\cancel{(c+9)}(c-4)}$$

$$\frac{2(c+4)}{c-4}, \; c \neq 4$$

14 $\quad \dfrac{\dfrac{3m-7}{m-8} - \dfrac{m-5}{m-8}}{\dfrac{m-6}{m-4} + \dfrac{m-6}{m-4}}$

$$\left(\frac{3m-7}{m-8} - \frac{m-5}{m-8}\right) \div \left(\frac{m-6}{m-4} + \frac{m-6}{m-4}\right)$$

$$\left(\frac{2m-12}{m-8}\right) \div \left(\frac{2m-12}{m-4}\right)$$

$$\left(\frac{2m-12}{m-8}\right) \cdot \left(\frac{m-4}{2m-12}\right)$$

$$\frac{\cancel{(2m-12)}(m-4)}{(m-8)\cancel{(2m-12)}}$$

$$\frac{m-4}{m-8}, \; m \neq 6, \; m \neq 8$$

CHAPTER 24

RATIONAL FUNCTIONS AND THEIR GRAPHS

1 $f(x) = \dfrac{2x}{x+7}$

x-intercept: $(0, 0)$

To find the x-intercept, set $y = f(x)$ equal to 0.

$0 = \dfrac{2x}{x+7}$

$0 = 2x$

$0 \div 2 = 2x \div 2$

$0 = x$

y-intercept: $(0, 0)$

To find the y-intercept, substitute 0 for x in the function f.

$f(0) = \dfrac{2(0)}{(0)+7}$

$f(0) = 0$

Vertical asymptote: $x = -7$

To find the vertical asymptote, set the denominator equal to 0.

$x + 7 = 0$

$x + 7 - 7 = 0 - 7$

$x = -7$

Horizontal asymptote: $y = 2$

The degree of the numerator *equals* the degree of the denominator. So, there is a horizontal asymptote of

$y = \dfrac{\text{leading coefficient of numerator}}{\text{leading coefficient of denominator}}$

$y = \dfrac{2}{1}$

$y = 2$

2 $f(x) = \dfrac{3x+8}{x^2-49}$

x-intercept: $\left(-\dfrac{8}{3}, 0\right)$

To find the x-intercept, set $y = f(x)$ equal to 0.

$0 = \dfrac{3x+8}{x^2-49}$

$0 = 3x + 8$

$0 - 8 = 3x + 8 - 8$

$-8 \div 3 = 3x \div 3$

$-\dfrac{8}{3} = x$

y-intercept: $\left(0, -\dfrac{8}{49}\right)$

To find the y-intercept, substitute 0 for x in the function f.

$f(0) = \dfrac{3(0)+8}{(0)^2-49}$

$f(0) = -\dfrac{8}{49}$

Vertical asymptotes: $x = 7$ and $x = -7$

To find the vertical asymptote, set the denominator equal to 0.

$x^2 - 49 = 0$
$x^2 - 49 + 49 = 0 + 49$
$x^2 = 49$
$x = \pm 7$

Horizontal asymptote: $y = 0$

The degree in the numerator is *less than* the degree of the denominator, so $y = 0$ is a horizontal asymptote of f.

③ $f(x) = \dfrac{x - 10}{x^2 + 4x - 5}$

x-intercept: $(10, 0)$

To find the x-intercept, set $y = f(x)$ equal to 0.

$0 = \dfrac{x - 10}{x^2 + 4x - 5}$

$0 = x - 10$
$0 + 10 = x - 10 + 10$
$10 = x$

y-intercept: $(0, 2)$

To find the y-intercept, substitute 0 for x in the function f:

$f(0) = \dfrac{(0) - 10}{(0)^2 + 4(0) - 5}$

$f(0) = \dfrac{-10}{-5} = 2$

Vertical asymptotes: $x = -5$ and $x = 1$

To find the vertical asymptote, set the denominator equal to 0.

$x^2 + 4x - 5 = 0$
$(x + 5)(x - 1) = 0$
$x + 5 = 0 \mid x - 1 = 0$
$x = -5 \quad x = 1$

Horizontal asymptote: $y = 0$

The degree in the numerator is *less than* the degree of the denominator, so $y = 0$ is a horizontal asymptote of f.

④ $f(x) = \dfrac{6x + 17}{x^2 - 25}$

x-intercept: $\left(-\dfrac{17}{6}, 0\right)$

To find the x-intercept, set $y = f(x)$ equal to 0.

$0 = \dfrac{6x + 17}{x^2 - 25}$

$0 = 6x + 17$
$0 - 17 = 6x + 17 - 17$
$-17 \div 6 = 6x \div 6$
$-\dfrac{17}{6} = x$

y-intercept: $\left(0, -\dfrac{17}{25}\right)$

To find the y-intercept, substitute 0 for x in the function f.

$f(0) = \frac{6(0) + 17}{(0)^2 - 25}$

$f(0) = -\frac{17}{25}$

Vertical asymptotes: $x = 5$ and $x = -5$

To find the vertical asymptote, set the denominator equal to 0.

$x^2 - 25 = 0$
$x^2 - 25 + 25 = 0 + 25$
$x^2 = 25$
$x = \pm 5$

Horizontal asymptote: $y = 0$

The degree in the numerator is *less than* the degree of the denominator, so $y = 0$ is a horizontal asymptote of f.

5 Graph B

$f(x) = \frac{x - 6}{5x}$

Vertical asymptote:
$5x = 0$
$x = 0$

Horizontal asymptote:

The degree of the numerator *equals* the degree of the

denominator. So, there is a horizontal asymptote of $y = \frac{1}{5}$.

6 Graph D

$f(x) = \frac{10}{2x + 3}$

Vertical asymptote:
$2x + 3 = 0$
$x = -\frac{3}{2}$

Horizontal asymptote:

The degree of the numerator is *less than* the degree of the denominator. So, there is a horizontal asymptote of $y = 0$.

7 Graph A

$f(x) = \frac{x}{x^2 - 49}$

Vertical asymptotes:
$x^2 - 49 = 0$
$(x - 7)(x + 7) = 0$
$x = 7$ and $x = -7$

Horizontal asymptote:

The degree of the numerator is *less than* the degree of the denominator. So, there is a horizontal asymptote of $y = 0$.

8 Graph C

$$f(x) = \frac{3x}{x^2 - 4}$$

Vertical asymptotes:
$$x^2 - 4 = 0$$
$$(x - 2)(x + 2) = 0$$
$$x = 2 \text{ and } x = -2$$

Horizontal asymptote:

The degree of the numerator is *less than* the degree of the denominator. So, there is a horizontal asymptote of $y = 0$.

9 $f(x) = \frac{4}{x - 2} + 1$

$$= \frac{4}{x - 2} + \frac{x - 2}{x - 2}$$

$$= \frac{x + 2}{x - 2}$$

Domain: $(-\infty, 2) \cup (2, \infty)$
Vertical asymptote: $x = 2$
Horizontal asymptote: $y = 1$

x-intercept: $(-2, 0)$
y-intercept: $(0, -1)$

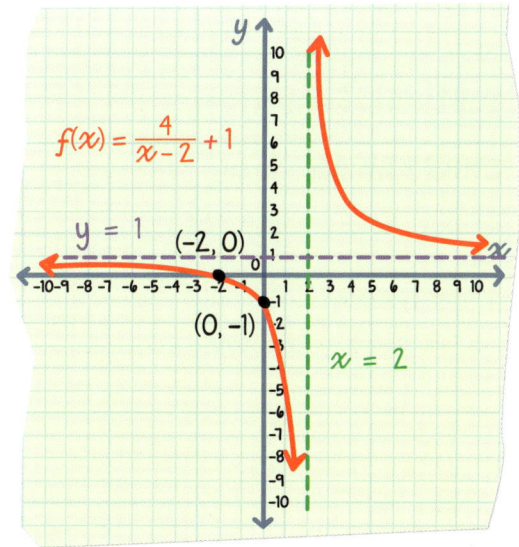

10 $f(x) = \frac{2x - 1}{x + 1}$

Domain: $(-\infty, -1) \cup (-1, \infty)$
Vertical asymptote: $x = -1$
Horizontal asymptote: $y = 2$

x-intercept: $(\frac{1}{2}, 0)$
y-intercept: $(0, -1)$

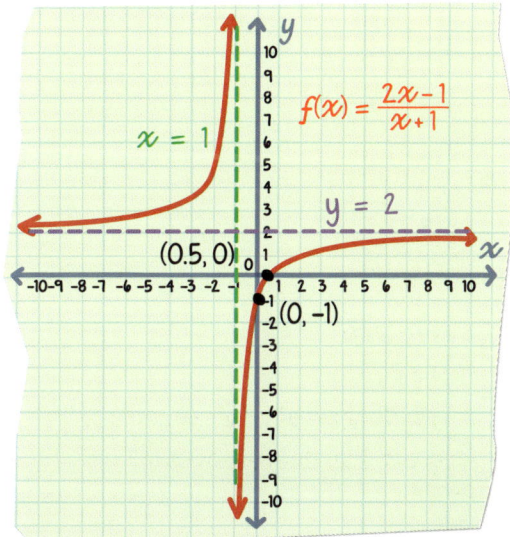

UNIT 6

Radical Functions

CHAPTER 25

OPERATIONS ON RADICALS

1 $-9\sqrt[6]{h} + 5\sqrt[6]{h}$
$(-9 + 5)\sqrt[6]{h}$
$-4\sqrt[6]{h}$

2 $2\sqrt{17} + 19\sqrt[3]{45} + 7\sqrt{17} + 3\sqrt[3]{45}$
$(2 + 7)\sqrt{17} + (19 + 3)\sqrt[3]{45}$
$9\sqrt{17} + 22\sqrt[3]{45}$

3 $4\sqrt{24} - \sqrt{54}$
$4\sqrt{4 \cdot 6} - \sqrt{9 \cdot 6}$
$4 \cdot 2\sqrt{6} - 3\sqrt{6}$
$8\sqrt{6} - 3\sqrt{6}$
$5\sqrt{6}$

4 $\sqrt{49} - 10\sqrt[3]{8} + \sqrt{48} + 8\sqrt[3]{27}$
$\sqrt{49} - 10\sqrt[3]{8} + \sqrt{16 \cdot 3} + 8\sqrt[3]{27}$
$7 - 10 \cdot 2 + 4\sqrt{3} + 8 \cdot 3$
$7 - 20 + 4\sqrt{3} + 24$
$11 + 4\sqrt{3}$

5 $6\sqrt[3]{29} \cdot 9\sqrt[3]{7}$
$6 \cdot 9\sqrt[3]{29 \cdot 7}$
$54\sqrt[3]{203}$

6 $12\sqrt[3]{2} \cdot \sqrt[3]{3}$
$12\sqrt[3]{2 \cdot 3}$
$12\sqrt[3]{6}$

7 $\dfrac{36\sqrt{64}}{6\sqrt{4}}$

$\left(\dfrac{36}{6}\right)\dfrac{\sqrt{64}}{\sqrt{4}}$

$6\sqrt{\dfrac{64}{4}}$

$6\sqrt{16}$

$6 \cdot 4$

24

8 $\dfrac{72\sqrt{96}}{9\sqrt{12}}$

$\left(\dfrac{72}{9}\right)\dfrac{\sqrt{96}}{\sqrt{12}}$

$8\sqrt{\dfrac{96}{12}}$

$8\sqrt{8}$

$8\sqrt{4 \cdot 2}$

$8 \cdot 2\sqrt{2}$

$16\sqrt{2}$

9 $\dfrac{85\sqrt{66}}{5\sqrt{6}} \cdot \sqrt{18}$

$\left(\dfrac{85}{5}\right)\dfrac{\sqrt{66}}{\sqrt{6}} \cdot \sqrt{9 \cdot 2}$

$17\sqrt{\dfrac{66}{6}} \cdot \sqrt{9 \cdot 2}$

$17\sqrt{11} \cdot 3\sqrt{2}$

$(17 \cdot 3)\sqrt{11 \cdot 2}$

$51\sqrt{22}$

10 $2\sqrt[3]{5} \left(6\sqrt[3]{200} + 9\sqrt[3]{25}\right)$
$2\sqrt[3]{5} \cdot 6\sqrt[3]{200} + 2\sqrt[3]{5} \cdot 9\sqrt[3]{25}$
$(2 \cdot 6)\sqrt[3]{5 \cdot 200} + (2 \cdot 9)\sqrt[3]{5 \cdot 25}$
$12\sqrt[3]{1000} + 18\sqrt[3]{125}$
$12 \cdot 10 + 18 \cdot 5$

$120 + 90$

210

11 $(\sqrt{7} + 8\sqrt{63})(2 - \sqrt{3})$

$2\sqrt{7} - \sqrt{21} + 16\sqrt{63} - 8\sqrt{189}$

$2\sqrt{7} - \sqrt{21} + 16\sqrt{9 \cdot 7} - 8\sqrt{9 \cdot 21}$

$2\sqrt{7} - \sqrt{21} + 16 \cdot 3\sqrt{7} - 8 \cdot 3\sqrt{21}$

$2\sqrt{7} - \sqrt{21} + 48\sqrt{7} - 24\sqrt{21}$

$50\sqrt{7} - 25\sqrt{21}$

12 $\dfrac{5x\sqrt{3}}{\sqrt{26}}$

$\dfrac{5x\sqrt{3}}{\sqrt{26}} \cdot \dfrac{\sqrt{26}}{\sqrt{26}}$

$\dfrac{5x\sqrt{3 \cdot 26}}{26}$

$\dfrac{5x\sqrt{78}}{26}$

CHAPTER 26

SOLVING RADICAL EQUATIONS

1 Solution: $x = 350$

$\sqrt{\dfrac{2x}{7}} = 10$

$\left(\sqrt{\dfrac{2x}{7}}\right)^2 = 10^2$

$\dfrac{2x}{7} = 100$

$\dfrac{2x}{7} \cdot 7 = 100 \cdot 7$

$2x \div 2 = 700 \div 2$

$x = 350$

Check:

$\sqrt{\dfrac{2(350)}{7}} = 10$

$\sqrt{\dfrac{700}{7}} = 10$

$\sqrt{100} = 10$

$10 = 10$ ✓ True

2 Solution: $y = 36$

$5\sqrt{y} - 9 = 21$

$5\sqrt{y} = 30$

$\sqrt{y} = 6$

$(\sqrt{y})^2 = 6^2$

$y = 36$

Check:

$5\sqrt{36} - 9 = 21$

$5(6) - 9 = 21$

$30 - 9 = 21$

$21 = 21$ ✓ True

3 Solution: $d = 62$

$\sqrt[3]{-d - 2} - 8 = -12$

$\sqrt[3]{-d - 2} = -4$

$(\sqrt[3]{-d - 2})^3 = (-4)^3$

$-d - 2 = -64$

$-d = -62$

$d = 62$

Check:

$\sqrt[3]{-62 - 2} - 8 = -12$

$\sqrt[3]{-64} - 8 = -12$

$-4 - 8 = -12$

$-12 = -12$ ✓ True

4 Solution: $w = -2$

$4\sqrt{2w + 13} - 1 = 11$

$4\sqrt{2w + 13} = 12$

$\sqrt{2w + 13} = 3$

$(\sqrt{2w + 13})^2 = 3^2$

$2w + 13 = 9$

$2w = -4$

$w = -2$

Check:

$4\sqrt{2(-2) + 13} - 1 = 11$

$4\sqrt{9} - 1 = 11$

$4(3) - 1 = 11$

$12 - 1 = 11$

$11 = 11$ ✓ True

5 Solution: $a = \dfrac{1}{6}$

$\sqrt{a + 4} = \sqrt{7a + 3}$

$(\sqrt{a + 4})^2 = (\sqrt{7a + 3})^2$

$a + 4 = 7a + 3$

$a - 7a = 3 - 4$

$-6a = -1$

$a = \dfrac{-1}{-6}$

$a = \dfrac{1}{6}$

Check:

$\sqrt{\dfrac{1}{6} + 4} = \sqrt{7(\dfrac{1}{6}) + 3}$

$\sqrt{\dfrac{25}{6}} = \sqrt{\dfrac{25}{6}}$ ✓ True

6 Solution: $c = 19$

$9 = \sqrt{4c + 5}$

$9^2 = (\sqrt{4c + 5})^2$

$81 = 4c + 5$

$76 = 4c$

$19 = c$

Check:

$9 = \sqrt{4(19) + 5}$

$9 = \sqrt{76 + 5}$

$9 = \sqrt{81}$

$9 = 9$ ✓ True

7 No solution

$10 + 2\sqrt{j} = 0$

$2\sqrt{j} = -10$

$\sqrt{j} = -5$

$\sqrt{j}^2 = (-5)^2$

$j = 25$

Check:

$10 + 2\sqrt{25} = 0$

$10 + 2(5) = 0$

$10 + 10 = 0$

$20 = 0$ ✗ False

8 Solution: $l = -8$

$\sqrt[3]{l + 9} = 1$

$(\sqrt[3]{l + 9})^3 = 1^3$

$l + 9 = 1$

$l = -8$

Check:

$\sqrt[3]{-8 + 9} = 1$

$\sqrt[3]{1} = 1$

$1 = 1$ ✓ True

9 Solutions: $p = -10$ and $p = 10$

$$\sqrt[3]{p + 28} = \sqrt[3]{p^2 + p - 72}$$
$$(\sqrt[3]{p + 28})^3 = (\sqrt[3]{p^2 + p - 72})^3$$
$$p + 28 = p^2 + p - 72$$
$$28 = p^2 - 72$$
$$100 = p^2$$
$$\pm\sqrt{100} = \sqrt{p^2}$$
$$\pm 10 = p$$

Check both possible solutions:

$$\sqrt[3]{10 + 28} = \sqrt[3]{10^2 + 10 - 72}$$
$$\sqrt[3]{38} = \sqrt[3]{38} \quad \checkmark \quad \text{True}$$

$$\sqrt[3]{-10 + 28} = \sqrt[3]{-10^2 - 10 - 72}$$
$$\sqrt[3]{18} = \sqrt[3]{18} \quad \checkmark \quad \text{True}$$

10 Solution: $b = 25$

$$7\sqrt{b} - 16 = 19$$
$$7\sqrt{b} = 35$$
$$\sqrt{b} = 5$$
$$(\sqrt{b})^2 = 5^2$$
$$b = 25$$

Check:
$$7\sqrt{25} - 16 = 19$$
$$7(5) - 16 = 19$$
$$35 - 16 = 19$$
$$19 = 19 \quad \checkmark \quad \text{True}$$

11 Solution: $f = -60$

$$\sqrt{-15f} - 6 = 24$$
$$\sqrt{-15f} - 6 + 6 = 24 + 6$$
$$\sqrt{-15f} = 30$$
$$\sqrt{-15f}^2 = 30^2$$
$$-15f = 900$$

$$-15f \div (-15) = 900 \div (-15)$$
$$f = -60$$

Check:
$$\sqrt{-15(-60)} - 6 = 24$$
$$\sqrt{900} - 6 = 24$$
$$30 - 6 = 24$$
$$24 = 24 \quad \checkmark \quad \text{True}$$

12 Solution: $g = 4$

$$\sqrt{g} + 5 = \sqrt{g + 45}$$
$$(\sqrt{g} + 5)^2 = (\sqrt{g + 45})^2$$
$$(\sqrt{g} + 5)(\sqrt{g} + 5) = (\sqrt{g + 45})^2$$
$$g + 10\sqrt{g} + 25 = g + 45$$
$$10\sqrt{g} + 25 = 45$$
$$10\sqrt{g} = 20$$
$$\sqrt{g} = 2$$
$$\sqrt{g}^2 = 2^2$$
$$g = 4$$

Check:
$$\sqrt{4} + 5 = \sqrt{4 + 45}$$
$$2 + 5 = \sqrt{49}$$
$$7 = 7 \quad \checkmark \quad \text{True}$$

13 No solution

$$\sqrt{18k} = \sqrt{2k - 32}$$
$$(\sqrt{18k})^2 = (\sqrt{2k - 32})^2$$
$$18k = 2k - 32$$
$$18k - 2k = -32$$
$$16k = -32$$
$$k = -2$$

Check:
$$\sqrt{18(-2)} = \sqrt{2(-2) - 32}$$
$$\sqrt{-36} = \sqrt{-36}$$

$\sqrt{-36}$ is not a real number, so there are no real solutions.

14 Solutions: $m = -4$ and $m = 3$

$\sqrt{m + 9} = \sqrt{m^2 + 2m - 3}$

$(\sqrt{m + 9})^2 = (\sqrt{m^2 + 2m - 3})^2$

$m + 9 = m^2 + 2m - 3$

$m = m^2 + 2m - 12$

$0 = m^2 + m - 12$

$0 = (m - 3)(m + 4)$

$m - 3 = 0 \qquad m + 4 = 0$

$m = 3 \qquad m = -4$

Check both possible solutions:

$\sqrt{3 + 9} = \sqrt{3^2 + 2(3) - 3}$

$\sqrt{12} = \sqrt{12}$ ✔ True

$\sqrt{-4 + 9} = \sqrt{(-4)^2 + 2(-4) - 3}$

$\sqrt{5} = \sqrt{5}$ ✔ True

CHAPTER 27

RADICAL FUNCTIONS AND THEIR GRAPHS

1 $h(x) = \sqrt{x - 8} - 2$

Step 1: Graph the function, $f(x) = \sqrt{x}$.

Step 2: Shift the graph of $f(x) = \sqrt{x - 8} - 2$ to the right 8 units.

Step 3: Shift the graph of $g(x) = \sqrt{x - 8}$ down 2 units.

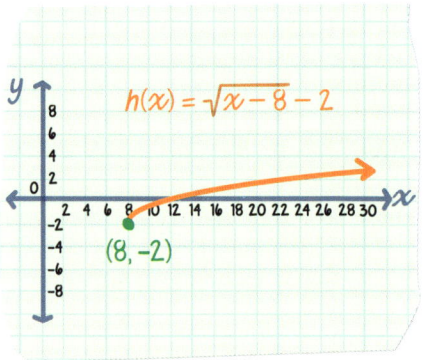

$h(x) = \sqrt{x - 8} - 2$

$(8, -2)$

2 $g(x) = 2\sqrt{x} + 4$

Step 1: Graph the function, $f(x) = \sqrt{x}$.

Step 2: Expand the graph of $f(x) = \sqrt{x}$ vertically by multiplying each output by 2.

Step 3: Shift the graph of $h(x) = 2\sqrt{x}$ up 4 units.

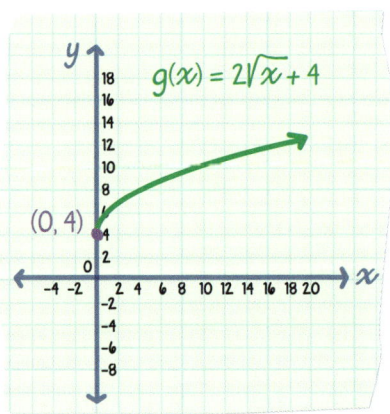

$g(x) = 2\sqrt{x} + 4$

$(0, 4)$

3 $j(x) = \sqrt{x+7} - 1$

Step 1: Graph the function, $f(x) = \sqrt{x}$.

Step 2: Shift the graph of $f(x) = \sqrt{x}$ to the left 7 units.

Step 3: Shift the graph of $k(x) = \sqrt{(x+7)}$ down 1 unit.

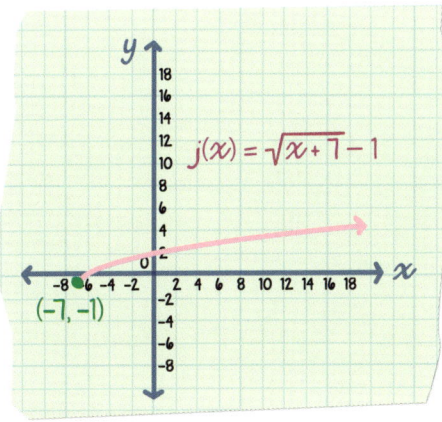

4 $k(x) = 5\sqrt{x} + 3$

Step 1: Graph the function, $f(x) = \sqrt{x}$.

Step 2: Expand the graph of $f(x) = \sqrt{x}$ vertically by multiplying each output by 5.

Step 3: Shift the graph of $j(x) = 5\sqrt{x}$ up 3 units

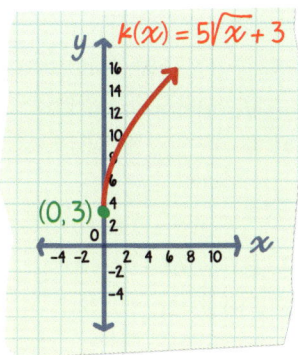

5 $h(x) = \sqrt[3]{x-6}$

Step 1: Graph the function, $f(x) = \sqrt[3]{x}$.

Step 2: Shift the graph of $g(x) = \sqrt[3]{x}$ to the right 6 units.

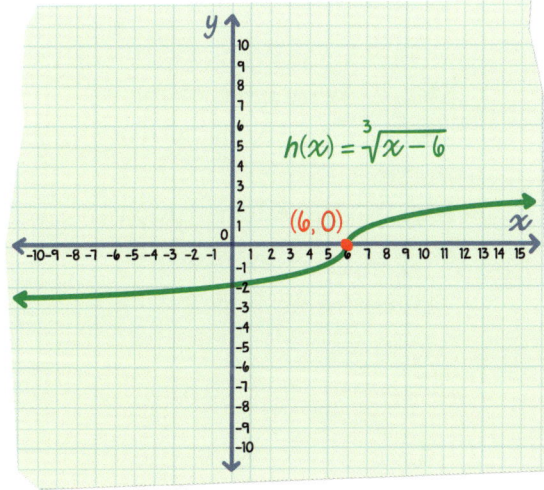

6 $g(x) = 4\sqrt[3]{x} + 12$

Step 1: Graph the function, $f(x) = \sqrt[3]{x}$.

Step 2: Expand the graph of $f(x) = \sqrt[3]{x}$ vertically by multiplying each output by 4.

Step 3: Shift the graph of $h(x) = 4\sqrt[3]{x}$ up 12 units.

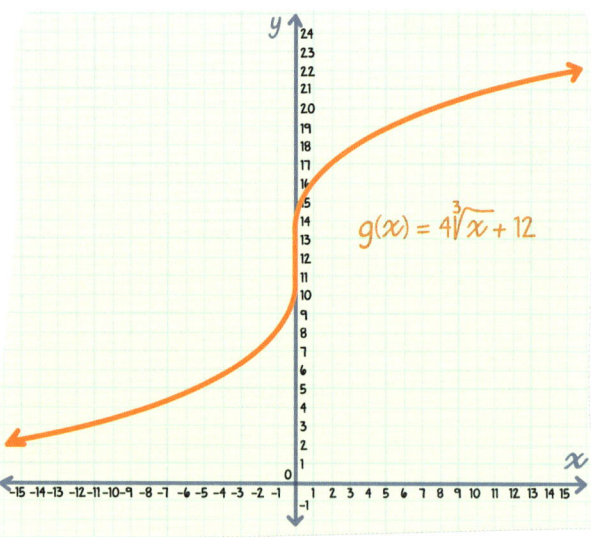

$g(x) = 4\sqrt[3]{x} + 12$

7 $j(x) = -8\sqrt[3]{x}$

Step 1: Graph the function, $f(x) = \sqrt[3]{x}$.

Step 2: Reflect the graph of $f(x) = \sqrt[3]{x}$ across the x-axis.

Step 3: Expand the graph of $g(x) = -\sqrt[3]{x}$ vertically by multiplying each output by 8.

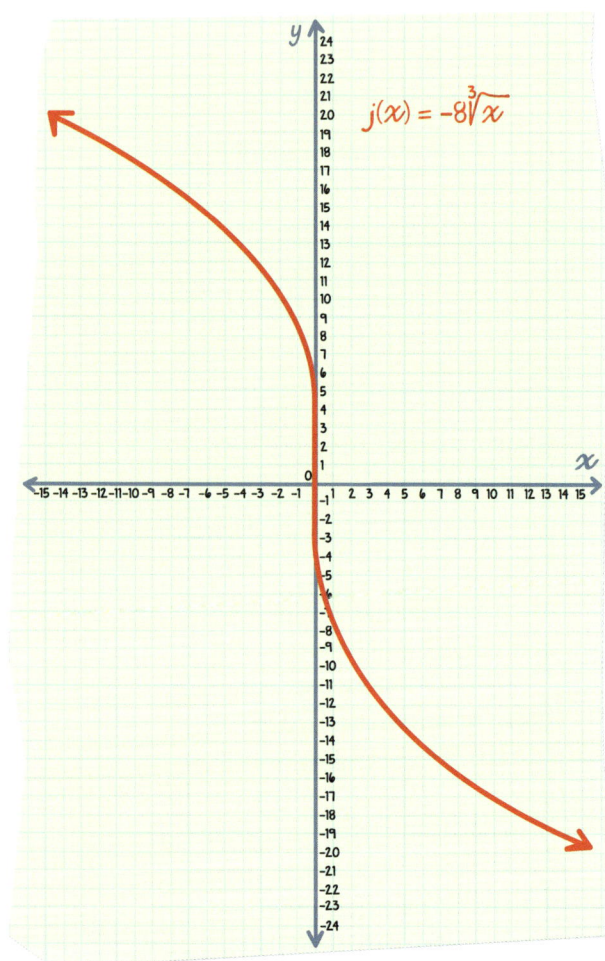

$j(x) = -8\sqrt[3]{x}$

CHAPTER 28

RATIONAL EXPONENTS

1 $32^{\frac{1}{2}}$

$\sqrt{32}$

$\sqrt{4^2 \cdot 2}$

$4\sqrt{2}$

2 $1{,}296^{-\frac{4}{3}}$

$\dfrac{1}{1{,}296^{\frac{4}{3}}}$

$\dfrac{1}{\sqrt[4]{(1{,}296)^3}}$

$\dfrac{1}{6^3}$

$\dfrac{1}{216}$

3 $\left(\dfrac{16}{25}\right)^{-\frac{3}{2}}$

$\left(\dfrac{25}{16}\right)^{\frac{3}{2}}$

$\left(\sqrt{\dfrac{25}{16}}\right)^3$

$\left(\dfrac{5}{4}\right)^3$

$\dfrac{125}{64}$

4 $256^{\frac{1}{4}}$

$\sqrt[4]{256}$

5 $\left(\dfrac{81}{36}\right)^{-\frac{1}{2}}$

$\left(\dfrac{36}{81}\right)^{\frac{1}{2}}$

$\sqrt{\dfrac{36}{81}}$

$\dfrac{6}{9}$

$\dfrac{2}{3}$

6 $\sqrt[3]{512}$

$512^{\frac{1}{3}}$

7 $\dfrac{1}{\sqrt{28}}$

$28^{\frac{1}{2}}$

8 $-\sqrt{\dfrac{16}{56}}$

$-\left(\dfrac{16}{56}\right)^{\frac{1}{2}}$

9 $\sqrt[3]{96}$

$96^{\frac{1}{3}}$

10 $27^{\frac{1}{2}} \cdot 75^{\frac{1}{2}}$

$\sqrt{27} \cdot \sqrt{75}$

$\sqrt{9 \cdot 3} \cdot \sqrt{25 \cdot 3}$

$3\sqrt{3} \cdot 5\sqrt{3}$

$15 \cdot 3$

45

11 $(343a^7b^{12})^{-\frac{1}{3}}$

$\left(\dfrac{1}{343a^7b^{12}}\right)^{\frac{1}{3}}$

$\dfrac{\sqrt[3]{1}}{\sqrt[3]{343a^6ab^{12}}}$

$\dfrac{1}{7a^2b^4\sqrt[3]{a}}$

12 $3(40)^{\frac{1}{2}} - 6(160)^{\frac{1}{2}} + 5(28)^{\frac{1}{2}}$

$3\sqrt{40} - 6\sqrt{160} + 5\sqrt{28}$

$3\sqrt{4 \cdot 10} - 6\sqrt{16 \cdot 10} + 5\sqrt{4 \cdot 7}$

$3 \cdot 2\sqrt{10} - 6 \cdot 4\sqrt{10} + 5 \cdot 2\sqrt{7}$

$6\sqrt{10} - 24\sqrt{10} + 10\sqrt{7}$

$-18\sqrt{10} + 10\sqrt{7}$

13 $(\sqrt[4]{gh})^3 \cdot (\sqrt[4]{gh})^6$

$(gh)^{\frac{3}{4}} \cdot (gh)^{\frac{6}{4}}$

$(gh)^{\frac{3}{4} + \frac{6}{4}}$

$(gh)^{\frac{9}{4}}$

$\sqrt[4]{(gh)^9}$

$\sqrt[4]{g^9 h^9}$

$g^2 h^2 \sqrt[4]{gh}$

14 $\dfrac{(\sqrt{c})^3}{(\sqrt[3]{c})^2}$

$\dfrac{c^{\frac{3}{2}}}{c^{\frac{2}{3}}}$

$c^{\frac{3}{2} - \frac{2}{3}}$

$c^{\frac{9}{6} - \frac{4}{6}}$

$c^{\frac{5}{6}}$

$\sqrt[6]{c^5}$

UNIT 7

Exponential and Logarithmic Functions

CHAPTER 29

EXPONENTIAL FUNCTIONS AND THEIR GRAPHS

1 $f(x) = 3^x$ and $g(x) = (\frac{1}{3})^x$

$f(x) = 3^x$

- Domain: $(-\infty, \infty)$
- Range: $(0, \infty)$
- y-intercept: $(0, 1)$
- Horizontal asymptote: the x-axis ($y = 0$)
- End behavior: As x approaches $-\infty$, y approaches 0; as x approaches ∞, y approaches ∞.
- The function is increasing. (The base is greater than 1.)

$g(x) = (\frac{1}{3})^x = 3^{-x}$

- Domain: $(-\infty, \infty)$
- Range: $(0, \infty)$
- y-intercept: $(0, 1)$
- Horizontal asymptote: the x-axis ($y = 0$)
- End behavior: As x approaches $-\infty$, y approaches ∞; as x approaches ∞, y approaches 0.

- The function is decreasing.
  (The base is between 0 and 1.)

$g(x) = (\frac{1}{3})^x = 3^{-x}$ is a **reflection** of $f(x) = 3^x$ across the y-axis.

2 $p(x) = 5e^x$ and $q(x) = -5e^{-x}$

$p(x) = 5e^x$

- Domain: $(-\infty, \infty)$
- Range: $(0, \infty)$
- Horizontal asymptote: the x-axis $(y = 0)$
- y-intercept: $(0, 5)$
- End behavior: As x approaches $-\infty$, y approaches 0; as x approaches ∞, y approaches ∞.
- The function is increasing. (The base is greater than 1.)

$q(x) = -5e^{-x}$

- Domain: $(-\infty, \infty)$
- Range: $(-\infty, 0)$
- Horizontal asymptote: the x-axis $(y = 0)$
- y-intercept: $(0, -5)$
- End behavior: As x approaches $-\infty$, y approaches $-\infty$; as x approaches ∞, y approaches 0.
- The function is increasing. (The base is greater than 1.)

$q(x) = -5e^{-x}$ is a **reflection** of $p(x) = 5e^x$ across the origin $(0, 0)$.

3 $h(x) = (\frac{2}{5})^x$ and $j(x) = (\frac{5}{2})^x$

$h(x) = (\frac{2}{5})^x$

- Domain: $(-\infty, \infty)$
- Range: $(0, \infty)$
- Horizontal asymptote: the x-axis $(y = 0)$
- y-intercept: $(0, 1)$
- End behavior: As x approaches $-\infty$, y approaches ∞; as x approaches ∞, y approaches 0.
- The function is decreasing. (The base is between 0 and 1.)

$j(x) = (\frac{5}{2})^x$

- Domain: $(-\infty, \infty)$
- Range: $(0, \infty)$
- Horizontal asymptote: the x-axis $(y = 0)$
- y-intercept: $(0, 1)$
- End behavior: As x approaches $-\infty$, y approaches 0; as x approaches ∞, y approaches ∞.
- The function is increasing. (The base is greater than 1.)

The graph of $j(x) = (\frac{5}{2})^x$ is a **reflection** of $h(x) = (\frac{2}{5})^x$ across the y-axis.

4 $k(x) = \frac{1}{2}e^x$ and $m(x) = -\frac{1}{2}e^{-x}$

$k(x) = \frac{1}{2}e^x$

- Domain: $(-\infty, \infty)$

- Range: $(0, \infty)$

- Horizontal asymptote:
  the x-axis ($y = 0$)

- y-intercept: $(0, \frac{1}{2})$

- End behavior: As x approaches
  $-\infty$, y approaches 0; as x
  approaches ∞, y approaches ∞.

- The function is increasing.
  (The base is greater than 1.)

$m(x) = -\frac{1}{2}e^{-x}$

- Domain: $(-\infty, \infty)$

- Range: $(-\infty, 0)$

- Horizontal asymptote:
  the x-axis ($y = 0$)

- y-intercept: $(0, -\frac{1}{2})$

- End behavior: As x approaches
  $-\infty$, y approaches $-\infty$; as x
  approaches ∞, y approaches 0.

- The function is increasing.
  (The base is greater than 1.)

The graph of $m(x) = -\frac{1}{2}e^{-x}$ is a
reflection of $k(x) = \frac{1}{2}e^x$ across
the origin $(0, 0)$.

5 $w(x) = -6^{5x}$

Step 1: Graph the parent
function, $f(x) = 6^x$.

Step 2: Reflect the graph of
$f(x) = 6^x$ across the x-axis.

Step 3: Horizontally shrink
the graph of $g(x) = -6^x$ by a
factor of 5.

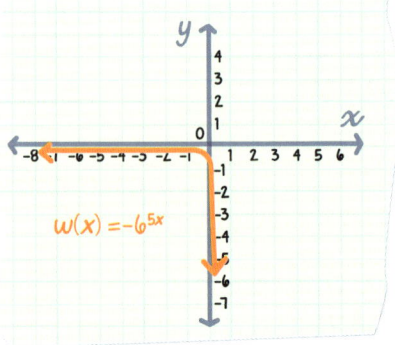

6 $j(x) = 7^{x-3} + 9$

Step 1: Graph the parent
function, $f(x) = 7^x$.

Step 2: Shift the graph of
$f(x) = 7^x$ to the right 3 units.

Step 3: Shift the graph of
$g(x) = 7^{x-3}$ up 9 units.

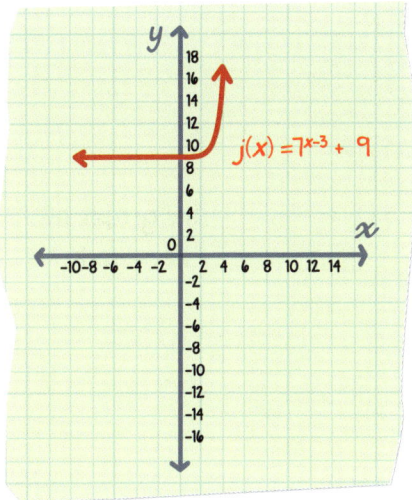

$j(x) = 7^{x-3} + 9$

7 $v(x) = 3^{8x}$

Step 1: Graph the parent function, $f(x) = 3^x$.

Step 2: Horizontally shrink the graph of $f(x) = 3^x$ by a factor of 8.

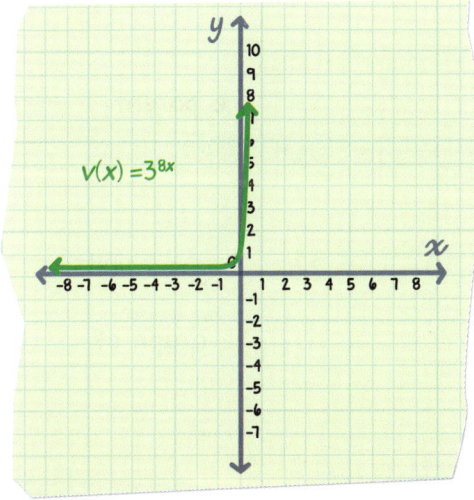

$v(x) = 3^{8x}$

8 $h(x) = 4^{x+8} - 2$

Step 1: Graph the parent function, $f(x) = 4^x$.

Step 2: Shift the graph of $f(x) = 4^x$ to the left 8 units.

Step 3: Shift the graph of $g(x) = 4^{x+8}$ down 2 units.

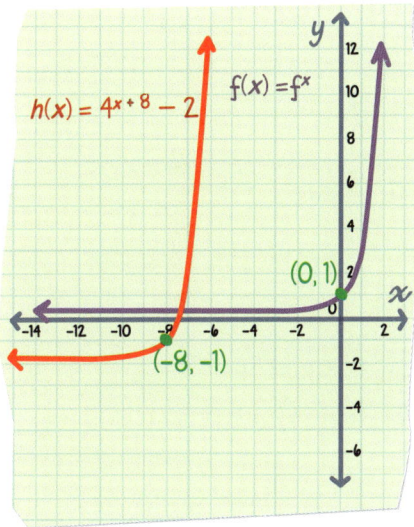

$h(x) = 4^{x+8} - 2$

$f(x) = f^x$

$(0, 1)$

$(-8, -1)$

CHAPTER 30

LOGARITHMIC FUNCTIONS AND THEIR GRAPHS

1 $4^3 = 64$
$\log_4 64 = 3$

2 $7^2 = 49$
$\log_7 49 = 2$

3 $2^{-5} = \dfrac{1}{32}$

$\log_2 \dfrac{1}{32} = -5$

4 $\log_3 81 = 4$
$3^4 = 81$

5 $\log_5 \dfrac{1}{25} = -2$

$5^{-2} = \dfrac{1}{25}$

6 $\log_g \dfrac{f}{h} = j$

$g^j = \dfrac{f}{h}$

7 $h(x) = \log_2(x + 8) - 5$

Step 1: Graph the function,
$f(x) = \log_2 x$.

Step 2: Shift the graph of
$f(x) = \log_2 x$ to the left 8 units.

Step 3: Shift the graph of
$g(x) = \log_2(x + 8)$ down 5 units.

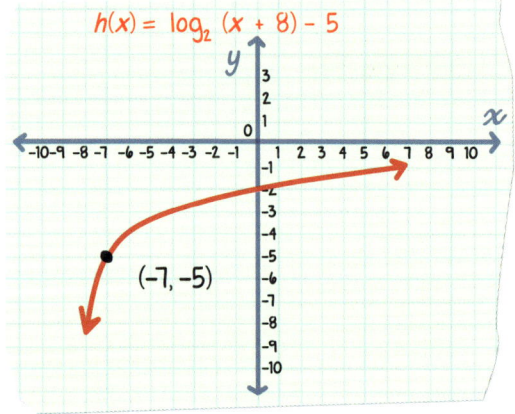

$h(x) = \log_2(x + 8) - 5$

$(-7, -5)$

8 $f(x) = \log_a x - 8$
$-5 = \log_a 8 - 8$
$3 = \log_a 8$
$a^3 = 8$
$a = 2$

9 $\log_5 75$
$\log_5 (25 \bullet 3)$
$\log_5 25 + \log_5 3$
$\log_5 5^2 + \log_5 3$
$2\log_5 5 + \log_5 3$

10 $\log_3 \sqrt{23g^7}$

$\log_3 (23g^7)^{\frac{1}{2}}$

$\dfrac{1}{2}(\log_3 23g^7)$

$\dfrac{1}{2}(\log_3 23 + \log_3 g^7)$

$\dfrac{1}{2}(\log_3 23 + 7\log_3 g)$

11 $\log_2 \left(\dfrac{jk^4}{h}\right)$

$\log_2 (jk^4) - \log_2 h$
$\log_2 j + \log_2 k^4 - \log_2 h$
$\log_2 j + 4\log_2 k - \log_2 h$

CHAPTER 31

**SOLVING EXPONENTIAL AND
LOGARITHMIC EQUATIONS**

1 $8^{6x} = 32^{3x-9}$
$(2^3)^{6x} = (2^5)^{3x-9}$
$2^{18x} = 2^{15x-45}$
$18x = 15x - 45$

$3x = -45$

$x = -15$

2 $5^{x+9} = 125$

$5^{x+9} = 5^3$

$x + 9 = 3$

$x = -6$

3 $4e^{3x} = 57$

$\dfrac{4e^{3x}}{4} = \dfrac{57}{4}$

$e^{3x} = \dfrac{57}{4}$

$\ln\dfrac{57}{4} = 3x$

$\dfrac{1}{3}\ln\dfrac{57}{4} = x$

4 $e^{2x} + 6e^x + 16 = 11$

$e^{2x} + 6e^x + 5 = 0$

$(e^x)^2 + 6e^x + 5 = 0$

$(e^x + 1)(e^x + 5) = 0$

$e^x + 1 = 0$ $\Big|$ $e^x + 5 = 0$

$e^x = -1$

−1 and −5 are not in the range of e^x.

There is NO SOLUTION to either of these equations.

5 $7^{12x} = 49^{x-15}$

$7^{12x} = (7^2)^{x-15}$

$7^{12x} = 7^{2x-30}$

$12x = 2x - 30$

$10x = -30$

$x = -3$

6 $2e^{13x} = 29$

$\dfrac{2e^{13x}}{2} = \dfrac{29}{2}$

$e^{13x} = \dfrac{29}{2}$

$\ln\dfrac{29}{2} = 13x$

$\dfrac{1}{13}\ln\dfrac{29}{2} = x$

7 $6x^2e^x + 18xe^x = 0$

$6xe^x(x + 3) = 0$

$6x = 0$ $\Big|$ $e^x = 0$ $\Big|$ $x + 3 = 0$

$x = 0$ ↑ $x = -3$

No solution. 0 is not in the range of e^x.

So, the solutions of the given exponential equation are $x = 0$ and $x = -3$.

8 Solution: $x = 3$

$\log_4(9x - 13) = \log_4(-2x + 20)$

$9x - 13 = -2x + 20$

$9x = -2x + 33$

$11x = 33$

$x = 3$

Check:

$\log_4(9x - 13) = \log_4(-2x + 20)$

$\log_4(9 \bullet 3 - 13) = \log_4(-2 \bullet 3 + 20)$

$\log_4(27 - 13) = \log_4(-6 + 20)$
$\log_4 14 = \log_4 14$ ✓

9 Solution: $x = 73$

$\log_3(x + 8) = 4$
$x + 8 = 81$
$x = 73$

Check:
$\log_3(x + 8) = 4$
$\log_3(73 + 8) = 4$
$\log_3 81 = 4$
$3^4 = 81$ ✓

10 Solution: $x = 2$

$\log_4(x + 6) + \log_4 x = 2$
$\log_4[x(x + 6)] = 2$
$\log_4(x^2 + 6x) = 2$
$x^2 + 6x = 4^2$
$x^2 + 6x - 16 = 0$
$(x + 8)(x - 2) = 0$

$x + 8 = 0$ $x - 2 = 0$
$x = -8$ $x = 2$

Check:
$x = 2$
$\log_4(2 + 6) + \log_4 2 = 2$
$\log_4 8 + \log_4 2 = 2$
$\dfrac{3}{2} + \dfrac{1}{2} = 2$
$2 = 2$ ✓

$x = -8$

$\log_4(-8 + 6) + \log_4(-8) = 2$
$\log_4(-2) + \log_4(-8) = 2$ ✗

Negative numbers are not in the domain of $f(x) = \log_4 x$, so the left-hand side is undefined.

$x = -8$ is an extraneous solution.

11 $\ln x = 7$
$\log_e x = 7$
$e^7 = x$

12 Solution: $x = 3$

$\ln x - \ln(6 - x) = 0$

$\ln\left(\dfrac{x}{6 - x}\right) = 0$

$\dfrac{x}{6 - x} = e^0$

$\dfrac{x}{6 - x} = 1$

$x = 6 - x$
$2x = 6$
$x = 3$

Check:
$\ln x - \ln(6 - x) = 0$
$\ln 3 - \ln(6 - 3) = 0$
$\ln 3 - \ln 3 = 0$
$0 = 0$ ✓

13 Solution: $x = 140$

$\log_2(x - 12) = 7$
$x - 12 = 128$
$x = 140$

Check:
$\log_2(x - 12) = 7$
$\log_2(140 - 12) = 7$
$\log_2(128) = 7$
$2^7 = 128$
$128 = 128$ ✓

14 Solution: $x = 7$

$\log_6(7x - 10) = \log_6(12x - 45)$
$7x - 10 = 12x - 45$
$7x = 12x - 35$
$-5x = -35$
$x = 7$

Check:
$\log_6(7x - 10) = \log_6(12x - 45)$
$\log_6(7 \bullet 7 - 10) = \log_6(12 \bullet 7 - 45)$
$\log_6(49 - 10) = \log_6(84 - 45)$
$\log_6(39) = \log_6(39)$ ✓

UNIT 8

Trigonometric Functions

CHAPTER 32

ANGLES AND THEIR MEASURE

1

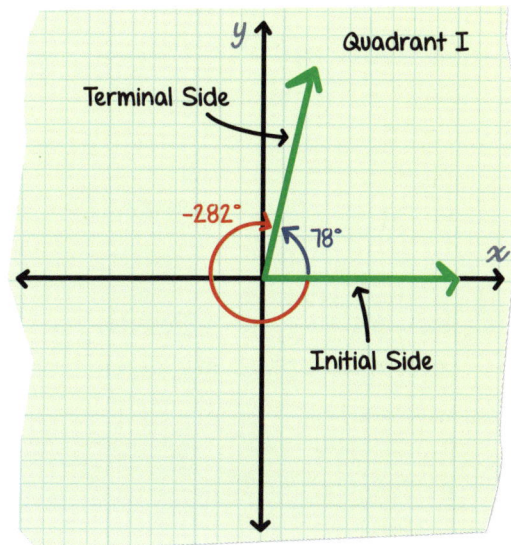

2

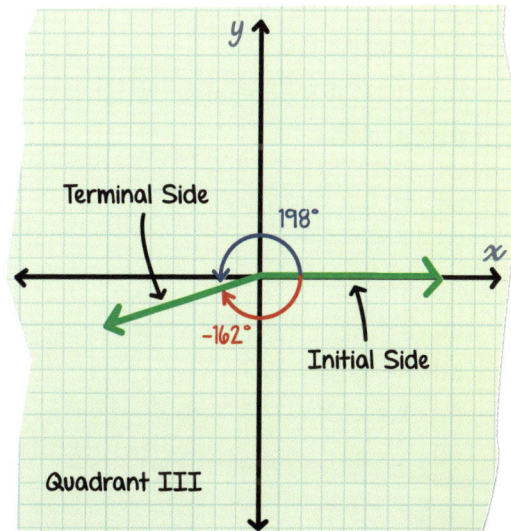

3

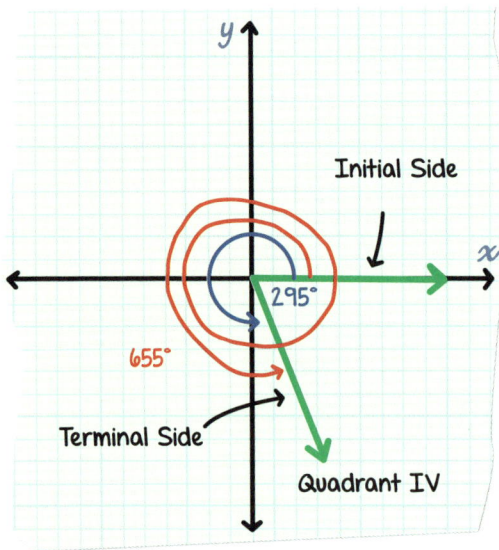

4 Answers may vary. Possible coterminal angles are given.

A. 775° and −665°
B. 450° and −630°
C. 1,000° and −80°

5 $m\overarc{HJK} + m\overarc{HK} = 360°$

$212° + m\overarc{HK} = 360°$
$212° − 212° + m\overarc{HK} = 360° − 212°$
$m\overarc{HK} = 148°$

6 $m\overarc{WX} + m\overarc{WZ} + m\overarc{ZY} + m\overarc{XY} = 360°$

$m\overarc{WX} + 113° + 90° + 90° = 360°$
$m\overarc{WX} + 293° = 360°$
$m\overarc{WX} + 293° − 293° = 360° − 293°$
$m\overarc{WX} = 67°$

$m\overarc{WZ} + m\overarc{ZY} = m\overarc{WZY}$
$113° + 90° = m\overarc{WZY}$
$203° = m\overarc{WZY}$

7 A. True
   B. False

8 $47° = \dfrac{47\pi}{180}$ radians

$47 \cdot \dfrac{\pi}{180}$

$\dfrac{47\pi}{180}$

9 $−126° = −\dfrac{7\pi}{10}$ radians

$−126 \cdot \dfrac{\pi}{180}$

$\dfrac{−126\pi}{180}$

$−\dfrac{7\pi}{10}$

10 $335° = \dfrac{67\pi}{36}$ radians

$335 \cdot \dfrac{\pi}{180}$

$\dfrac{335\pi}{180}$

$\dfrac{67\pi}{36}$

11 $\dfrac{\pi}{15} = 12°$

$\dfrac{\pi}{15} \cdot \dfrac{180}{\pi}$

$\dfrac{180\pi}{15\pi}$

12

12 $-\frac{5\pi}{2} = -450°$

$-\frac{5\pi}{2} \cdot \frac{180}{\pi}$

$-\frac{900\pi}{2\pi}$

-450

13 $\frac{8\pi}{15} = 96°$

$\frac{8\pi}{15} \cdot \frac{180}{\pi}$

$\frac{1440\pi}{15\pi}$

96

CHAPTER 33

TRIGONOMETRY OF THE UNIT CIRCLE

1 $W(\frac{9\pi}{2})$

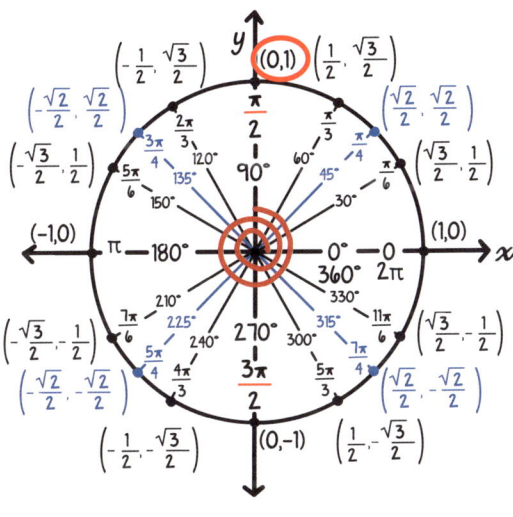

$(0, 1)$

2 $W(\frac{14\pi}{3})$

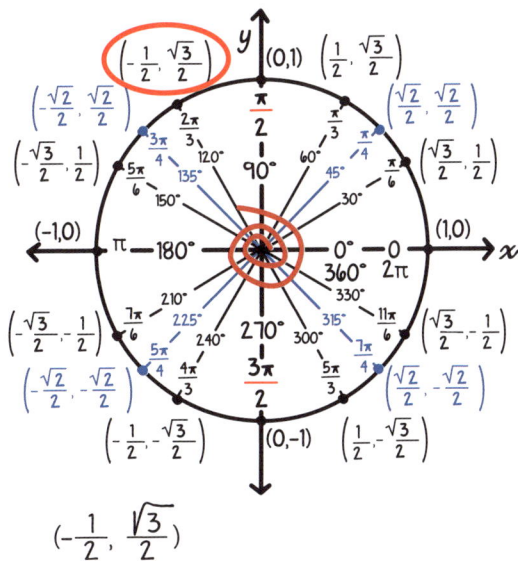

$(-\frac{1}{2}, \frac{\sqrt{3}}{2})$

3 $W(-\frac{7\pi}{4})$

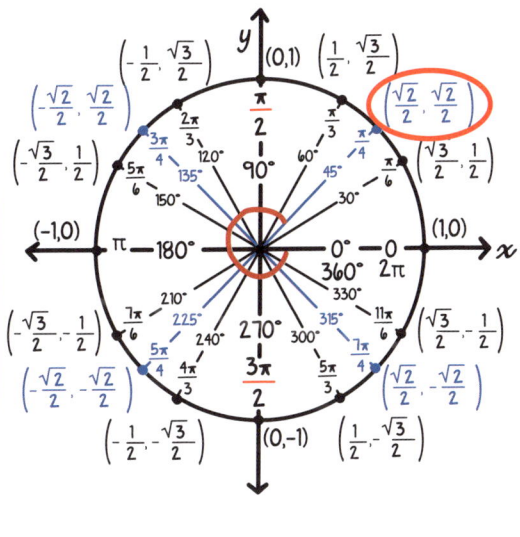

$(\frac{\sqrt{2}}{2}, \frac{\sqrt{2}}{2})$

4 $\cos \dfrac{3\pi}{4}$

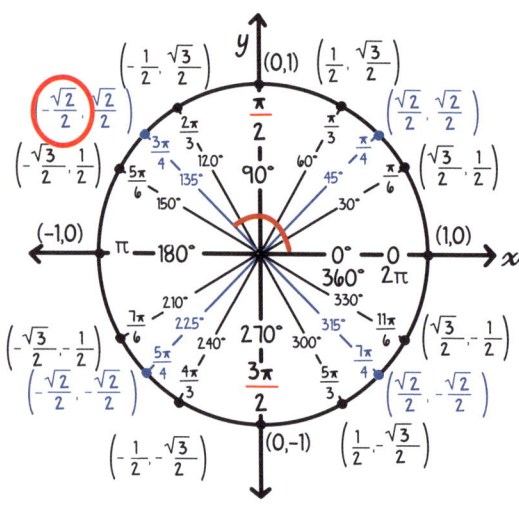

$$\cos \theta = x$$

$$\cos \dfrac{3\pi}{4} = -\dfrac{\sqrt{2}}{2}$$

5 $\sin \dfrac{\pi}{3}$

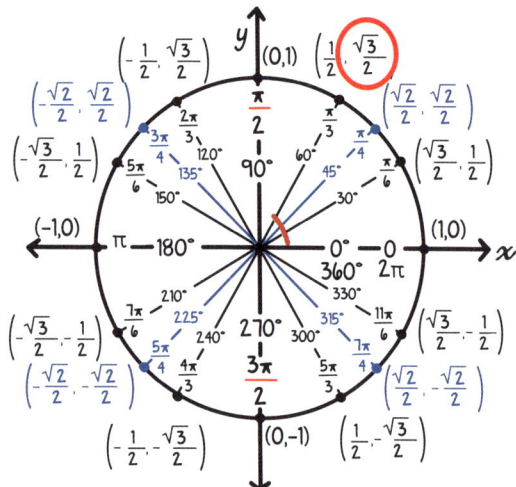

$$\sin \theta = y$$

$$\sin \dfrac{\pi}{3} = \dfrac{\sqrt{3}}{2}$$

6 $\sin(-4\pi)$

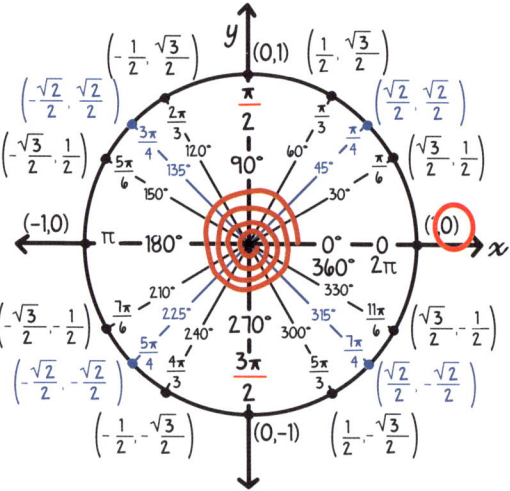

$$\sin \theta = y$$

$$\sin(-4\pi) = 0$$

7 $\cot \dfrac{2\pi}{3}$

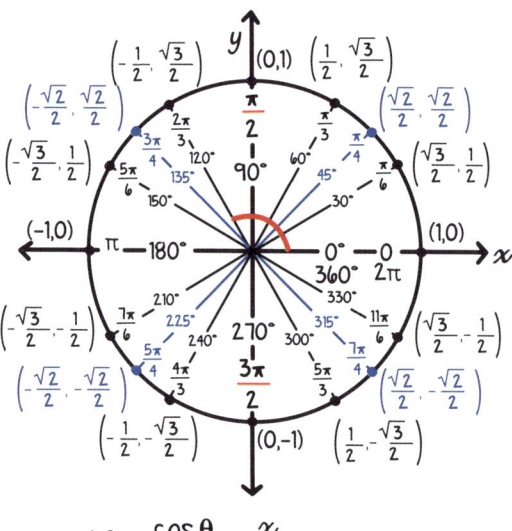

$$\cot \theta = \dfrac{\cos \theta}{\sin \theta} = \dfrac{x}{y}$$

$$\cot \frac{2\pi}{3} = \frac{\cos \frac{2\pi}{3}}{\sin \frac{2\pi}{3}} = \frac{-\frac{1}{2}}{\frac{\sqrt{3}}{2}} =$$

$$-\frac{1}{2} \div \frac{\sqrt{3}}{2} = -\frac{1}{2} \cdot \frac{2}{\sqrt{3}} = -\frac{1}{\sqrt{3}} =$$

$$-\frac{1}{\sqrt{3}} \cdot \frac{\sqrt{3}}{\sqrt{3}} = -\frac{\sqrt{3}}{3}$$

8 $\sec \frac{\pi}{4}$

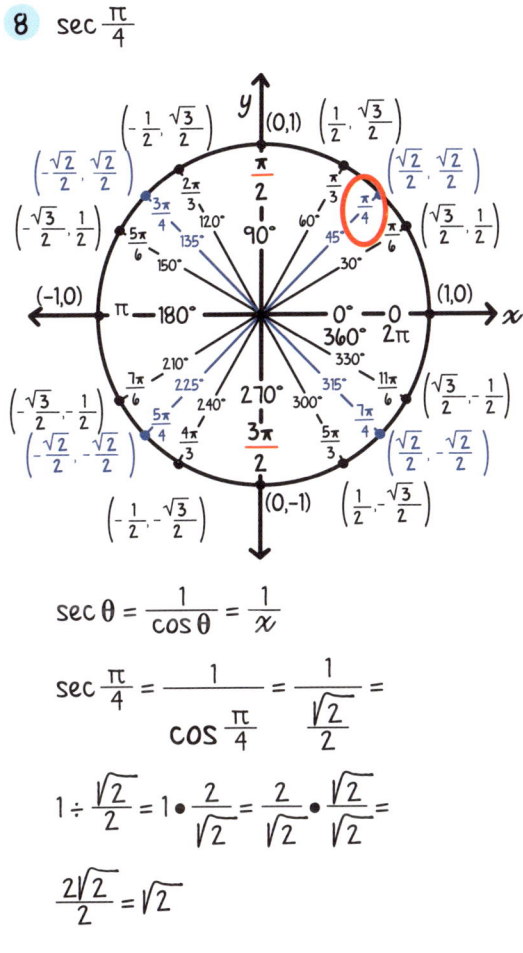

$$\sec \theta = \frac{1}{\cos \theta} = \frac{1}{x}$$

$$\sec \frac{\pi}{4} = \frac{1}{\cos \frac{\pi}{4}} = \frac{1}{\frac{\sqrt{2}}{2}} =$$

$$1 \div \frac{\sqrt{2}}{2} = 1 \cdot \frac{2}{\sqrt{2}} = \frac{2}{\sqrt{2}} \cdot \frac{\sqrt{2}}{\sqrt{2}} =$$

$$\frac{2\sqrt{2}}{2} = \sqrt{2}$$

9 $W\left(\frac{7\pi}{6}\right)$

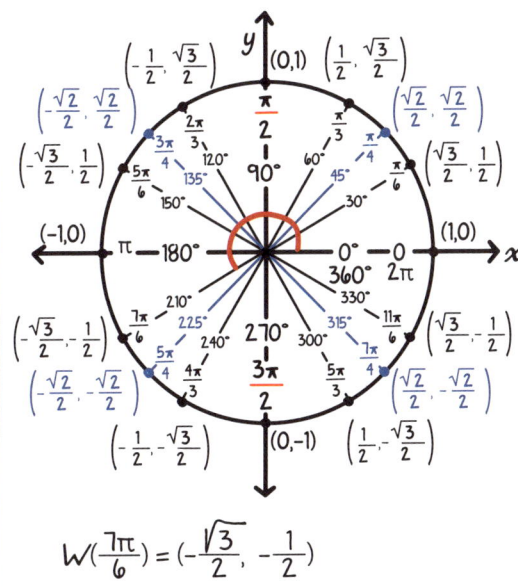

$$W\left(\frac{7\pi}{6}\right) = \left(-\frac{\sqrt{3}}{2}, -\frac{1}{2}\right)$$

10 $\sin\left(-\frac{5\pi}{2}\right)$

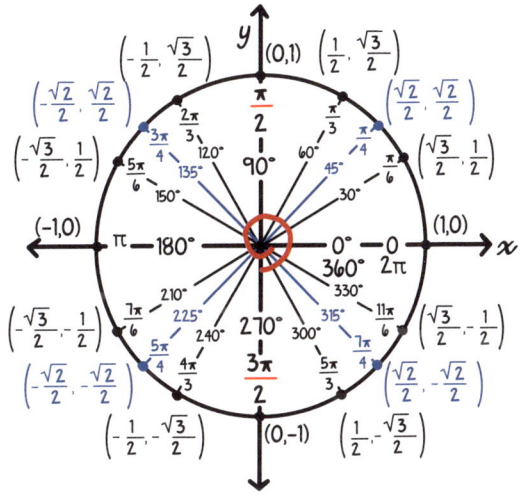

$$\sin \theta = y$$

$$\sin\left(-\frac{5\pi}{2}\right) = -1$$

11 $\cos 7\pi$

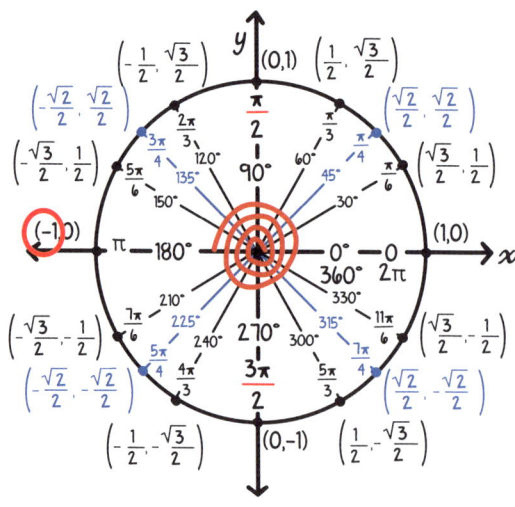

$$\cos \theta = x$$
$$\cos 7\pi = -1$$

12 $\sec\left(-\dfrac{3\pi}{4}\right)$

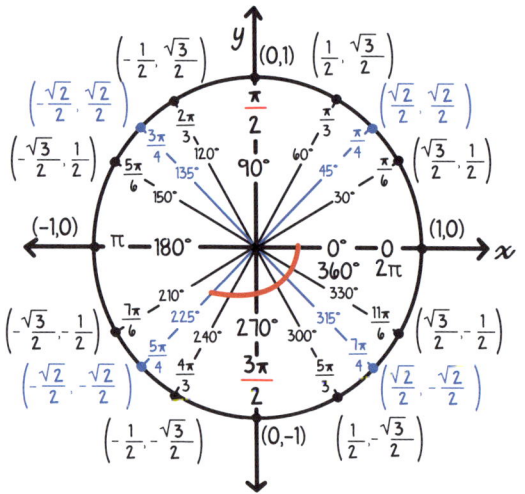

$$\sec \theta = \frac{1}{\cos \theta} = \frac{1}{x}$$

$$\sec\left(-\frac{3\pi}{4}\right) = \frac{1}{\cos\left(-\frac{3\pi}{4}\right)} = \frac{1}{-\dfrac{\sqrt{2}}{2}} =$$

$$1 \div \left(-\frac{\sqrt{2}}{2}\right) = 1 \bullet \left(-\frac{2}{\sqrt{2}}\right) = -\frac{2}{\sqrt{2}} \bullet \frac{\sqrt{2}}{\sqrt{2}} =$$

$$-\frac{2\sqrt{2}}{\sqrt{2}} = -\sqrt{2}$$

13 $\cot\left(-\dfrac{\pi}{6}\right)$

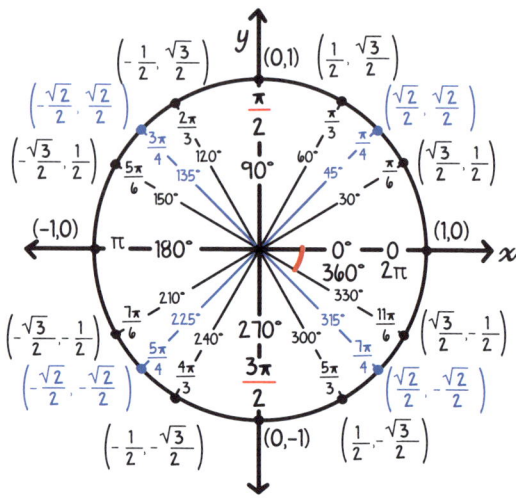

$$\cot \theta = \frac{\cos \theta}{\sin \theta} = \frac{x}{y}$$

$$\cot\left(-\frac{\pi}{6}\right) = \frac{\cos\left(-\frac{\pi}{6}\right)}{\sin\left(-\frac{\pi}{6}\right)} = \frac{\dfrac{\sqrt{3}}{2}}{-\dfrac{1}{2}} =$$

$$\frac{\sqrt{3}}{2} \div \left(-\frac{1}{2}\right) = \frac{\sqrt{3}}{2} \bullet \left(-\frac{2}{1}\right) =$$

$$-\frac{2\sqrt{3}}{\sqrt{2}} = -\sqrt{3}$$

14 $\sin\left(-\frac{9\pi}{2}\right)$

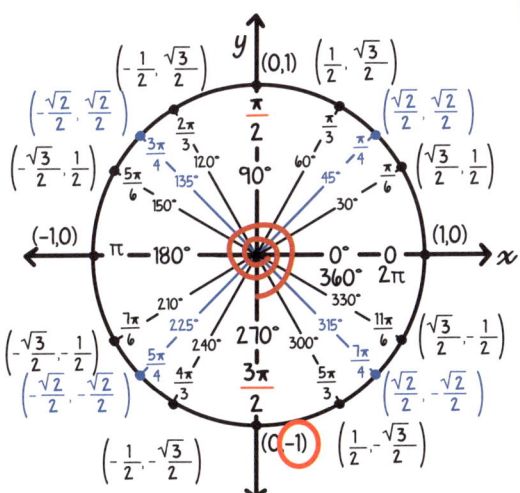

$$\sin\theta = y$$

$$\sin\left(-\frac{9\pi}{2}\right) = -1$$

CHAPTER 34

RIGHT TRIANGLE TRIGONOMETRY

1 Find the length of the missing side.

$$3^2 + b^2 = 5^2$$
$$9 + b^2 = 25$$
$$9 - 9 + b^2 = 25 - 9$$
$$b^2 = 16$$
$$b = 4$$

$$\sin\theta = \frac{OPP}{HYP} = \frac{3}{5}$$

$$\csc\theta = \frac{HYP}{OPP} = \frac{5}{3}$$

$$\cos\theta = \frac{ADJ}{HYP} = \frac{4}{5}$$

$$\sec\theta = \frac{HYP}{ADJ} = \frac{5}{4}$$

$$\tan\theta = \frac{OPP}{ADJ} = \frac{3}{4}$$

$$\cot\theta = \frac{ADJ}{OPP} = \frac{4}{3}$$

2

$\sin 45° = \frac{1}{\sqrt{2}}$	$\cot 60° = \frac{1}{\sqrt{3}}$
$\sec 60° = 2$	$\csc 30° = 2$
$\tan 30° = \frac{1}{\sqrt{3}}$	$\tan 45° = 1$

3 This is a 45°-45°-90° triangle, so we know the following:

- The length of each leg is x.

- The length of the hypotenuse is $x\sqrt{2} = 8\sqrt{2}$.

$$x\sqrt{2} = 8\sqrt{2}$$

$$\frac{x\sqrt{2}}{\sqrt{2}} = \frac{8\sqrt{2}}{\sqrt{2}}$$

$$x = 8$$

Therefore, the length of each leg is 8 cm.

4 This is a 30°-60°-90° triangle, so we know the following:

- The length of the longer leg is $x\sqrt{3} = 7\sqrt{3}$.

- The length of the shorter leg is x.

- The length of the hypotenuse is $2x$.

$$x\sqrt{3} = 7\sqrt{3}$$

$$\frac{x\sqrt{3}}{\sqrt{3}} = \frac{7\sqrt{3}}{\sqrt{3}}$$

$$x = 7$$

Therefore, the length of the shorter leg is 7 cm.

The length of the hypotenuse is $2x = 2(7) = 14$ cm.

5 215°
$$215° - 180° = 35°$$

6 $\frac{7\pi}{6}$
$$\frac{7\pi}{6} - \pi = \frac{\pi}{6}$$

7 $\frac{3\pi}{5}$
$$\pi - \frac{3\pi}{5} = \frac{2\pi}{5}$$

8 78°

9 $\csc\frac{5\pi}{3}$

Find the reference angle.

$$2\pi - \frac{5\pi}{3} = \frac{6\pi}{3} - \frac{5\pi}{3} = \frac{\pi}{3}$$

Evaluate the cosecant of the reference angle.

$$\csc\frac{\pi}{3} = \frac{2}{\sqrt{3}} = \frac{2\sqrt{3}}{3}$$

Since the given angle is in Quadrant IV, the cosecant is negative.

Therefore, $\csc\frac{5\pi}{3} = -\frac{2\sqrt{3}}{3}$.

10 $\cot\frac{9\pi}{4}$

Find the reference angle.

$$\frac{9\pi}{4} - 2\pi = \frac{9\pi}{4} - \frac{8\pi}{4} = \frac{\pi}{4}$$

Evaluate the cotangent of the reference angle.

$$\cot\frac{\pi}{4} = 1$$

Since the given angle is in Quadrant I, the cotangent is positive.

Therefore, $\cot\frac{9\pi}{4} = 1$.

11 $\cos\frac{4\pi}{3}$

Find the reference angle.

$$\frac{4\pi}{3} - \pi = \frac{4\pi}{3} - \frac{3\pi}{3} = \frac{\pi}{3}$$

Evaluate the cosine of the reference angle.

$$\cos\frac{\pi}{3} = \frac{1}{2}$$

Since the given angle is in Quadrant III, the cosine is negative.

Therefore, $\cos\frac{4\pi}{3} = -\frac{1}{2}$.

12 $\sec\frac{\pi}{4}$

$\sec\frac{\pi}{4} = \sqrt{2}$

13 $\sin 30° = \frac{OPP}{HYP} = \frac{x}{12}$

$12 \cdot \sin 30° = \frac{x}{12} \cdot 12$

$12 \cdot \frac{1}{2} = x$

$6 = x$

So, the height of the slide's ladder is 6 feet.

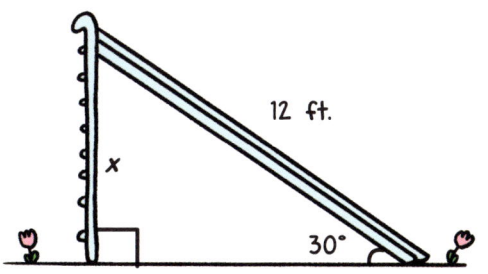

12 ft.

x

30°

CHAPTER 35

GRAPHS OF TRIGONOMETRIC FUNCTIONS

1 C

2 B

3 D

4 E

5 A

6 $f(x) = \frac{1}{4}\cos 2x$

Amplitude: $\frac{1}{4}$

Period: $\frac{2\pi}{B} = \frac{2\pi}{2} = \pi$

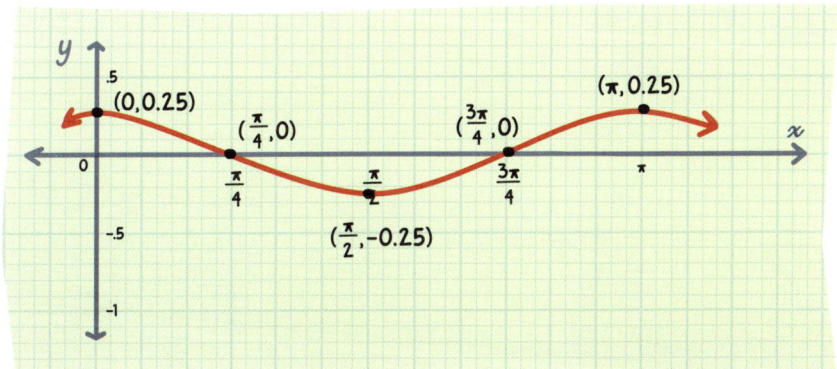

7 $h(x) = \sin(3x) + 4$

Amplitude: 1

Period: $\dfrac{2\pi}{B} = \dfrac{2\pi}{3}$

Vertical shift: up 4 units

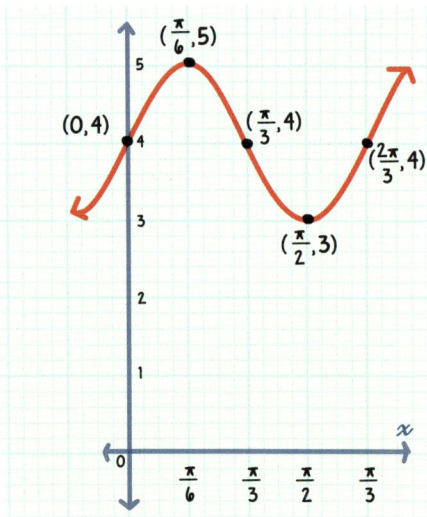

8 $w(x) = \cos(x - \pi)$

Amplitude: 1
Period: 2π

Phase shift: to
the right π units

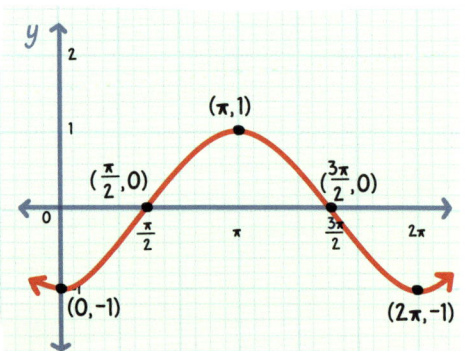

9 $g(x) = 2\sin\left(x - \dfrac{\pi}{2}\right) + 1$

Amplitude: 2
Period: 2π

Horizontal shift: to the right
$\dfrac{\pi}{2}$ units

Vertical shift: up 1 unit

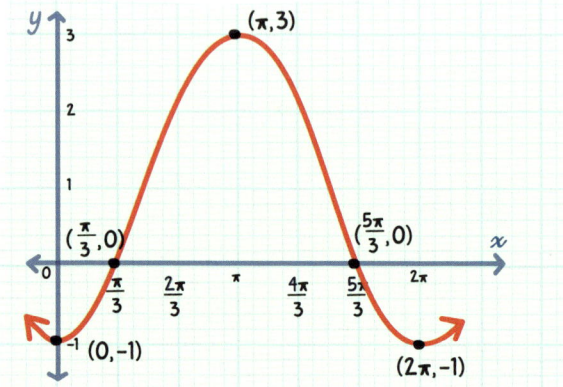

10 $j(x) = \sin 2x - 2$

Amplitude: 1

Period: $\dfrac{2\pi}{B} = \pi$

Vertical shift: down 2 units

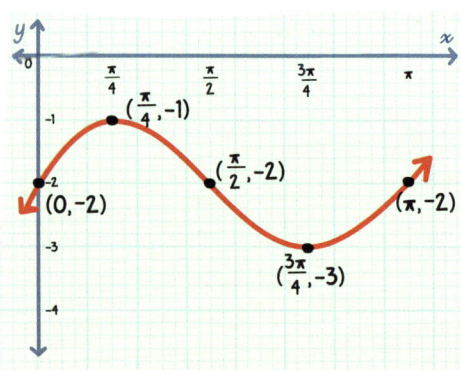

11 $v(x) = \cos(x + \frac{\pi}{2})$

Amplitude: 1
Period: 2π

Horizontal shift: to the left
$\frac{\pi}{2}$ units

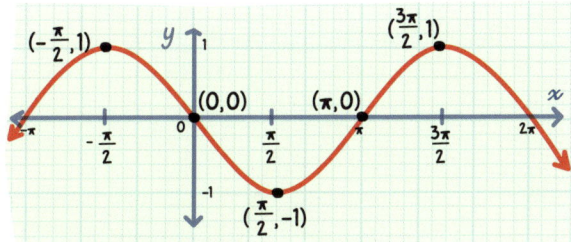

12 $c(x) = 3\sin(x - \pi) - 2$

Amplitude: 3
Period: 2π

Horizontal shift: to the right
π units

Vertical shift: down 2 units

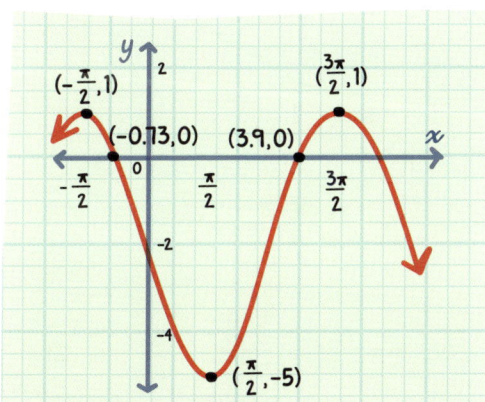

CHAPTER 36

INVERSE TRIGONOMETRIC FUNCTIONS

1 $\sin^{-1}\frac{\sqrt{3}}{2}$

$\theta = \sin^{-1}\frac{\sqrt{3}}{2}$ if and only if

$\sin\theta = \frac{\sqrt{3}}{2}$ and $-\frac{\pi}{2} \leq \theta \leq \frac{\pi}{2}$.

Since $\sin\frac{\pi}{3} = \frac{\sqrt{3}}{2}$ and

$-\frac{\pi}{2} \leq \frac{\pi}{3} \leq \frac{\pi}{2}$, $\sin^{-1}\frac{\sqrt{3}}{2} = \frac{\pi}{3}$.

2 $\arccos(-\frac{\sqrt{2}}{2})$

$\theta = \arccos(-\frac{\sqrt{2}}{2})$ if and only if

$\cos\theta = -\frac{\sqrt{2}}{2}$ and $0 \leq \theta \leq \pi$.

Since $\cos\frac{3\pi}{4} = -\frac{\sqrt{2}}{2}$ and

$0 \leq \frac{3\pi}{4} \leq \pi$, $\arccos(-\frac{\sqrt{2}}{2}) = \frac{3\pi}{4}$.

3 $\arcsin 2$

Since there is no angle θ
such that $\sin\theta = 2$, $\arcsin 2$
is **undefined**.

4 $\arctan(-1)$

$\theta = \arctan(-1)$ if and only if

$\tan\theta = -1$ and $-\frac{\pi}{2} < \theta < \frac{\pi}{2}$.

Since $\tan(-\frac{\pi}{4}) = -1$ and
$-\frac{\pi}{2} < -\frac{\pi}{4} < \frac{\pi}{2}$, $\arctan(-1) = -\frac{\pi}{4}$.

5 $\cos^{-1}(\frac{\sqrt{3}}{2})$

$\theta = \cos^{-1}\frac{\sqrt{3}}{2}$ if and only if

$\cos\theta = \frac{\sqrt{3}}{2}$ and $0 \le \theta \le \pi$.

Since $\cos\frac{\pi}{6} = \frac{\sqrt{3}}{2}$ and

$0 \le \frac{\pi}{6} \le \pi$, $\cos^{-1}\frac{\sqrt{3}}{2} = \frac{\pi}{6}$.

6 $\tan^{-1}(\frac{1}{\sqrt{3}})$

$\theta = \tan^{-1}\frac{1}{\sqrt{3}}$ if and only if

$\tan\theta = \frac{1}{\sqrt{3}}$ and $-\frac{\pi}{2} < \theta < \frac{\pi}{2}$.

Since $\tan\frac{\pi}{6} = \frac{1}{\sqrt{3}}$ and

$-\frac{\pi}{2} < \frac{\pi}{6} < \frac{\pi}{2}$, $\tan^{-1}(\frac{1}{\sqrt{3}}) = \frac{\pi}{6}$.

7 $\sin\theta = \frac{OPP}{HYP} = \frac{5}{19}$

$\theta = \sin^{-1}\frac{5}{19}$

$\theta \approx 15.2575°$

$\theta \approx 15°$

8 $\tan\theta = \frac{OPP}{ADJ} = \frac{4}{6} = \frac{2}{3}$

$\theta = \tan^{-1}\frac{2}{3}$

$\theta \approx 33.69°$

$\theta \approx 34°$

9 $\cos 0 = \frac{ADJ}{HYP} = \frac{21}{43}$

$\theta = \cos^{-1}\frac{21}{43}$

$\theta \approx 60.7664°$

$\theta \approx 61°$

10 $\cos\theta = \frac{ADJ}{HYP} = \frac{3}{12}$

$\theta = \cos^{-1}\frac{3}{12}$

$\theta \approx 75.52248°$

$\theta \approx 76°$

11 $\cos(\sin^{-1}\frac{1}{4})$

Recall that $\sin^{-1}\frac{1}{4}$ is an angle. If we call this angle θ, then $\theta = \sin^{-1}\frac{1}{4}$, and so $\sin\theta = \frac{1}{4}$.

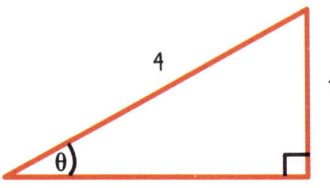

$1^2 + b^2 = 4^2$

$1 + b^2 = 16$

$b^2 = 15$

$b = \sqrt{15}$

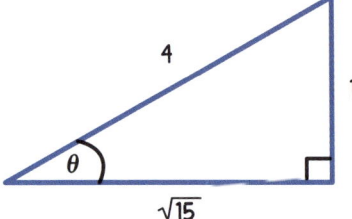

$\cos\theta = \frac{ADJ}{HYP} = \frac{\sqrt{15}}{4}$

Therefore, $\cos(\sin^{-1}\frac{1}{4}) = \frac{\sqrt{15}}{4}$.

12 $\sin\left(\tan^{-1}\frac{7}{2}\right)$

Recall that $\tan^{-1}\frac{7}{2}$ is an angle. If we call this angle θ, then $\theta = \tan^{-1}\frac{7}{2}$, and so $\tan\theta = \frac{7}{2}$.

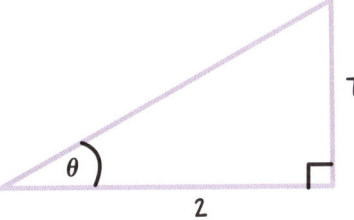

$2^2 + 7^2 = c^2$

$4 + 49 = c^2$

$53 = c^2$

$c = \sqrt{53}$

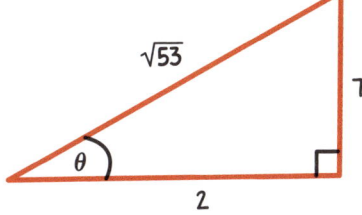

$\sin\theta = \frac{OPP}{HYP} = \frac{7}{\sqrt{53}} = \frac{7\sqrt{53}}{53}$

Therefore, $\sin\left(\tan^{-1}\frac{7}{2}\right) = \frac{7\sqrt{53}}{53}$.

13 $\tan\left(\cos^{-1}\frac{1}{2}\right)$

Recall that $\cos^{-1}\frac{1}{2}$ is an angle. If we call this angle θ, then $\theta = \cos^{-1}\frac{1}{2}$, and so $\cos\theta = \frac{1}{2}$.

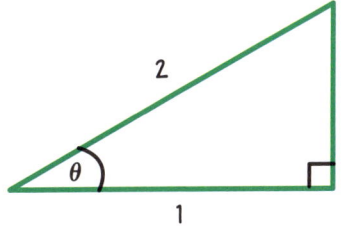

$a^2 + 1^2 = 2^2$

$a^2 + 1 = 4$

$a^2 = 3$

$a = \sqrt{3}$

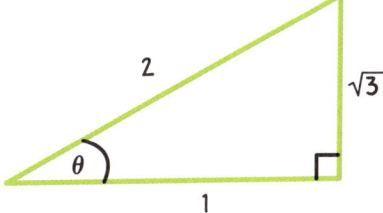

$\tan\theta = \frac{OPP}{ADJ} = \frac{\sqrt{3}}{1} = \sqrt{3}$

Therefore, $\tan\left(\cos^{-1}\frac{1}{2}\right) = \sqrt{3}$.

14 $\tan\left(\sin^{-1}\frac{5}{8}\right)$

Recall that $\sin^{-1}\frac{5}{8}$ is an angle. If we call this angle θ, then $\theta = \sin^{-1}\frac{5}{8}$, and so $\sin\theta = \frac{5}{8}$.

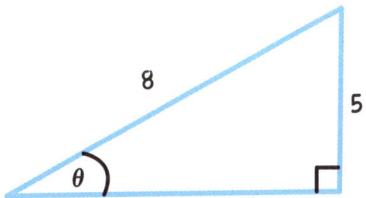

$5^2 + b^2 = 8^2$

$25 + b^2 = 64$

$b^2 = 39$

$b = \sqrt{39}$

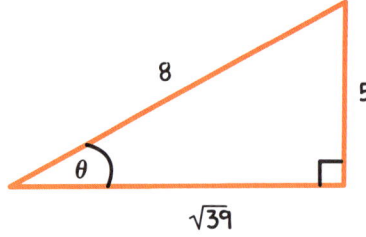

$\tan \theta = \dfrac{OPP}{ADJ} = \dfrac{5}{\sqrt{39}} = \dfrac{5\sqrt{39}}{39}$

Therefore, $\tan(\sin^{-1}\frac{5}{8}) = \dfrac{5\sqrt{39}}{39}$.

CHAPTER 37

TRIGONOMETRIC IDENTITIES

1 $\dfrac{\sin(-x)}{\cos(-x)}$

$= \dfrac{-\sin x}{\cos x}$

$= -\dfrac{\sin x}{\cos x}$

$= -\tan x$

2 $\dfrac{\sec x}{\tan x}$

$= \dfrac{\dfrac{1}{\cos x}}{\dfrac{\sin x}{\cos x}}$

$= \dfrac{1}{\cos x} \div \dfrac{\sin x}{\cos x}$

$= \dfrac{1}{\cos x} \bullet \dfrac{\cos x}{\sin x}$

$= \dfrac{1}{\sin x}$

$= \csc x$

3 $\dfrac{\tan(\frac{\pi}{2} - \theta)}{\sec \theta}$

$= \dfrac{\cot \theta}{\dfrac{1}{\cos \theta}}$

$= \dfrac{\cos \theta}{\sin \theta} \div \dfrac{1}{\cos \theta}$

$= \dfrac{\cos \theta}{\sin \theta} \bullet \dfrac{\cos \theta}{1}$

$= \cot \theta \cos \theta$

4 $\dfrac{\cos^2(-x)}{\cot^2 x}$

$= \dfrac{(\cos^2(-x))^2}{\cot^2 x}$

$= \dfrac{(\cos x)^2}{(\dfrac{\cos x}{\sin x})^2}$

$= \dfrac{(\cos x)^2}{\dfrac{(\cos x)^2}{(\sin x)^2}}$

$= \dfrac{\cos^2 x}{\dfrac{\cos^2 x}{\sin^2 x}}$

$= \dfrac{\cos^2 x}{1} \div \dfrac{\cos^2 x}{\sin^2 x}$

$= \dfrac{\cos^2 x}{1} \bullet \dfrac{\sin^2 x}{\cos^2 x} = \sin^2 x$

5 $\csc x \tan x = \sec x$

$$\frac{1}{\sin x} \cdot \frac{\sin x}{\cos x} = \sec x$$

$$\frac{1}{\cos x} = \sec x$$

$$\sec x = \sec x \ \checkmark$$

6 $\frac{\cos^2\theta}{1 + \sin\theta} = 1 - \sin\theta$

Use the Pythagorean Identity $\sin^2 x + \cos^2 x = 1$ or $\cos^2 x = 1 - \sin^2 x$.

$$\frac{1 - \sin^2\theta}{1 + \sin\theta} = 1 - \sin\theta$$

Factor the numerator as the difference of two squares.

$$\frac{(1 - \sin\theta)\cancel{(1 + \sin\theta)}}{\cancel{1 + \sin\theta}} = 1 - \sin\theta$$

$$1 - \sin\theta = 1 - \sin\theta \ \checkmark$$

7 $\sin\left(\frac{\pi}{2} - x\right)\tan x = \sin x$

$$\cos x \cdot \frac{\sin x}{\cos x} = \sin x$$

$$\frac{\cos x}{1} \cdot \frac{\sin x}{\cos x} = \sin x$$

$$\sin x = \sin x \ \checkmark$$

8 $\frac{\cos^2(-x)}{\cot^2 x} = \sin^2 x$

$$\frac{(\cos(-x))^2}{\left(\frac{\cos x}{\sin x}\right)^2} = \sin^2 x$$

Use the Negative Identity $\cos(-x) = \cos x$.

$$\cos^2 x \div \frac{\cos^2 x}{\sin^2 x} = \sin^2 x$$

$$\cos^2 x \cdot \frac{\sin^2 x}{\cos^2 x} = \sin^2 x$$

$$\sin^2 x = \sin^2 x \ \checkmark$$

9 $\frac{\tan\theta - \cot\theta}{\sec\theta + \csc\theta} = \sin\theta - \cos\theta$

$$\frac{\frac{\sin\theta}{\cos\theta} - \frac{\cos\theta}{\sin\theta}}{\frac{1}{\cos\theta} + \frac{1}{\sin\theta}} = \sin\theta - \cos\theta$$

Rewrite the fractions with a common denominator in both the numerator and denominator.

$$\frac{\frac{\sin\theta \sin\theta}{\cos\theta \sin\theta} - \frac{\cos\theta \cos\theta}{\cos\theta \sin\theta}}{\frac{\sin\theta}{\cos\theta \sin\theta} + \frac{\cos\theta}{\cos\theta \sin\theta}} = \sin\theta - \cos\theta$$

$$\frac{\frac{\sin^2\theta - \cos^2\theta}{\cos\theta \sin\theta}}{\frac{\sin\theta + \cos\theta}{\cos\theta \sin\theta}} = \sin\theta - \cos\theta$$

$$\frac{\sin^2\theta - \cos^2\theta}{\cancel{\cos\theta \sin\theta}} \cdot \frac{\cancel{\cos\theta \sin\theta}}{\sin\theta + \cos\theta} = \sin\theta - \cos\theta$$

$$\frac{\sin^2\theta - \cos^2\theta}{\sin\theta + \cos\theta} = \sin\theta - \cos\theta$$

Factor the numerator as the difference of two squares.

$$\frac{(\sin\theta + \cos\theta)(\sin\theta - \cos\theta)}{\sin\theta + \cos\theta} =$$

$$\sin\theta - \cos\theta$$

$$\sin\theta - \cos\theta = \sin\theta - \cos\theta \checkmark$$

10 $\frac{1 + \sin x}{\cos x} = \frac{\cos x}{1 - \sin x}$

Introduce $1 - \sin x$ to the left side of the equation.

$$\frac{(1 + \sin x)(1 - \sin x)}{(\cos x)(1 - \sin x)} = \frac{\cos x}{1 - \sin x}$$

Multiply the numerator on the left side.

$$\frac{1 - \sin^2 x}{(\cos x)(1 - \sin x)} = \frac{\cos x}{1 - \sin x}$$

Use the Pythagorean Identity: $\sin^2 x + \cos^2 x = 1$ or $\cos^2 x = 1 - \sin^2 x$.

$$\frac{\cos^2 x}{(\cos x)(1 - \sin x)} = \frac{\cos x}{1 - \sin x}$$

$$\frac{\cancel{\cos x} \cdot \cos x}{\cancel{(\cos x)}(1 - \sin x)} = \frac{\cos x}{1 - \sin x}$$

$$\frac{\cos x}{1 - \sin x} = \frac{\cos x}{1 - \sin x} \checkmark$$

CHAPTER 38

SOLVING TRIGONOMETRIC EQUATIONS

1 $2\cos x - 1 = 0$

$2\cos x = 1$

$\cos x = \frac{1}{2}$

Since $\frac{1}{2} > 0$ and cosine is positive in the first and fourth

quadrants, we need to find two solutions: one between 0 and $\frac{\pi}{2}$ (the Quadrant I solution) and another between $\frac{3\pi}{2}$ and 2π (the Quadrant IV solution).

The Quadrant I solution is $x = \cos^{-1}(\frac{1}{2}) = \frac{\pi}{3}$.

The Quadrant IV solution is $x = 2\pi - \frac{\pi}{3} = \frac{6\pi}{3} - \frac{\pi}{3} = \frac{5\pi}{3}$.

So, on the interval $[0, 2\pi]$, the solutions are $\frac{\pi}{3}$ and $\frac{5\pi}{3}$.

2 $3\sin x - 3 = 0$

$3\sin x = 3$

$\sin x = 1$

$x = \sin^{-1}(1) = \frac{\pi}{2}$

So, on the interval $[0, 2\pi]$, the solution is $\frac{\pi}{2}$.

3 $8\sin^2 x - 6 = 0$

$8\sin^2 x = 6$

$\sin^2 x = \frac{6}{8}$

$\sin^2 x = \frac{3}{4}$

$\sin x = \pm\frac{\sqrt{3}}{2}$

Between 0 and 2π, $\sin x = \frac{\sqrt{3}}{2}$ when $x = \frac{\pi}{3}$ and $x = \pi - \frac{\pi}{3} = \frac{2\pi}{3}$.

Similarly, between 0 and 2π, $\sin x = -\frac{\sqrt{3}}{2}$ when $x = \pi + \frac{\pi}{3} = \frac{4\pi}{3}$ and $x = 2\pi - \frac{\pi}{3} = \frac{5\pi}{3}$.

So, on the interval $[0, 2\pi)$, the solutions are $\frac{\pi}{3}$, $\frac{2\pi}{3}$, $\frac{4\pi}{3}$, and $\frac{5\pi}{3}$.

4 $\sin x = \sqrt{2} - \sin x$

$2 \sin x = \sqrt{2}$

$\sin x = \frac{\sqrt{2}}{2}$

Since $\frac{\sqrt{2}}{2} > 0$ and sine is positive in the first and second quadrants, we need to find two solutions: one between 0 and $\frac{\pi}{2}$ (the Quadrant I solution) and another between $\frac{\pi}{2}$ and π (the Quadrant II solution).

The Quadrant I solution is simply $x = \sin\frac{\sqrt{2}}{2} = \frac{\pi}{4}$.

The Quadrant II solution is $x = \pi - \frac{\pi}{4} = \frac{4\pi}{4} - \frac{\pi}{4} = \frac{3\pi}{4}$.

So, on the interval $[0, 2\pi)$, the solutions are $\frac{\pi}{4}$ and $\frac{3\pi}{4}$.

5 $\sin^2 x + 1 = 2 \sin x$

$\sin^2 x - 2 \sin x + 1 = 0$

Use quadratic factoring, treating this equation as if it were $a^2 - 2a + 1 = 0$.

$(\sin x - 1)(\sin x - 1) = 0$

$(\sin x - 1)^2 = 0$

Use the Square Root Property.

$\sin x - 1 = 0$

$\sin x = 1$

$x = \frac{\pi}{2}$

So, on the interval $[0, 2\pi)$, the only solution is $x = \frac{\pi}{2}$.

6 $4 \sin^2 x \cos x - 2 \cos x = 0$

Factor out the GCF: $2 \cos x$.

$2 \cos x (2 \sin^2 x - 1) = 0$

Use the Zero-Product Principle.

$2 \cos x = 0$

$\cos x = 0$

$x = \frac{\pi}{2}$ or $x = \frac{3\pi}{2}$

$2 \sin^2 x - 1 = 0$

$2 \sin^2 x = 1$

$\sin^2 x = \frac{1}{2}$

$\sin x = \pm \frac{\sqrt{2}}{2}$

Between 0 and 2π, $\sin x = \frac{\sqrt{2}}{2}$ when $x = \frac{\pi}{4}$ and $x = \pi - \frac{\pi}{4} = \frac{3\pi}{4}$.

Similarly, between 0 and 2π, $\sin x = -\frac{\sqrt{2}}{2}$ when $x = \pi + \frac{\pi}{4} = \frac{5\pi}{4}$ and $x = 2\pi - \frac{\pi}{4} = \frac{7\pi}{4}$.

So, on the interval $[0, 2\pi)$, the solutions are $\frac{\pi}{2}$, $\frac{3\pi}{2}$, $\frac{\pi}{4}$, $\frac{3\pi}{4}$, $\frac{5\pi}{4}$, and $\frac{7\pi}{4}$.

7 $2\sin x + \sin^2 x - 3 = 0$

$\sin^2 x + 2\sin x - 3 = 0$

Use quadratic factoring, treating this equation as if it were $a^2 + 2a - 3 = 0$.

$(\sin x - 1)(\sin x + 3) = 0$

Use the Zero-Product Principle.

$\sin x - 1 = 0$
$\sin x = 1$
$x = \dfrac{\pi}{2}$
$\sin x + 3 = 0$
$\sin x = -3$
No solution

So, on the interval $[0, 2\pi)$, the only solution is $\dfrac{\pi}{2}$.

8 $2\cot x + 2\cos x = \cot x$

Use trigonometric identities to rewrite the equation with sines and cosines.

$2\dfrac{\cos x}{\sin x} + 2\cos x = \dfrac{\cos x}{\sin x}$

Multiply by $\sin x$ to eliminate the fractions.

$\sin x \bullet (2\dfrac{\cos x}{\sin x} + 2\cos x) =$

$(\dfrac{\cos x}{\sin x}) \bullet \sin x$

$2\cos x + 2\sin x \cos x = \cos x$

$2\sin x \cos x + \cos x = 0$

Factor out the GCF: $\cos x$.

$\cos x(2\sin x + 1) = 0$

Use the Zero-Product Principle.

$\cos x = 0$
$x = \dfrac{\pi}{2}$ or $x = \dfrac{3\pi}{2}$

$2\sin x + 1 = 0$
$2\sin x + 1 - 1 = 0 - 1$
$2\sin x = -1$
$\sin x = -\dfrac{1}{2}$
Since $-\dfrac{1}{2} < 0$ and sine is negative in the third and fourth quadrants, we need to find two solutions: one between π and $\dfrac{3\pi}{2}$ (the Quadrant III solution) and another between $\dfrac{3\pi}{2}$ and 2π (the Quadrant IV solution).
Since $\sin^{-1}(\dfrac{1}{2}) = \dfrac{\pi}{6}$, it follows that the Quadrant III solution is $x = \pi + \dfrac{\pi}{6} = \dfrac{6\pi}{6} + \dfrac{\pi}{6} = \dfrac{7\pi}{6}$ and the Quadrant IV solution is $2\pi - \dfrac{\pi}{6} = \dfrac{12\pi}{6} - \dfrac{\pi}{6} = \dfrac{11\pi}{6}$.

So, on the interval $[0, 2\pi)$, the solutions are $\dfrac{\pi}{2}$, $\dfrac{3\pi}{2}$, $\dfrac{7\pi}{6}$, and $\dfrac{11\pi}{6}$.

9 $\cos^2 x = 2\sin x + 2$

$\cos^2 x - 2\sin x - 2 = 0$

Rewrite using the Pythagorean Identity $\sin^2 x + \cos^2 x = 1$ or $\cos^2 x = 1 - \sin^2 x$.

$(1 - \sin^2 x) - 2\sin x - 2 = 0$

$-\sin^2 x - 2\sin x - 1 = 0$

$\sin^2 x + 2\sin x + 1 = 0$

Use quadratic factoring, treating this equation as if it were $a^2 + 2a + 1 = 0$.

$(\sin x + 1)(\sin x + 1) = 0$

Use the Square Root Property.

$(\sin x + 1)^2 = 0$

$\sin x + 1 = 0$

$\sin x = -1$

$x = \dfrac{3\pi}{2}$

So, on the interval $[0, 2\pi)$, the only solution is $\dfrac{3\pi}{2}$.

10 $2\cos x + 1 = \sec x$

$2\cos x + 1 = \dfrac{1}{\cos x}$

Multiply by $\cos x$ to eliminate the fraction.

$\cos x (2\cos x + 1) = \dfrac{1}{\cos x} \cdot \cos x$

$2\cos^2 x + \cos x = 1$

$2\cos^2 x + \cos x - 1 = 0$

Use quadratic factoring, treating this equation as if it were $2a^2 + a - 1 = 0$.

$(2\cos x - 1)(\cos x + 1) = 0$

Use the Zero-Product Principle.

$2\cos x - 1 = 0$

$2\cos x = 1$

$\cos x = \dfrac{1}{2}$

Since $\dfrac{1}{2} > 0$ and cosine is positive in the first and fourth quadrants, we need to find two solutions: one between 0 and $\dfrac{\pi}{2}$ (the Quadrant I solution) and another between $\dfrac{3\pi}{2}$ and 2π (the Quadrant IV solution).

The Quadrant I solution is simply $x = \cos^{-1}\left(\dfrac{1}{2}\right) = \dfrac{\pi}{3}$.

The Quadrant IV solution is $x = 2\pi - \dfrac{\pi}{3} = \dfrac{5\pi}{3}$.

$\cos x + 1 = 0$

$\cos x = -1$

$x = \pi$

So, on the interval $[0, 2\pi)$, the solutions are π, $\dfrac{\pi}{3}$, and $\dfrac{5\pi}{3}$.

11 $4\cos^2 x - 3 = 0$

$4\cos^2 x = 3$

$\cos^2 x = \dfrac{3}{4}$

$\cos x = \pm \dfrac{\sqrt{3}}{2}$

Between 0 and 2π, $\cos x = \dfrac{\sqrt{3}}{2}$ when $x = \dfrac{\pi}{6}$ and $x = 2\pi - \dfrac{\pi}{6} = \dfrac{11\pi}{6}$.

Similarly, between 0 and 2π, $\cos x = -\dfrac{\sqrt{3}}{2}$ when $x = \pi - \dfrac{\pi}{6} = \dfrac{5\pi}{6}$ and $x = \pi + \dfrac{\pi}{6} = \dfrac{7\pi}{6}$.

So, on the interval $[0, 2\pi)$, the solutions are $\dfrac{\pi}{6}$, $\dfrac{5\pi}{6}$, $\dfrac{7\pi}{6}$, and $\dfrac{11\pi}{6}$.

12 $2\sin x = \tan x$

Use a Quotient Identity to rewrite the right-hand side of the equation with sine and cosine.

$2\sin x = \dfrac{\sin x}{\cos x}$

$2\sin x \cos x = \dfrac{\sin x}{\cos x} \cdot \cos x$

$2\sin x \cos x = \sin x$

$2\sin x \cos x - \sin x = 0$

Factor out the GCF: $\sin x$.

$\sin x(2\cos x - 1) = 0$

Use the Zero-Product Principle.

$\sin x = 0$

$x = 0,\ \pi,\ \text{or}\ 2\pi$

$2\cos x - 1 = 0$

$2\cos x - 1 + 1 = 0 + 1$

$2\cos x = 1$

$\dfrac{2\cos x}{2} = \dfrac{1}{2}$

$\cos x = \dfrac{1}{2}$

Since $\dfrac{1}{2} > 0$ and cosine is positive in the first and fourth quadrants, we need to find two solutions: one between 0 and $\dfrac{\pi}{2}$ (the Quadrant I solution) and another between $\dfrac{3\pi}{2}$ and 2π (the Quadrant IV solution).

The Quadrant I solution is $x = \cos^{-1}(\dfrac{1}{2}) = \dfrac{\pi}{3}$.

The fourth quadrant solution is $x = 2\pi - \dfrac{\pi}{3} = \dfrac{5\pi}{3}$.

So, on the interval $[0, 2\pi)$, the solutions are 0, π, 2π, $\dfrac{\pi}{3}$, and $\dfrac{5\pi}{3}$.

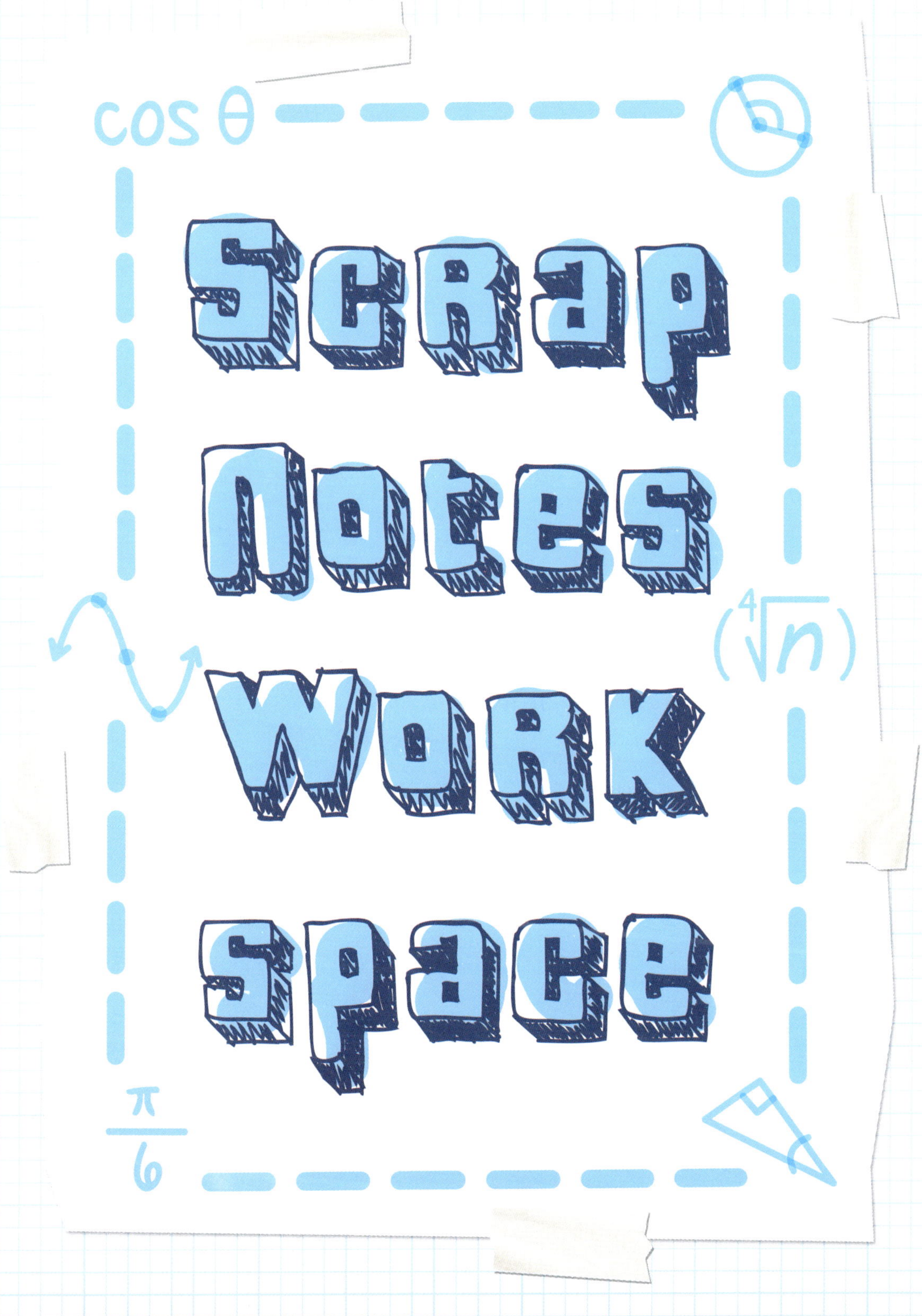
cos θ
Scrap
Notes
Work
space
(∜n)
π/6

Everything You Need to Ace Algebra 2 is right here!

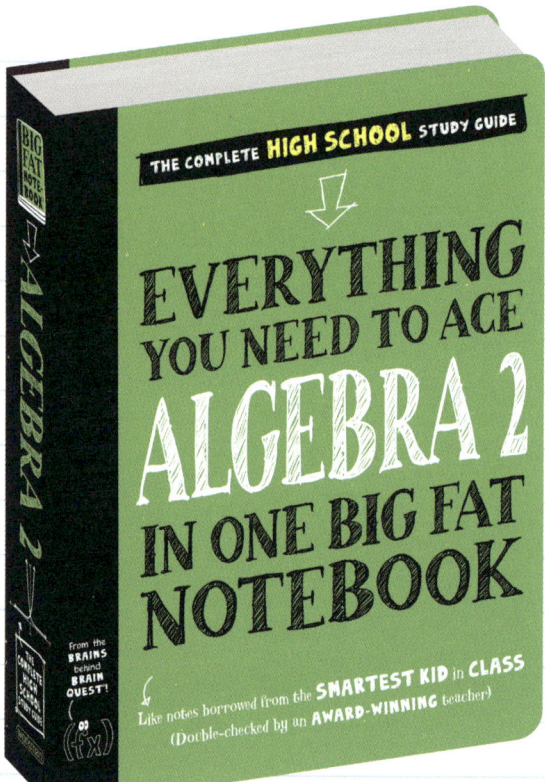

This **Big Fat Notebook** helps makes sense of all the stuff you need to know with **step-by-step examples, easy-to-understand definitions, fun doodles, and more!**

Ace all your high school math classes with
BIG FAT NOTEBOOKS!

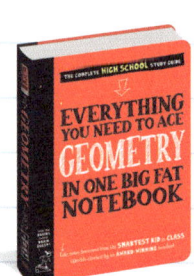
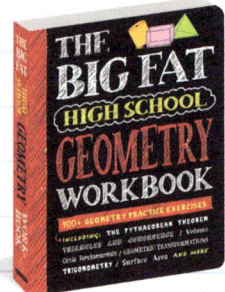
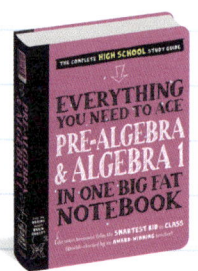
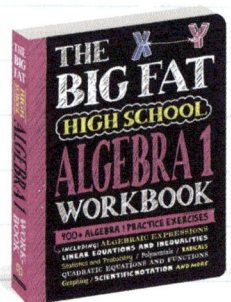